# THEY PLAYED FOR DAVID PLEAT AT LUTON TOWN – VOLUME 1

# CONTENTS

# ACKNOWLEDGEMENTS

This book has been made possible thanks to the people listed below who have supported me during the past two and a half years to bring this project to life in documenting this important time in the history of, not only Luton Town Football Club, but also an era in the final two decades before the formation of the English Premier League which changed the footballing landscape for players and fans alike almost beyond recognition from this era when the game still very much had its place at the heart of working-class culture across the country.

I would like to thank my wife Angie, our children Josh and Lottie (all passionate lifelong Hatters) for their enthusiasm, encouragement and their understanding whilst I spent many hours meeting, zoom calling, face timing or plain old time 'gassing' on the phone with the players. Also, my incredible father in law, Brian Shepherd who has followed the Hatters since 1947 home and away, big love to you 'Pops'. Thanks also to my brother Stephen who gave me the desire to follow him and 'those Duncan boys from next door' onto the Oak Road terrace back in 1977.

Not least to the players themselves, as well as Physio John Sheridan and Coach Trevor Hartley for their time, recollections, stories, photo's and for being so open and incredibly welcoming; without them there would be no project in the first place had they not shared their memories and stories first-hand from the men who were there, as a band of brothers, all in it together and under the stewardship of their manager, David Pleat.

I am truly grateful for the all the support and the hours of proof reading by my friend Adrian Shotbolt. Also, giving their time on proof reading duties was Luton Town Historian, Roger Wash. Thank you Roger for your advice and guidance as well as being so welcoming in opening up the huge archive of match reports and photographs held under the fine stewardship of the Hatters Heritage charity organisation. https://www.hattersheritage.co.uk thanks and acknowledgment also to Gareth Owen gareth@go-photo.co.uk, Home Counties Newspapers Group for the provision of photographs.

To my editor Kathryn CJ Hall for the hours of zoom calls to help put some structure to my enthusiastic but sometimes wayward writing. To Stuart and Aidy at Curtis Sport, the publishers, for believing in the project and to my friend and former footballer Garry Thompson for introducing us.

Lastly to David Pleat himself, although having no direct input into this book, but purely for having put together this incredible band of brothers during his tenure of the club in the 1970s and 1980s

This book is dedicated to those lads who played for the club in this era but who are sadly no longer with us. Here's to you, all fine footballers and men; ***Raddy Antic, Tony 'Paddy' Grealish, Les Sealey, David Preece, Marc North, Andy King, John 'Woody' Woodward, Milija Aleksic, Chris Turner, David Carr, Paul Futcher, as well as Rodney Fern, Alan Garner, Billy Holmes, John 'Maxi' Faulkner, Bobby Thomson and Graham Horn*** who all would have played for David Pleat whilst he was in charge of the reserves at Kenilworth Road.



*First published in 2022 by Curtis Sport*

*ISBN: 978-1-7398342-1-0*

*Photographic acknowledgements:*

*Hatters Heritage, Gareth Owen, Home Counties Newspapers Group*

*Every effort has been made to trace copyright. Any oversight will be rectified in future editions.*

*Cover design & Production Editor: Aidy Hewlett*

*Design and production by Curtis Sport*

*"They Played for David Pleat at Luton Town; Football, from an era, when its place was still very much at the heart of working-class culture. An invitation to look back at a time from within the dressing room and the corridors of Kenilworth Road. The memories and stories of the men who were there, as a band of brothers, all in it together and under the stewardship of their manager, David Pleat."*

# FOREWORD

## TV PRESENTER, FORMER CHAIRMAN OF LUTON TOWN FC AND LIFELONG HATTERS FAN, NICK OWEN

The David Pleat era is memorable for its flowing, attacking football from the wonderful talent he signed. Who can forget the 3-3 draw at Liverpool or the 4-4 at Stoke? He got us up to the top flight in glorious style in 1982, famously kept us up in 1983 and created the squad that kept the Town amongst the elite for a decade, the club's most successful period. It was a brilliant time to be a fan and his legacy, of course, included the highpoint in the club's history - winning the League Cup in April 1988, with mostly his squad, shortly after he had moved on to Tottenham. Certainly, the most thrilling moment in my sporting lifetime and I am sure that applies to all Hatters of a certain age.

Now, how interesting it is to hear from the men who served under Pleat! Philip Duffy has interviewed so many players and staff from David's first spell at the club and it is fascinating to read their thoughts now, as they look back with the benefit of maturity and hindsight. We are all inevitably more reflective as we get older and sometimes see episodes in our personal history in a different light, with pleasure, in some cases, or with regret.

Remember those thrilling bursts down the wing by David Moss in his seven years at Kenilworth Road? We loved him, didn't we? I find some of his remarks in the book very telling. He says he appreciates his years at Luton now more than he did at the time. And, overall in his whole career, he says, " I enjoy it more now when I think back than when I actually experienced it at the time." Also, "...I probably didn't enjoy it as much as I should have done."

How many of us are guilty of not appreciating the 'now' because we are in such a rush to get on to the next thing, anxious about the future and how things are going to pan out? It is very easy to let the moment slip by and not appreciate what you are part of at any one time. David Moss was integral to those exhilarating years and it is interesting that, after the roller coaster has come to a halt, he now appreciates just how enjoyable a time it was at a happy and successful football club.

It seems to me that almost all the people Philip has spoken to look back on their time at Kenilworth Road with enormous affection. A great atmosphere in the club that has to come down from the top. They mostly see David Pleat as a towering influence on their careers and later lives. Wherever else he worked in his own long career, David is essentially Luton through and through. He lives locally and he is a frequent visitor to our games. We, the fans who were there, owe him so much for a glorious period in the club's history. This book will confirm that the people who were lucky enough to work with him feel the same.

Nick Owen

(BORN 12TH FEBRUARY 1959, SUNDERLAND)

# MICHAEL GORDON HARFORD

LUTON TOWN FC 1984 TO 1990 (& 1991/92)

*Born in Sunderland, Michael, known as Mick, grew up as a devoted fan of his home town club, Sunderland, then based at Roker Park, a place that he dearly loved. As a youngster, Mick only ever wanted one thing: to become a professional footballer and if possible, with his beloved Sunderland AFC.*

My earliest football memories are of playing in the street in Stamford Avenue, Humbledon, with my friends Jimmy and Ian Lambert. I continued to play, representing my school teams at both St Cuthbert's and St Joseph's. Our school team was very good as it contained both Kevin Dillon (Birmingham City, Portsmouth, Newcastle United, Reading) and Micky Hazard (Spurs, Chelsea, Swindon Town), as well as myself and the other lads. We had a great teacher, Mr. McCorluck, who would arrange games at lunchtimes. He threatened to drop me from the school team one time as I was going home for my dinner, but he insisted that I stayed to have school dinners and play football immediately afterwards.

My family were huge Sunderland supporters - me and my sister used to go all the time, so, it was very much ingrained into me at a very young age. One of the best days of my life was going to London for the first time as a fourteen-year old boy on May 5th, 1973 to see Sunderland win the FA Cup Final against Leeds United, who at the time were the best team in England whilst we were in the English Second Division. We won 1-0! I remember taking a swim in the fountains at Trafalgar Square after that famous victory.

It was such a shame that the three of us, me, Micky and Kevin, all being local lads, slipped through the net at that time and didn't play for Sunderland, although I did briefly much later in my career. It was especially so for Micky as he was such a brilliant footballer – he would have been fantastic for Sunderland in those early to mid-1980s.

I played for Sunderland schools and then had trials with Sunderland when Jimmy Adamson was the manager. I was sixteen at the time and devastated when I wasn't offered an apprenticeship at Roker Park and for a while, I have to admit, that I gave up on the dream and of playing altogether.

I took on an apprenticeship as a plumber, which I did for two years. I packed in football just to follow the team, I was such a big fan, and I'd follow them across the country with my mates. We didn't have any money so we would hitchhike to see Sunderland when they were away, then try and jump on the supporters' coaches on the way back home.

By now I was seventeen and still not playing football, but then I had a knock on the door and I was asked if I wanted to come back playing as they were building a good young side over at Lambton Street Boys' Club. I jumped at the chance to get back to football. From there, we got picked up by a scout and four of us from Lambton Street ended up going down to Lincoln City.

I was at Lincoln for just over three years before having an opportunity of a move to Newcastle United. I didn't really think about it too much, I was a footballer, I felt that I had earned this chance to go to a massive club. The rivalry with Sunderland and with me being a Sunderland fan didn't come into it for me. I have the utmost respect for Newcastle United. The manager who signed me, Arthur Cox, was brilliant for me. In fact, Arthur signed me again later in our careers when he took me from Luton Town to Derby County – Arthur is a great guy. He's, well, he's getting on in years but we still keep in touch on the phone.

At Newcastle United, to be honest, I went there too young. I couldn't handle the situation with having the famous Number 9 shirt of Newcastle United on my back and I just didn't cope with it very well. Perhaps if I'd gone there just a few years later then it would have been the perfect move for me. I lasted around twenty games. Nearing the end of the season I scored two goals against Preston so I thought I might be okay there after all, but I then went on a scoreless run until I finally scored one more solitary goal in what turned out to be my final game at home to Orient in May 1981. Arthur called me in and told me he'd accepted a bid from Bristol City, he wanted me to go and thought it would be a good move for me because I was a good professional and I was still young. He believed in me but he just knew the fans weren't going to accept me; it wasn't working.

I was transferred to Bristol City that summer. So, I just missed out on Kevin Keegan, Terry McDermott and Peter Beardsley all coming in the following year in 1982, still as players back then under Arthur Cox. Newcastle United were on their way up and I was on my way to Bristol City!

When I was at Bristol City we played Aston Villa down at Ashton Gate in an FA Cup tie early 1982, so it must have been the third or the fourth round. Now, unbeknown to me, at the time Ron Saunders, who was still the Villa manager then, had taken a liking to me and how I played.

In March 1982, due to the awful financial situation at Bristol City, my player registration was returned to Newcastle United and later that same day Ron Saunders came in for me. Ron had resigned from Villa but he took me to his new club, First Division Birmingham City. I had the notorious honour of being on three football league clubs' books in one single day. I will always be indebted to Ron as he was a great football man and he taught me how to properly play the centre forward role in my time with him at Birmingham.

One night when I was out with Mark Dennis and our ladies for a meal and a few drinks, we got back to my house in Birmingham and I decided I would demonstrate the workings of my brand-new lawn mower that I was particularly proud of. I proceeded to cut my front lawn at two o'clock in the morning, no doubt endearing me to my neighbours. Nobody directly complained to me about it, but I know that when a potential Birmingham City player coming into the club was looking for a house in the same road, he asked the guy what the neighbours were like. The guy selling the house replied, "Oh, everyone around here are really nice, but watch out for the guy over at number 14, he's often out cutting his bloody grass at two in the morning!"

I'll always remember a home game with Liverpool at St Andrews. It was a league match in the 1983/84 season. Bizarrely enough, Muhammad Ali was there being paraded around the ground and was brought into our dressing room about forty minutes before kick-off. He walked around to us all individually and shook everyone's hand and then he signed all of our programmes. I don't think he really knew what was going on or if he'd even been to a football match before. To this day, I'm really not sure what he was doing there but at least I can say that I met Muhammad Ali once and shook his hand. I think I could have taken him (winks).

There wasn't any fall out between myself and Ron Saunders. He felt that I wasn't the same player, not quite so fearless, after my horrific injury sustained in a clash with Sam Allardyce where he split my mouth wide open. Sam was playing for Coventry City, I turned to run and he elbowed me, totally off the ball. I woke up in hospital with my kit and my boots still on and I was clear as a bell. No headache at all. I asked what was going on here and the hospital staff said, "You've got a nasty cut. You're going for an operation." A hundred stitches and plastic surgery later and I was up and away again. But I was left with a scar where people think I've got a hair lip. Ron was right, to a certain degree, as it took me a long time to get over that mentally.

I had the chance to join QPR that summer in 1984. I went down there but it wasn't right for me so I stayed at St Andrews. Ron Saunders, however, had decided to go in a different direction with his options upfront and also Birmingham City really needed the finances that selling me would bring in. They were in the same boat as Luton Town, producing good sides but always having to balance the books as well, with no rich owners around in those days

The move to Luton was as simple as it gets in that it was a case of get your boots and off you go on your drive down to Luton. No haggling with agents, you're just in the room with the two managers, Ron Saunders and David Pleat, the fee was agreed and Ron told me to just get myself down there and get playing.

When I look back it's arguably the best move that I ever made for my career. Coming to Luton, the team were struggling a little bit at the time. I'll never forget my first three or four days there. I stayed in a hotel in Leagrave with Steve Foster and a guy called Sledge who was Fozzie's driver. Me and Foz had had loads of battles over the years but once we were at Luton together we became best mates. A year after joining Luton I moved into a flat in Harpenden, which is where Foz lived. It's a really nice small town right on the outskirts of the south side of Luton, so Fozzie and I became neighbours as well as team mates. I had a golden retriever called Sam, that was great and certainly helped to keep me fit.

Boxing Day 1984; Mick comes up against Coventry City and former Luton favourite Kirk Stephens

I've got the utmost admiration for Fozzie and in my opinion, arguably he's the best player to ever play for Luton in terms of what he did for the club as a captain. I'm not saying that he was the most skilful but as a captain he was very genial.

He was a leader, and we followed him; he certainly did great things at Luton Town football club. When I turned up at the club to start training, I walked into the dressing room and it was full of international footballers. Ricky Hill, Brian Stein, Mal Donaghy, Ashley Grimes as well as Fozzie, there was a lot of seasoned and really good pro's including Les 'The Cat' Sealey and another international player in Andy Dibble.

The club was already carrying a very good squad of players. Some great young lads coming through with the likes of Garry Parker, Rob Johnson, Mitchell Thomas and Tim Breacker, as well as Meka Nwajiobi. That side just needed of bit of guidance in my opinion. Luton were already a fantastic football team but it was a case of winning 5-2 one week but getting beat 4-0 the next week, then a win of 4-3 the following week. They just couldn't keep clean sheets. The games were always on a knife edge. Fozzie brought that stability to the club in terms of getting a hold of the two full backs, keeping them in and then telling them when to go. You certainly didn't want Steve Foster exposed in the wide areas where Mitchell Thomas or Tim Breacker had galloped up the wing. You'd want Fozzie in the middle of the pitch when the opposition delivered the ball into our penalty area as he had a natural positional sense which led to the ball, seemingly, landing on his head all of the time. He certainly galvanised us as a team. It didn't stop us from playing our free-flowing football but it stopped, or I say it reduced the goals going in our own net. Talking to Mitchell and Tim even now, we still talk about how we used to play with their willingness to get forward but with Steve holding them back at the right times, and in those struggles the captain invariably won and kept the line together. It's a pleasure to talk about these times with those lads as it was arguably one of the best sides that I ever played in.

We managed to turn the league form around and I don't think we ever looked like being relegated in the end. That season was also memorable for the FA Cup run that we had – of course, we were only minutes from going out at the first hurdle in the third round tie at home where Fozzie kept us in the competition with a very late equaliser at home to Stoke City, earning us a replay, which we won and which set up another home tie this time against Huddersfield Town. This gave me the chance to seek some revenge on Sam Allardyce as he was by now playing in the heart of the Huddersfield Town defence. I admit that I did try to hurt him, to be honest. I went in two-footed and threw elbows until I caught him, and there was some blood on his forehead. That was probably when I was at my most vindictive on a football pitch. Sam and I have no issues with each other, it's just the way it was back then. We won the game 2-0 and so that led us to the three-game almighty struggle with Watford, as we needed two replays before we beat them 1-0 at home with Wayne Turner getting his legendary goal on his birthday. The three games were played so quickly over just five or six days and then there was only three or four days from winning that second replay before we played the quarter final, again at home, this time with Millwall as the visitors.

We'll never forget that Millwall match, but for the wrong reasons, of course. All those morons running onto the pitch, it was one of the craziest football games that I've ever been involved in. All the players had to go off the pitch three or four times, billiard balls being thrown into our goalmouth and God knows what else! Those scenes will never be forgotten with our ground being ripped apart as they came onto the pitch again ripping up and throwing anything they could get their hands on. It did take the shine off what should have been a massive celebration of winning the game to reach a Villa Park FA Cup semi-final against Everton. But as footballers you get on with it and quickly the excitement sets in with the prospect of an FA Cup semi-final. It was a level of the competition that a lot of us hadn't yet played in during our careers. Fozzie had with Brighton though, two years earlier, so I guess we leaned on him a little bit.

We went up to Crick on the night before the game. We didn't do anything special in that we treated it as just another game. We drove to Villa Park on the morning of the match and to be fair to us we put on a really good performance. I think we did that because we never really changed our routine to fit the occasion. We were missing two key players in midfield as Peter Nicholas and David Preece were both cup-tied. They'd already played earlier that season in the competition for their clubs just prior to joining Luton Town but we already got this far without them. The two lads who did come in, Garry Parker and Wayne Turner, did brilliantly, and if I was picking my all-time Luton Town XI that I played with, Garry Parker would be in it. So, even with Nico and Preecey missing we were bringing in really good players to replace them.

On our day we believed that we could beat anyone and regularly did in both the league and cup over the years at Luton. We put in a hell of a performance until right at the end when we were cheated out of a place in an FA Cup Final in terms on the decision by the referee, John Martin (Alton, Hants), which was totally nonsensical really. Then we didn't defend the free kick well enough. I had to go off as I'd broke a bone in my foot so I had no option but to miss out for the second half of extra time. Mossy came on in my place and then the guy that I would have been marking scored in extra time to put Everton through at our expense, but to be fair to David Moss he wasn't on the pitch to defend free kicks and corners. Ultimately, it was a massively disappointing day but a few things still stick out in my mind. Obviously, there's Ricky Hill's goal as I was placed right behind him. As soon as he'd hit it I knew the ball was going nowhere but in the goal. To see all the Luton Town fans go up in the air as they were in the Holte end where we scored was a truly euphoric moment shared with the fans. The way they got behind the team was incredible. I was so disappointed for the Luton fans on that day because it was a performance that deserved to take us to Wembley and we truly believed that on our day we could beat anyone. We weren't scared of any opposition be it home or away; we just really enjoyed playing together as a team. We had a good spirit and great camaraderie and we genuinely weren't fearful of anyone. Obviously, we had respect for teams that we played against but we just went out there and enjoyed every challenge.

We bounced back with two home wins in the league immediately after the Villa Park semi-final – we beat Norwich City in midweek on the Tuesday night, just three days after the Everton defeat! Then five days after that, on the following Sunday, there was the memorable 2-1 home win, broadcast live on ITV, over Manchester United. I'd scored a penalty to put us 1-0 up with twenty minutes left, only for Norman Whiteside to equalise just three minutes later. Again, that determination and belief that flowed through the team carried us over the line and we won the match in

Mick Harford powers in a header to give Luton a 2-1 win against Manchester United April 1985

the 90th minute: Steve Foster smashed a free kick onto the United crossbar and I managed to react quickest and get above everyone in the box to the rebound and head it downwards into the net to score the winner down at the Oak Road end of the ground. Just one of many great memories of playing at Kenilworth Road. It really was and still is such a special place.

We were safe from relegation and as we moved closer to the end of the season we, the players, started to hear rumours that the club were going to change the pitch at Kenilworth Road and install an artificial surface. To be honest, I quite enjoyed it. I liked playing on it and it certainly developed your technique. I wouldn't go as far as to say that it made you a better player. I think that nowadays, the artificial surfaces are much different to the one laid at Kenilworth Road, and to the one that had been laid in 1981 at QPR. The one that we played on was certainly harder and firmer and the ball certainly travelled a hell of a lot quicker than it does on 3 and 4G pitches now.

Mick and David Preece celebrate a last minute winner versus Manchester United

Let's be honest about it, it was a massive advantage to us, especially as we knew exactly how to play on it. We had a plan, how to play, how to start the game as we would always try to start a match very quickly on the astroturf pitch. If I had a choice, I wouldn't have played on it. But in those days, you just got on with it. The biggest conundrum that I and the other lads faced was what boots to wear. Les Sealey used to wear studs on it, but we all ended up wearing moulds on it, it was that good. Initially, we started off by wearing traditional training shoes with pimples on the bottom. At the first home game against Nottingham Forest, there was still a lot of sand on the pitch yet to bed in, but at least Dick Wassell got Groundsman of the Year that season (smiling, tongue in cheek); with no games being called off, he won it by a mile. I still carry the scars of playing on that surface on my knees and elbows that you got from going to ground on it and the marks are still there all these years later. I had knee issues during my career but my injuries weren't down to playing on the artificial pitch, that wasn't a factor. My knee issues were simply down to cumulative knocks, whacks and injuries that you pick up as a footballer over the years.

On the social side of things, we simply went where Fozzie told us to go! We had some amazing trips away, once we went to America for a week, we did a bit of golf, we did a bit of everything really… including a bit of drinking down in Florida, this was end of season, mind you!

The best story that I've got from our end of season team holidays, though, is from when we went to Cyprus. I'm not sure which resort we were in but it must have been 1985. It was one of those surreal moments that just unfolded before me. I was sat at a beach bar with David Pleat, David Evans, and Emeka Nwajiobi. Thinking back to it I have to ask myself how did us four end up sitting on a beach bar like that together? Within five minutes we just heard this roar of motorbikes. They came into view and then right over to us where the bar was. On the three bikes were Mitchell Thomas, Brian Stein, and Ricky Hill. The lads were in front of us revving the bikes up without any helmets on, just in t-shirts, pair of shorts and flip-flops on their feet. I shouted over, "Hey, Rick, how are you boys getting on?" They stayed there chatting for two or three minutes, all the time continuing to rev the throttle on the bikes. Suddenly, they pulled away, skidding about as they rode off. The next thing I heard was David Evans kicking off at David Pleat. "You call yourself a fucking manager?" he shouted. "You've got our best three players there on the motorbikes, think of how much they're worth?" All I could see was Pleaty sinking lower and lower into his seat. David Evans continued: "You're a disgrace! There's no discipline, that's three of our best players revving off on those bikes. If they come off them are they insured?" David Pleat was still going lower and lower. Then I swear to god the next moment there was one of those big parachutes coming into view flying over the top of us. We could see someone waving to us from the parachute and he's shouting, "Mr Chairman, how are you doing? Alright Mr Chairman?" It was Steve Foster, the club captain, on one of those paragliders. With this David Evans had had enough, he just shook his head, finished his drink and got up to walk off. The timing of it was comical genius from Foz. All the while, Meka was sat there, keeping quiet, enjoying the spectacle of this comedic moment.

Fozzie was also great at arranging nights out close to home, too, and at Christmas or anytime he felt there was a lull, so to speak, around the place and the team, he'd arrange a night out. We'd go somewhere special, into town, invariably we'd stay in Luton. We'd always be made very welcome at Mr Man's Chinese restaurant, The Sun-Do in Bute Street, where we'd have a good meal and a few drinks. Fozzie would make sure that the young lads came down and were included too, not just the senior pro's, as he wanted everyone to be together, getting them involved in the various drinking games. Mike Newell at the time, didn't drink so he quickly became Fozzie's number one target. There would be fancy dress, too, at Christmas time where Foz would dress up as a nun or something like that. He was a really good leader of the group.

Speaking of Mike Newell, he was still really young when he came in, about twenty or just twenty-one, I think, but he was one hundred per cent dedicated. He trained like a trojan every day, as most of us did. He worked hard as he wanted to get better and turned himself into a really good footballer through sheer hard work. He'd always be looking to do extra work after training with the other coaches like Trevor Hartley and John Moore. A lot of us did, to be fair. Mike came into the club from Wigan Athletic, who I think were in the Fourth Division then, and he transformed himself in all fairness into a top player. I did my knee in and so had an operation at the start of the 1986/87 season and Mike came in and was ever present that season. If I remember correctly, he played every game under John Moore that year as I was out for a long time until December. I was watching a few clips just the other day from that season and Mike took my Number 9 shirt. Even when I came back from injury he kept the 9 and I was in the 10 as there was no squad numbering allocated in those days. Mike was brilliant and for a young lad making the big jump up the divisions with his move to us at Luton, he became a big part of the spirit and camaraderie at the football club.

On one occasion, Steve Foster came in for training one morning wearing a hat and dark glasses to cover cuts that he'd mysteriously obtained on his face and head following a team night out in Luton at Mr Man's Chinese Restaurant. It was really strange, I was watching him and I saw him put out the plate glass window. It was really weird because, as we were making a move to leave, he just lost his balance, his shoulder went into the window and the glass went out. As the window went out he somehow defied gravity at a 45-degree angle and managed to pull himself back into the room of the restaurant so he never went fully out through the window and onto the street. I know because I was there.

He didn't get all of those cuts ending up out on the street outside the restaurant, but there probably is some truth in what he tells of later that night in challenging the taxi driver to a press-up competition to pay off the taxi bill or something. Fozzie was certainly quite unique on his nights out in some of the things that he did. So, when he came in the next day with a hat and dark glasses on, nobody knew what happened later that night but it definitely wasn't from going through the window at Mr Man's. But yeah, it is true that he fell into it which resulted in the window being put through. These things over time gather momentum and became almost like urban myths, like the one of myself and Tony Coton (Watford player) in a pub in Watford where we had been started upon and I supposedly ran over and locked the door so that nobody could leave – like I say, a lot of urban myths, but then, to be fair, a lot of the stories were true, too (smiling with a wink).

When David Pleat left Luton Town, it wasn't a surprise. Things do get into the papers as the team was doing well and so he was a wanted man within football. David, when he was a young manager and I was playing for him, reminds me of Nathan Jones a little bit, how he is now, in terms of his desire, his passion, the way that he works on the training ground very, very thorough, very hard working, drilling the players and putting the structures into them. David Pleat did that on a daily basis with us and he puts me so much in mind of Nathan in the way that they both worked hard and go about their business in a similar way. So, no, I definitely wasn't surprised that David left the football club in 1986 to go to Tottenham. But it's like anything, we were footballers and you just get on with it. You have to trust and to believe in yourself so if a new manager is coming in, you've got to work hard and prove that you're a good player to get in the team. One of the big things for me, as a footballer, no matter who I was playing for, was that I always wanted to prove to my team mates that I was good. That was important to me; I would want to prove myself to my team mates before I did to the manager. It was the respect of my team mates that I wanted. To me, it didn't really bother me who the manager was as long as I was getting picked. You just had to be selfish and single-minded, because at the time, the teams that I played in at Luton, to be honest with you, it used to manage itself.

In the 1986 World Cup at Mexico, it looked as though Luton Town Football Club might have three or maybe even four players in the squad and on the plane to Mexico, with Ricky Hill, Brian Stein, Mitchell Thomas and myself all in the frame at one point or another during that season, which turned out to be David Pleat's final season before moving to White Hart Lane. It was really disappointing that eventually none of us went, especially when you talk about Ricky, Brian and Mitchell. They were all top players so for me to be in that bracket it was brilliant. I still have my letter from the England manager, Bobby Robson, which read, Mick, unfortunately you haven't made the final squad that I will be taking to the World Cup in Mexico this summer but you're officially on 'standby' should we need to call upon you. I was due to have an operation on my knee so as soon as I received that letter in the post I went ahead and proceeded with it in preparation for the following season. For me, it was an honour to be on standby for a World Cup. It was such a good England squad and was a privilege to be a part of it and to train with the likes of those players. There were a lot of really good players around in those days but it was still disappointing in the end not to go. However, Luton Town did have one representative of the club at those finals with Mal Donaghy playing in his second successive World Cup Finals with Northern Ireland.

The following season in 1986/87 under John Moore, we carried on doing really well in the league and in the FA Cup with yet another three-game battle with two replays, this time against Liverpool. Me and the majority of the squad had the utmost respect for John Moore, he's a legend in his own right at the football club. I wish that every football club could have a 'John Moore' in my opinion. The discipline he would bring and the way that he brought the young lads through the youth and reserves was truly legendary. At one point we looked like we might get fourth or fifth place in the league. That season when we played Tottenham at home beating them 3-1, my old school mate from Sunderland, Micky Hazard, who by then had left Spurs to go to Chelsea, said to me, "Mick, I'm telling you, you've got a chance of winning the league." That's how decent we were in those days.

There always seemed to be that extra spice to matches when we played teams in and from London, and obviously with Luton being situated where it is so close to London they had an element of a derby feel to them, both at home and away. It was always special playing in the Capital at those big grounds with full houses. They were great times especially as we'd always give them a game, no matter who the opposition was, and we quite often came away with something from those games. I have to say that I did love playing in London.

I always felt that the best place to play was in England. A lot of the young lads when I was making my way in the game at Lincoln City and then at Newcastle United were being lured out to play during the summer months in America in various teams in the NASL but I never did. There was an occasion in the late 1980s when I was still at Luton before I went to Derby County, when an agent contacted me at home. I still don't know how on earth he got hold of my number! We spoke a further four or five times as he wanted me and Chris Waddle to go to Marseille in France; history tells its story, I don't know if the agent was full of it in wanting to get me out there too, or if he was just trying to get to Chris as I'd played with him when we were both very young at Newcastle United and again in the England set up under Bobby Robson. But Chris did go there, he had a brilliant time and became a legend in French football, but my move out there never transpired. I didn't want to leave Luton for Marseille and have to live in the South of France…

The story that is in Sir Alex Ferguson's book about David Pleat blocking his move to take me to Manchester United where he said that David was difficult to deal with on that occasion, I was totally unaware of at the time. In fact, I only found out about his interest when I was told about it when Sir Alex's book came out. If that had been nowadays, no doubt I would have been a Manchester United player because the agents would have gotten hold of it, they would have got into the club and approached the manager. However, back then when it was directly between manager and manager, and on that occasion David Pleat stuck to his word that he wasn't selling me and that was basically the end of it. Whether Sir Alex ever came back in with another offer I don't know, but I genuinely only ever found out about the whole thing when I read his book years later. David denies the whole episode and I still see him quite regularly and we keep in touch with regular phone calls.

I had a great time as a player and then later on in various roles, including first team manager, and I still remain on the staff to this day. It's a really special club, one that has become very close to my heart and I would like to go on record to thank the fans for making the club what it is. They truly are the lifeblood of Luton Town Football Club.

(BORN 18TH DECEMBER 1951, HYDE, CHESHIRE)

# ALAN WEST

LUTON TOWN FC 1973-81

*Alan began his career at Burnley, a product of the club's prolific youth system that culminated in winning the prestigious FA Youth Cup in 1968. Amongst his team mates were Steve Kindon, Dave Thomas, Eddie Cliff, Mick Docherty and Eric Probert. Alan had always played as a forward at school in Hyde and for the Northeast Cheshire County side but when he signed for Burnley as a fifteen-year-old, having been spotted playing as a striker for his school side, the Turf Moor club turned Alan into a midfielder. He was spotted aged fourteen playing for his school team from Hyde against a team in nearby Stalybridge.*

I was approached by a scout after the game and invited along to Burnley for a week-long trial. I jumped at the chance as playing professionally had always been my dream. I trained with them for the week and was then offered an apprenticeship following on from that trial.

It was the summer of 1967 when I joined Burnley. I went there straight from school, still just a kid, physically immature really as I was a late developer. Steve Kindon, a fellow youth team player back then was unstoppable. He was an ex rugby player, already six-feet tall and twelve stone and could run 100 metres in ten seconds. I admired him; he was prolific in front of goal, especially at that age. A really great lad.

Another player in those days, Dave Thomas, was just a brilliant footballer, a real all-rounder. He could play either as a forward, a winger, or as a midfielder. He made it into the full England side, and he played quite a bit when Don Revie was the manager. Revie really appreciated Dave.

Along the pathway to winning the FA Youth Cup in 1968, me and my team mates disposed of Manchester City and Manchester United, Sheffield United and Everton before beating Coventry City in a two-legged final. (I hadn't been in touch with Steve Kindon or Dave Thomas for forty years until 2018 when Burnley put together a fifty-year reunion back to mark us winning the FA Youth Cup. It was the first and only time that Burnley had won that competition. So, Burnley FC wanted us all to meet up and mark the occasion. I've stayed in touch with both Steve and Dave over the past few years, which has been really brilliant.)

When I was nineteen and still at Burnley, I had the honour of being awarded an Under 23's England cap. We played against Wales at Swindon Town's County Ground. I was also in the squad for the following two games against Scotland and East Germany having got into that squad after Alf Ramsay had seen me playing away at QPR (I believe it was). That was on the Saturday. Then the following day, Alf phoned my manager, Jimmy Adamson, who then, in turn, informed me that I would be in the side and playing for England Under 23s on the Tuesday. I leapfrogged from nowhere and straight into the team, which all felt surreal.

Getting into the England set up was brilliant for me personally, but it was also the beginning of a very strange time, too as coming to the end of that season, having played nearly the whole of the First Division campaign with Burnley and getting into the England squad, I then had a huge fall out with Burnley and the management there because they'd offered me a new contract which equated to only an extra five pounds a week. That led to a massive bust up and that was it, I never played for Burnley again.

Tommy Docherty had tried to sign me for Manchester United but Burnley wouldn't let me go, and this was never made public knowledge. I was sad that it ended this way as I'd always enjoyed my time at Burnley.

It was when I left Turf Moor that I signed for Sunderland, just after they'd won the FA Cup in May 1973. Bob Stokoe signed me, however, I failed a medical! After three days, they found that I had a back problem which consisted of a floating vertebra that I'd actually been born with and unfortunately, it's still there today. The deal was called off as their specialist announced I would have a very serious back problem in the future and as a football club they couldn't afford to take that risk. In fact, he told me personally that if I carried on playing I would be in a wheelchair within two years.

I had a lot of X-rays during my medical at Sunderland as they'd had a difficult time earlier in the year when, in January 1973, if I remember correctly, they had signed a player from Crystal Palace by the name of John Hughes, who was one of the famous Celtic 'Lisbon Lions' from their European Cup triumph in 1967. He only lasted forty-five minutes of his first game for Sunderland as he, apparently, had gone to Roker Park with an undiagnosed knee problem. They'd paid a fair amount of money for him and so that episode prompted them to have an incredibly stringent medical process in place when signing players in future.

So, this condition which was picked up by Sunderland, was also found during my medical in 1981 when I went from Luton to Millwall so they weren't going to sign me there, either. Peter Anderson, by this time, was the manager at Millwall and told the board at there, "Look, I've played with Alan for years, he's one of the fittest players I've ever known and we're signing him!" Suffice to say, Peter over rode the medical staff.

Following the medical issue raised by the Sunderland specialist at Roker Park I disappointingly returned to Burnley, but my contract was up at Turf Moor so the club were understandably keen to move me on.

A few weeks later, after I failed my medical at Sunderland, Luton Town came in for me offering the same amount of money that had been agreed between Burnley and Sunderland and I stayed at Luton Town right up until I almost finished my playing career. What's more, I never had a single day off with a bad back! I actually very rarely missed any games through injury throughout my whole career. I wasn't in any pain and didn't even know that I had it until it showed up on the Sunderland medical tests.

I signed for Harry Haslam in October 1973. When I arrived, Harry was like a general manager with Roy McCrohan being his coach. Roy took all the coaching and training sessions whilst Harry, who was more of an office manager, came down occasionally to watch but allowed Roy to get on with the training. Reg Game was the physio, Danny Bergara the youth coach and the reserve team coach was Ken Whitfield, but I never really got to know him as he left fairly soon after I signed, along with another coach called Ray King. The staff at football clubs back in those days were very small to what you have today. They have more nutritionists these days at clubs than we had as a whole backroom staff!

I made my debut for Luton Town away at Orient on October 20th, 1973 in an unconvincing 2-0 loss. Keith Barber kept the scoreline respectable in making a number of brave saves. The Luton Town side that

Alan, white shirt on the left, on his Luton debut at Orient in October 1973

day was Keith Barber, Don Shanks, Bobby Thompson, Peter Anderson, John Faulkner, Alan Garner, Jimmy Ryan, John Ryan, Barry Butlin, myself and John Aston. That was really some team to be joining, one that would be celebrating promotion to the First Division come the end of the 1973/74 season.

I do remember David Pleat coming down from Nuneaton to join the staff at Luton around 1975 or 1976. To be honest, when he first joined us, and I assume that Harry knew him somehow prior to David joining us, Harry had him doing everything and anything that needed doing around the club. I say that with the greatest respect as it shows that David was happy to be involved at that level doing anything. He did get involved with coaching the youth team and a bit later with the reserves, but he was often in the office driving and pushing fund raising projects, selling lottery tickets, anything that he could put his hand really. Basically, you name it David would do it; nothing was too much trouble for him.

In time, David got more involved with coaching and running the reserve team and when Harry left to go Sheffield United in January 1978, I can clearly remember that a lot of the players, particularly the senior ones, were all left wondering what was going to happen next with Harry gone. As he'd signed most of those senior players, they were left guessing who the club would appoint next as the first team manager. It was all done very quickly when Harry left, and it was quite a shock. I was Captain of the club at the time and I was very close to him but before we knew what was happening, he was gone. I never even had the chance to have a conversation with him about it.

Almost out of nowhere, the club announced they were giving the job to David Pleat. As the reserve team manager, the players knew him a little, but a lot of the senior players were surprised and shocked that the directors had given David the job. However, as they say the rest is history, and he took that opportunity that was given to him in January 1978 and did an amazing job over the following eight years at Kenilworth Road.

David almost immediately set about restructuring not only the playing staff but also his back-room staff, too. He brought in his mate Ken Gutteridge. I won't say anything more about that though, just that the appointment of Ken didn't work out. But these things happen in life. Also, soon after, I think David Coates and John Moore joined the staff.

A lot of players were sold very early in David's time as manager, ones that the club could get good money for. Steve Buckley had actually just been sold, going to Derby County in early January 1978, not long before the change of management from Harry Haslam to David Pleat towards the end of that month. The Futcher Brothers went to Manchester City, Phil Boersma moved on and many more of what I would call the older, senior players moved on as well with the likes of Jimmy Ryan, John Aston, Jimmy Husband, John Faulkner. These were all players who, to be fair, were all in their thirties and probably coming towards the end of their playing career, whereas I was still only twenty-six or twenty-seven and was right in the prime of my career.

I think the great thing in David's favour was that when he took over, he had some outstanding young players already at the club coming through, including Brian Stein, Ricky Hill and Godfrey Ingram. These lads were quality players and I felt that part of my role was to encourage those youngsters by staying at Luton myself as well. I was at a time in my own career where I was honestly thinking should I stay or should I move?

I was playing in the States at the time for Minnesota Kicks, and they were always trying to sign me to stay on so that was always an option, but when you saw the young raw talent that David was starting to bring into the club including Mal Donaghy, Kirk Stephens, Jake Findlay and Mark Aizlewood, you could clearly see the direction the club was going in. It really was one after another and also some real quality like David Moss, too. He picked up some of those lads for absolute peanuts which was fantastic business for the club financially, but also you had these youngsters coming through into the first team along with a few players like myself and Lilly Fuccillo, who were already established and in our prime.

Bob Hatton was a great signing in the summer of 1978 from Blackpool after they were narrowly relegated from the Second Division, and we got on really well. David was always looking to bring in the right player at the right time even knowing that it might not necessarily be a long term solution. He was sure it would benefit the team not only in the here and now but also in playing the long game, and that down the line the club

Alan mid 70's in the glorious Admiral kit – truly Mr Luton Town

would benefit from the up and coming youngsters in the side gaining a wealth of knowledge and know-how from playing with these guys. Another example was David bringing in Alan Birchenall, the ex-Chelsea and Leicester City player. He only played ten games in the 1978/79 season but he was confident, with a wealth of experience, which really helped to bring on the younger players coming through. So, with Bob and Birch we had a touch of real experience within our side, just for a short while, but it worked a treat.

Bit by bit you could see David Pleat adding great quality to the team and he did again in the next summer of 1979, signing and spending large amounts of money on quality players such as Mick Saxby and Tony Grealish.

Those types of players came and went, then the club made some changes in the boardroom with some new directors and from that, David had some money to spend. They never had any money when I was there. No real money to speak of, but the club built bit by bit and later, after I'd left, they were able to buy in the likes of talented young player Paul Walsh, who they could never have attracted just a few years earlier. Going back a few short years the club almost went to the wall in 1976 and relied on cut-price last-minute sales of Andy King to Everton and Peter Anderson to Antwerp in Belgium. Both were sold way under their market value but the horrible part of it was that both clubs buying, knew the position that Luton Town were in and exploited the situation. But that's how it was at the club, always looking to sell the odd player just to keep things afloat.

Slowly, things did change, and Luton would start paying reasonable money for quality players. I remember Raddy Antic coming in and David saying to me, "I've been to Spain, Alan, I've been watching this fantastic player." He was absolutely raving about trying to sign him. Nobody knew who this guy Raddy was, but David did. He knew players all over; he was, and still to this day is, a football nut! I would talk to David on a Monday and we'd talk about the game at the weekend and he'd talk about this and that. Then I would ask him about something and he'd say, no, I've not had time to get around to that yet because I was off watching games in

Northern Ireland or in Barcelona, Spain or somewhere like that. Straight after our games at Kenilworth Road on a Saturday he'd be immediately off on a flight somewhere. He was always off watching games elsewhere, scouting for any potential targets. He was unbelievably driven to improve his team.

Going back to my days playing in America, I have Harry Haslam to thank for that. In the summer of 1976, my wife's parents were living in Christchurch, New Zealand. In talking to Harry, I was saying that I'd really like to go to New Zealand to take Cathie to see her mum and dad, as she hadn't seen her parents for three or four years now. So, Harry set about thinking of setting me up with some coaching in Christchurch during the close season in May, June and July.

Then, out of the blue, he came to me one day and said that something had cropped up and wondered if I'd be interested. Upon asking what it was, Harry told me a new team was starting up in the NASL and the manager there, Freddie Goodwin, had asked if we had any players that he could 'loan' for the upcoming season, which starts in May and finishes at the end of August. He went on to add that I might miss a game or two but would I be interested. I didn't see this offer coming; it was completely out of left field, so to speak. I said to Harry, "Well, I might be interested, but are you willing to let me go out there and play through the summer?" Harry said, "Yes, but just this once!" And so, that's how that all came about, and as far as I know the club let Steve Litt and Ron Futcher go over as well as myself.

Cathie and I went out to Minnesota at the end of the 1975/76 season. In the middle of the NASL season was the bicentennial celebrations of the US independence so there was to be a two-week break. This had all been agreed before I went out there with Minnesota's manager, Freddie Goodwin, so Cathie and I spent those two weeks over in New Zealand with her mum and dad. Cathie stayed on for another week or two with her parents after I travelled back for the re-start of the NASL season.

The team was so successful we actually made it to the final of the cup. We'd won our league, the conference, as they called it. In the final, we came up against Toronto, which we lost, but the season for us overall was still considered to be a great success. I came out on the statistics table with being their top player in 'Goal Assists'. Whereas, back in those days in England, nobody was counting assists, unlike in the modern game. But back then in America, they were already heavily into the data and statistics such as assists etc., so when I left there and came back home, Minnesota arranged a deal with Luton Town for me to return to play for them in the NASL every year for the next three years. That's how the whole thing came about, initially from a conversation with Harry about mine and Cathie's desire to get out to New Zealand and then on the back of the team doing so well in 1976. Minnesota were keen to keep that team together and bring back the other lads as well as myself.

Steve Litt went there permanently and he stayed. He's still living in the States now. Ron Futcher went back and he stayed there until the club packed in around 1981. I went there every summer from 1976 until 1979 and I really enjoyed it out there, it was a fantastic experience. In the NASL back then it was a 50/50 mix in terms of the pitches being traditional grass or astroturf, which, at the time, nobody played on in the English football league. The most amazing aspect of my time out there was the players that I played against, absolute legends of the game. I played against them all: Pele, Beckenbauer, Cruyff, Eusebio and George Best. Even better was to come in 1977 when I got chosen to play in the 'All-Star' team with those players as one of the midfield three, which to me was quite remarkable, consisting of George Best, Franz Beckenbauer, and me!

I played across two generations of Luton sides really, but I think my best Luton XI that I personally played with, and it's not easy as I've had to leave out some very good players, was a 4-3-3 formation. Jake Findlay in goal, back four of John Ryan, Steve Buckley, Paul Futcher, Mal Donaghy, midfield three of Ricky Hill, Peter Anderson, Lil Fuccillo (before he broke his leg, he was a brilliant left-sided midfield player), front three David Moss, Brian Stein and Jimmy Husband. I have to say that Ricky Hill was the best midfielder that I ever saw at Luton, and had he played for Arsenal or Manchester United he would have had a lot more senior England caps than what he did get playing at Luton.

Before Ricky came into the first team that day over Easter 1976, Harry Haslam had told me about this young lad that he'd seen playing on a Saturday morning in the youth team. I used to go along to watch the games as well, played up on Stockingstone Road at the old Co-op pitch. Harry would like me, as club Captain, to go along and encourage the kids coming through. Ricky stood out in those games; a fantastic talent!

Having got so close to getting promotion back to the First Division in both 1979/80 and 1980/81, the resolve was still there within the group, both in the players and the staff, that we'd do it at the next attempt. The

younger players that had been coming through by now had a couple of years' league experience under their belts and were able to stand their own ground, maturing into really good football league players.

The two seasons previously we were so nearly there, but just not quite there in getting over the line. David Pleat knew that he still needed one or two players to really make sure we could maintain and achieve our ultimate goal of promotion over a whole season. The key to this was bringing in Brian Horton. That was a brilliant move and the gamble was there for all to see as David let Paddy Grealish go the other way with Tony leaving to join Brighton. David knew that we needed a little bit of extra toughness in the centre of the park as around Brian, all the other players would improve and grow in stature.

I reached a point of asking myself again, do I stay or not? I had a long chat with David about this. He really wanted me to stay but he was totally honest in saying that he couldn't guarantee I would be in the team every week, of which I understood, and as I was thirty/thirty-one by then, I knew I was past my very best. I was still in the squad though, and in and out of the team during the season (1980/81) that had just ended. I still felt I had a lot to offer and I still wanted to play at this stage, I wasn't quite sure about my future, whether or not I would go into coaching or managing, but I certainly didn't want to be sat on the bench.

I was still in contract at Luton and felt like I still had a year or two left in me as a player. During this time, I had my former team mate at Luton Town, Peter Anderson, ringing me every day, asking if I'd made my mind up yet and saying that he'd got a lot of good young players there with him at Millwall and that I would be ideal to help him to bring them through. He'd just got the manager's job and never stopped badgering me, which was nice in a way of course, but you'd never get that today with managers phoning players directly, not with agents and other people in place around top players these days in the modern game. It just wouldn't be allowed.

'Westy' launches another Luton Town attack at Kenilworth Road against Shrewsbury also in April 1980

Luton had put it out there in the football circles letting it be known that they were willing to listen to offers for me, and there was interest from around ten clubs who wanted to sign me. I felt torn wondering what to do. I was settled in Luton as I'd been in the town for almost ten years, so it was a really difficult decision to make. I think what swayed it for me was that I still had this desire to play for a while longer and so I decided in the end to leave and join my old mate Peter at Millwall.

Having joined Millwall, it was ironic that in one of the pre-season friendly games in that summer of 1981 when I moved, Luton Town came down for a friendly match against us. It was nothing to do with my going there; I think it was already arranged with David Pleat through his obvious Luton connection with my new manager Peter Anderson. I recall talking to Brian just before that game, obviously I'd played against him in the past, and he told me that in coming to Luton he was looking forward to at long last playing with me and not having to kick me! I kind of think we would have made a good team, that he would have won the ball and played it off to me. Brian was a very good player and a great professional.

It was okay at Millwall, but it didn't work out for Peter as he got sacked after about eighteen months. At this point, with around eighteen months remaining on my contract, George Graham came in. George wanted to change everything, and he did a good job, though in my opinion he just brought in a load of runners and kickers to get the job done in Division 3.

With regards to the ongoing contract discussions with George Graham, Millwall were willing to let me go but without honouring the remainder of my contract. I said, "Look George, I'm married with two little boys, I have a lot of responsibility – you owe me eighteen months contract plus the signing on fee still – and you just want me to leave, think about it again and come back to me with a sensible, reasonable offer." I didn't expect all of the money they owed me, but something decent.

The on and off discussions continued back and forth until one Tuesday morning when I was in for training. After the session George said to me, "I've had another chat with the Chairman, Alan. Have you got ten minutes to talk it over?" I followed him into his office and during this conversation he made me a reasonable offer. I told him straight away that I'd accept and we should call it a day.George said, "Alan, you've been a really great player but this type of football at this level is just not for you," and so we came to an agreement and I left Millwall. By then I was really suffering with terrible Achilles tendon trouble and as I was thirty-two going on thirty-three, I was obviously past my best so it was the right time for me to go.

I left home that morning as a Millwall player and I returned home later on to inform Cathie that I was no longer. I explained that we'd agreed a settlement on my remaining contract and the outstanding signing on fee but had to break the news that I was now out of a job! She just looked at me with a shocked expression at the finality and suddenness it had come to an end. But in the evening of that very same day, Cyril Buck, the Secretary of Hitchin Town rang me out of the blue. "Alan," he said, "I know that this is a far-fetched question but we are in a bit of a pickle here at Hitchin as we're right down near the bottom of the league. Is there absolutely any chance that you might come to Hitchin Town as our player/manager?" I said to him, "Cyril, do you know what's happened today?" When he said he didn't, I explained to him about me leaving Millwall.

I didn't take Cyril up on his offer that day, on principal, because they already had a manager. But I did say to him, "Hopefully, you'll stay up in the league by getting enough points in the six games or so that you have left to play. If you still want me, talk to me again at the end of the season when you've spoken to the manager that you have in place there now."

Hitchin Town managed to stay up. They sorted out their existing manager and he left the club, then they came back with another approach for me to join them, to which I happily accepted, and stayed there for four years.

I really enjoyed my time at Hitchin, where we had a steady flow of the young lads that hadn't quite made it at Luton Town and with Hitchin being so close geographically to Luton, we were well placed for the lads to carry on playing football at a decent standard of non-league whilst they found their feet outside the environment of being at a full-time football club. Some coped better than others; lads like Mark Burke and Les Harriott. Les was at Barnet with Barry Fry but when he wasn't playing for them Barry would let him come and play for us so he was in and out of our side for about a season or so. Audley Baker joined us too, and his son, Lewis, who played for Chelsea, is currently at Stoke City. Young

John Woodward had come across a little earlier from Luton, however, bless him, John sadly passed away in 2020. Neil Madden had also found the path to Top Field, too. David Pleat had high hopes for 'Mads' at one point. He really rated Neil and ultimately, I think he saw him as a natural replacement for me in my role in the Luton Town side as he was a similar(ish) type of player to myself. He was a very clever footballer but for whatever reasons never made it in league football. Another very clever player who came to Hitchin from Luton was Ray Brammer, who spent one or two seasons with us. David had also hoped that Ray would be a natural replacement for David Moss on the left wing in a similar vein that he'd hoped Neil Madden would succeed myself. David certainly thought he had a player in Ray. He was a good player, but he was a classic case of getting in with the wrong crowd very early on and he just lost his way. Again, he was another player who was in and out of the side at Hitchin. I could never really put my finger on it but he just didn't have that commitment or desire to knuckle down, which was a shame really, and I've not heard from him in years.

People still to this day send me those Topps chewing gum cards from the mid to late 1970s and ask me to sign them. I never received a penny in image rights from those cards and stickers whereas players these days would sue if their image was being used for commercial gain without their permission. I don't really know why I seemed to always be selected for the card sets back then, but thought it was because I'd come from the First Division with Burnley, having played for the England Under 23s and was now Captain at Luton Town.

Whenever I've been asked the question over the years, why did I stay at Luton Town for so long when I could have moved on and back up to the First Division especially when the club were in dire financial straits under Harry Haslam around 1975/76 and again when David Pleat took over midway through the 1977/78 season, I tell them that I stayed on because it was a family club with a great bunch of players and the fans were really loyal. I really enjoyed my time playing for Luton. Being part of the football family, we share something beautiful and very special.

(BORN 14 MAY 1960, KINGSBURY, LONDON BOROUGH OF BRENT)

# ALAN GRAHAM JUDGE

## LUTON TOWN FC 1976-1983

*In 1976, sixteen-year-old Alan was playing for a youth side in Welwyn Garden City when his coach suggested that he attend midweek coaching sessions at Luton Town, together with future fellow Luton Town apprentices, Nigel Johnson and Phil Driver. Signed up on schoolboy forms by Harry Haslam, all three were eventually offered apprenticeships or young professional contracts. David Pleat gave Alan his first full professional contract soon after he became manager, in January 1978, on the advice of Danny Bergara.*

My impression of David Pleat was that he was very open to ideas from home and abroad and willing to give youth a chance. I credit my long career in the professional game to the disciplines instilled into me during those early years at Luton. I travelled to Luton with Nigel and Phil as they lived close to each other, and then I moved in with Wayne Turner and his family in 1981, staying there until I moved to Reading in 1983. A lad called Kerry Dixon would pick me up from Wayne's house and give me a lift to the Elm Park club. Kerry was a local Luton lad, who was overlooked by Luton Town as a youth player and later went on from Reading to become something of a legend with Chelsea.

The team spirit at Luton was excellent; something David Pleat was keen to foster. There were very few clashes of personality, however, so it didn't matter who I roomed with when travelling for away games. As goalkeepers, we had to get on as we spent a lot of time training together and so we were often teamed up in the same room.

One of my roommates was Milija Aleksic, a great guy, always willing to

Alan Judge, media day in the Summer of 1982

pass on tips and help me improve. Others such as Jake Findlay, Tony Godden and Andy Beasley had a more competitive edge, but I enjoyed working with them all, nonetheless.

Fairly early into the 1978/79 season, David Pleat signed Jake Findlay. I'll always remember Jake's first morning coming into the club. He was really nervous, he'd come from Aston Villa reserves and nobody had ever really heard of him. So, Jake walked in and immediately Milija, with a big smile on his face, went up to him, shook his hand welcoming him in to the club and then started singing, 'You say hello, and I say goodbye' to the tune of The Beatles song 'Hello Goodbye'. But that was Milija, he was just class, he was great, and perhaps he knew that he was moving to Tottenham so maybe that's why he was in such a good mood.

David Pleat did occasionally watch reserve and youth games, monitoring the progress of all players and taking many younger players through the system and into the first team: Clive Goodyear, Wayne Turner, Rob Johnson, Mitchell Thomas and Garry Parker to name just a few. Garry Parker still often reminds me that he used to clean my boots!

My first team debut was away at Newcastle United on the last game of the 1979/80 season. I had a serious ankle injury a couple of months earlier and was asked if I felt fit enough to play. I still had a slight limp but I said yes, anyway. It was sore but I got through okay. David Peat said the Newcastle United manager, Bill McGarry, had said I looked like a goalkeeper, which made me believe then that I might have a career in the game, and to this day I still appreciate the chance that Pleat gave me. My debut ended in a 2-2 draw with Bob Hatton scoring both the Luton goals that day. In the championship winning season of 1981/82 the draw, played against Rotherham, stood out because of my penalty save. I really don't know what the fuss was about. I was always going to save it!

The coaching staff at Luton, Danny Bergara, Trevor Hartley and David Coates, had a fabulous passion and great amount of knowledge that gave me a springboard into a long career in football. They were demanding when they needed to be, but always up for a joke at the right time. Plenty of humour would take place in the changing rooms and we

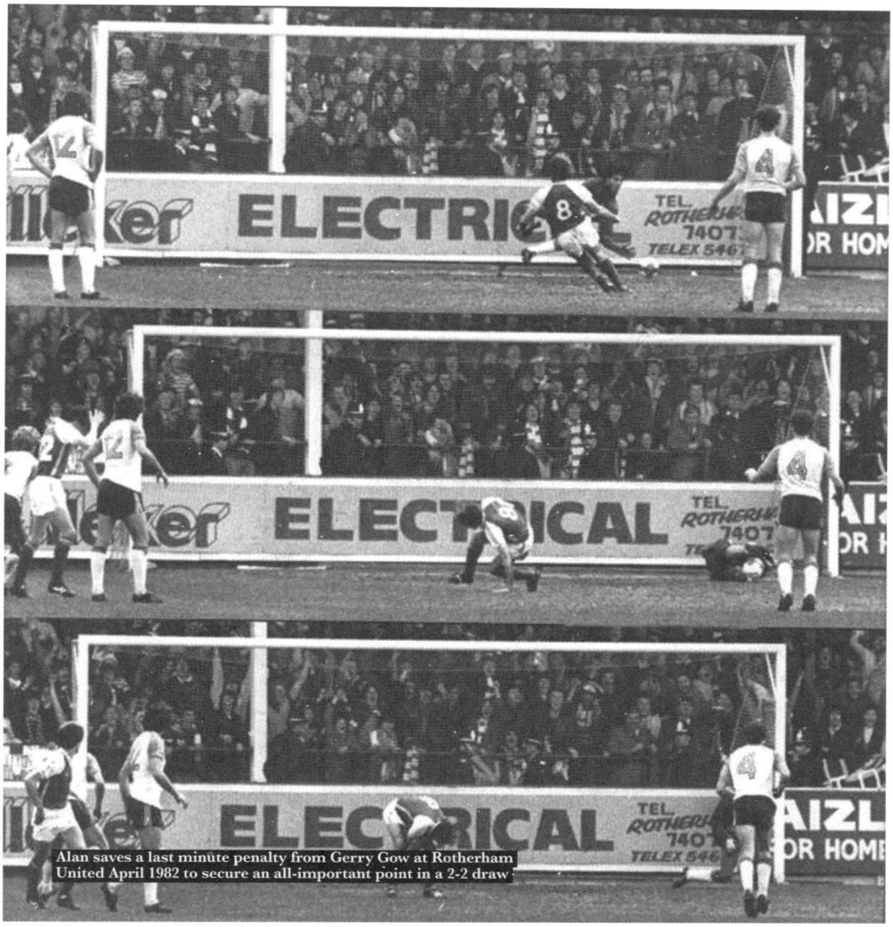


Alan saves a last minute penalty from Gerry Gow at Rotherham United April 1982 to secure an all-important point in a 2-2 draw

all had nicknames, some more flattering than others! We were occasionally taken away for team bonding and we always had a healthy respect and appreciation for what we could bring to the team.

When I looked around the changing room and saw players like Mal Donaghy, Kirk Stephens, Ricky Hill and David Moss, how could you not feel confident going into the game? They exuded an air of invincibility in the promotion season.

I was pleased with my contribution to the team in the 1981/82 season. But Jake Findlay was firmly the number 1 at the time and rightly so. He was a very good keeper and I had little experience back then. The experienced players always had time for the younger players, though. We socialised away from football and many lifelong friendships were formed. The time I spent with Wayne Turner's family and friends was a particularly special time for me. In fact, he introduced me to my wife thirty-three years ago!

After an initial loan period in the latter stages of the 1982/83 season, I left Luton for Reading in the summer of 1983. I was unable to break into the first team and we all knew the time had come for me to leave. I was a late developer and didn't feel I had the physicality to succeed at the top level until I was in my mid-twenties.

My proudest achievement, though, was to play for the Oxford United first team at the age of forty-four after having survived bowel cancer four years earlier. Peter Rhodes Brown, a former team mate of mine, recently told me I was in the top ten list of the oldest players to have played league football. Something to tell the grandkids! The game was away at Southend United on November 6th, 2004

I now own a driver-trainer school and live in Bicester, in Oxfordshire. Driving has always been a passion of mine since I was a kid, along with football, of course. But mainly I love being my own boss. I enjoy motorsport too, particularly F1, and I got a class 1 LGV licence when I was in my late twenties and went on to drive trucks in between football seasons to supplement my income. I coached at the Oxford United Centre of Excellence, including goalkeepers from youth to first team level up until I was forty-nine. I kept myself fit and continued to play for local teams managed by former team mates at southern league level up until that time. When I stopped playing, however, I stopped coaching, too. It became clear I just liked the 'playing football' part.

Regrettably, I have no memorabilia from my time at Luton Town. The only things I've kept from back then is my shirt and the Milk Cup final winners' medal when I was at Oxford United.

(BORN 26TH OCTOBER 1959, LUTON, BEDFORDSHIRE)

# GODFREY PATRICK INGRAM

LUTON TOWN FC 1977 - 1982

*Born at the Luton & Dunstable hospital, Godfrey went to Northfields Upper School as his family lived on the Dunstable side of Poynters Road in the town. In 1975 he played for England Schoolboys against West Germany in front of a crowd of 90,000 to 100,000 spectators. He scored a couple of goals and was being hailed as the English Pele!*

*Living up to the superstar reviews he got as a fifteen-year-old, Godfrey Ingram was a world beater. While playing at Wembley he destroyed the West German Schoolboys with a two-goal performance that so impressed their National Team manager, Helmut Schon, he wanted to recruit Godfrey there and then and place him with a top German club.*

In that England schoolboys team with me that day was Billy Gilbert who went on to play for Crystal Palace, Jerry Murphy and Paul Waddington, also both with Crystal Palace, and Ray Ranson who later played for Manchester City. Also, a very gifted lad called Jason Seacole, who played for Oxford United. What I didn't know at the time was that David Pleat had also played for England Schoolboys.

At Wembley, when I got those two goals, one of which I scored when I, seemingly, went around everybody, shortly afterwards Shalke 04 announced they wanted to sign me. Back then Shalke and other teams didn't have any easy way of getting in contact with me so they literally sent somebody over from Germany. The representative in question had a limousine and was driven around the Luton area asking everyone where I lived! Finally, he tracked me down and on arrival said, "We'd love to sign you for Schalke and as a gift we'd like to give you this show dog." The dog was a really beautiful pedigree poodle.

Helmut Schon was the West German National Team manager and after he'd seen me in that game at Wembley, he'd set about trying to get me into a top German side. The guy who stood on our doorstep holding the Poodle added, "Helmut Schon sends his best regards, he thinks that you're a wonderful player and we'd really love for you to come and play and to see Germany." I was already on schoolboy forms by then with Luton Town but as ordinary folk, me and my family were intrigued and agreed to go.

They took us out to Schalke where I met and trained with some great players like Branko Oblak and Klaus Fischer. It was just incredible, but I think what stopped me pursuing this amazing opportunity was that firstly Luton Town was my team, having supported them for as long as I could remember, but also the thought of leaving my family and friends at that age was just too much. I couldn't imagine it. With the benefit of hindsight, and seeing the success of players such as Jadon Sancho, I often wonder what might have happened had I taken up the offer. They offered me a lot of money, too, a lot more than I would ever be on in Luton's first team. But playing for Luton was my dream. I remember watching Ian Buxton, Malcolm MacDonald, Terry Branston and Graham French, of course. Graham French was fantastic. The first time that I actually realised a ball could be 'curled' was watching him near the touchline down the Oak Road end. I was amazed with the technique that you could actually make the ball spin and that stayed with me as I started practising all of the techniques I was seeing first hand out there on the football pitch. My adopted dad, Eric, who has now passed, used to spend hour upon and hour dedicated to just kicking the ball backwards and forwards to me. It wasn't necessarily that he wanted me to be a footballer but he was very supportive of whatever I wanted to do, and so he was prepared to stay out there to pass the ball and throw it up in the air, that sort of thing. I really did have a great upbringing.

I grew up playing for a local team called Luton Dynamos where Alan Slough was the honorary head of the team. I had Luton in my blood for as long as I can remember. In fact, around 1969/70 when I was about ten years old, I was a mascot at a home match at Kenilworth Road. From being a kid on the terraces standing in the crowd one year to being able to play out there the following year was a dream come true.

Luton Town already had me on schoolboy forms and recognised my potential. David Pleat said I had some very special talents which included pace, control, finishing, and the balance which seemed to be a gift.

When I signed for Luton Town, I was an apprentice, but only for about six months before signing up as a junior professional. We only had three apprentices at the time; a lad called Nigel Johnson, who sadly passed away around twenty or so years ago, and Phil Driver who went on to play for Chelsea. They, along with goalkeeper Alan Judge, were all from the Welwyn Garden City area.

At the time when I signed as junior pro, David Pleat was the reserve team coach and the youth team was looked after by Danny Bergara. Danny was amazing, he'd had a fantastic playing career and as a South American (Uruguayan), the techniques and skills that he taught us were fantastic. I really owe a lot to him.

As I came out of the youth team, I started playing for the reserves under David Pleat and that's where my tactical and game management education started.

It's a massive step up from youth team football to playing in the reserves where you are suddenly playing against opposition players who are hardened experienced first team players, and you have to learn fast how to play the game. Up until that time I was still a very raw player. Nobody had really coached me because, as a kid, I was so far ahead of everybody and scoring goals for fun. Getting some technical coaching from Danny Bergara and then tactical ideas from David was amazing, a real eye-opening time for me.

I got my chance in the first team mid-way through the 1977/78 season when Harry Haslam put me in for a series of games where we played Oldham Athletic three times in a week: once in the league and two FA Cup games in January 1978. Later that season I remember coming on from the bench, away at Millwall, and then starting and scoring a 25-yarder away at Burnley, but by that time David Pleat was the Manager. The main thing that I remember about that game at Turf Moor was the sheer size of Burnley's Steve Kindon. He really was the biggest human that I had ever seen in my entire young life up until that point. He was also unbelievably quick for a big guy. Then you had Ralph Coates with his comb over hair flaying in the wind and there I was, looking at these guys and thinking that these are real men that I'm playing against now.

I was really saddened by the departure of both Harry Haslam and

Danny Bergara when they took up the reins at Sheffield United, because Harry had signed me as an apprentice. Harry had such a jovial approach it was almost like he wasn't a football manager yet was more like a friend. Harry, like everyone back then, would say stuff that would now be considered racist, things like, "Don't hide in the dark corners" But I never took it to be derogatory at all; it was just the way things were back then. By joking around and bringing a smile, he kind of brought me out of my shell a little bit. There I was, sitting with first team players, and we'd all be laughing and joking so the fact that he'd recognised me, I found at the time, was quite amazing.

For me, Harry Haslam was fantastic and as I'd already played for David in the reserve team, he knew what I could do, so when he became the first team manager I expected to get lots of games. I would say that Harry and Danny leaving was hard on a lot of players, not just myself, because we loved them both. It's not an exaggeration to say that Harry Haslam was 'Mr Luton Town'. If my memory serves me correctly Danny may have mentioned to me in passing about joining them at Bramall Lane, but again, at that time, I would never have considered leaving Luton Town.

People ask me about that first game of the 1978/79 season, when I lined up as the sub on the opening day alongside seven or so of David Pleat's new signings. We went in 1-0 down at half time but scored six in the second half, yet I have absolutely no recollection of this game. I ended up playing most of my career and scoring all the goals over in America so when I try to think back to specific games and who they were against I have to say that I do struggle with the details at times. I was expecting to play more under David, but in those first couple of seasons I only got a handful of games in the first team and in his second season in 1979/80, I only played in one game which was away at West Ham. The West Ham game was a real battle, we won 2-1 and Mick Saxby got the winner. West Ham had some great players, they were a footballing team and we were a footballing team as well, but we were better…

The first time I went to America was in the summer of 1979 where I played for New York Cosmos. With Luton Town's wage bill, they really had to off load players in the 'off-season'. At the time, Cosmos had a policy of trying to select the best young players from around the world and putting them together with some absolutely sensational established footballers. When I arrived there we were due to play Argentina's national team as they were touring. I arrived on the Tuesday and we were due to play them on the Thursday. The club told their kitman, "Put Ingram's name over the top of the first shirt that you can find as he's going to go on the bench." Years later when I went to wash that shirt, inside I found Johan Cryuff's name with mine hastily sewn over it. I am pleased to say that I've still got the shirt. I did get to keep quite a few from my time playing in the States as they weren't as stingy as our kitman, George Rogers, at Luton. He was a wonderful man, but he was also wonderfully mean with the kit, though thinking about it, with us lot he had to be!

Steve White was then bought from Bristol Rovers, for a lot of money. He was a great goalscorer and although I felt that he struggled at first, when a Second Division club paid £200,000 back then (in 1979) for a player, they must keep playing them. I felt that perhaps nobody valued me here and I might have to move on after all. Another forward player was brought in, Andy Harrow from Scotland, but he was soon returned north of the border.

I did go out on loan in the 1979/80 season to Northampton Town where I played around ten or so games and scored four goals. They made an offer for me to sign on a permanent basis but I genuinely can't remember if I turned it down or if it wasn't enough for Luton Town to let me go. That loan spell really woke me up to the fact that I wanted to be playing first team football and that I really didn't want to be messing about playing reserve team football anymore. It was the first time I thought that if things weren't going to work out at Luton Town then I'll have to move on.

A local newspaper reported at the time that Northampton Town boss, Dave Bowen, offered £55,000 and Luton Town accepted. But I refused, much to David Pleat's surprise. I wasn't happy to sign for Northampton on a permanent deal, preferring instead to stay and fight for my place in Luton's first team. Pleat was quoted as saying, "For the first time I sensed he was prepared to fight for something."

I was soon back in the squad and enjoyed my extended run in the team when Steve White twisted his ankle midway through the 1980/81 season. I was duly selected for the following game, which was at home to Preston, and promptly scored a spectacular solo goal enabling a 4-2 victory. David Pleat purred in his post-match interview, "Here's something you don't see often in the English Second Division, lovely skills, lovely touches, there was fear in the Preston defenders' eyes."

The thing with David was that he certainly had an eye for a bargain,

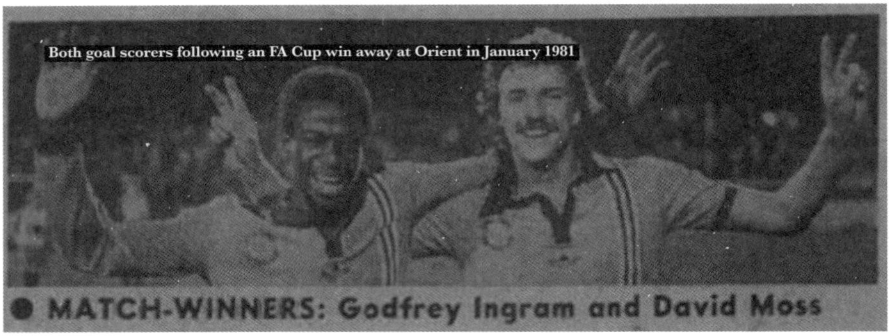


picking up the likes of Steiny and more than one or two others along the way; it's all competition. But, for a player like me, I got a little discouraged. I was thinking how hard I was training, listening to instructions, yet feeling like I wasn't getting anywhere. So, going to Northampton, even though it was a drop of one or two divisions, it rekindled my belief in myself that I was a bloody good player and I knew that I'd got a tonne of goals in me. It was unfortunate but it was a realisation that my long-term future may not involve scoring goals for Luton Town and, as the record books show, I went on to score 270 goals later in my career. The funny thing is I always knew I could get goals no matter what level I played at. I played one or two games up front with Bob Hatton and in that formation, I felt that I could score a bunch of goals no matter the opposition. I've got good memories generally as a player at Luton, and remember scoring away at Newcastle United in an FA Cup tie and some other really nice goals, and I just didn't get enough opportunities in the first team.

I loved scoring at Kenilworth Road and jumping on the bars, it was really special because there were loads of my mates in there celebrating the goal with me. I got into a bit of trouble with the referees for doing it, though I don't think I got booked, just told off occasionally.

There were other challenges playing back then, too. The misconceptions, especially as a black player, people would say, "Oh, Ingram, he's good, but he doesn't like a kick." I would say who DOES like getting kicked? Centre halves of the day were scared of my pace and the way that I used to receive the ball. I wasn't a typical centre forward and would move left or right, and as centre backs don't like moving laterally I'd do that, get the ball and I'd be gone. There weren't many defenders who could keep up with me. I played a couple of games on the wing when Mossy was still in Tampa at the start of the 1981/82 season and you'd know what was coming, first half of the game, the full back is going to steam into you. I learnt a little trick watching Pele, where he'd be off the ground but kind of left his foot in so as the guy goes underneath you, your studs would go right across his rib cage. I was never naturally like that, I didn't want to hurt anybody, but it was only when people started trying to destroy me I thought okay, have this… I'd ride the tackle but they'd have my studs instead so they didn't get to break my legs.

Sir Alex Ferguson, he wasn't a sir at the time though of course, saw me as a potential player to join him at Aberdeen in the Scottish Premier League so I went up there for them to take a closer look at me in November 1980. The funny thing was that I left Luton Airport in just a sports jacket but when I arrived in Aberdeen in was below zero, and was truly the coldest that I'd ever been in my life. The club put me into digs in Aberdeen and that first night when I got into bed I was that cold I stayed fully clothed under the bed covers. Sir Alex was fantastic with me, he saw my potential and I was really excited at the possibility of maybe joining them. Mark McGhee was paired with me to show me around as I guess Sir Alex thought we'd make a good pairing and would complement each other up front, so he wanted us the gel off the pitch as well, which we did; we got on really well. I took part in a trial game and trained with the first team for around four days. I gave a really good account of myself scoring a bunch of goals in practice and in a trial match, and I felt very sharp. My overriding memory of that week was not only one of just being cold, but also the bars and restaurants that were quite interesting because they were full of Americans from the oil industry. That was another eye opener for me that's for sure, as I was this young kid from Luton finding myself away from home and suddenly surrounded by American accents everywhere in Aberdeen up in the northeast of Scotland. These were big hairy oil driller guys with big moustaches, beards and arms as thick as tree trunks. I felt like I was in the middle of a music video for the Village People! It was quite surreal but that was pretty much my experience of Aberdeen at the time.

Aberdeen had a really good team and you could see they were building something there and were looking to cement the foundations by bringing in really good young players. In fact, the club won three league championships, four Scottish Cups, one League Cup, the European Cup Winner's Cup and the European Super Cup in and around the years that followed leading to Sir Alex taking up his role at Manchester United late in 1986. Sir Alex told me that he was very impressed with me but ultimately,

I think that, well at least the papers reported at the time, Luton wanted a little bit too much for me (a reported £120,000 figure) so that deal didn't go through which was a real shame. That's certainly chalked up as another 'what could have been'.

The stuff that David did with the team, tactically, was really fantastic; tactics didn't really exist so much under Harry. But David brought in different formations and gave us different things to think about. Counter attacking for instance, I think we were the first team that planned to counter attack and the way that he described it was completely out of the blue during a training session up at Stopsley. He said, "Jake, the moment you get the ball in your hands from a corner or when you cut out a cross during open play, I want Kirk to sprint out on the right side and David Carr, I want you to sprint out to the left hand side. Jake, you get the ball to them and then just drive on with it." I remember us doing that so well that we became a team that could counter attack with devastating effect. I scored a goal away at Derby where it went from Jake and we worked it all the way down the field, a cross centre pass out on the left from David Moss, and my pace got me clear of the defenders. I planted the ball in the back of the net whilst my momentum took me backwards, which made the ball rise. Thankfully it hit the net and didn't sail over the bar, and this was all captured by the Match of the Day cameras and shown to the nation later that evening. It was a really big thing to be selected as one of the three of four games that they would show. We were also up against former Luton players Steve Buckley and Alan Biley, who were both in the Derby County side that day. That kind of tactical genius is what David brought to Luton Town and everyone in the team knew what to do when the oppositions attack broke down. We were so quick to counter it was fantastic.

The first game on astroturf in English football, in which we played and won away at QPR in the early part of the 1981/82 season was incredible. I was just amazed at the speed of the ball and like I said, we were a footballing team so were used to knocking it into feet, but some players who just weren't used to doing that would find that the ball would skip away from them and it would be gone.

The situation during the 1981/82 season was that I was still under contract at Luton for another year or two but I'd only played two or three games at the beginning of the season before Mossy came back and then I was out of the team again.There was a lot of newspaper talk about Chelsea preparing to put an offer in for me. Then, one day, David pulled

Godfrey up against QPR's John Burridge in April 1981, Godfrey had earlier scored a bullet header past the legendary keeper in the first half

me to one side and told me there was a team really interested in me. So, I'm thinking, You little beauty, here it comes, I'm going to be playing with players like Clive Walker at 'The Bridge'... However, David then told me the club was San Jose. I was taken aback and really didn't know what to make of it. The amusing thing is that I went straight home where I still lived with my folks, and looked it up in an encyclopaedia Britannica. The first thing that came up told me that San Jose was in Costa Rica.

I was adamant that I wasn't going there, I didn't even know where it was on the map! I went back to Pleaty and said, "Hey, it's a really interesting offer, thanks for thinking of me, but I ain't going to Costa Rica." David looked me, sighed and said, "It's San Jose in California!"

In the back of my mind I thought, Okay, Chelsea, with all these rumours in the newspapers, I know they want to sign me so there's been some tapping up and all that nod, wink and a promise sort of stuff going on here…I'll go to California for the rest of the 1981/82 season and then I'll come back. That's all I had in mind when I went out to the States, a few months then Chelsea here I come. Then, I arrived in San Jose and the first person I met was George Best. It was now a case of Wow, I'm playing with Besty here! not to mention San Jose had tripled the wages I was on at Luton Town. I was still very much thinking that I'd prefer to have the rest of the year here and then see what happens. However, before the end of the season, San Jose came to me out of the blue and doubled the wages again! I just didn't know what to do and of course back then I had no way of contacting anyone at Chelsea to find out if they were still interested in me. Then, in the off season, I came back to England and got married, went back to California, and that's how I ended up staying in the States.

I would have really liked to have joined Chelsea but in my first season at San Jose I was scoring goals for fun, broke George Best's previous goal scoring record, was being mobbed by fans, interviewed on TV after every game and I was loving life. From there I just kept going. It's a funny old world how things work out!

I played out the rest of the 1981/82 season with San Jose scoring seventeen goals in thirty-one games and came back to England in the late summer of 1982. That was the time I joined Cardiff City. The number one reason that I came back was that my adopted mother was only expected to live a few more weeks or months at best, so San Jose were good enough to sell me to Cardiff, albeit retaining an option to buy me back. Cardiff City were brilliant with me, they let me stay in Luton near my mother and train with Luton Town on the Monday, Tuesday and maybe even the Wednesday, too, and then I'd drive all the way back to Cardiff in a car that Chris Green from Tricentrol lent me. I'd then take part in training or a practice match with City on the Thursday, rest on the Friday, play the match on the Saturday and then straight afterwards I'd be back to Luton to see my mum on the Sunday. That was kind of a cool thing that Pleaty allowed me to do, and I always appreciated the kindness he showed to me during that time in my life.

A side story to this is whenever I came back to the UK, Chris at Tricentrol would always do me a deal whereby I would buy a secondhand car, and then he would buy it back from me for the same price. The first time I did this, myself and my wife at the time toured the South of France and went onto Spain a few times, putting about 10,000 miles on the clock. Fair to say that I was called a few expletives by Chris when I returned the car, but he'd agreed to buy it back at the same price, no questions asked! He was, and still is, a great guy.

During my stay at Cardiff, San Jose looked for another striker to replace me but they couldn't find one and so they exercised their contractual right to buy me back. I enjoyed my short time playing for Cardiff City, they had a tremendous crowd and support, plus I got to train with a very young up and coming goalkeeper by the name of Andy Dibble, who a few years later would go on to write his name in legendary status at Wembley in helping Luton Town defeat Arsenal in the League Cup Final. I returned to playing for Golden Bay Earthquakes (San Jose had changed their name) in the 1982/83 Indoor season scoring a further thirty-four goals in thirty-eight games.

So there I was, playing for and really enjoying San Jose. I was living the dream, but then they traded me to Minnesota Strikers. Now, bearing in mind this was 1984, Minnesota offered me a three-year contract worth £250,000 a year improving to £300,000 and then to £350,000 the following year. However, I really loved San Jose so I ripped up the

Godfrey in pre-season photo shoot in the summer of 1981

contract in front of Joe Robbie Jr. of the Robbie family, who owned the Miami Dolphins. I said there just wasn't enough money to keep me in this town and I just threw it back at him. Years later, I met him again, and I apologised for being such a stupid brat at the time.

Later on, after I had been in the States for a few years, around the mid-1980s I came back to England and had a pre-season trial with West Ham. I really wanted to come back as I'd matured as a player and got even faster. I remember at the time Peter Beardsley had been playing for the Vancouver Whitecaps and was making a successful return for Newcastle. Peter and I used to play against each other and, although I never like to compare myself, I felt that I was far ahead of him technically and had become a match winner. Afterall, I had been playing and learning from top world class players like Carlos Alberto, Franz Beckenbauer and Johan Neeskens with New York Cosmos, and previously I'd learnt so much from George Best that I thought if I come , I might have a chance to push into the England squad with the Mexico World Cup in 1986.

I came over for pre-season with West Ham. Paul Ince and Frank McAvennie were there under Lou Macari. It was very enjoyable at West Ham and they had the same footballing philosophy as Luton; Billy Bonds had already retired but he was still as fit as a fiddle. Billy would take us for the running sessions and he'd leave us all for dead, he was amazingly fit. It was a good team and the sort of side that I felt I would score a bunch of goals for. I played a few friendly games, notched a few goals and they offered me a contract, but I could earn in a week what they were offering me for a month. Football is a short career; I'd worked my way up to the top in the States and would have been starting again at the bottom back in England, albeit probably with a chance to make the world cup squad. In the end, the timing just wasn't quite right for me to come back to England.

Milan Mandarić, who had founded San Jose Earthquakes and would later become well known as a club owner in England with various clubs including Portsmouth and Leicester City, came to me and said, "Godfrey, you're earning top money, you really need to talk to my accountant." The accountant advised me to buy something substantial that would be tax deductible and help me reduce my tax. I returned a week later to happily inform him I'd followed his advice. "I've just bought a nice big boat," I announced. The accountant wasn't best pleased said, "I meant buy a goddam house!" And yes, this was in Silicon Valley where homes are now selling for millions, but I was just a naïve kid from Luton who had gone from being a home town reserve team player, half in and half out of the first team at Luton Town FC, to starring for San Jose playing with the likes of George Best in a very short space of time. My intellect had not kept pace and I soon caught on. But that episode still makes me laugh.

The end result was Hey, here I am in California, spending gorgeous afternoons on my boat in San Francisco Bay, earning a world class wage, and then, out of the blue, I get an amazing chance to come back to England to join West Ham. I really wanted to join them but I had to weigh things up and in the end, financially, it made no sense and that's why I never returned to play in England.

As it turned out, staying in the States was a blessing in disguise in that all owners of the clubs I played for had one thing in common: they were all owned by very successful entrepreneurs and all of them encouraged me as their top player to learn a little about business. They would say, "Please come and spend some time with us and we'll teach you how our businesses works." That was the catalyst for me going into business. It was like going to a free business school and I feel extremely fortunate that it worked out the way that it did. Of course, I do have a few regrets, I would have loved to have played in the 1986 World Cup, I'd have loved to play for Chelsea, Schalke and West Ham, but at least I achieved what I set out to do as a six-year-old and that was to play for my home-town team, Luton Town.

Years later, I was fortunate enough to be in a position to help the club financially when I was asked to be an investor in the 20/20 group. Gary Sweet's family and my family used to go to the Stopsley Working Men's club, we'd met as kids, but the initial message about the 20/20 Group came through my brother. He phoned me to say that Gary Sweet contacted him to see if I would be interested. I said, "Are you nuts?!" then added, "I will listen to what he has to say." Ultimately, I invested alongside Mick Pattinson, who lived a couple of miles away from me in San Diego and some other dedicated Luton Town supporters and businessmen. I was pleased I got to play a part in saving the club, but it's definitely easier to be out there on the pitch than watching and it felt like it was the right thing emotionally to do.

We had a little get together recently back in England with a number of former players and of course David Pleat. It was lovely to see David. Over the years we'd knock into each other once in a while, but this was the first time that I got to sit down with him in a very long time. We chatted endlessly about football. He had a hundred questions for me about California and my career, he has such an inquisitive mind. David takes information in and he pulls it back at will. I think that's one of the things that made him such a great manager. He's a very good listener, insightful, a shrewd operator, and he really knows his stuff.

When we, as players, all look back at our time under David, we honestly believe that those were some really special times. It was the team spirit that perhaps Harry Haslam started and David added to in the following years, along with Danny Bergara, John Moore, John Sheridan, David Coates, right through to the kit men, the ground staff with Dickie Wassell, Irene and the kit ladies. That was Luton, everyone had a value and everyone contributed something, it really was a special moment in time to be in and around Luton Town Football Club. I have nothing but love and fond memories of living out my dream of playing for my boyhood club.

(BORN 18TH MARCH 1964, LEWISHAM, SOUTH LONDON)

# PAUL MARCELLUS ELLIOTT

## LUTON TOWN FC 1983-85

*Paul trialled at Luton as a youngster back in 1978 aged just fourteen, playing for a team called Yarnton FC, the manager of that team, Mike Dove, being a very dear friend of his. Living in Thamesmead at the time, Mike, who was also a West Ham scout, discovered Paul and gave him that chance to begin his career.*

Yarnton Way was an actual road going up and around a large roundabout and Mike lived just off that road so he put together a Sunday team called Yarnton FC. Paul Walsh also lived off this road, having grown up on Basildon Road in Abbey Wood. I played for them for many years as a kid in an independent league, and in those years, I was playing against the likes of Paul Walsh, Tony Cascarino, Andy Townsend, Danny Wallace, David Rocastle and Paul Davis who were all top players coming through in South East London. This league was the top league to play in, the highest level to play Sunday football in the area.

Mike Dove used to arrange trial matches for us as it was an opportunity for us to play against professional opposition but without the added pressure. We'd play in tournaments, some of the matches being against teams from the likes of Chelsea and Arsenal. Then he arranged a game for us where we travelled up to Bedfordshire and played against Luton Town. I think I scored a couple of goals in that game too, as I was playing as an attacking right winger then. The match was played on Luton Town's main pitch as well; it was an unbelievable experience to have that chance to play within that environment. I didn't get taken on but isn't it ironic that four years later, in the very same club that you had a trial with previously, they end up signing you for a lot of money? I had a great time in my career there.

During my time with Yarnton FC I also had trials at Chelsea and West Ham, but they all said I wasn't good enough and with every rejection, you start to lose your confidence. I was playing on cow field pitches on a common for my local Sunday side in South East London when a scout for Charlton spotted me randomly. He approached me and said, "Paul, we like you, we think you've got something. Why don't you come down to The Valley and try out for us at Charlton?" I was a speedy little right winger back then. I hadn't grown physically yet but I was fast, mobile and nimble. At this stage I had become disillusioned with becoming a professional footballer, and nobody likes rejection, being told again and again that you're not good enough. It's true though, that adversity builds character and I just kept plugging away, chasing my aspirations and dreams. I was taken on at Charlton Athletic at aged fifteen and within seven or eight months I was in the youth team, moving up into the reserve team within days of leaving school, which was very unusual. I made my debut in the first team against Crystal Palace. I literally went in there as a boy and became a man almost overnight from being in that structured environment, mixing with players who were twenty-seven and twenty-eight, whereas I was just sixteen/seventeen. I was big and strong for my age, and had physically matured, though not emotionally, and I felt that being integrated into the football club at that age was really good for me. I learned so much.

My family were the biggest influence on my early career. My mum and my grandma called me 'Tet' as a nickname from as long as I could remember. Apparently it, came from birth when I was in the cot and started mumbling words, and I just used to lay there saying 'tet, tet, tet 'over and over! The nickname stuck so much that even now all the people that I'm close to, family, as well as friends in the game that you build those relationships with, all know me as Tet.

Mum always said to me from a young age, "Paul, you need to be twice as good just to be even." And that always spurred me on even more. I used it as a catalyst to fulfil my career dream. I also had the nickname of 'Leroy' after the character in the TV show, 'Fame', which was huge at the time. I remember turning up with my hair in plaits on a Saturday morning at Luton before a game and David saying to me, "Have I signed a nutter?" Laughing, I said, "No, David, you've signed a dude!" My elder brothers, Jeff and Tony, were also a big influence. Jeff showed all the signs of making the grade as a professional, and many people thought if anyone was going to make it in football from our family, it would be him as he was an exceptional talent. He got on very well with Paul Walsh as both he and Walshy played for Blackheath District. That's where my relationship with Paul goes back from having known him since I was ten years old.

The standard of youth football within South East London at the time was extremely high. Jeff was such a talented footballer, what you might call a 'real' centre forward. He had great feet, left foot, right foot, he had a bit of that Stan Collymore about his game. You never knew which one was his stronger foot and he was exceedingly quick, though he could get talked out of a game a little bit by a dominant centre half. But technically he was a very good player. He went to West Ham when he was fifteen or sixteen and played alongside Paul Allen and Bobby Barnes; he was on the periphery of some great things there. Then he broke his leg: a devastating injury for a footballer especially. He tried to come back but had to have the leg re-set which unfortunately led to him not pursuing football as a career. He never achieved the same standard where he was before the injury. It was very sad as he was so talented and had all the ability to make it to the very top but, realising that talent alone wasn't enough, Jeff was well aware application and luck was needed, too. I'm terribly proud of him in any event as he went on to have a magnificent career in Retail and has been an unbelievable role model for me during and post-career. This made me realise that football is all about ups and downs, and the real test of character comes when things in football aren't going well for you.

I had a few managers at Charlton. When I signed as an apprentice Andy Nelson was there, then Mike Bailey, Alan Mullery, Ken Craggs and finally Lennie Lawrence came in towards the end of my time at The Valley. A great club and Lennie was a great man, I've got a lot of time for him. They were all good people. Charlton was my first club and I've done a lot of work with them, still very active with them now, and I set up their charitable community trust. I love Charlton, geographically, as I was raised nearby and went to school there. My in-laws still live 500 metres from the stadium. My wife lived just up the road from me when we grew up as kids, so I know the area and I loved it there. Later, I realised just how great a move it was for me going to Luton because I felt exactly the same way as I did at Charlton. There was no difficult bedding-in period, because of the dressing room and the way I was made to feel joining that group of players and staff, it was a home-from-home welcome.

Up against the team that he thought that he was leaving Charlton before signing for Luton in March 1983. Paul tussles with Pat Jennings and David O'Leary in a league match at Highbury in 1983

Whilst at Charlton there were rumours circulating that Arsenal wanted to sign me. I'd heard that they'd come to watch me and I was so excited. Then a headline and story appeared in the London Evening Standard stating that Arsenal were preparing a £450,000 bid for young Charlton starlet Paul Elliott. As a young man I believed all that, I wasn't mature enough to understand all the nuances that go along with paper talk. Charlton, at that time, had a lot of issues, financial problems. Lennie Lawrence called me into the dressing room after training and said they were dreadfully sorry but they'd have to sell me as the club was in a lot of financial problems. Then he added, "There's a club that wants to buy you. Meet me back at the ground at 2pm and I'm going to drive you to a hotel in Cockfosters to meet with them and for you to talk over the details of the move." So, I went home to put on my suit and tie, all the time thinking This is a dream come true, it's Arsenal, it's Arsenal! But Lennie hadn't told me which club it was, and I hadn't stopped to ask, until we arrived at the hotel.

I was so excited that I couldn't even talk to my mum. The chatter in the car on the way there still had me thinking I was meeting with Don Howe and Terry Neill, then we arrived at the hotel and I was told the club wasn't Arsenal at all, it was Luton Town and David Pleat would like to speak to me. My heart just sank because I had this expectation in my head that this was leading to happy days at Arsenal. But I have to say, after listening to David Pleat for just fifteen minutes, I knew that Luton Town was the club I wanted to join. He made a massive impression on me, telling me how much he wanted me, valued me, saying, "Paul, you have the potential to become a full England international." He was saying all the right things and as they say thereafter, the rest is history.

It was a big opportunity for me as a young eighteen-year-old and it was one that I embraced, flourished and grew.

I was thrown straight in and played a tough, competitive, bruising encounter coming up against the excellent Garry Thompson for West

Brom in a 0-0 draw at Kenilworth Road. I think I had Thommo where I wanted him that day on my debut for Luton; I remember the game clearly. Thommo was really aggressive but I knew I could compete with him because I was very athletic. I knew he was never going to run away from me, and I felt that I could dominate him in the air. He was one of the tough guys, a brave man, and he always played fairly. He's a good man, I like him very much as a person. I played against him and then with him when I went to Aston Villa. I seem to remember John Wile was playing that day as well in one of his last games, as he came towards the end of his own amazing career with West Brom. I should have scored in that game, too, with a header from a corner. I beat Paul Barron in the Albion goal to the ball and with him stranded, the ball sailed just wide of the post with the goal wide open.

It was a big move for me in 1983 and David Pleat was building a great side at Luton Town. I initially moved into the same digs as Walshy, with a really nice lady looking after us, though that was just for that first game. It was the day before we played West Brom, I got all the deal done with the club the day before when I came up on the Thursday. We trained that day and again the next day so I stayed in those digs on the Thursday and Friday. Thereafter, I stayed with a lovely woman called Elsie Brown. I called her Mrs B, and she really took great care of me. I absolutely loved it there. David always made sure the lads had a home-from-home experience, he was very much like that. I think he aligned himself with Brian Clough in that type of management, very much ahead of his curve in thinking and player management.

October 1983; Paul competes with future Aston Villa team mate Mark Walters

I signed with Luton just before my nineteenth birthday. Once I got there I quickly settled in. The people there weren't just top class players, but top class people, too. People like Brian Horton, who I loved, Nobby, the best Captain that I ever played under, Mal Donaghy; what top player he was, made very few mistakes, always an 8 out of 10 performance. There was Kirk (Stephens) on the right and Mitchell Thomas on the left coming through the ranks, Ricky Hill, a top-class player who could attack and defend. We had Brian (Stein) up front, with Emeka Nwajiobi coming in, Mick Harford, David Preece, God rest his soul. What a wizard Mini was, he had unbelievable technical ability. Vince Hilaire was with us briefly but what a talent he was, we called him the Prince, a great guy. Peter Nicholas also came in and you could see that David was always so far ahead of the curve. Going to Luton was a great move and not just from a professional sense but socially as well. It was great camaraderie; a great dressing room and I think it's only been during the last eight to ten months when the group reconnected that David Pleat has discovered just how bad we were; he found out about all the things that we can't put into print. Our nights out at Mr Man's restaurant and Ronelles Night Club in the town, to name but a few. They were the players' regular places to relax and bond, away from the football club.

What a rollercoaster that last part of the 1982/83 season turned out to be when we had the games leading up to the final day showdown at Manchester City. I played in every game of the run in after I joined up until that final home game of the season against Everton, when I was unfortunately injured. Also, I think David knew that the Manchester City game was coming and it would be our chance to get those three points that we needed to stay up. So yes, I sat out the Everton game on the Saturday, which ended in a heavy defeat and at a touch, I could have played at Manchester United on the following Monday night. Had it been a cup final I certainly would have declared myself fit but David wanted to rest me and a few others at Old Trafford, so we would be as fresh as possible for the upcoming Saturday at Maine Road.

Leading up to that game I didn't really feel the pressure. What I do recall though, is on the Friday, while training at Kenilworth Road, we were all walking around the pitch, David was doing some drills along with Trevor Hartley and David Coates. He was just telling the players to go and walk around the pitch and talk to each other. As this was going on, David would come and have a one-to-one with each player. It was just his way of managing the situation. It came to my turn and we continued to walk around the pitch whilst training was going on. He said, "Paul, listen, you've been remarkable since you've come in with what you've done and you've settled in here at the club, and if we get beat tomorrow, IF we get beat, you're young enough to come back." I turned to him. "David," I replied, "we, Luton, will be playing in the First Division next season, don't think about that, we WILL be playing there. You don't have to say that to me, I feel that positive and confident!" David looked at me and said, "You're a winner son!" I answered him with genuine modesty: "I try to be." I remember David looking at me with so much respect, this young nineteen-year-old boy with confidence, belief and very much on the front foot. That was as interesting moment as I don't know to this day if he was testing me mentally to see how I was thinking. But I just KNEW we weren't going to get relegated, whatever that looked like!

I remember the pressure started that evening when we drove up to Manchester, it became relentless; you could feel it.

David was very astute in keeping routines as normal as possible in an attempt to aleviate as much pressure as he could. I guess the real pressure was on Manchester City in that respect as there was huge pressure for them to stay in the top flight. Tactically, they weren't sure what to do. You sensed their lads like dear old Tommy Caton, God rest his soul, a good lad, were caught between a rock and a hard place. Phsycologically, as well as tactically, they approached the game in the wrong way thinking they only needed a draw to stay up in the Division, whereas we needed all three points on offer.

I remember the feeling after getting the result, following David's unbelievable substitution to bring on Raddy Antic late in the game and hitting that winner with only minutes remaining. And even though I got into a fight on the pitch when some City fans came on to try and give me a smack, we quickly got off the pitch and into the dressing room where we all went a bit mad. On the coach after leaving the ground, we all had to duck down as there were bricks being thrown at our bus.

The drive back, there were Luton Town fans in their cars and mini-buses on the M6 and the M1 everywhere; it was amazing. We stopped off at a pub and I've never had that same feeling of elation ever since in my career thereafter, especially that night when we got back into Luton, then out for the night in Ronelles club in town. Just talking about it I feel the happiness now, almost forty years on. I didn't realise how much it meant to people because at the time you don't think like that, you just focus on getting the right outcome. It's not until you have the release that you truly appreciate what it meant to people. People talk about David Pleat's jig across the pitch shown on Match of the Day on the following day and I honestly think that was one of the best moments of my career.

It was the whole experience, not just the game, that in itself was amazing to play in. A huge stadium crackling with intensity and a full house at Maine Road. It was a great moment for the club and a truly great moment for David as he'd kept his team playing in that emphatic style that had achieved them promotion the season before playing wonderful football, pleasing on the eye. Everything in that team was what David was about as a coach and as a manager: his values of how we used to train and play. He got his just rewards in playing the right way and keeping Luton Town up in the top flight.

That result was so important to us at Luton Town FC as it gave us so much confidence and a level of self-belief going into the 1983/84 season. We evolved and used it as a catlyst to say we belonged here, we've earned the right to be here, we're comfortable, we CAN play at this level. We could play this offensive, attractive style that David wanted us to play to really go at the opposition. It was even more impressive when you look at the team that he'd built, the players that came in from lower divisions, or those that were home grown. He certainly wasn't about buying ready made top level players. He was very good at buying players to bring through the system or he'd buy good, mature players at the right age with miles left on the clock. Like any manager, he didn't get every one of his purchases right but he was good at recognising and accepting that and moving them back out of the club quickly. I remember a lovely lad, Steve Elliott, who came in from Preston in the summer of 1984. He was a centre forward but he just couldn't fit into the style that David wanted him to play in at Luton so he realised that and moved him on, and from that transfer he brought in David Preece from Walsall as part of that deal. Preecey was unbelievable; what a player 'Mini' was. He had a left foot like a wand. He couldn't run, but he didn't have to as he had spacial awareness and a range of passing that was amazing. But in training in the runs he'd always be at the back of the queue, he was behind everybody else, but when it came to all the drills and finding space he was just off the scale.

Another good midfield player around then was a home grown player, Garry Parker, who had come through the ranks at Luton. I remember getting on the end of his cross at QPR to head in a winner, I didn't get too many but I certainly remember that one. He just couldn't get a regular place in the team with Ricky, Mini and Nico ahead of him and it was such a shame, that he left Luton because 'Parks' had such confidence, a great arrogance on the ball with a real self-belief. The things he could do with a ball, he made the game look easy and was a very good footballer. He got a great move a few years after leaving Luton when Brian Clough came in for him at Forest after he spent some time under Brian Horton at Hull City, and I was pleased that later he went into management. He certainly was a tremendous talent, he had a sweet strike, he could ping the ball like a golfer, and he had wonderful technique.

David Pleat was so true to his values. He would tell us flatly if he hadn't enjoyed watching us play in some games, even when we'd won! Probably my biggest disappointment for him was that he perhaps should have got the England job instead of Graham Taylor. Not only for what he achieved at Luton but also how he set up Tottenham tactically in a 4-5-1 formation in the 1986/87 season.

Going back to Walshy, I'm extremely indebted to him actually, as my move to Luton Town was born out of a strong recommendation by him to David Pleat. Luton had been promoted to the First Division and you could see that under David they played in such a carefree, open, expansive way and beautiful on the eye. That reflected how David Pleat was as a coach and how he wanted his team to play. He'd rather win a 5-4 than 1-0, that was his mindset. David told Walshy we were leaking goals, giving them away for fun like Christmas presents. Then he asked, "Who's the best centre half that you've played against?" To be fair to Walshy he said, "Tet is one of the hardest that I've ever played against, I could never get away from him, he was very competitive, quick and athletic, but also comfortable on the ball as well and could dominate play." That activated David's interest in me, and to this day, Walshy still wants to claim 15% of my signing on fee, which, by the way, wasn't a lot back then. I said, "Walshy, you're not having it but I'll settle for the recommendation!" He'd certainly done me a turn, so to speak. I think what also went in my favour was that in Luton's promotion year I had played for Charlton against Luton and again in two league cup games earlier in the 1982/83 season against Brian Stein who was a top player and just on the threshold of international recognition. I got to know Brian well later and he'd also been asked by David about potential centre halves to bring in. Although Brian didn't know me well at the time he said, "That lad Paul Elliott, at Charlton." David had very cleverly spoken to Brian and Walshy separately and they both gave me a ringing endorsement as to who was the best they'd come up against and why.

David Pleat was always that kind of guy who liked young outstanding players. He always had an emphasis on buying and/or developing youth along with, wherever possible, bringing in the senior players as well. That whole move to Luton Town was a fascinating time.

I had already made my England debut at youth level, my first game against Austria. I ended up with eight England youth caps, and my long-term ambition was to get one-hundred full caps and captain my country with the World Cup in Mexico only a couple of years away when I joined Luton. However, I ended up with three England Under 21 caps between 1984 and 1986, scoring one goal. I recall one time when I played for the Under 21 team along with Mitchell Thomas whilst David took the rest of the first team for a three-day break to the West Indies. Later in my career I was called up to the England B team to play Switzerland at Walsall's Bescot Stadium in May 1991.

The team reflected the town at the time. It was very diverse with English, Scottish, Irish and black players, very inclusive and representative of the communities within and across the town. I think there was one time, I believe against Southampton away at The Dell in February 1984, that there must have been about six black players in the side with myself, Mitchell Thomas, Ray Daniel, Emeka Nwajiobi, Brian Stein, and Ricky Hill. I don't think David got the credit that he deserved with the evolution of black players; he was certainly one of the leaders in doing so.

Most importantly, he educated us to play the game in the right way. He always encouraged me to come out from the back with the ball, and wanted us to play and pass the ball from defence. It's quite interesting that when I was a young lad playing for Yarnton FC I was a right winger or a centre forward, but I always knew, long term, that I wanted to be a centre half because I was quick, and back then you didn't have a lot of athletic defenders. I was naturally that way. I had done a lot of athletics back at school but I could also play football as well. So, along with those attributes, I also had a good growth spurt at about seventeen years of age: I was about six-feet-one then. With the ability to attack the ball, I could run and play the ball from defence and it all just joined up, and that's why I think that I made that rapid progress getting into Charlton's first team at aged sixteen before getting a huge move to Luton Town at eighteen.

David Pleat spoke highly of me early in the 1983/84 season, saying, "I was impressed with him when I bought him, and I'm even more impressed with him now. He's excellent in the air, like most good centre halves, but he also has tremendous pace, and a great deal of skill, too – which isn't nearly so common in central defenders." David acknowledged my arrival in March wasn't exactly the smoothest of settling in periods at the club as Luton narrowly avoided relegation.

I only played briefly with Steve Foster, but the centre half who I played alongside who was brilliant for me as an eighteen-year-old moving to the top division in England, was Mal Donaghy. He was like a Dennis Irwin-type player where he could switch seamlessly between centre half and left back or as a holding midfield player. He was top class international and he really brought me through. Mal was unbelievably consistent and didn't make many mistakes, he was that steady hand next to me, he knew what I could do well: I was good on the ball, I could tackle. When you're young you're a little bit impetuous. I liked to play as an attacking centre half and he was that steady hand next to me. I had a similar player next to me at Charlton where I had the experienced Welsh international, Leighton Phillips. I was very lucky as a young player as I always had very mature centre halves next to me.

Disastrously, I broke my leg in a League Cup tie with Leicester City in October 1984. Colin Todd was making his debut for Luton next to me in the centre of the Luton defence that night at Kenilworth Road, with Mal Donaghy being moved out to the left back role. However, the partnership only lasted thirty-two minutes when I made a challenge which I actually received a yellow card for from referee John Martin, against Leicester City's Alan Smith. It left me with a broken leg and facing a lengthy period out of action. I was in a lot of bloody pain, I can tell you. It was from my own challenge going through the back of Smudger. On the way to the Luton & Dunstable hospital I remember the ambulance went off a kerb, I jolted back and my leg went up and I was screaming and my goodness, that's when I realised that I was in a lot of pain!

That period following the leg break was a tough time for me. David was great, I was young and it was my youth that got me back as well as my mental strength. Those were the kind of injuries that players were retiring from especially at that time in the mid-1980s. I worked with our brilliant physio, John Sheridan, a great man, but surgery techniques weren't like they are now. I had to have a huge plaster cast the length of my leg and had to keep it elevated. You didn't have anything like today where you could have a boot that would be weight bearing. Because of that I just lost so much muscle, it was like a chicken's leg to be honest when the cast was finally removed and that was the hardest thing, not just the psychological side so much, like it is for most players. But it was the building up of those muscle groups again as I'd had to stay in full plaster for so long. There simply wasn't the advanced techniques that are common place today.

I seem to remember that my first game on returning was against Oxford United in a friendly and I'd worked so hard to get back playing. Trevor Hartley was there and he was really pleased with me as I'd gotten over the psychological part of getting back playing, too. I'd had a pin inserted in my shin, used as a healing catalyst to knit the bone back, and then I had to have another operation to have it removed, which added to the time away before being able to build it back up again. So, not only my youth but I also had my mental strength to help deal with the adversity, along with my single mindedness. John Sheridan knew I wasn't that kind of guy that he had to watch over. I was conscientious in that I would do whatever it took to get back playing again. That's just the way I was. I would say, in that respect, I was probably very easy to manage.

Coming back from that injury in 1985 I also had, added into the mix, the laying of Luton Town's artificial surface at Kenilworth Road. Two things that really bothered me initially about the pitch was, 1) the bounce, because it was like a springboard, and 2) the burns that you'd get on the side of your legs if you were going to slide tackle on that surface. But what it did do was teach me to think about my game more. As I was a fairly good athlete a lot of the time I could read the flight of the ball, so if it was a really long ball most of the time it would just skid right off the surface and straight out of play. I knew I could conserve my energy with not chasing balls that otherwise may have stayed in play.

Also, when we played against the good teams, I found that quite easy because I could read the play and nip in front of them to regain possession of the ball. Undoubtedly, we gained an advantage because we could train on it day in and day out. We had a lot of teams that would just come down and train on it for an hour or so on the Friday before the match and it was a disadvantage for them. But, personally for me, technically it definitely improved my game.

I was back to full fitness for the start of the 1985/86 season but in my absence, Fozzie and Mal had forged a great partnership and with Mitchell Thomas doing so well out at left back, there was no room for me. I only got three starts along with a handful of substitute appearances in the early months of the season, which was obviously frustrating because I wanted to play, like every player does.

David was very kind to me but at the end of the day he knew after achieving so much already by rising through the ranks at Charlton and getting a move to the first division with Luton, that I wanted to play. To David's credit, bringing in Fozzie soon after my injury from Aston Villa reserves was the right thing to do. Initially, as a short-term solution with no guarantees, as David had said to Foz that long term there were no promises.

I had played twelve games for the reserves and that was not where I wanted to be. I was putting David under pressure by handing in a transfer request as I wanted to play first team football. Everton came in for me but they were only offering to take me on a loan deal. David wasn't going to let me go out on loan. I was frank with him, saying that I had to think about my career and it was no good to me at the age of twenty-one not playing first team football. We had a bit of an 'interesting' conversation at the point when Everton showed an interest in me, but having blocked the loan move David said, "No, you're staying here, Paul" to which I replied, "I am happy for you to keep me here but put me in the first team, you can't have it both ways and I have to think of my career." We had a bit of a disagreement on that front but in the end, it worked out with Aston Villa coming in with an offer which was a lot of money and to which David elected to accept, and so I moved on. I came back in for Fozzie for what turned out to be my farewell appearance for Luton at home to Manchester City on November 30th, 1985 and it was all in the papers that I had a decision to make the day after with the offer on the table having already been accepted by Luton. However, I do remember being slightly unsure as I think I was in the last year of my contract at Luton, so part of me was wondering if I should sit it out and wait till the end of the season to see what happens, then be a free agent. But then I thought it's Aston Villa, it's a big club, the royal family of the midlands, so I took the decision in the end to leave Luton Town and move to the midlands.

I enjoyed it at Villa Park, it was certainly challenging and then on the back of that I got the move to Italy eighteen months after leaving Luton, which to be honest with you was just off the scale. It was amazing to be playing in the same league, in Serie A, up against the likes of Baresi, Maradona, Gullit, Van Basten, Maldini, Costacurta, Enzo Scifo to name but a few. Enzo Scifo was an unbelievable talent – very similar in technical ability and range of pass to the great Ray Wilkins, but, Scifo had the additional ability to make those killer clever-weighted passes in the final third of the pitch similar to Kevin De Bruyne. Believe it or not, playing at Pisa, as a club they were just like Luton Town, because they'd just come up from Serie B. They were a very young team where the majority of the players had come up through the ranks. Pisa were punching above their weight so it felt like a very similar alignment with Luton in terms of the evolution of the club. I had two brilliant years in Italy, it was easily the best league in the world back then in 1987.

Then, in 1989, I came back to the UK and onto even bigger things by going to Scotland, joining up again with my old boss from Aston Villa, Billy McNeil, but this time up at Celtic. That was an absolutely fabulous move for me going there. At this time, over at Rangers, Souness was building his side with Chris Woods in goal, Gary Stevens at right back, Terry Butcher, Richard Gough, John Brown, Trevor Steven, Terry Hurlock, Ally McCoist, Mo Johnston and Mark Hateley. What a team that was to be competing against with my Celtic team mates. I was so proud to be voted Scottish Footballer of the year in my final season at Parkhead.

Following on from my time in Scotland, I had yet another great move heading back to London, but this time with Chelsea where I became the West London club's first black captain and won Player of the Year award in the early 1990s.

When I look back, and I know that you have to look forwards, but sometimes I have to stop and say to myself, my goodness, Paul, you've actually had a bloody good career. I was very lucky and privileged to have worked with some brilliant people. Speaking of brilliant people, it's interesting to note that in that game at Anfield in September 1992, alongside me in the Chelsea team, were none other than my old Luton Town team mates Mal Donaghy and Mick Harford. In fact, looking at the footage, Mal was one of the first players ever to check on me which I wasn't surprised by as I've always loved Mal and he's always been brilliant with me. He saw how I was and immediately knew that it was a serious injury straight away as it was an awful challenge. It was like an assault on me but I always say it didn't take away my life or my ability to do other things. I've used it as a springboard to go and do all those others things that I've done with my work.

Luton Town was a wonderful club and although it was over thirty-five years ago, I still keep in touch with David Pleat. When I saw him recently at Wembley for the FA Cup final I said to him, "David, I played for a lot of clubs, but I can't tell you how happy I was to play for Luton, not just on the pitch but also off the field and in the dressing room." Training with David and in that environment was fantastic for my growth in the game. David came from a Jewish background so he understood prejudice with the anti-semitism having been a Jewish footballer and then a Jewish manager. Going back to that game against Southampton in February 1984, we had six black players in the Luton Town starting eleven that day! It was unbelievable at the time, people must have been thinking where all the diversity had come from with all these brilliant black players in the same team!

Paul in pre-season for media shoot in 1984

David was very much a pioneer in his time. He gave everyone the chance with equal opportunities and that was what the ethos of the club was all about regardless of race, colour or creed. He is simply a wonderful man and so my time at Luton Town was brilliant as we were regularly playing with four or five black players in the team. We had Ricky Hill, Brian and Mark Stein, Emeka Nwajiobi, Ray Daniel, and Mitchell Thomas as well as myself. He was a game changer, he was brave to do that as he would have been under a lot of pressure, but that's how you change culture.

In David Pleat's programme's notes immediately following Paul's departure from the club he wrote; "For Paul Elliott to leave this club took him much heart-searching. He knows the potential, the standards and the environment. But times change and players move on for whatever reasons. We wish Paul every success – he has been a gentleman and an excellent professional during his stay at Luton and we are sure that he will continue to develop."

(BORN 1 OCTOBER 1962, PLUMSTEAD)

# PAUL ANTHONY WALSH

## LUTON TOWN FC 1982 - 1984

*Paul began his senior football career in 1979 at the age of sixteen where he played for Charlton Athletic. After helping Charlton get promotion from the Third Division to the Second, he was signed by Luton Town in 1982 and went on to win PFA Young Player of the Year in 1984.*

There were no agents back in the days when I was doing well at Charlton and you used to get snippets in the papers, mainly in the Sunday papers in those transfer gossip columns. I'd been linked with Villa, Everton, Manchester United and all sorts of clubs so you start to get a little bit carried away in your own head in terms of where you would like to go. I had been out one evening in the early summer just after the end of the 1981/82 season, when, following this night out, my mum came into my bedroom to tell me a certain David Pleat was on the phone asking to speak to me. Oh, right, that's the Luton manager, isn't it? I thought. My mum didn't know him from Adam. I went downstairs to the phone and said hello. The voice on the other end said, "Hello, David Pleat here, I want you to come to Luton Town, would you be interested in joining us?" Perhaps he shouldn't have been contacting me directly as it could have been looked at as tapping me up, I don't know, but I told him of course I'd been interested. Secretly, I was hoping to go somewhere bigger but Luton Town made the bid for me, Charlton Athletic accepted the offer, so I went up to Luton. I think I was half way through a two-year contract at the time with Charlton but in those days it didn't matter, because even if your contract was up, they still kept hold of your registration until a fee was agreed and that was it, deal done, with Steve White going the other way from Luton to Charlton.

Steve White didn't know anything about it, he was in the other room about to be ambushed by Pleaty and Ken Craggs who had taken over at Charlton after Alan Mullery had left. I went in first, as they had to agree terms with me for starters. I went in and met Pleaty and Craggs, obviously very inexperienced, and I'd taken a bit of guidance from Leighton Phillips at Charlton about what to ask for and all the rest of it. I blurted my number out and they said, "What, he's talking telephone numbers?" This left me thinking that Leighton had chewed me right up! He hadn't, but they were just grafting on me. Psychologically, that put me on the back foot, which is what they were trying to do I suppose. They told me to go into the other room while they had a bit of a chat, but they left the door slightly open because they wanted me to hear what was going on. It was a lot of bullshit being spoke for my benefit and all I could think was that I didn't want to fuck this up. Eventually, I was called back in and we agreed on a little bit less, and once they had me secured they sent me back out of one door so they could then bring in Steve White through the other, adjoining from another room. There were three doors, one into the main lounge, one into the bedroom and one out of the bedroom and onto the landing. When Steve came in I closed the door and left. The next thing they had to do was ambush Steve and let him know they wanted to sell him, then it was down to Charlton to look after him to get him to go. He took some convincing, and I think he was a bit devastated at the time. No doubt it wasn't a nice experience for him, he might have gone in there thinking that he was going to get the offer of a new contract but he ended up being sold by Luton just before the new season up in the First Division, where he'd played a big part in helping them to gain promotion.

When I signed for Luton I already had my own flat in Sidcup in South East London, I wasn't living in it but I'd bought it just to get on the property market. Pleaty asked me as a favour to him to just try living locally in digs organised by the club. I had a great landlady, Madge, up near Sundon Park, and had her to talk to when I was there in the evenings as well as her

Paul Walsh signing for Luton in July 1982 – David would later be getting Paul from behind bars after an night out in Dunstable

son, Barry occasionally. I had a free reign there to do what I wanted. I had people around me, my dinner was made, my washing was done, so Pleaty was spot on; it was the right thing to do rather than being left to my own devices in a flat. I wasn't homesick, I could go home every week if I wanted to as I was only an hour and a half from home, but what it was doing was keeping me out of trouble. If I'd be kicking my heels every night on my own and getting a bit bored, maybe, I'm only saying maybe, I might have 'ventured out' a bit. So, the digs system certainly helped to keep me nice and straight.

It was a massively exciting time moving to a new club. I was nervous and excited all rolled into one because you're meeting a new group of people, stepping into a new and higher Division, and everyone was experiencing the top flight of English football for the first time. I think that Brian Horton had played previously in the top flight but I'm not sure if anyone else had. It was brand new for all of us together and there was a great feeling around the place.

Going training and meeting the other players on your first day is always a little bit nerve wracking. You know that everyone is looking at you. The club had just got rid of one of the previous season's top strikers in Steve White and replaced him with a nineteen-year-old who's not proven. But I'd played 100 games already at Charlton Athletic so I was well on my way.

The first pre-season at Luton in 1982 was hilarious looking back on it. We went out to play some games in Sweden and it was great fun, that's when being in football was more fun. (Over the years it got a little more serious with the amount of money coming into the game, and became more professional.) I'm not saying that we weren't professional, although what we were doing might be deemed as unprofessional now, because we had a laugh, we had a beer, and we did silly things.

Coming back from a night out in Sweden, during that first pre-season tour, I was trying to get a girl that I had with me back into the hotel, but I didn't have the key. We found a window that was open, so I pushed this girl up through it and then climbed in myself, not knowing whose room it was. I was just making my way out of the room and there he was, Pleaty! "What are you doing?" he asked. I replied, "I'm going to bed, we've got training in the morning, ain't we?" I just left the girl there in David's room! I don't think that Pleaty knew what to do, he'd just signed me and we were on pre-season.

Paul gets in a shot at Kenilworth Road against local rivals Watford in 1984

Brian Stein and I were looking good as a partnership and I felt that I was still convincing everyone, but I was also starting to feel that I was winning the players over in terms that I was going to be a good player, though I still had to produce the goods in the games. There was a nervous anticipation about the place, that's how it felt.

The second pre-season saw Brian Horton and David Moss in the room next to us. I was rooming with Wayne (Turner) then. Brian and David were like a couple of kids themselves and one night when we'd been out for a drink, they were throwing sweets through the windows at us so I don't what made me do this… Well, I do know, drink, that's what made me do what I did next: I went out on the balcony and threw the plastic furniture down into the side of the swimming pool below. The next day the owners of the hotel weren't best pleased when they found it smashed and in bits, lying around the pool area. Those sorts of things never got massively blown out of proportion and maybe that was because the club had paid whatever it was, £400-500 grand on this player. I think it was a little bit accepted but there were consequences and I had to pay the damages of about three hundred quid, which really pissed me off at time. Mossy and Nobby were laughing at me the next day as they knew I was in the shit, but at the same time it was just all part of how it was back then.

At that time, I think I might have already played for England by then as well as I played at the end of my first year at Luton on that Australia tour. If you can imagine that within the space of a year I went from a transfer, striking up a new partnership with Steiny at a new club, to get a whole bunch of new team mates; it was massively exciting but it wasn't always going how we'd want it, as we'd have great games and poor games, and were at the wrong end of the table. Then, at the end of the season, I went on tour with England and got three senior caps. It was a massive year for me, but from my point of view it was all moving so fast. I was nineteen when I signed in July and then a year later, at twenty, I got my

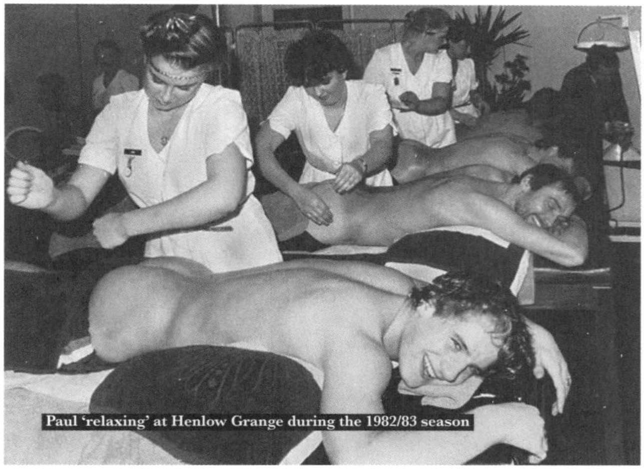

Paul 'relaxing' at Henlow Grange during the 1982/83 season

first full England caps, so a lot was happening for me. We could have a life back then, we had a good time, and there were no camera phones back then, either. We went over the top a bit at times and did things that we shouldn't have done,but it made life exciting. Being brutally honest, it was bordering on unprofessional conduct for a top-flight footballer but it was just the way it was.

I've got great memories from those two years, absolutely phenomenal, having a good time with great team mates, great camaraderie. That last game of my first season at Manchester City, you just can't describe it. The euphoria following that game, the way that it unfolded. Their fans on the pitch, a few of our players getting a hit, players fighting up the tunnel, Brian Horton and Dennis Tueart. Walking around the inside of Maine Road, we had this euphoric feeling, but it was like we were at a funeral because everyone else there were Man City players, staff and fans and they'd all just been relegated. We were cock-a-hoop and I don't think that was going down too well. We had to lay down on the bus with all the curtains pulled as we were going to get bricked by their fans lying in wait for us. We got clear and back to the hotel in Stafford and had a good old jolly-up. Pleaty was very good in the week leading up to that game and I think we went to Henlow Grange, though I can't remember the exact day. I've got pictures in my scrap book of us all having a lovely massage. Of course, we also played Manchester United away early in that week as well and got beat 3-0, so that wasn't the greatest warm up. We also honoured an agreement to play a testimonial at Watford that week, too, I can't remember much about that though, it's a sketchy memory and I don't suppose that any of us would have wanted to be there. I felt that Pleaty didn't really want to be there either given the circumstances of how our season was mapping out, but at the same time he wanted to keep his word and stick to the agreement of the testimonial held at Vicarage Road.

The actual game at Maine Road kind of passed me by, I didn't play very well. The main thing that I remember is having a row with Nicky Reid, the Manchester City player. I had history with him from the home game back in December 1982 where he tried to elbow me in the face and I remember chasing him down following that. So, there's a little bit going on between me and him and he said to me, "You're fucking well going down, you little cunt," and at that time, he was right. It was 0-0 with fifteen minutes to go. I have to admit that I gave him so much abuse after the game, I couldn't leave him alone. You just never know how these things will turn out. Raddy, bless him, he hit the shot and it went in. They are lifelong binding friendships that are born out of going through those situations together. I'm so glad there was a dinner evening put on for Pleaty a few years ago, as Raddy attended along with his wife Vera, and I got to see him again, which was the last time that I saw him so I'm really glad that we did that. A lot of us from that group keep in touch, including the likes of Mossy and Nobby Horton, who I go to visit now and then. We're close probably more than any other group than I was part of throughout my whole career; they certainly were special times. I know we were fighting relegation but it was still special.

Trevor Aylott was a great lad, he came in when Steiny broke a bone in his foot. Me and Wayne used to hammer Trev, he'd always threaten to beat us up! It was one of those situations where we'd massively take the piss out of him, he'd laugh it off to a point but then he'd bite and look like he could hurt us, so we knew just when to back off. He knew that it was just all banter and good fun but sometimes we'd push things a bit too far. I think that he's a taxi driver these days.

Throughout the Luton period we were young and reckless and a bit mad at times, but we had fun and sometimes we pushed our luck, especially me and Wayne when we were out. We were naughty boys around town a little bit. Wayne did get picked on a little when we were out being a local Luton lad himself, which perhaps made him a target for other lads who were jealous of us. However, Wayne was brilliant, he was hilariously funny, gobby, and he was quick witted too, so if anyone came up to him intent on giving him some grief he used to rinse them with his fast mouth; it was funny because these people couldn't handle him on that level. There was one night in The Hatters nightclub when I could see this bloke out of the corner of my eye. I knew he was getting closer and closer, just waiting for Wayne to bump into him and as he did, the bloke threw his drink on the floor. The bloke got in Wayne's face and said, "What are you going to do about that then?" I think that Wayne, quick as you like, popped a fiver into the guy's top pocket and carried on dancing but the bloke still lumped him. He'd already decided that he was going to take a swing at him regardless, he was just looking for any reason to start something. Then there was my twenty-first birthday party down at Ronelles where we were all in fancy dress and Wayne was dressed up like Hitler. You couldn't get away with doing that these days. I've got all the photos. Something kicked off that night as well and someone ended up getting bashed with Wayne's helmet. It was just part of what used to go on during a night out.

There was a time that David Pleat had to come to Dunstable Police Station to get me out after a bit of bother at Cinderella's in the town. My mates were up from South London, they were very smartly dressed, but one of them didn't have a tie on. So, the bouncer, who was always an absolute prick, always made it hard for me and Wayne and insisted on the tie as part of the dress code. This kid walks up beside us, and I'm not joking, he was dressed like a sack of shit but because he had a tie, the bouncer let him in. My mate had got a mohair coat on and a nice crisp white shirt, he looked the 'nuts', but he wasn't letting him in, so they started scrapping. I thought to myself, What am I going to do here, I can't get involved in that, so I took a step back. But every time I stuck my head in the door this big bouncer would come towards me. He opened the door slightly and I just booted it back at him a little bit; it was nothing really. He knew he couldn't step off the premises and I knew what would happen if I took one step inside. I still ended up getting done for criminal damage, which was a farce really, but when you're playing top level football and for England, then people will love all of that shit.

For training days, Pleaty would sometimes get in a guy called Roger Spry and we would do something a bit different, with some alternative types of training with a philosophy based on power, balance, flair and agility, assisted by music and rhythm. If you didn't have a game it would be Monday train, Tuesday train harder, Wednesday off, so could be a game of golf and a beer or quite a few beers. If there was a game on the Tuesday we'd try to squeeze in a night out afterwards depending on where it was. I remember when I scored my hat-trick away at West Ham on an absolute mud heap of a pitch and after it, David Pleat even came to Ronelles with us when we got back to Luton for a couple of drinks.

Two of my proudest moments I recollect are when I scored a hat-trick against West Ham with my father watching from the stands and then in my Liverpool debut again against West Ham, when I scored just fourteen seconds into the match, playing alongside Kenny Dalglish.

We'd got a brilliant 3-3 draw at Anfield in my first season at Luton, then a year later we got absolutely turned over 6-0 when Ian Rush scored five of the goals. It was always a bit of a mixed bag of emotions with that one. The first one in 1982 was amazing for me as it was my first time playing at Anfield. It was all just so brand new, exciting and exhilarating, along with a bit of pressure, but great fun all the same. That September in 1982 was just amazing. I scored a hat-trick at Kenilworth Road in a 5-3 win over Notts County, then we had the 3-3 draw at Anfield followed by thumping Brighton 5-0 at home. Then, a week later, we draw 4-4 away at Stoke City, which could have been 5-4 with Mossy putting a penalty against the post in the last minute against Derek Parkin, who had, by then, taken over in goal with no sub goalkeepers on the bench in those days. My 'second' goal should have stood when their keeper, Peter Fox, was sent off. The referee should have just given the goal; we had the advantage after he'd handled

Iconic players, John Burridge and Andy Gray are powerless against a rampaging Paul Walsh as Luton put Wolves to the sword 4-0 in September 1983

outside the box so he should have just allowed play to continue but he didn't, so that may have made a difference.

By the end of the 1983/84 season I already knew that I was leaving as I had been to meet Liverpool. Pleaty drove me to meet the Liverpool representatives and ended up asking me to drive. Although he eventually sold me. When we played Luton at Liverpool, I scored two in one game a season or two after leaving. That was satisfying because you just change, you want to do well against your former club and former team mates. Your mindset changes when you move on to a new club.

It was a great two years and its always great when we get back together. I really like that people have softened up over time. Mick Saxby for instance, he was angry and unhappy but you see him now, he's a pleasure to talk to, a really nice bloke. Football can bring the best and the worst out in people. I see Sax on Twitter every now and then but I don't do much on there anymore as it seemed that I only posted when somebody died, people like Raddy, Michael Robinson, Jim Smith, just loads of people who I knew and that I really liked. People started hammering me for my Twitter account reading like an obituary column.

It is really hard for players when their careers get cut short. My last contract was for three years but I lost out on the last two and a half years of it because of injury, though looking at the bigger picture I did well. Gary Shaw at Aston Villa, Champions of England, European Cup Winner, but then he got injured at twenty-four and he really struggles getting his head around it all and how his life has turned out since. That must have been so hard for Gary. I just can't even begin to imagine what I would have been like had that happened to me at a similar age. I count myself really lucky. I did have a few injuries at the wrong time as well but again, looking at the bigger picture, if you'd said to me at fourteen when Charlton were considering letting me go because they said I was too small, I'd have bitten your hand off with the career that I had. Whilst at the same time I do have just a little regret that I could have done a little bit more in the game as well, but twenty years in the game is not easy.

When I signed for Manchester City much later in my career, I mentioned the 1983 game in my press conference to get the elephant in the room out there, so to speak. I went to Man City and was thirty-two by then, and they thought I was over the hill, even the fans didn't want me. I'd had eighteen months at Portsmouth and then Nobby signed me as he was manager at City by then. There was huge pressure on me as there was

Paul drives Luton forward during the 1-1 draw at Notts County in April 1983

massive question marks over my signing. However, it was another satisfying period as it worked out well for me. I felt there was negativity, not so much hostility over my signing, perhaps a hangover from the 1983 game, but mainly because of my age at the time I think. Steve Lomas tells a good story: 'We're facing a fucking relegation battle and this little 5 ft 5" midget walks through the door and I thought to myself what the fuck is he going to do for us' He told me this retrospectively as it was quite a funny point, because, for my size, I was half decent in the air and he couldn't believe how many goals that I scored with my head. He's a good lad Steve, I'm good mates with him. I do feel that I got a lot of respect for my play at Man City and those are the satisfying things that you take out of the game.

Me, Mossy and Wayne go on a golf holiday every year. If I'm up in Manchester I'll pop in to see Mossy as well as Nobby. It was always lovely to see Raddy. Me, the wife and two kids were staying at a friend's villa in Puerto Banús one time. We were walking along the marina one morning looking at the cars, boats and the luxury yachts, when lo and behold, Raddy was just sat there reading a newspaper outside one of the cafés in the port. So, I shouted, "Raddy, what are you doing, munchy, munchy?" He was delighted to see us and invited us to have dinner with him. He had this magnificent four-bedroom apartment looking right over the beach at Marbella, and he welcomed us into his home with his family, including his son and his son's girlfriend. Raddy and Vera looked after us something fantastic and I'll never forget that. I'd always tried to keep, loosely, in touch with him over the years as it was always going to be hard, but he had an incredible career himself in management after he stopped playing at Luton at the same time that I left in 1984.

Sometimes it's not until you come out of the game that you realise you haven't maintained those friendships. I think now that a lot of us, all these years later, have just realised you've got to do that and keep in touch more. Not only do I feel I've got to do, I want to do it, too. Pleaty rang me the other day, so I had a chat with him, he wanted me to do an article with someone, which I did. I think that at least he's writing his memoirs. I went to visit David Coates a few years ago who was unfortunately diagnosed with dementia. I took him out for some lunch up in Leicester. I often meet up to take Chris Nicholl out for a stroll as he's also suffering with dementia. You go out for an hour walk and it's a ten-minute conversation that you have five or six times over. Chris has now been admitted to a care home so I can't take him out for a walk any more but I do still go to see him. I didn't really know Chris but I just wanted to be there for him and take him out whenever I could. I did get to know him a little bit and having played for Luton as well, but before my time at the club, we had that in common. I also played against him for Luton when he was in his last season playing at Southampton.

I was walking along with my missus, as I walk ten miles every day, and I happened to bump into Matt Le Tissier (who I'm pals with from our time on Sky Sports together) and Chris Nicholl, who was also out for a walk. I'd heard that Chris wasn't doing so good and I'd always got on well with him whenever we'd meet. He was always on the gold trip to La Manga that a load of us would go on so I felt a little bit of a connection with him through the golf. I found out that he was living with his sister and it wasn't a million miles away from where I live, so I went round there and we'd enjoy our walks together.

I've taken part in the dementia study with the FA because my memory's not brilliant. I did the test but I lost my confidence a little bit afterwards. Most of the test, I thought, was quite easy when it was just quick-fire questions like what day is it, what is the date. That was a lot of it until we moved onto naming ten inanimate objects and then I had to name them back. I could only remember five of the ten. Then, five minutes later, I was asked to name them again and I could only name three. So, my short term memory is not the best. I don't know if that's just naturally down to getting a bit older or whether it's from the bangs on the head that I've had in football, not only with the ball but quite a few clashes of heads coming together during games. I did also have a cycle accident where I hit the car with my arm and shoulder, then followed through head butting the top of the car as I didn't have a bike helmet on. When I fucked up that last part of the test, and as it's in my nature that if I wasn't good at something, it got me down a bit and I have to say that I lost a bit of confidence. I keep myself as busy as I can, I talk to a lot of people as I've not got that much to do so I'm keeping my mind working to avoid it stagnating. Every day you pick the paper up and you read about a different player, mostly from the generation slightly before my time, but that's because they were from that age when you were heading those really heavy old laced up balls, made even worse when they were wet becoming really heavy as it must have been like heading a brick. The white Mitre ball in our day wasn't great either though, when it was wet. By the time I was at Liverpool we'd play with the Adidas Tango, which was great, a bit of a softer coating on it, much nicer to play with and easier to head. Ultimately, with the FA tests, I think the idea is to put a number of former professional footballers through all of the set tests and then to do the same with say one hundred or so 'normal Joes' who didn't play the game for a living but are of the same age and then compare the results to see if there's a link between heading the ball so much as a younger man to developing dementia in later life.

Looking back on my time at Luton, at that time in my head, I was in a rush. If I'm honest I wanted a bigger club than Luton, but it turned out that going to Kenilworth Road was the best thing that ever happened to me because it gave me the chance to grow and develop. Pleaty left me alone to play, he was never disciplining me too much, though maybe he should have done. However, he was never really on my case. I've only got to look at the return on that where I had two great years, I was PFA Young Player of the Year, and five senior England caps, ten Under 21 caps too, and that all happened whilst I was at Luton Town. I didn't appreciate it at the time, but that one hundred games with Luton was the perfect learning ground for what was happening to me at that point, yet in my greedy, impatient head, I wanted a bigger club. I was ambitious and I wanted to get there yesterday, and that's just how it was, but Luton Town was a massive part of my life.

(BORN 8 MAY 1965, CWMBRAN, WALES)

# ANDREW GERALD DIBBLE

LUTON TOWN FC 1984 – 1988

*Andy took the first step of his footballing career when, at 12 years of age, he signed associate schoolboy forms in 1977 with Cardiff City. His early football ability went in parallel with his rugby being capped by Wales at Under 15 in both sports. In 1981 Andy signed apprentice forms with Cardiff before signing pro forms a year later in 1982. Making his full debut in the football league on his seventeenth birthday on May 8th, 1982 at Ninian Park in home match with Crystal Palace in a 0-1 loss.*

I went on to play over sixty league games. I loved my early years there in this three year period after signing as an apprentice and then a two-year pro contract. I got to play with former Luton Town favourite Godfrey Ingram, when he came to Cardiff in 1982 on some record fee-signing fanfare, but it turned out to be more of an elaborate loan and he soon went back to the US to continue playing. He is still well thought of at Cardiff City as he scored a fair few goals in his short time with us in Wales and we actually met up recently at the club.

A teenage Andy Dibble just before turning down Graham Taylor at Watford to join Luton Town in 1984 instead.

My contract was running out with Cardiff City in the summer of 1984 and a number of clubs had shown an interest in signing me. Little known fact, I was actually training with Watford two to three days a week. I really liked their manager, Graham Taylor, and for a while it looked like I would be joining

Watford. However right at the last-minute, David Pleat came in for me. His attention to detail was amazing! He knew everything about me, about my schooling and my family. My dad and I met with him at the Chiltern Hotel in Luton but we'd also met previously in a hotel in Coventry. During the meeting in Luton David Pleat completely sold Luton Town FC to me. But I was still very young at just nineteen and it was a big decision to make. I felt bad letting Graham Taylor down after he had invested quite a bit of time in me.

So, I signed a four-year contract with Luton Town and moved in to club digs Where I was placed with the Brown's on Dallow Road in Luton. They were great, a really lovely family and made me feel very welcome, helping me settle with the move from Wales. I stayed there for just under a year before I bought my first house in Westoning. I really loved it there and stayed up until I left Luton in 1988.

My first impression of the club was that it had a real family feel about it along with the excellent attacking brand of football that the manager and coaches were insisting upon being played.

I signed at the same time as three other lads: Vince Hilaire from Crystal Palace, Steve Elliott from Preston, and Ashley Grimes from Coventry City, with both Vince and Steve being moved on by the club quite quickly after failing to make the grade at that level and not quite fitting in the style of play, which was unfortunate for those two lads but that's football sometimes. As for the other lad, Ashley, we all know the part he was to play a few years later in April 1988 at Wembley.

I was really happy to start the 1984/85 season as first choice keeper

Young Andy cannot stop a heavy 4-0 defeat at West Brom in September 1984

ahead of the experienced pairing of Les Sealey and Jake Findlay, and I was pleased on a personal level with my performances until I got injured on 17th November at Old Trafford against Manchester United. It wasn't a particularly heavy challenge on me but I just caught my boot in the turf and turned, resulting in knee ligament injury which ended my season just as it was beginning. I think I got back towards the end of the 1984/85 season in time to play some reserve team games, but I ended up missing out on the amazing FA Cup run which ended up taking Luton Town to Villa Park and that famous semi-final encounter against the all-conquering Everton side, the best team in the country at that time. We came so close to getting to the final it was a real heartbreak for everyone.

I continued with my return to fitness in the summer of 1985 and into pre-season training. I had a new apprentice looking after me, a young man named Marvin Johnson. He'd joined the club and had been allocated to Steve Foster and myself, so I would look for Marvin every morning as the Welshman in me would be crying out for a cup of tea before I could get going. Marvin was a great lad and obviously went on to have a great career at Luton Town; it must have been mine and Foz's influence on his early days that set him up!

After the usual set of friendly games, we were back to business in the league and once again I started the season with the Number 1 shirt on my back. Unfortunately for me, that summer the club laid the infamous plastic pitch which personally I didn't like. It was good for the club financially, I understand that, but for me as a goalkeeper it wasn't such a good thing. I ended up badly injuring my elbow on that surface quite soon into the new season and after only seven league games, I was out injured again.

We were a really social group of players, not drinking to excess and a couple of Tuesdays a month, if there was no game of course, and with Wednesday's being our day off, there would be a big group of us who would go for a meal, a Chinese at Mr Man's in Luton. There would be myself, Mitchell Thomas, Micky Harford, Steiny, Ricky, Steve Foster, Ashley Grimes and most of the others. On player night's out we didn't really get bothered too much as most of the attention was reserved for the two glamour guys in the team: Ricky Hill and Brian Stein. They were always the favourites on night's out.

At Luton, I didn't really have a particular roommate for away games or tours, I quite liked to room with different players as it helped to get to know everyone better. I was comfortable with whomever I roomed with as I like

Andy at White Hart Lane vs Tottenham in 1984

to think of myself as a sociable guy.

With the form of Les Sealey coming in after I was injured again I was out of the side, and in those days there was never a sub keeper on the bench as you could still only name one sub, so a chance to get some competitive first team football came about with Lawrie McMenemy and his Sunderland side. Bob Bolder came down making the reverse journey from Sunderland as I believe that he was looking to move to London, so he was brought in to cover me in the reserves. I really enjoyed my time up at Sunderland. I found Lawrie McMenemy to be another excellent manager and with great coaching staff around him. I played about fifteen to twenty games there and was even voted Player of the Month by their supporters' club during my short stay at Roker Park.

In the summer of 1986 David Pleat left the club and went to Tottenham, taking some of the staff with him as well as Mitchell Thomas. John Moore took over in what was to be his only season in charge as first team manager. I was suffering with injuries again and also due to the excellent form of Les in goal, I played only one first team game that season away at Watford in a 2-0 defeat. I think John Barnes scored that night which was probably one of his last appearances before joining Liverpool. I also went out on loan again to Huddersfield playing five league games for them before being recalled to play in the game at Vicarage Road against Watford.

My last season at Luton obviously ended on a massive high with the win in the Littlewoods Cup Final at Wembley against Arsenal, but overall I was disappointed with the number of games that I played in my four years at the club. After a long spell on the side lines and in the reserves, I'd returned to the first team in the FA Cup semi-final at White Hart Lane against Wimbledon. I was disappointed with the result, obviously, but I was happy with my own performance, especially in the first half when I came out on top in a number of one-on-one situations. However, we conceded two goals in the second half missing the chance to play Liverpool in the FA Cup Final. It was a tough game to come back in to as I'd only played once before that season away at Everton in the Simod Cup and I would have preferred some league games first, leading into the semi-final. I was unsettled with only playing reserve team football and Luton Town

Andy diving bravely at the feet of Chelsea striker Kerry Dixon in 1985

as a football club had come a long way since I had first joined them as a nineteen-year-old back in 1984. At this point in my career and at the age of twenty-three I needed regular first team football so I took the remaining part of the season where I played every game, to consider my options and I would have been happy to stay. However, talks didn't go how I had hoped and the chance to move to Manchester City came along. I dropped a division to move to Maine Road but the promise of a first team spot was really what I was looking for at this stage of my career. But Luton now had a fit Les Sealey and the club also signed Alec Chamberlain from Everton that summer to compete for the Number 1 jersey.

I now split my time living between Wilmslow in Cheshire and my home in Wales and I've worked for a number of clubs as a goalkeeping coach.

(BORN 15 SEPTEMBER 1958,
HALTWHISTLE, NORTHUMBERLAND)

# STEPHEN BLAIN ELLIOTT

## LUTON TOWN FC 1984

Although he'd loved his time at Preston North End, in the summer of 1984 Steve was excited by the prospect of signing for Luton Town and to be playing in First Division alongside fellow new signings, Andy Dibble from Cardiff, Vince Hilaire from Crystal Palace, and Ashley Grimes from Coventry City.

He was in the habit of scoring against David Pleat's Luton teams in their Second Division tussles with Preston in the late 1970s and early 1980s, scoring at Kenilworth Road in a 1-1 draw in October 1979. He also scored the only goal of the game at Deepdale a year later in October 1980 followed up in the same season with another goal at Kenilworth Road for Preston in an eventful 4-2 win for Luton.

David Pleat didn't make a great impression on Stephen, recalls Steve's wife, Mags - he was only there for about five months - he enjoyed meeting and playing with the other lads at Luton Town. There were some big names at that time in the likes of Mal Donaghy, Ricky Hill, and Brian Stein.

Initially, he went to a guest house/B&B along with Ashley Grimes. Then he went to live with a lovely family in Luton which the club paid for. Mags was still working in Preston at that time. They sold their house to move down to Luton, the club then put them into a house in Harpenden.

Steve got off to the perfect start, with a goal just three minutes into his First Division debut for the Hatters in an eventual 2-0 home opening day victory over Stoke City. Unfortunately, there would be only two further

On the cover of the Watford home game; a 3-2 victory for the Hatters with Steve hitting the winner

league goals scored by him. Away at QPR, Steve got Luton's first goal of the game in a thrilling 3-2 win at Loftus Road. The other was a brilliant drive in the second half at home to Watford in October 1984. Steve's goal turned out to be the winner in another 3-2 victory for Luton Town.

He did find the net a further three times in a Luton shirt that season, all coming in the League (Milk) Cup campaign that year. A goal in the home leg of the second-round tie against Orient, then a late brace at Hillsborough in the fourth round, as the Hatters bowed out of the competition 4-2 on a bizarre evening with Sheffield Wednesday being awarded three penalties that night, all of which were dispatched past Jake Findlay in the Town goal by Andy Blair.

Steve's twelfth and final league appearance in a Luton Town shirt came in an away fixture at Highbury against Arsenal on December 1st in a spirited display, but one that ultimately ended in a 3-1 defeat with Steve very unlucky not to score late on in the game with a well-timed run and effort. Coincidentally, this fixture also marked the debut of Steve Foster in the centre of Luton's defence.

Following this fixture, his wife said the Luton manager wanted rid of him. He said to Stephen, "If you don't sign for Walsall you will never play for the first team again and I will let you rot in the reserves."

The week following the Arsenal match the deal was done which saw Stephen heading to the West Midlands and David Preece heading south from Walsall to Kenilworth Road. David made his debut that Saturday on December 8th at home to Aston Villa and scored the only goal of the game. Mags added, "Steve wasn't that bothered as he wanted to leave the club by then as he wasn't enjoying it."

Steve, number 9, puts pressure on the West Ham defence during a 2-2 draw November 1984

After he signed for Walsall he went to Kenilworth Road to collect his boots to find them thrown in the bin!

The day he signed for Walsall his wife, Mags, had started at a new job in St Albans as a nurse so when they both arrived back home that day, he told her that he'd signed for Walsall. Mags returned to work only to hand her notice in the next day! She said, "I misunderstood the transfer to Walsall; I thought he meant we were going to Poland!"

*Stephen wasn't interviewed directly due to being tragically diagnosed with Head Trauma Alzheimer's at the age of fifty-nine, but Mags very kindly spoke on his behalf.*

(BORN 2ND AUGUST 1955, GILLINGHAM)

# ANTHONY LEONARD GODDEN

## LUTON TOWN FC 1983 ON LOAN FROM WEST BROMWICH ALBION

*After five years of being the number one goalkeeper, the record holder for the most consecutive first team games, 228, at West Bromwich Albion, Tony Godden found himself out of favour and out of the team as the football club underwent a change within the backroom staff as a new first team coach came in from Gillingham. Tony had started out at his home town club of Gillingham going through all of the youth ranks and signing as an apprentice in 1971, but after three months he hated it. He spoke to his dad about the situation as he felt he wasn't getting enough coaching. It was an old school apprenticeship where he was spending most of his days sweeping, mending, and painting the terraces and stands at Priestfield. His father agreed and Tony went to Ashford Town where the manager, Reg Elliott told him if he got through the pre-season, he'd set him up with some trials. It turned out that Reg was scout for a number of Midlands football league clubs. True to his word, Reg set Tony up with a trial, ironically with Wolverhampton Wanderers, but the then Wolves manager, Bill McGarry said he didn't think he was good enough and passed up on the chance to sign Tony.*

I went on trial at West Brom and played in a friendly against Tottenham reserves where I saved a penalty. After just three days on trial at West Brom I signed on for the princely sum of £35 a week. Spurs also wanted to sign me after that trial game but West Brom had first refusal on me, so to speak. I was Johnny Giles' first signing after he left Leeds United to take over as player manager at West Brom. Quiz question for you there...and his second signing was? Geoff Hurst. I remember I was a nineteen-year-old lad from Gillingham in the presence of the man who scored a hat trick in the World Cup Final nine years earlier. It didn't work out for Geoff at the

Hawthorns and he was quickly off to Stoke City.

I had a great career at West Brom and hold the record of playing the most consecutive games in the first team. When Ron Atkinson went to Manchester United he wanted to sign me, but the club blocked it. We were at Old Trafford and I was chatting to Ron before the game when he suddenly said, "Hadn't you better go and get changed?" But I was out of the team with Paul Barron arriving at the club, which he couldn't believe. He then asked where I was sitting to watch the game, to which I told him I didn't know yet. Ron insisted that I sat next to him on the Man United bench, which I did, whilst still a West Brom player. In the players' bar after the game, Ron Atkinson came over to me and said he'd just struck a deal with West Brom and he wanted me to join him at Manchester United, that I should come back up the next day, bring my things and we'd get it all signed up. However, I got a call the next day saying that the West Brom board had blocked it as they didn't want a fans' revolt if yet another terrace favourite was allowed to follow Ron from the Hawthorns to Old Trafford, after Bryan Robson and Remi Moses had followed Ron up the M6.

I'd already had a phone call from a player who was still at Gillingham himself at the time to say watch your back with this new guy. Sure enough, as soon as the new guy came in he killed it for me, so I was out of the team. Soon after, and whilst I was at Bisham Abbey on a goalkeeping seminar which was being run by Bob Wilson, I got a message through from West Brom to say that the Luton Town manager, David Pleat, wanted to speak to me as their first-choice keeper, Jake Findlay, had fractured his finger the previous Saturday away at Arsenal and wanted to know if I'd like to join for the remainder of the season. I hadn't been out of the team long at West Brom but with that guy in situ at The Hawthorns, I knew I wouldn't be getting any first team football and all that I wanted to do was play. I left the seminar early and drove straight to Kenilworth Road to meet with David Pleat where I was happy to sign.

At the time I came in at Luton there were some really good players and I just couldn't understand that with the team spirit and togetherness in the dressing room on top of the quality on the pitch, why they were struggling. After playing my first few games, we lost the first three culminating in the 2-5 loss at Watford after being at 2-2 going in at half time. Raddy was sent off for a nothing challenge, Watford then took full advantage of the extra man and scored three more goals. Following that, the senior players decided to call a meeting between ourselves, away from the club in a local

pub in Luton, whose name escapes me. Brian Horton was the main voice during this meeting and it became clear to me that he would go on to be an excellent manager. Other players were very vocal during the meeting including, Ricky Hill, Mal Donaghy, and David Moss. The basis of the meeting was to make us harder to beat and to start defending from the front. Trevor Aylott had joined the club at the same time as me and we became firm friends, he was a really great guy and he was perfect for implementing this plan, as, with all due respect to David Pleat, with all the flair and attacking play that he implemented and insisted upon us playing, defensive coaching was not his strong point.

The plan worked and we won three and drew three of the next six games, which we thought made us safe with three games remaining as we needed just one more win. Then it all fell apart in our final home game with Everton. I think we took the lead in the first half through Ricky Hill, but it was almost like you could feel a defeat coming. I can't really put my finger on it, just that some of the lads froze. We conceded two quick goals just before half time, but we never recovered and disastrously conceded a further three goals in the second half to end up losing 1-5. To make matters worse it seemed that all the teams around us won that day, which dropped us right back in meaning we needed to win one of our last two games, both away, and both in Manchester, first at Man Utd. We lost 0-3 and David Pleat discussed with Brian Horton about resting a couple of players and therefore giving debuts at Old Trafford to youngsters Garry Parker and Ray Daniel. This was a gamble they thought worth taking as they felt that with a fresher starting eleven on the Saturday at Maine Road, we had a better chance of collecting the three points.

That Friday, after training on the day before the game away at Manchester City where we had to win to stay in the First Division, David Pleat called me into his office and gave me the thanks for everything that you've done while you've been with us speech. I was on £400 a week, which was my contracted wage at West Brom, and they would pay me as normal then invoice Luton for the money.

I told David Pleat that I would be more than happy to stay at Luton Town beyond my loan period as I really liked the club and the fans, that we had a great dressing room with a great set of lads, but David just said no, we can't afford you. I said that I couldn't believe he was telling me this now. "Why?" Pleat asked. I told him he must be either the stupidest manager ever or he must think I was the best of pro's to tell me this the day before the biggest game in Luton Town's history. Pleat replied, "Well, of course I know you're the best of professionals…" letting his words hang in the air between us. David Pleat was a weird and wonderful man.

I went back to Birmingham that night and was picked up the next day on the way to Maine Road. There was a calmness and confidence of having the quality of players and the right starting eleven to get what was required from the game. Wayne Turner was a wonderful bulldog of a player, and perhaps some people would have raised an eyebrow in having Raddy Antic on the bench but Pleat got it right and later in the game replaced Wayne with Raddy, of which we all know the result after that substitution. I looked around at the kick off and a few of the lads looked a bit tentative, but nobody was a bag of nerves. I think we soon lost possession and Ray Ranson surged forward and put a real tester into the box towards my far post, which I took cleanly and certainly settled me down. That seemed to spread through the team and truth be said, I don't remember actually having a great deal to do that day.

Tony Godden, next to Ricky Hill, face extreme aggression on the Maine Road pitch in May 1983

At the end of the game Ricky came over to congratulate me and before we knew it there was a number of a very unhappy Manchester City supporters on the pitch who had just suffered relegation as a result of us winning and staying up ourselves. They were coming at us.

Paul Elliott threw a few defensive punches then Ricky told me to run, but I knew that if we ran and were chased that they'd trip us up then the boots would really be flying in and around us. "No," I said, "we stand our ground." We did and then a police horse appeared behind us to lead us off the pitch. We had a police officer at every window on the team coach as we left the ground.

Tony, central on the right of the photo, in between Ricky Hill and Paul Elliott, Wayne Turner behind them.

As some of the lads had managed to keep their shirts as a memento of such an achievement, I asked to keep my goalkeepers' shirt from that day, which I would have loved, especially as I knew that it was to be my last game for Luton, but it was met with a flat no and I was dropped off in Birmingham on the way back. I ended up in Coventry that night as I had been invited to a party thrown by Kirk Stephens' parents. I got on really well with them, seeing them at every Luton match that I played in during my loan spell. Kirk wasn't there though, I think he was partying with the rest of lads somewhere.

As a reward for staying up we had a little break for a few days straight after in Magaluf, all laid on by the club, where we had some real fun letting off steam. Some of the staff also joined us but I don't recall David Pleat being there. And that was it, no more talks on staying at Luton, which I would have really liked to have done as I could feel something building there if they kept the team together and made a couple of good additions. However, I was back at West Brom, and thankfully there had been another change on the coaching staff and I was back in the team.

I really enjoyed my loan spell at Luton and I appreciate that I'm still well thought of by the fans thirty-nine years later. I recall the local newspaper reporting at the time of my arrival at the club that they'll either hang me in the town square or raise a statue. Thankfully, neither happened!

Ron Saunders came in at West Brom and was stone cold honest with me, saying he didn't want me as his keeper and that he'd be moving me on. Soon after that Ron called me back into his office and told me that Chelsea had come in for me to take me on loan. I told him no, I'm not going out on loan again and if I go there it has to be a permanent move. Ron looked me in the eye and said, "Look, go there now for the remainder of the season and I'll promise you I'll let you go on a free transfer at the end of the season." And so, I went to Chelsea and did well. Ron was many things to many players that he came into contact with over the years but on this occasion he made good on his promise, which allowed me to go to Chelsea on a free transfer.

As well as Chelsea, I also went on to play at a number of clubs including Birmingham City and Peterborough United. Whilst I was at the Stamford Bridge outfit, under John Hollins, I had another memorable game in Manchester, this time at United where I pulled off two penalty saves against two different takers, Gordon Strachan and Jesper Olsen. This helped us to hang on to a 1-0 win.

I managed some local non-league clubs, Kings Lynn and Wisbech, as I'd settled with my family in the Peterborough area. I coached at Peterborough United with Barry Fry and Wayne Turner with whom I was friends from our time together in the trenches, so to speak, in 1983 at Luton. I was also goalkeeper coach at Northampton Town under Ian Atkins, which led to two Wembley appearances. Also, Derby County under John Gregory, then my last coaching job was with Gus Poyet at Brighton, which was around ten years ago.

I'd got to the point where I decided I just didn't want to do it anymore with so much time away from my family, who were now settled in Peterborough. It had begun to feel very far away from where I was in Brighton. I was in training at 9am on a Christmas morning, then back on my own in the afternoon to an empty flat in Eastbourne before we headed to Reading, I think it was, on Boxing Day. That really was the moment I decided to leave football and spend more time with the family, which has turned out great as I've seen so much more of the grandchildren than I ever would have done if I was still in football.

I now live in Whittlesey near Peterborough. After leaving football I joined the prison service where I'm still employed on a part time basis as a custody transport officer. It keeps the old brain cells ticking over!

(BORN 26TH NOVEMBER 1957, BERMONDSEY, LONDON)

# TREVOR KEITH CHARLES AYLOTT

LUTON TOWN FC 1983 - 1984

*Hailing from Bermondsey in South East London Trevor Aylott has a natural affinity with his local club Millwall, although he admits to being a long-term fan on Manchester United and states Bobby Charlton as the best footballer he has ever seen. Yes, even better than Wayne Turner, he proclaimed, when pushed on the subject whilst chuckling with admiration for his former team mate and, along with Paul Walsh, his (mostly friendly) tormentor off the pitch during the trio's time together in the corridors of Kenilworth Road.*

I came through the ranks at Chelsea making my debut at nineteen. Looking back I probably made too good a start by scoring a goal in each of my first two games. In my first game I came on as a sub at St James Park against Newcastle United. A week later, I made my full league debut against Bristol City and I scored with a header. Funnily enough, Norman Hunter was playing at centre half that day and I went on later to play with him when he was the player/manager at Barnsley. Norman was coming to the end of his career but they had some real players in that Bristol City side then including Norman, Gerry Gow, and Clive Whitehead. The strangest thing about the two goals I scored were that they were both scored in the 55th minute, both at the same end and both at the Bridge. The header was a long way out around the penalty spot. I have a picture of the goal, Norman Hunter is there in the shot but also Ray Wilkins, and they are both looking at me heading in from way out. Ray was a couple of years older than me so I didn't come through the same youth team as him at Chelsea. I came through with Tommy Langley, he was a good friend of mine and, in those days, Chelsea certainly weren't the club that they are now. A lot of young players did get an opportunity, a lot of lads coming through the youth side. There were three Wilkins brothers coming through at one point. Two of them, Graham and Ray, both played first team football, then there was Ray Lewington, he was a year older than me. Tommy (Langley), Eddie Maybank, and Johnny Bumstead amongst them. It was great that a lot of players came through at The Bridge and like them I got my chance in the first team, too.

The following week I did it again, scoring at The Bridge, and this time against the great Peter Shilton and his Nottingham Forest side. There were still some of the old Chelsea greats in that side too, with Ron Harris, Charlie Cooke and Peter Bonetti who were also playing in that game along with a sprinkling of really young players; it was a special Nottingham Forest side. They were European champions at the time under Brian Clough, and they won it and then defended it the following year too, which was very difficult and a great achievement, especially for a club like Forest as at the time they weren't one of the established 'big boys' so to speak.

From Chelsea I headed north to Yorkshire and Barnsley, where Allan Clarke signed me. He was there in a player-manager role so I actually got to play alongside him, which was amazing for me personally. He was thirty-six years old by then but he was still the best goal scorer that I ever played with. Considering he was in his mid-thirties at the time, he was phenomenal. He had Norman Hunter playing at the back, so the pair of them had come over from Leeds United at the same time. A young Mick McCarthy was coming through in the Barnsley first team at the time also. Ronnie Glavin was the best goal scoring midfield player that I had the pleasure of playing with in my career. When I look back, it's amazing how many England centre forwards that I played with: Peter Osgood, Allan Clarke, Brian Stein, Paul Walsh, and Luther Blissett.

We had a very good team at Barnsley then, and we had many good battles with Luton Town. We just got pipped for promotion and we had a really good cup run as well. We made it to the quarter finals of the League Cup where we came up against Liverpool losing in a replay as we'd drawn 0-0 at Anfield in front of almost 34,000 people in January 1982, but we lost the tie back at Oakwell going down 1-3.

We were strong but, like Luton Town, we were also a skilful team who liked to play good football – games against David Pleat's Luton sides were always enjoyable. The season of 1981/82, we almost made promotion but were pipped by Norwich City by three or four points in the end. We did very well against Luton that season, unlike most teams in the Second Division, as Luton won the league by a mile. We won 4-3 at Oakwell and drew 1-1 on a hot day in May. We came within three minutes of being the only team to do the double over Luton that season but Brian Stein scored a screamer to level the score. Luton were parading the league trophy around the pitch before the game and we really wanted to spoil the party. I failed to score in either game that season, but I must have put myself on David Pleat's radar as he came in for me within a year.

I actually went to Millwall from Barnsley, which didn't turn out to be the best move for me. It was a case of the heart ruling the head as Millwall were my local team and I wanted to move back down to London, despite receiving a number of offers on better pay elsewhere. I love Millwall but it turned out to be a mistake for my career. There were a couple of Luton Town connections with Peter Anderson, who was the manager at Millwall when I signed there, as well as midfielder Alan West. The chairman had put in a fair amount of money so Peter was able to sign not only myself but Sam Allardyce and Willie Carr from Wolves.

It wasn't meant to be, Millwall were in the Third Division at the time and, unfortunately, Peter Anderson was soon sacked as manager to be replaced by George Graham. Not long afterwards we were away at a training camp on transfer deadline day. I was called in by George who said that he'd had an offer from David Pleat at Luton Town to take me back to the First Division. George said that the club were happy to let me go so they could bring some money in to help rebuild the team and it would obviously be good for me going back to play in the top division. I was keen on the move as I felt that my career was in a bit of a slump at the time so it was a massive confidence boost for me that David wanted to sign me for Luton.

I really enjoyed playing up front with both Paul Walsh and Brian Stein, when he returned from injury. in those days it was traditional to have big target man up front playing alongside a smaller, quicker, strike partner. There were occasions when David Pleat played all three of us together. I loved playing with Walshy as he was like a little terrier. Brian Stein was brilliant to play with too, as he was a naturally talented forward player, a great goalscorer. It was a pleasure to play with both of them. It was a shame that more often than not it would be two out of the three of us in the starting line-up. Mossy was great for us playing up front as he was a terrific winger; he really was a dream to play with. He wasn't lightening quick over distance, but he had that knack of dropping the shoulder to get himself that extra bit of space. He'd never needed acres of space to be able to deliver the ball, he'd pull it to one side and you knew that the ball in would be perfect. He was the best crosser of a ball that I ever played with and he could use both feet equally well. There were some wingers that I didn't like playing with as I never knew when they were going to cross it, and it was making me look bad every week. But Mossy was different, he'd get the ball and you knew what he was going to do and that it would be a good quality cross coming over for me to time my run for.

When I moved to Luton I rented a two bedroom flat in Harpenden. I became neighbours with both Raddy Antic and Brian Horton so we would travel in together every day for training and on match days too. That really helped me to settle in straight away. I had been in the process of buying a house in Bromley in South London whilst I was playing for Millwall as I hadn't been there long enough to put down firm roots again, so when the move to Luton came along I was in a good position that I didn't have anything to sell, although the people that I pulled out on buying their house in Bromley were less than happy with me that's for sure, as we were pretty close to completion. I was already married to Liz by then. We've been married forty-odd years now!

AYLOTT strikes it rich

TWENTY-two-year-old Trevor Aylott has had more than his fair share of triumph and despair. He desperately wanted to become a Chelsea star. Instead, they chose to sell him to Barnsley for £50,000 this season.

But then Trevor's luck changed. He scored the winning goal in Barnsley's F.A. Cup victory over Hartlepool — and has recently married Elizabeth Stead, aged 22, from Bermondsey, London.

**Trevor's wedding picture from the newspaper story that was run on their wedding being arranged around the football fixtures**

When I moved up to Barnsley, we were due to get married the following summer of 1980 and our wedding picture made the Sun newspaper in the football pages. We actually bought the wedding forward and ended up getting married on my birthday in November 1979, which turned out to be a cold Monday night. We'd played a cup game on the Saturday, and Allan Clarke had allowed me to have time off to get married. So, following the game on Saturday, I would then be away from the club and Alan had asked me to be back by the Thursday. They say it takes months, even years to arrange a wedding, but we did it in just four days. What we didn't think about or realise was that it was a cup game on the Saturday and if it had been replayed then we would have been facing a replay on the day that we were due to be back in London to get married. We played Hartlepool at Oakwell on the Saturday, then the plan was to head back to London with the registry office and the reception hall with the drink all booked and paid for on my birthday the following Monday.

On the day of the match Allan Clarke pulled me up and said, "If it's a draw today you'll have to call the wedding off and re-arrange it all again." That was going through my mind the whole game thinking of having to cancel everything. The game was going that way at 2-2 with about twenty minutes left, then I scored a cracking volley from the edge of their box. We ended up getting another two so ended up winning the tie 5-2, but at the time when I scored it was still 2-2 and looking like my wedding was going to have to be re-arranged. It became a feel-good story that The Sun newspaper picked up on with the headline showing me scoring the winning goal and striking it rich with the wedding. Liz and I were just so pleased that it turned out alright with the game being won and we could go ahead and get married.

When I moved to Luton, Tony Godden and I became roommates in the digs that we were put into initially by the club. We'd both moved to club at the same so were the new guys in together. I think Jake Findlay had been injured the week before so Tony was brought in on loan from West Brom to cover and we were signed on the old deadline day which, back then, was in March. We came in really deep into the 1982/83 season. I'd met up with David Pleat and his coach, David Coates at the Tower Hotel just by Tower Bridge in London and signed the contract right there and then. I think it was at least an eighteen-month contract, perhaps even a two-year deal but I can't for the life of me remember it exactly now. David Pleat certainly gave me a new lease of life.

Tony and I were made to feel really welcome by the other lads straight away at Luton, which was brilliant as it's not always the case when you go into a new dressing room, especially like we did from signing on deadline day deals and straight into a relegation scrap. It really helped us to settle as we both felt we had something to prove: for me it was my chance back in the First Division and for Tony as well, as after years of being the first-choice keeper he was out of the side at West Brom.

Walking into a dressing room for the first time can be really difficult as you're more often than not there to replace somebody who may have been tight with the players. As I was coming up from the Third Division with Millwall, I really felt that I had something to prove, even though I'd played against most of the lads previously when I was at Barnsley during Luton's promotion season when we were one of only a few clubs to take four points off of Luton that year. So, like I say, it's not always the easiest thing to do but those lads really made us welcome.

That first game though, where both Tony Godden and myself made our debuts, didn't turn out to be a fairy tale story for us as we got turned over 3-1 at home to Sunderland. They had Frank Worthington playing for them that day, also Leighton James tore us apart in the second half. They had a good side with Jimmy Nicholl, Nick Pickering, Barry Venison and Chris Turner in goal, too.

We lost the next two as well; first one at home to Norwich City by the single goal and then the disastrously crazy away game at Watford, although I scored early with a diving header, if I remember correctly, to level the score after Luther Blissett had put them ahead in the first five minutes. Nobby Horton scored to put us 2-1 up but then it all fell apart in the second half culminating in Raddy Antic being sent off for a second yellow card with half an hour still to play in the second half. We ended up on the wrong end of a 5-2 defeat and away at Vicarage Road of all places. I almost made it worse that day by attempting a ludicrous back pass from the half-way line that was way short, but Tony Godden was alert to it and got me out of trouble on that occasion.

That Watford side did really well that year with the likes of Nigel Callaghan, Luther Blissett and John Barnes amongst others, taking a lot of the top teams by surprise as they were newly promoted along with ourselves at Luton.

Wayne Turner and Paul Walsh were a right pair together. I knew of them both having played against them, but I didn't know anything about them until we shared a dressing room. I got on well with Wayne Turner and I stay in touch with him now. I love him, he's so funny, such a character, but when I first went to the club I didn't quite know what to make of him at the start, I couldn't work out if he was taking the mick or not because I might have slapped him! And I told him that many times. He, along with Walshy especially, did get on my nerves and certainly Walshy did push it too far on occasions. Don't get me wrong, I get on great with Paul but there were a few times it went over the line. So, I'd grab him and he'd look up at me with that look on his face and I couldn't help but burst out laughing, and Wayne would be cracking up too at the sight of a guy my size getting hold of Walshy. It brings tears to my eyes now just thinking about some of the scraps that we got into. The pair of them at times would be right at it and even Wayne, who I had in a head lock, would still be laughing even though I knew it was hurting him. But he wouldn't let me see that, the daft sod! Both great lads. Wayne was always upbeat and he could lift the spirts of the other lads. He loved playing for Luton, they were his team, and he showed such resilience and determination as it seemed that he would always be the one to get substituted or he'd be the first to be dropped from the starting line-up as soon as other players were available again. To coin a phrase, he was certainly a lad that you'd want in the trenches with you, that's for sure. He'd always give everything he had in every game that he played.

Speaking of Walshy, I recall playing against him at The Valley when he was still a seventeen-year-old kid with Charlton Athletic. I was at Barnsley then and I think that it was the 1980/81 season. I remember thinking what a good player he was even at that age; you could see he was special. I was even interviewed by Match Magazine and did all of those usual questions and answer things that were popular, and in the Young Player for the Future section I tipped Paul Walsh to go on to be a big star player. David Pleat saw that too and knew what he was doing when moving on Steve White in order to sign Walshy from Charlton. With Steve White going and within two years, Luton then made a lot of money on the deal by selling him on to Liverpool after David Pleat had turned him into a full England international player whilst he was at Luton.

The strangest thing about that last game at Maine Road was, it was going to be one of the two teams playing each other on the day going down. It would either be ourselves or Manchester City who would be relegated alongside Brighton and Swansea City, who were already confirmed for the drop. It was quite incredible that after forty-two league games, as we played in the top division back then, for it to come down to a straight winner-takes-all on the final day really was something amazing to be involved in. The twist was though, City only needed a point to save themselves whereas we needed all three points.

There was a full house and as the prize was survival in the First Division, I'd say that was the biggest game that I played in with the weight hanging in the balance on the outcome of the match. To have to get the win away from home as well, then have the fairy tale ending with Raddy Antic coming off the bench, with Wayne Tuner getting the hook again late on in the game to score the winner with only five minutes left to play.

You can imagine the tension before the game, you just want to get on with it and play, but you have to deal with the whole week leading up to it to get the big moment not only in your career, but also the fortunes of two football clubs. I think we were single minded and focused in that we knew we had to win, it was as simple as that! A point wouldn't have been enough for us. Manchester City possibly felt that they had the upper hand with home advantage and they only needed a point, but I think all the pressure was on them really as nobody outside of our camp gave us a chance. But, as I said, Raddy got the winner and David Pleat come dancing across the pitch at the final whistle in his beige slip on shoes. I thought he was running towards me so I put my arms out to greet him only for him to run straight past me to cuddle Nobby Horton! Then we had the City fans rushing onto the pitch to get at us players to vent their frustration and anger at being relegated in their own back garden by us, Luton Town! Our dancing on the pitch with the joy of the moment was short lived as it became clear very quickly that the City fans was hostile supporters; they didn't want to pat me on the back as a sporting gesture, they wanted to deck me one, and any of the other Luton lads that they could get to. We had to get off the pitch as quickly as possible. Funny thing that I remember in that moment as I was running towards the tunnel, one lone Manchester City supporter decided to jump in my way off the pitch. I replay it in my mind now, it's was quite comical like a cartoon, as he put his hands out and steadied himself as if he was going to rugby tackle me. At the time I was a pretty big, fit fella, so I assumed he would see sense and move out of the way otherwise I'd run over him. Well, he never moved, so that's just what I did, ran straight through and over him and he went down flat like a cardboard cut-out in the mud. I just left him laid out on the floor and headed straight down the tunnel. I'll never forget it, I was looking around and they had a really big tunnel at Maine Road that led into a big square room used as a training area, so I looked over to see the comedian, and Manchester City fan Eddie Large, was sitting in the corner by himself crying. I always think back to that moment and think, Well, that's the only time he ever made me laugh!

It was a fantastic day for us, and I have to say that the celebrations afterwards were just as good! I've got to be honest with you, though, with the pressure off and the prize of staying up in the top division we really enjoyed ourselves after that and we really deserved our place in that league. We had some top-quality lads there with Walshy, Brian Stein, Ricky Hill, Mal Donaghy, young Paul Elliott and the not so young Brian Horton. Kirk Stephens was a class right back, top drawer, no-nonsense defender and boy, could he bomb forward to join in with the attack, too. I think he hit the bar in the Maine Road game in the second half if I remember it

Trevor wheels away after scoring in the important 2-1 win at home to Aston Villa in April 1983

correctly and people have to be mindful that back in the early 1980s in English football as most teams played with a traditional back four with the two full backs hardly ever going over the half way line, so we were ahead of the curve under David Pleat and his staff with deploying over-lapping attacking full backs like Kirk. He had a great career at Luton, then what you might have thought was his dream move back to his home town club Coventry City, but he soon picked up a career-ending injury which was a real shame.

You couldn't say that Raddy was unreliable, the staff couldn't tie him down to do something specific, whereas they could say do this or do that with other players like Ricky Hill or David Moss, just for example. Raddy had loads of ability but he had that maverick element to him in that you were never really sure what you would get from him. He had all the skills and when you played with him he could frustrate the life out of you, whilst other times he'd be an absolute genius on the pitch. He was almost certainly, in technical ability, our best player. But whereas if Ricky Hill lost the ball he would do everything to fight to win the ball back, if Raddy lost the ball he wouldn't, he would get annoyed with himself and throw his arms up in the air first before he reacted, to attempt to get the ball back. There's no getting away from it, he was an outrageously talented player and ultimately that ability saved the club from what would have been a disastrous relegation back on that day in May 1983 at Maine Road.

Had Luton gone down that day, two FA Cup semi-finals in 1985 and 1988, consistent top 10 finishes in the First Division may never have happened. Most of David's side made up the starting eleven when the club beat Arsenal in the league cup final at Wembley in 1988. Also, David got the Tottenham job on the back of Luton Town staying in the First Division and flourishing under him. He carried on doing well at Tottenham as he would always get his teams playing attractive football. Obviously, his aim was to win football matches but he always insisted on winning well. By playing what he would call 'good football' he would often say, "You won, but I didn't enjoy watching you play today." Nothing gave him greater pleasure than leaving the ground feeling that we'd won it well. He didn't want his teams to grind out results. Entertain and win, that's what he always wanted. However, sometimes that's not always possible and you have to win 'ugly' as they say. David would always look to buy players who could play the game the way he wanted it to be played.

We were playing at West Ham, it was a night game on a Tuesday towards the end of the 1983/84 season and we got beat, but I hadn't played. We had the next day off then on the Thursday, we were back in for light training, a bit of physio and to start preparing for the weekend's game at home to Notts County. Then I got called into the manager's office. David said to me, "Trevor, I'm leaving Walshy out on Saturday so you'll be starting." I just replied saying, "Okay, brilliant, thanks, gaffer," and that was it, short and sweet. We trained again on the Friday, then, match day on the Saturday, we got into the ground's dressing room, we all started getting changed and suddenly David came in. He looked at me and then called me over to him. "Follow me to the boot room, Trevor," he instructed. I did as he asked and then he said, "Trevor, I'm sorry but I've changed my mind, I'm going to stick with Walshy." I was not best pleased to say the least, to be frank I was absolutely raging. I said, "How the hell am I going to go back into that changing room and hand my kit back to someone else now I've got it on and everyone else is in there changed as well?" Had he done it a little earlier before we'd all got changed saying he'd had a change of heart and was pulling me from the game then fine, but he didn't, he told me he meant to but he'd gotten waylaid. I said, "David, I'm going to feel such a burke now going back in there having to change and putting Number 12 shirt on!" It got worse for me personally though, as I was then told that I wasn't even the sub! Remember that we still only had one sub on the bench back then. Raddy Antic was staying as the named sub. In the end we won the match, so for the team it turned out to be the right decision, but I was made to feel a prize burke as we used to say back then.

After the game I was still fuming. I'd been up to the players bar for a quick drink along with my missus Liz, then as we were walking out David Pleat was walking straight towards us. I have to be honest, in that moment my intention was to have a real go at him but Liz beat me to it! She absolutely tore strips off him. No swearing or anything but she absolutely let him have it. David just stood there and took it, so did I, like a ventriloquist's dummy. Everything she said was exactly what I wanted to say to him in that moment. To be fair to David Pleat, he couldn't really have a go back at Liz. He didn't really know what to do, he just looked at us both and started to apologise saying it was a decision made for the team, but I just grabbed Liz's hand and said, "Come on, let's go!" As I was driving home, I told her never to do that to me again, when in reality I was just frustrated that she'd beaten me to it and said everything that I wanted to. I was shocked at Liz as I'd never seen her be so passionate about my football career before like that. We got back home and it was all still rolling around in my head so I decided to phone David Pleat right there and then, which I did. David said, "Trevor, you don't have to ring, you don't have to apologise." I was quick to say that I wasn't calling to apologise as I agreed with everything that she said, but that I wanted him to know that it should have been me that said it. "Trevor, that's great," he replied. "Always stick up for your family!" So, he even managed to turn that one around on me. But it was quite a humiliating experience.

We'd started really well in the first part of the 1983/84 season and perhaps it was a little bit of the case after the Lord Mayor's show and all that, but when all is said and done Luton Town in the First Division were a small club punching above their weight and once injuries set in, especially to key players, as well as players hitting a loss of form, all of those factors can be very damaging to confidence and we lost our momentum in the second part of the season. We couldn't pay out money to replace injured players such as Ricky Hill and David Moss, and we had a few suspensions hurting us too, with Mal Donaghy and Paul Elliott missing games. Young kids like Mitchell Thomas, Tim Breacker, Garry Parker, Mark Stein, and Ray Daniel were thrown into the first team. Young Stacey North came in to make his debut on the last day of the season with Kirk Stephens out injured. That turned out to not only be my final game, but it was also the last games in a Luton Town shirt for Brian Horton, Clive Goodyear, Raddy Antic and of course Paul Walsh, with his transfer to Liverpool. Also, Kirk Stephens was sold to Coventry City soon afterwards.

David Pleat knew he had to refresh his Luton side at the end of the season, as his captain and general, Brian Horton moved on to manage Hull City. I also left the club that summer in 1984 and was called into David Pleat's office where he told me I'd done really well for the club in my time there but as part of his changes to the playing staff, he was really keen to sign Vince Hilaire from Crystal Palace and that Palace wanted me in return as part of the deal. That was Steve Coppell on the other end of the deal at Palace and I was his first ever signing as a manager where he'd gotten his first job in management. By chance his assistant manager was Ian Evans who was a big mate of mine from our days at Barnsley together. I'm sure that a lot of my move there would have been on Ian's recommendation as Steve was just finding his way following early retirement from his playing days. I think he was only about two years older than I was at the time. I was sad to be leaving Luton but when the manager is as honest and up front about it with you as David was there's really not a lot that you can do about it. It certainly wasn't my decision to leave but when it's laid out to you like that what's the point in arguing? Ultimately, it was David's decision and in the world of football you have to accept that.

I went back to South London, once again with Vince Hilaire heading the other way to Kenilworth Road. David Pleat continued bringing in the right men to re-invigorate the side a little later in the next season by signing Mick Harford, Steve Foster and David Preece, along with Peter Nicholas from my new club, Crystal Palace.

I have to say that Brian Clough was a genius, and I do think that David Pleat did try to model his approach in the Brian Clough way, so to speak, in as much that David was quite witty. He certainly said some things that made you sit up and think to yourself, Is he serious? Did he mean that? David Pleat could be very much like that at times in a similar way to how Cloughie was. David was and still is very sharp and quick witted. It was lovely to bump into him and all the lads again a short while ago, initially at the Elite 80's evening held at Luton Hoo in 2018 and more recently with the occasional reunion that we have with some of the lads, and David Pleat is always there. I think that it's a mark of respect for David how so many of the lads from the Luton side back then still regularly attend these gatherings.

It's always nice to meet up with them, especially with Brian Horton who signed me when he was manager at Oxford United and Mossy was his assistant. I'd gone from Bournemouth to Birmingham City, where I stayed for half a season and then Brian Horton signed me at Oxford United, where I also only spent half a season. Oxford were in the old Second Division at the time, which is now The Championship. We had another scenario in that we had to win the last game of the season to stay up, like we did when the three of us were together in 1983 at Luton, with the must-win game against Manchester City at Maine Road.

April 1984; Trevor and Brian Stein cause a moment of mayhem in the Spurs defence at White Hart Lane

However, this game was away to Tranmere Rovers at Prenton Park. It wasn't quite the same as the Manchester City game in that one of either team on the pitch would go down that day, but it was really strange how the three of us were back together again and needing to get that last day win again, which we did, winning 2-1 to keep Oxford United up. Steve Foster was at Oxford United then as well to make another Luton connection, although we actually just missed each other at Kenilworth Road with me going to Crystal Palace in the summer of 1984 and Vince Hilaire coming the other way in the deal. Fozzie didn't join Luton until later in the 1984/85 season so we missed each other by a few months there under David Pleat.

I have a real soft spot and a fondness for my time at Luton. And the social side of the club was fantastic. As I said, I lived nearby to Nobby and Raddy in Harpenden and I truly believe that I became good friends with not only them but with all of the lads, really. The lads enjoyed socialising with each other away from the club, which believe me doesn't always happen at every club that you go to. It really was a terrific place to be and I thoroughly enjoyed my time at Kenilworth Road.

(BORN 4TH FEBRUARY 1949, HEDNESFORD)

# BRIAN HORTON

LUTON TOWN FC 1981 TO 1984

*Brian Horton was born and bred in the West Midlands in Hednesford, Staffordshire and was inspired by watching the great Stan Cullis Wolves sides of the 1950s from the Molineux terraces. Brian was installed as Luton Town's club captain and became a close ally to David Pleat as his midfield general on the pitch and in the changing room. David spoke of Brian as a terrific bloke, and although he underrates his own contribution, he was the catalyst in a way as he was the captain, and a right hand in the dressing room. He was a real football person playing the enforcing midfield role, without fouling. He led players by example and it's not surprising that he was a successful manager. Brian was a winner who couldn't bear losing. He got everyone else around him on the pitch going; a skipper in every sense of the word, and having led Brighton to two promotions he was exactly what was required. Not only was he a fine player himself but he was also a tremendous inspiration to those around him. Brian provided those fighting qualities that may have lacked in previous seasons before he joined Luton Town. He earned the respect of his fellow professionals in every division of the football league that he played in and that's what David wanted to rub off onto the rest of the team.*

There were times I thought I'd never make it to become a first division player, my biggest fear being that I was getting too old.

But after more than two-hundred games at Port Vale, then in the Third Division, Peter Taylor took me to Brighton for a modest £30,000.

Following five very successful years and two promotions as skipper with Brighton and Hove Albion and therefore achieving my ambition to play in the English First Division, I joined the Hatters in the summer of 1981

I had a year left on my contract at Brighton, but with Alan Mullery leaving over the sale of Mark Lawrenson to Liverpool and Mike Bailey coming in and saying that he wanted to replace me, I didn't want to stay under those circumstances. There were a few clubs interested, Newcastle United came in and Alan wanted to take me with him to Charlton Athletic, but David Pleat came in for me too, so I went for talks and liked what David had to say on how he wanted his team to play. There were a few players leaving that summer too, with Alan West, Paul Price and Paddy Grealish all moving on. I knew a lot of the players still at the club as I had played against them, so I knew that it would be a good team.

'The changing of the guard' Pre-Season August 1981; Brian Horton for Luton up against the Hatters former club captain Alan West of Millwall

Kenilworth Road; 1981 photo call for the newly signed Skipper

What really stood out for me in my first year at Kenilworth Road was how we started the season. We played Charlton in our first game at home and there was a certain sense of irony about that game with Alan Mullery going to Charlton and me having gone to Luton that summer of 1981. Alan wanted me to go to Charlton but I'd already done the deal with David Pleat so we got them first game and beat them 3-0. We played so well, and of course Mossy hadn't come back from America by then as he'd spent the summer on loan to Tampa Bay Rowdies. Then we went to QPR for a midweek game and the first ever competitive game on their new astroturf pitch and beat them 2-1. That game for me was the start of what we were about to achieve that season. There was so many other games that stick out, we were the best team in the division by a mile. We were scoring loads of goals and playing good football and obviously the fans were loving it. That's what I really like about David Pleat's philosophy: his way was just so attacking, whereby I was the holding midfield player with Ricky (Hill) and Lil Fuccillo, with Mossy outside left and with the two strikers up front.

David certainly became one of my managerial mentors, along with Gordon Lee during my time at Port Vale, and Ron Bullas, who was a coach of mine at school. Having spent five years at Brighton with Alan Mullery, I left at the same time as Alan did in 1981. I still had a year left in my contract at Brighton but I got the offer from Luton to join them and to be honest it couldn't have worked out any better for all of us really, because we had a fantastic team who played good football. I learnt an awful lot from David in terms of, well, everything about him really, he was a great psychologist, and he'd study processes and behaviour by observing, interpreting, and recording how people related to one another.

David's football standards were very high; he wanted us to play well, he would never accept us just kicking the ball long. Training sessions were excellent and I certainly learnt a lot from him. It actually turned out to be one of the best things that I ever did because it's great to pick different pieces from different managers, which I did with him. I didn't have many different managers throughout my playing career to be fair, but David was way above the rest and I think he should have managed the England team at one point, I really do. He was as good as that. He had us getting the ball down and we would always try to play, very much in a modern way to today's style. The club signed some good players as well as bringing some very good young lads through the youth ranks, and he loved putting the kids in alongside the senior players. He just wanted them to come into the side and enjoy their football, and the likes of Garry Parker, Ray Daniel, Frankie Bunn and people like that all went on to have good careers. In fact, those three I've mentioned all joined me at one point in my first managerial position up at Hull City, although David did take us to tribunal over Frankie Bunn.

David always wanted us to enjoy playing and for both himself and the crowd to enjoy watching us, too. There were times that we'd come in and even after winning a game, he'd basically say to us, "I haven't enjoyed watching you play today." He wanted to enjoy it and he gave us the freedom to play that way, especially with players like Ricky Hill who was a fantastic player alongside me. He did all of my running for me for two years, did Ricky. Then there were others, David Moss, Brian Stein and Walshy who came in and of course Lil Fuccillo in the midfield; the three of us, that's how we played. I was in the holding role which was new, playing

4-3-3 with just one out and out winger. That first season I was at the club we won the Championship. We were a fantastic team scoring goals for fun, and it was a team that was a joy to play in.

Brian Horton majestic in Midfield during a 3-0 away win at Leicester City in August 1983

In the summer of 1982 I had hoped to head out to America to play in the North American Soccer League. I'd been negotiating with the manger of San Jose Earthquakes but unfortunately, for both him and myself, he was sacked before the deal could be done. It was a shame as I would have loved to have the opportunity to play out there in the NASL.

In our first season, following our promotion to the First Division, people called us 'Mad Hatters' because of the way we all poured forward to attack the other team, no matter who they were, and leaving huge holes at the back to be exploited. After surviving with the win on the last day at Maine Road in our second season, 1983/84, we toughened up. We had a lot more grit about us across the back line and became more controlled in our approach to matches. You're never finished learning in football and I believed that we showed that and learnt from our mistakes from the previous season. By Christmas 1983 we were near the top of the league. We certainly didn't go defensive, by any means, David Pleat would never had gone back on his commitment to us playing attacking football, especially with the squad that we had put together. It was just a case of doing our attacking in the right way and at the right time. I was thirty-four then and was certainly looked upon as a father figure in the side, and I was delighted to stay another year after my initial two-year contract had run out after that incredible day away at Manchester City. I was out of contract and I had a few clubs interested. I nearly joined John Neal at Chelsea, despite it meaning dropping back into the Second Division, but it appealed to me as I still had a home in Brighton and I could easily commute to Stamford Bridge. But when David came back to ask if I had got myself sorted with another club and would I consider another year with him at Luton Town in the First Division, I was delighted, and at my age, staying in the First Division for one more season was so very special. I knew I wasn't getting any younger but I also knew that had I turned down the offer, I would have regretted it.

Speaking of the last gasp final day win at Maine Road in May 1983, everywhere I go now in Manchester I get asked about it as I still attend a lot of their supporters' club evenings having been associated with the club as manager later in my career, and every time I go, that's the match they want to know about what went on that day. Leading up to that match we hadn't been in a relegation battle, we were out of it, but then we lost to Everton and Man United. Then, all of a sudden, we had to go to Man City on that last Saturday of the season and win the game. David was fantastic, he kept it all low key. He'd actually agreed, much earlier in the season, for us to play in a testimonial for Ross Jenkins at Watford on the Wednesday night of that week presuming we wouldn't be in a relegation battle. I didn't play, but we lost that game as well. Leading up from Wednesday night to Saturday I felt the important thing was that he drummed into us we had to win, as a draw was no good to us. City only needed a draw. I think it's hard to play for a draw, but they nearly got it, too. However, we all know that Raddy Antic scores late on after coming on as substitute late in the game. Wayne Turner said that he came off for Raddy Antic to come on and get the winner. Wayne reckoned that David Pleat fainted in the dugout because he was so emotional and then he made that run across the pitch towards me at the end. That moment became famous! I think David gets a bit embarrassed by it all but why shouldn't you show emotions like that? He ran over to me, kissed me on the cheek and said, "Brian, you can go anywhere you want!" Those were his words, I don't know if he remembers that but I replied, "Gaffer, I know I can because my contract's up!" I'd only signed a two-year deal when I came to the club in 1981. Players don't do that these days; they want new contracts when there's still two years left to run. David then talked me into staying for another year and then after that he helped me to get my first management job at Hull City in the summer of 1984. But I wouldn't have swapped that for anything after the major decision that I took to leave Brighton because at the time, they were still in the equivalent of the Premier League and to leave after captaining them from the Third Division up to the first was a big wrench. But I couldn't have gone to a better club or a better manager.

When the new manager came in (following Alan Mullery's departure) he didn't want me whereas David Pleat did. It did me great in terms of the fact I had three great managers. Gordon Lee at Port Vale worked the budget on a shoe string and taught me a lot about that side of the game.

December 1983; The pure joy of slotting home a penalty at the Oak Road end versus West Brom in a 2-0 win

Alan Mullery at Brighton, even though Peter Taylor had actually signed me but left after ten games. I played under Alan for five years and his type of football was very demanding and then of course, came David Pleat. I speak to David all the time, he became my major mentor, really. He changed the way that I played. He also changed the shape of the team so instead of playing 4-4-2 we played 4-3-3 and I'd never played that system before. I was the holding midfield player in front of the back four with Lil Fuccillo on one side and Ricky Hill on the other. Mossy was on the outside and in my first year at Luton it was Brian Stein and Whitey, and then Walshy came in for Whitey the following season. The back four were tremendous. Jake Findlay in goal with Kirk Stephens, Mal Donaghy, Mike Saxby and Mark Aizlewood, and then Richard Money. It was a tremendous side and we had the younger fringe players coming through with Wayne Turner, Frankie Bunn, Mitchell Thomas and Ray Daniel. It was just a special time to join Luton Town and it played a massive part of my life in football.

My time at Luton ranks right up there in my playing career and I finished as player/manager at Hull City, which was a job that David helped me to get after I'd done three years at Luton Town where we got promotion with by far the best side. We won the league by a mile and then the following season we stayed up by winning the last game of the season away at Manchester City. David then talked me into signing a new deal with Luton. My contract was up after that day at Man City so had we gone down I might not have got a new contract. I signed for two more years but after one year it was time to move on as I was thinking about my next stage in football, and then he helped me to get the Hull City job. Brighton had the special days and Luton had special days as well, but I also had five years from 1971 to 1976 in the old Third Division with Port Vale. They were special times for me too, so it's hard to pick one time out over the other. Obviously, the football that we played at Luton was exceptional. I just used to stand there and watch it sometimes, as I was the holding midfield player. Ricky Hill was a magnificent player as was left-footed player Lil Fuccillo, so our balance of that midfield three was great. Mossy could have been anything really and played top level and so could Brian Stein. Obviously Walshy did (referring to playing for England, Liverpool, Spurs and Manchester City) and I signed him eventually at Maine Road. Mal Donaghy was a top international player, Jake was a good keeper and Saxby was excellent in the centre. I went through all the players I played with at Kenilworth Road: Kirk Stephens was a great attacking right back, he was the one that maybe had the problem with our formation really as we played with a left winger, but nobody out there in front of Kirk. He would always say, "What happens if their left back comes down with the left winger, where does that leave me?" What we used to do was to simply push Ricky over on the left back and I would come over to cover so it was quite simple really, but it could be complicated when playing one of the top sides as they might expose you a bit more, which on occasion they did in the First Division.

Luton have always been a side where their fans want them to play football. I wouldn't have liked to have played in a team that by-passed midfield with a long ball style of play. I was very fortunate to play in two teams where the managers wanted to play in an attacking style; the first with Alan Mullery's team at Brighton for five years where I was the attacking midfield player and Steve Piper was the holding player. We had two wingers and two strikers but never a big target striker; we never played that way and even less so with David Pleat at Luton. Even when we'd won the game he would sometimes say, "I've not enjoyed watching you play today, you haven't really played the football that I want you to play." Yet we could get beat somewhere, sometimes heavily, and he wouldn't change his principles. "You've done okay today," he'd say, adding, "yes, you got beat but you played some good football." In that first season particularly, the team was just full of goals. Mossy got twenty-odd, Steiny and Steve White got twenty or so, Ricky Hill weighed in with a few, Lil not so many, but he was a good left-sided footballer. David just changed the way that I looked at the game, he basically changed my philosophy on playing football and then when I went into management I always kept that style of football where I wanted my team to play not to just hit the front players being like the so called 'long ball teams'.

I did come back down to Luton to talk about the vacant manager's job. I had about an hour with the chairman, but his own words were that he thought I would be too strong for him. I was quite a strong determined person and I had my own opinions, so clearly if he didn't want that then it would have been pointless appointing me. It was something that I would've liked to have done. I lived in Harpenden when I played for Luton and I loved living there, it was a great place to live and the club was a great place to be. The team was fantastic and we have a reunion every now and then which is pretty unique in that we all get together and still do that after all this time. The gaffer loves to be there in amongst the players, the team that he put together, it was just such a very special place to play football. I loved his philosophy in the way that he wanted us to play the game. The supporters enjoyed the way we played and scored goals as well as the entertaining style. We were competing with Watford down the road and were very much 'bang' at each other, which was incredible. It was just a fantastic time in my life from being thirty-one to thirty-four years old.

David and I speak regularly and all he ever does is talk football, football, football, which I love. We get on great just like we did as captain and manger. I think you have to have that relationship and I certainly tried to do that when I became a manager myself. David would let me air my views, as well as other players to be fair, generally asking the younger players too when we were having team meetings. He always wanted them to speak up first before the senior players, but what I learnt from him in terms of the coaching was fantastic.

(BORN 13 JANUARY 1966, BELFAST)

# CAHAL McCONVILLE

## LUTON TOWN FC 1982 - 1984

*Cahal was born in Belfast in January 1966. His family moved to Luton in 1969 when he was three years old. He came to the attention of Luton Town whilst playing for a local kids' Sunday League side, Luton North End. John Moore watched him in a county cup final played at Dunstable Town's Creasey Park where he helped himself to five of his team's six goals that day without reply from the opposition. Cahal was approached after the game by John Moore but his mum was reluctant for him to sign and commit to Luton at the time. However, the club put a clause in the contract that if he was approached by another club he was free to talk to them. His family were happy to sign this contract and Cahal himself was keen to sign for his local home town side. Despite late interest from Chelsea, Spurs and Manchester United, all three offered Cahal's family all sorts of incentives for him to sign for their clubs, and in the end he signed apprenticeship forms with Luton Town in 1982. Originally, the club were going to sign him on the YTS scheme, as this enabled Luton to sign more players, but with John Moore having seen him slot those five cup final goals in, David Pleat insisted that he should be signed on full apprentice forms.*

*He first appeared for Luton Town in the Combination team whilst still a pupil at Luton's Stockwood High School during the 1981/82 season, playing against Tottenham Hotspur. Cahal was fouled by former Hatters' keeper Milija Aleksic for the game's only goal, with the resulting penalty being dispatched by Lil Fuccillo. Another early appearance was away at Arsenal at their London Colney training ground, when he scored two goals a 3-1 win. The centre backs for Arsenal that day were a young pairing, Tony Adams and Martin Keown.*

In the early days at Luton Town, fellow apprentice, Mark Stein would

CAHAL McCONVILLE

1982; Fresh faced youngster, scoring the goals in Luton's youth team

travel up from his home in Barnet and during the week pretty much lived with me and my family. We then became good friends. They were a great bunch of lads coming through in that youth team at the time, too good really, as the side was never settled. Some lads were away up in the reserve team playing a good level in the Combination League and some were in and around the first team squad, too. I loved the early days training at the Brache. We'd all get in the mini bus and be driven to Warden Hills for the long runs, which I really liked. Mitchell Thomas was good with the distance running too, but Garry Parker was terrible when it came to the long runs. What a player he was though, having great vision and ability with the ball. Mark Stein was also more about his burst of quickness over a shorter distance and the long runs were not his favourite thing, either. The worse one for these runs though was Jake Findlay. I honestly don't think I ever saw him run for more than twenty seconds in all my time at Luton. Jake would start the run, but then he would walk until reaching his 'taxi pick up point' as he always had someone to call a taxi to pick him up and bring him back while we all did the run. I don't know how he got away with it!

I was allocated to Mick Saxby and then also Clive Goodyear as their apprentice, and I would look after all of their kit and boots etc. It was a shame that Mick got injured in the promotion season as I don't think Clive would have achieved his place in the first team without Mick's injury. I remember Mick coming back and playing some games with us in the reserves but he'd lost the leap that he had previously; he used to win almost everything in the air in both boxes.

I mainly knocked around with Garry Parker and Marc North. Garry was from Oxford and Mark was even more local hailing from Stevenage. We'd go out in Luton a lot on a Saturday night after we'd played in the afternoon for the reserves, or the youth team in the morning. Casa Bianca's and Tropicana's were our favourite haunts, on the Malibu and Coke, as even then I wasn't too keen on beer. These days I don't drink at all, but they were some great nights out back then.

When we played in the mornings, we'd then be back at Kenilworth Road in the afternoon for a ringside view of the first team's home matches. At half time we were part of the army helping club groundsman Dick Wassell to replace all the divots with our pitch forks during the break. It was a great education being able to watch that fantastic Luton first team back then in their first season after promotion back to the First Division.

For the apprentices and YTS lads, it was our job immediately after the first team home matches, to help George Rogers, our kitman, with all the gear. Some of us would be on the players' boots straight away and the worse job was cleaning the big sunken bath in the dressing room; that was a job you'd try to avoid if you could. Actually, thinking about it, the away dressing room was the worse job as the opponents treated their changing room with utter contempt. They left their rubbish wherever it dropped, the sinks, toilets and baths would be thick from mud off their boots as were the walls, splattered with mud where they'd bang the mud off their boots and leave it where it fell.

After the season finished we'd get about a week off and then it was straight back to Kenilworth Road for all the jobs around the ground that needed doing during the close season. Mending fences, gates, seats, toilets, and painting everywhere: the barriers on the terraces and the perimeter fencing as the 'cages' were still up at the Oak Road and Kenilworth Road ends of the ground

John Moore was always our head coach with the Youth Team, but we also had great coaching from Trevor Hartley, David Coates, and of course David Pleat. Pleat was such a clever tactician and wanted the game played on the ground, as he hated seeing the ball launched up in the air. Training was always one and two touch football, and five-a-side would be one touch to get you to open up your body to receive the ball and to see and play the pass early; it was fantastic, really.

Something that stuck with me always was that Pleat would say to the forwards, "Expect the defenders to miss the ball." This improved my anticipation of the game, I lived by it when I played and it got me a lot of goals by not waiting for the defender to make the mistake but to expect them to do so and then you were on them and, more often than not, in on goal.

I was on £25 a week at first as a full apprentice. The YTS lads got less, plus there was £25 'digs' payment, but as I still lived at home in the town they bumped my money up to £50 a week. By the last year of my apprenticeship the club had put my money up by a further £40 a week. There was a bonus scheme in place. With the youth team the win bonus was £2, £1 for a draw and nothing for a loss. In the reserves the win bonus went up to £30, and a draw would earn you £15 and again, nothing for a loss. If you made the first team at that time the win bonus was £320, half that for a draw and nothing for a loss. I think there was a £500 bonus after you made your first ten full first team starts.

We didn't stay over for matches with the youth and reserves, we'd always drive to games in the mini bus on the day and come straight back, sometimes arriving very late or even in the early hours. I remember the third round of the FA Youth Cup we were away at Newport County. We stopped in a hotel a few miles from the ground just to relax and have a meal, then we went on to the ground for the game, which we won 2-0 with Mark Watts and Stacey North getting the goals. Both of these players would progress to Luton Town's first team. We headed straight back to the mini bus after getting showered and changed, then it was the long road trip back from South Wales to Luton, arriving back in the wee small hours of the following morning.

The only times we were away and roomed together was on the post-season tours of Holland that I went on for two consecutive years. The first year I roomed with Mitchell Thomas and Ray Daniel and the second year I roomed with Stacey North and again with Mitchell Thomas, so both years I was with the Marsh Farm boys as all three of them were from there. They'd all played together for the brilliant Limbury Boys' Club, and were unbeatable when we were all back in schools' football.

Speaking of Mitchell and Stacey, there's a story where we were coming to the end of the season and a few weeks before the players would get that call in to the office to be told if they were to be kept on or if they'd need to be looking to find themselves another club. Mitchell had been told that Luton would not being keeping him on after his YTS came to an end, however, fate would play its part in changing all of that. The first team was going away on a tour and Pleat wanted to take Stacey North as cover for the squad as Richard Money was injured. But, just before they were due to go, Stacey informed the club that he didn't have a current passport and therefore couldn't go. Pleat was furious with him as Stacey had been on the fringes of the first team and was rumoured all season to be the one to make the step up. Mitchell Thomas was pulled into the tour, and he did well,

Cahal in 1981/82 whilst still at school, front row, crouching, 2nd from the left.

coming back and earning himself a two-year contract, right place at the right time. I often wonder what would have happened to Mitchell had he been released at that age by the club.

Our run in the FA Youth Cup that year took us all the way to a two-legged semi-final home and away against Norwich City, whose side included the lightning-fast Louie Donowa, Tony Spearing and Jeremy Goss, all who went on to play a big part in Norwich City's first team. They also had a lad called Paul Clayton who scored six goals for them in their run up to the final, including a goal against us in the semi-final first leg at Kenilworth Road. The irony was that this guy, Clayton, was a local lad from Dunstable but had ended up at Norwich. We'd beaten St Albans, Cambridge United, Newport County, Oxford United and Leicester City in our run to the semi-final. However, in the first leg at home we froze and found ourselves 0-3 down before I scored to pull one back to go to Carrow Road in the second leg, chasing a 1-3 deficit.

In the second leg we felt that if we got at them and notched an early goal to bring the aggregate score to 2-3 as quickly as possible, then we knew we'd have a chance against them. We took quite a decent following to Carrow Road and I think the attendance was over 8,000. Unfortunately, my folks were not in the crowd that night, despite fully intending to be there. They were travelling on a hired coach carrying around forty people on board, but it broke down and never made it to Norwich.

The game itself started well enough and early on I was taken out for a stonewall penalty. The ref awarded it but then, for no apparent reason, he changed his mind and at half time our coaches were going mad at the officials. It was an even first twenty minutes or so but then we really got on top and felt we'd played them off the park, but we just couldn't find that elusive goal and the away leg at Norwich ended 0-0. The home defeat had cost us a place in the FA Youth Cup Final against Everton. Norwich City went on to win the final that year beating Everton 1-0 in a replay after the two-legged final had finished 5-5 on aggregate, with local Dunstable lad Paul Clayton, who else, scoring the solitary goal in the replay to win the cup for City.

On the day of that famous Raddy Antic goal up at Manchester City on the final day of the 1982/83 season, we were far away from that match. We'd played away at Tottenham with an earlier kick off time than the first team game. On the way home in the mini bus from North London, we were able to follow the game on the radio. As we pulled up in Maple Road, the game still at 0-0, we thought that was it, we'd be relegated back to the Second Division after only one season, but as the mini bus engine was turned off it came over the radio that Raddy had slammed a goal into the Man City net and that the game was over, we were staying up! The mini bus erupted and things were thrown everywhere. At the same time that David Pleat was enacting his now famous 'run/shuffle' across the Maine Road pitch in Manchester, and we all sat back at the club in the changing room celebrating with a bottle of beer each that John Moore had allowed us to have. Even to this day I remember that the beer was rank!

I was capped at international level for Northern Ireland whilst I was at Luton. I would travel over with Mal Donaghy and his wife as he'd be in the senior National side and I would often be taken to Mal's mum's house for dinner. He was a fantastic player and a really nice, quiet family guy; a great

Luton Town's youth team that went to the semi finals of the FA Youth Cup in 1982/83; Cahal is crouching 3rd from the right

role model.

I had a few mementos from my playing time, it was all at my mum's house, but I've moved a few times and god only knows where the stuff is now. It was only a few programmes, cuttings etc., we never got to keep the shirts back then, there was only just enough to go round as it was. There was none of the swapping shirts at the end of matches that goes on today where clubs have got multiple sets of kits to use. We just had the one and our kitman, George Rogers, kept a tight rein on it, that's for sure.

We didn't get any actual caps issued from the internationals that I played in, unlike the lads playing for England at the same level, but I did get a shirt from an Under 21's game in Turkey, where we'd travelled to Ankara in October 1983, on the same plane as the full National side due to the fact we were both playing at the same ground on the same day. I got to travel with Mal Donaghy, Pat Jennings and Norman Whiteside amongst others. There were 95,000 in the stadium and you came up to the pitch from underneath the stands; the noise was incredible. The Turkish supporters were throwing anything they could at you whilst entering up from the tunnel. I shook off the hail storm of cans, cigarette packets and banana skins to score a hat-trick in a 4-1 win. I got my shirt signed by all the lads on the plane coming back but over time that, too, has been misplaced. Shame, as it would be great framed, taking pride of place on the wall. We did also get to keep our warm-up tops with the fixture you were playing in printed around the crest and we used to get a little badge every time we played for the country, too.

I never felt I was near the reckoning for the first team, although my goals scored and performances in the youth and reserves should, I felt, have given me a chance. I spoke to John Moore about it but he said I should just keep my head down and perhaps my chance would come. It never did.

At the end of the 1983/84 season, I was offered the chance to sign for another year by David Coates, who was the assistant manager at the time, when I came to the end of my apprenticeship at Luton Town. He told me he liked me and wanted me to stay, but I'd become disallusioned at getting a place in the first team ahead of the competition at the club.

There was interest from a Swedish Second Division team, KIF Örebro, whose biggest local rivals at the time were managed by the future England manager, Roy Hodgson. KIF had already come over to watch me train and play at Luton. They offered me a two-year pro contract to join them

Cahal in 2019 with the Dunstable Road Runners club

in Sweden, which I did. I enjoyed playing and living out there. I would stay for the whole season and only come back home when the season had finished, then head back out to Sweden for pre-season training. The Swedish league don't play like we do in Britain – August through to early May – but play their league during the middle of the year as the winters in parts of Sweden are severe. I picked up the Swedish language okay while I was there but everyone spoke great English, so there was never any language barrier to overcome.

David Coates phoned me soon after I left during my first season playing in Sweden to ask how I was doing, he also said that I would be welcome back anytime to Luton Town. In total, I actually ended up playing–for three years between 1984 - 1987, professionally out in Sweden with the one club, where I actually had the same ligament injury as Mick Saxby. It happened in the morning during training and by the afternoon I was in plaster, thankfully no need for an operation. The medical science had advanced in just a few years and the team out in Sweden were brilliant, which meant I was back playing soon after.

At the end of the third season in Sweden I suddenly felt that I no longer wanted to play football for a living. It was like I'd woken up one morning and thought what am I doing. I didn't love it like I did growing up or in the early days at Luton Town. So I moved back to England and stopped playing.

I did play for a friend, however, who was running a football team for a little while in the local Saturday league and I was offered a chance to play for local non-league sides like Barton Rovers, but I didn't want to play football anymore. If I was going to carry on playing back in England I would have looked to play at football league level and not at non-league, meaning no disrespect but I had just fallen out of love with playing.

Upon reflection, I think that I regret not taking one of the offers to sign up with another club after I left school. I suppose if I'd lived in digs and moved away from home earlier, I might have pushed myself more. As it was, I enjoyed living with the comforts of home and family and having my circle of friends around me whilst still residing in Luton.

However, looking back, I can definitely say I had a great time in football, despite how things turned out. I live just outside Luton now with my wife, Sandra, and our family, and I'm a self employed window fitter. I'm also a very keen distance runner with the Dunstable Road Runners club.

(BORN 15 JANUARY 1961, LINCOLN)

# CLIVE GOODYEAR

## LUTON TOWN FC 1978 - 1984

*Clive signed for Luton Town in October 1978 from non-league Lincoln United. He was seventeen at the time and had been playing locally whilst undertaking a plumber's apprenticeship. All of this happened after he had previously been released by Graham Taylor at Lincoln City where Clive had been signed by the future Watford, Aston Villa and England manager on schoolboy forms.*

When I was seventeen, a year after I had been playing for non-league Lincoln United, I was contacted to attend two trials, one at Coventry City and the other at Luton Town. I didn't even go to the trial at Coventry. I went to Luton and had two trial games for them after which I was offered a professional contract at Kenilworth Road. Graham Clapham was the coach at Lincoln United, he knew David Pleat from a few years previously so I think he'd recommended that I was perhaps worth a look at in a trial match situation. I played on a Saturday morning in the youth team and I did okay so they invited me back to play in a midweek game, the Eastern Junior Cup Final that had been held over from the previous season against Ipswich Town. I had a very good game, we won the cup 3-2 and David offered me a contract straight after. That initial contract was only to the end of that season, which was the remainder of 1978/79. Coaching staff, John Moore, David Coates and Ken Gutteridge, who was also the assistant manager at the time, made me feel welcome straight away and that really helped make the move into being a young professional a very easy transition. There were a lot of nice people in and around the club that did a good job in looking after you. I was on my own in digs on Stoneygate Road for my first season, then in the summer of 1979 I was offered a three-year contract and moved into another of the club's digs up on Poynters Road with the well-known landlady, Mrs Gough, where Frankie Bunn also stayed. I'd gone from £30/£40 a week as an apprentice plumber whilst playing in the non-league with Lincoln United and now I was being offered a full-time contract over three years. I certainly wasn't going to haggle over the money or anything like that as I just wanted to play football.

In those days, you had the youth team, the reserve team, and the first team, so you had a monetary incentive to get up into the reserve squad and then into the first team squad where you would get a little bit extra in bonuses. As I came straight into Luton Town as a pro, I was never assigned to jobs and tasks that the young apprentices had to do but as I had already begun an apprenticeship as a plumber, I had done far worse jobs there than any of the ones given to the apprentices at Kenilworth Road. Cleaning out drains and sewage is far worse, I would say, than cleaning somebody's boots and getting their cup of tea in the morning.

I played a mixture of youth team and reserve team fixtures when I joined. We also had a Midlands Midweek League where the team was run between John Moore and David Coates. We'd play against the likes of Birmingham City, West Brom and Wolves, all of which had good young players coming through. They were always good sides to play against so that was a decent league to be playing in. Training at the start of the week began with all the squads put in together but then, towards the end of the week, as all the sides played on the same day (a Saturday), the reserves and the first teams would mostly train separately come the Thursday and Friday. But generally for training, we were all mixed in a lot of the time, which really helped to gain confidence and experience training with really good pro's.

I made my first team debut against Wrexham at home towards the end of the 1979/80 season. Neil Madden also made his debut in the first team that day as well. However, I had been in line to make my first team debut on my eighteenth birthday back in January 1979 but the game against Bristol Rovers was postponed on the morning of the match due to a really icy pitch. My chance went with other players coming back in from either injury or suspension, which meant that I had to wait patiently for another chance that didn't come until over a year later in May 1980. Two or three days before, David Pleat told me and Neil Madden that we'd be in to make our debuts against Wrexham as he was going to rest both Mick Saxby and Alan West. It was very exciting times and I remember the game really well as Wrexham had Dixie McNeil playing at centre-forward and I used to watch him play for Lincoln City, so I was playing against my home town hero! He'd scored around twenty goals in the league that year for Wrexham who also had Dai Davies and Joey Jones at the time; they were a good side. We kept a clean sheet, winning the game 2-0 and I also remember that I had a chance to score in the second half with a header but I miss-headed it as it came off the corner of the nugget and missed the target down at the Kenilworth Road end. Both Neil and myself played the full ninety minutes as there was only one sub named back in those days. Steve White was on the bench that day so it was unlikely that he would replace either of us, which turned out to be the case. Steve was warming up to come on but then Mossy scored a spectacular goal mid-way through the second half, Steiny got a second later in the game. Steve White didn't get on the pitch in the end.

Although both myself and Neil had done well in the Wrexham game, both Saxby and Westy were back in the team the following week for the final game of the season away at Newcastle United. David Pleat gave another young player his debut as our friend from the youth team, Alan Judge played in goal as Jake was out injured. Bob Hatton signed off his time as a Hatter scoring both of our goals at St James Park that day in a 2-2 draw.

I did get my first senior goal the following season away at Cambridge United with a header in a 3-1 win at the Abbey Stadium. It was the game where Jake Findlay received a rib injury after a challenge from George Reilly, with Mal Donaghy putting on the goalkeeper's gloves. We went down to ten men as Raddy Antic had already come on for David Moss. Mal didn't concede any and another late Steiny goal wrapped up the win for us. I played in five consecutive games that year, then I got a bad facial injury to my mouth away at QPR, which unfortunately knocked my confidence a bit. It took me a little while to get back into it again.

As a young player back then coming into that environment with the likes of Mal Donaghy, Paul Price, Mike Saxby and also Mark Aizlewood, who could also play at centre half, there was very much a 'first team' dressing toom and a reserve team dressing room and you had to earn their respect to make your way into the first team dressing room. All around the club it was a very friendly atmosphere, with the older pro's like Bob Hatton looking after you, and there was definitely some good banter amongst the lads. It was a great time to be at the club.

1980 Players Fancy dress night out, Clive is in school uniform 2nd from the right

In the Championship winning season of 1981/82 I was already in the side playing next to Sax for two or three games prior to when he got injured at home to Crystal Palace that October. I suppose you could say I ended up taking his place, although it was very unfortunate for him because he was doing so well. I thought we'd done quite well together in those few games leading up to that incident. Mark Aizlewood was out of the side at the time and Mal Donaghy was next to us over at left back.

Having not been a regular in the side and just being a part of the teams that went close in the previous two seasons, when I did come into the side and stayed there in the 1981/82, there was already that belief in and around the club amongst both the staff and the players that this was going to be the year the club got promotion back to the First Division. There was no fear really, I just think that David Pleat felt we would always score more goals than other teams with the way we were playing. We felt really confident every time we went out and I'm very proud of the fact that I only played in two losing games in the whole of that season in the league, both high scoring away games going down 4-3 at Barnsley and 3-2 at Newcastle United, with Varadi getting a late winner against us.

We'd always have a Christmas party and an end-of-season do in which the player fine's kitty from throughout the season for things such as turning up late for training or late for the team bus, etc., would go towards a good night like the fancy dress parties up at Cesar's Palace. I remember us also having a player's fancy dress party in a pub out in Westoning or out Flitwick way one time as well. The social side off the pitch definitely helped to build a great team spirit, which carries out onto the pitch meaning you can rely on your team mates to have your back if you're having a hard time.

Clive ready for the first division in the summer of 1982

Going into that first season up in the top division in 1982, I was still a relatively young player so it was quite a baptism coming up against top footballing sides almost every week, No criticism of David Pleat, but we never did a massive amount in training towards defending as a team; it was all about going forward, can we score goals. At times, we left defending to our own devices, which sometimes led to being exposed with 2v2 at the back with Kirk Stephens bombing up on one side of the pitch and Richard Money, at that time when we went up, on the other side. But it was certainly a great time to be playing even though I didn't like letting in the goals, obviously.

I remember the heavy defeat at home to Everton towards the end of the season, and I admit that my own performance was shocking that day. I think confidence was at a low all round by then. That was probably the biggest down point of that season for me.

The week immediately after the Everton defeat we had the game away at Manchester United on the following Monday, then we played a testimonial for Ross Jenkins at Vicarage Road, before, if I recall, going back up to Manchester on the Thursday. I feel that David Pleat was quite clever in carrying on with that testimonial, as opposed to just training and getting wound up about the task that lay before us, it took our minds off the City game coming up on the Saturday, and so in playing this game midweek it took the pressure off a little bit.

The ironic thing about that game, was that I was a big Manchester City fan for a lot of my younger years while I was growing up so I found myself playing against the likes of Asa Hartford and Dennis Tueart, who were heroes that I had watched in the 1970s. People said to me 'well you supported Man City, and you relegated them at Maine Road' to which I responded, "Well, it was my job!" Brian Stein got the better of Paul Power to get his cross in at the second attempt, then with Alex Williams palming the cross to the edge of the box for Raddy to get that all important goal, it was just amazing to be on the pitch at that moment. The pure elation as you could see from the television pictures was an unbelievable feeling, but with time added on we probably still had ten minutes to go after the goal. It was probably worse watching than it was playing, as it always is, as at least on the pitch you feel that you have a bit of control over what is happening. We had the goal to defend and that was it, just get your head and body in the way of everything that came at you. Then, at the final whistle, there was a couple of tussles with some threatening behaviour from some Manchester City fans who'd come onto the pitch. Fortunately, the police were on the pitch pretty quickly and we were ushered off, but it did turn into quite a frightening experience for a few moments at the time.

During the Match of the Day interview with John Motson, where the whole team were involved, Brian Stein was asked for a few words and when he started speaking, I think it was Jake Findlay or Kirk Stephens who started mimicking a snoring sound, which cracked everyone up. But those two were like that with everyone all the time during interviews and the such like, the real characters of the team, they were non stop, and that really helped build up the team spirit to what it was.

I roomed with Mal Donaghy a lot through the actual season but for end of season tours, invariably Mal would be away on international duty with Northern Ireland so I would room with Wayne (Turner) or Rob Johnson instead. Mal was a quiet and family orientated man but he did like to socialise with the rest of the group, just not in full view of everybody immediately after games.

The home game with Tottenham in January 1983, which, co-incidentally, was also the day of my twenty-second birthday, there was a massive crowd with something close to 22,000 at Kenilworth Road that day. We drew the game 1-1 and it looked like I'd got the perfect birthday present by getting onto the end of a cross that came in at the Oak Road End from young Mark Watts. If I remember correctly, Mark was in the team making his debut in place for David Moss who was injured. However, it was given as an own goal with the history books crediting it as an 'OG' to Gary O'Reilly, but I still say to this day that I felt something come off my head to help it on its way past Ray Clemence and into the Spurs net, though whether it was the ball or not I certainly did my best to try to claim it. You wouldn't expect anything less from a footballer than for them to claim that they'd got a touch and to be fair to Gary O'Reilly, he wouldn't

December 1982, Clive goes agonisingly close to beating Joe Corrigan in the Manchester City goal

have begrudged the goal going down to me rather than as an OG against him. The goal put us 1-0 up at half time and it looked like it would be good enough to record a win against Spurs. It would have done except for a certain Glenn Hoddle equalising later in the second half after coming on as a sub.

I did manage to score that season past another England goalkeeper when I scored in the fog during the 3-3 home game with Southampton in November 1982. It was an 87th minute equaliser and from looking at his face that must have been the worst goal that Peter Shilton ever conceded, I think. We'd come back from being 0-2 down at half time only for David Armstrong to put Southampton back in the lead in the 84th minute down in front of the travelling support in the open terrace at the Kenilworth Road end of the ground, so they must have thought they'd wrapped up the points. All this was played out in front of the Match of the Day cameras to be shown to the nation later on that Saturday night.

The following season, in 1983/84, I only played thirteen games. It wasn't down to injury but more to do with young Paul Elliott coming through and becoming the recognised centre half pairing alongside Mal

Donaghy. I just couldn't force my way back in the starting line-up so I became a kind of bits and pieces player in and around the first team. The season before had been tough and as a defender in a team that was letting a lot of goals in it did take something out of me, confidence-wise I think, and I do believe that it followed on from the first season up in the First Division and into the next. It's just one of those things that happens in football, where you fall out of favour a little bit. At the time you don't think it's happening and you're angry when you're not in the team when you think you should be, but you have to accept that it's part of the game.

I never got to keep the shirt from the Manchester City game in 1983, George Rogers, the Luton Town kitman wasn't having any of it. It was like getting blood out of a stone at the best of times to get kit from George! In fact, I never got to keep any of my Luton Town shirts, I do have a photo with Eric Morecambe and the Second Division Championship trophy though, tucked away in the loft somewhere, but I do have shirts from my Plymouth Argyle days and the full kit from when I was fortunate enough to win the FA Cup Final with Wimbledon against Liverpool in 1988 when, ironically, we beat Luton Town in the semi-final at White Hart Lane to reach the final. It was a game, I hasten to add, that in which I was not a part of as I wasn't in the Wimbledon line up that day. I also have international kits from my time playing in Hong Kong.

In the summer of 1984, I still had a year left on my contract with Luton

Clive on the right of the image, number 5, scores the games only goal at home to Watford in December 1982

and I am in the squad team photo taken for the upcoming 1984/85 season. I'd been up against a very young Teddy Sheringham when we played a pre-season friendly away at Millwall on the Friday night in mid-August, which was just a week before the start of the new season. But then, come Monday morning, I was called into David Pleat's office and told, "You're going to Plymouth!" That was it, no discussion of an offer coming in, would you like to talk to Plymouth... To be fair, I would say that it was probably time to move on anyway but there may have been some other things going on in the background, though I don't know for sure. So, I was told on the Monday, went down to Plymouth and signed for them on the Wednesday, travelled to Burnley on the Friday, then made my debut in a 1-1 draw at Turf Moor on the Saturday and scored my first goal for Plymouth the following Monday at home to Torquay United in a Milk Cup tie.

After having been released by Wimbledon, I went to Brentford for three months but we failed in the play offs so they decided to release me there as well. The story goes that when I was at Wimbledon we used to go, as a team, to a Chinese restaurant in Wimbledon village and the owners of that restaurant were in contact with the teams in Hong Kong. They asked me if I was interested in going out there, to which I agreed. I was there for two years with a team called Ernest Borel. It was a decent standard out there, this was 1991 to 1993, and I would compare it to National League level here in England nowadays. I'd had my knee injury by then so the lighter schedule was good for me, and as there were only ten teams we only played every ten days or so. It was good money and a good contract and a nice combination with a lot of younger players from England out there and older players like myself coming to the end of their playing careers.

As a result of my knee injury I began studying physiotherapy and when I qualified I joined Luton Town as the assistant physiotherapist, later on becoming the club's head physio. I've also worked at both Cardiff City and Chester City and in June 2006 I set up my own physiotherapy/sports injury clinic based in Bletchley, Milton Keynes. In addition to this, I've also held surgeries with Argos, Homebase, and the Abbey Bank, who all had their head offices near my clinic, to provide physiotherapy for their staff. I also helped out at the 2008 and 2009 London Marathons attending to the runners who were raising money for Progressive Supranuclear Palsy with their post marathon treatment.

In 2018, I retired from my physiotherapy practice and now enjoy splitting my retirement between both here in the UK and in Portugal, where I have a second home.

Even though there's a lot of talk about the 'Crazy Gang' days down at Wimbledon and winning the FA Cup, I would say that still my favourite time in my playing career was that period at Luton Town. It was so good because of the team mates, the camaraderie that we had both on and off the pitch, it was certainly the best that I came across, and was definitely my favourite period as a player. A lot is made of the so-called team spirit at Wimbledon, but it was nothing compared to what I personally experienced at Luton Town.

(BORN 12 AUGUST 1957, CLIPSTONE)

# MICHAEL SAXBY

LUTON TOWN FC 1979-1984

*Mick was born in Clipstone, in a small ex-coal mining village in north Nottinghamshire built on the site of an old army base and likely to be the site of a medieval royal palace. Almost straight from school in 1974, Mick started playing for Mansfield Town even though he also had a full-time job. Playing and training at night on Tuesdays and Thursdays became a bit overwhelming and so his dad asked Dave Smith, the then-manager, if he was intending to sign his son on a full-time contract. Smith did sign him and Mick stayed at Mansfield until 1979 when he joined Luton Town.*

Towards the end of what turned out to be my last season at Mansfield Town in 1978/79, there was a lot of local paper talk that Leeds United were interested and the rumour was they had been to watch the last six or seven of our home games that season. There was also talk of West Ham being interested, too. However, no approach was made by either club and as I was out of contract, manager at that time, Billy Bingham, put off his holiday for a week to ensure that he tied me to a new contract. I signed the new contract and Billy went happily away on holiday. However, unknown to Billy, Luton Town then made an approach so I told my dad there was an offer to go to Luton and asked would he come with me to meet them. There were no agents back then and my dad told me to stay quiet and let him do all the talking when we got there. Dad had spent his whole working life working down in the local coal mining pit and knew nothing about football business.

Upon arriving at Leicester Forest East Services, we went into reception and said we were there to meet with a Mr David Pleat. Ken Gutteridge,

Mike Saxby with a young photographer on Media day Summer 1979

the Luton Town assistant manager at the time appeared in the foyer to meet us and took us to the room where we would meet with the delegation from Luton. As we walked in, my dad once again reminded me to leave all the talking to him. We entered the room to be greeted by a party of three waiting for us: Dennis Mortimer, the Luton Town chairman of the time, David Pleat and… Eric Morecambe! Now, there was no bigger Morecambe & Wise fan than my dad, every Christmas TV special they would have him in absolute fits of laughter, so when he saw his hero sat there he was unable to say another word for the duration of the meeting; I had to do all the talking myself! There was me, this twenty-one year old lad who'd never lived outside of Mansfield and thinking I needed a passport to do so, having to thrash out the deal on my own. David Pleat offered me the terms, a five-year contract. I told him I didn't want to sign a contract for that long, but Pleat said, "Look, if we're paying £200,000 for you then it's going to be a five-year deal." Back in 1979, £200,000 was a lot of money to pay for a player, at the time it was Luton's record fee paid, and that stood until 1982 when they bought Walshy from Charlton Athletic. It was also a record fee received by Mansfield Town and that stood for about another ten years after that. I signed with Luton Town there and then, Mansfield were very happy with the fee and sold me behind their manager's back. As we left the services, my dad, who had continued to remain silent throughout the entire meeting, nudged me and said, "See, son, I did alright for you there, didn't I!" Billy Bingham joked with me afterwards that I had cost him his job at Mansfield Town, to which I replied, "No, Billy, I got you to two World Cup Finals." Billy had returned to the Northern Ireland manager's role in 1980 guiding them to two consecutive World Cups whose squad included a certain Mal Donaghy, and we all know what happened one night in Valencia against the Spanish, in June 1982...

I was happy, too, with the basic wage plus, that was the last year the player got five per cent of the fee and there was a loyalty bonus as well, all to be paid in instalments at the end of every season for the duration of the five-year contract. Mum and Dad had always followed me everywhere I played so when I moved down to Luton they came with me to look around. I can still see my mum's face as we drove through to the ground up Oak Road and into the players car park in Maple Road, she looked at me and said, "Oh, where have you come to?" When I first joined Luton Town, I was put into digs with Mrs G. (Mrs Gough) where I found that I was lucky enough to be in digs with Ricky Hill and his walk-in, Cecil Gee filled wardrobe in the 'west wing' at Mrs G's! We had a great time at Mrs G's on the Luton side of Poynters Road, especially with Cesar's Palace being so close!

As neither Ricky nor Paddy Grealish drove, we picked up Paddy on the way to training, me being the chauffeur every day. I drove a Ford Cortina MK II when I first moved down from Mansfield but once I started earning a few pay cheques I bought a Black Austin Princess, though soon realised it was a bit of a family car so I upgraded to a Ford Capri, 2L Sport, which I got a good deal through the club sponsor, Tricentrol. Not as good a deal as Jake Findlay would have got though, that man was the king of getting things for free. I got a good deal but I still had to pay for it myself.

A good pub quiz question is, when did Mick Saxby first play at Kenilworth Road in a Luton Town shirt? Most people may say, Gillingham at home in the League Cup in August 1979 or the league game at home to Orient later that month (as I was suspended for the first home league fixture of the season with Cambridge United), but it was actually much earlier and whilst I was still playing for Mansfield Town. We'd arrived at Kenilworth Road in December 1977 to play against Luton Town. I was the sub that day but I did come on later in the game. The kitman had packed our normal home kit, which clashed with Luton's kit, so we ended up wearing the Luton away shirts on the day. So, I played at Kenilworth Road in a Luton shirt almost two years before actually signing for them.

Relaxing at home with wife Glenis and some quality LP's

My first league game for Luton Town was away at Bristol Rovers in August 1979, this was actually the second game of the new season as I'd missed the first game at home to Cambridge United due to still serving a one-match suspension from the previous season with Mansfield Town. We lost the game at Bristol Rovers 2-3 and a future Hatter, Steve White, who would join us later on that season, absolutely destroyed us. Pleat probably signed him on the back of this performance against Luton that day. We were 0-3 down going into the last ten minutes before Mossy pulled two late goals back to make the score line more respectable. I scored my first goal for Luton away at West Ham in October that year, it turned out to be the winner after Steiny had scored the first to put us 2-0 up at half time. West Ham pulled one back in the second half but we got the points, and it was nice to get the decisive goal. I got four goals in my first season, along with this one, and I also scored against QPR, Chelsea on New Year's Day, and Notts County - all at home.

Paddy Grealish had arrived at Luton at the same time as I did in the summer of 1979 for another big fee at the time from Orient. It was lucky that we did join together as we became firm friends and ended up living opposite each other when I finally moved out of Mrs G's digs on Poynters Road and bought myself a house in Westoning. My mum was much happier when she saw where I was living after this move.

In the week leading up to New Year's Day 1980, there was a game on the pitch at Kenilworth Road two/three days before we were due to play Chelsea at home on the Monday. Unfortunately, before Dick Wassell had the chance to replace all the divots, there was a freeze. We tried to train on the pitch and it was terrible so after training, David Pleat told us to report as usual for the Chelsea game on New Year's Day, but said he was 99.9% sure that the game would be off. Taking David Pleat's word and with it being New Year's Eve, Ricky and I were invited over the street on Poynters Road where Colin Ball and his wife lived. Colin ran the Century Club at Luton Town so we thought why not, which led to us drinking until 2am, thinking the game would be off the next morning, also I think it was an early kick too, on police advice to keep the fans away from the boozers before the game. How wrong I was.

Arriving at Kenilworth Road, I can't vouch for how Ricky felt, but I had a stinking hangover, only to be told by Pleat the referee had passed the pitch as playable and the game was on. The pitch was still terrible and we all had to wear hockey boots or pimpled trainers. There was still trouble down in the open Kenilworth Road end, I'm not sure if some Luton lads got in there amongst the Chelsea crowd but it kicked off and spilled over onto the pitch. Some of the poor souls found themselves being picked up and tossed back over the fence and into the crowd. The pitch was terrible but it led to an all-out end-to-end slugfest of a match. I scored a header, even with my hangover, rising above Colin Pates to head in at the far post for our second goal of the game in front of the Chelsea fans at the Kenilworth Road end. Chelsea got a corner and the player I was marking whispered to me, "Your breath stinks of ale, but our lads have been on it until 4am this morning as well." The Chelsea players had all assumed the game would be off too, so they'd all seen in the New Year, and the new decade for that matter, with a skin-full. It led to a memorable match with the final score of 3-3 to which supporters would regale of having been there for years to come with Mal Donaghy and David Moss scoring the other two goals for the Hatters.

We were a very social group with golf, snooker and the pub, but I never drank two nights before a game, except for one occasion where Brian Horton arranged a players' night out early in the season in 1981/82 and we all ended up in The Vine on Castle Street in Luton and drank about four or five pints of Stella. We weren't falling down drunk but we had a decent amount that night, and we played away at Filbert Street, Leicester City on the Saturday. They were with us as the early pacesetters in the Division and we played them off the park winning 2-1, but that was the only time I drank that close before a game. We enjoyed a drink afterwards and from Westoning myself, Paddy Grealish and Steiny, who was in Flitwick, would frequent the Old Bell in Greenfield, near Flitwick. This pub was run by the former Luton Town goalkeeper, Tony Read, who had retired a few years earlier in 1972.

At home with the Saxby's; 'Get 'Orf my land!'

I used to go home to Mum and Dad's house every weekend after matches. When I'd arrive, my mum would be so pleased to see me and the first thing my dad would say to me was, "Have you got the papers?" By this he meant the excellent coverage

'Our Sax' scores his first goal for Luton Town in the 2-1 away win at West Ham in 1979

from the local Luton papers, The Herald, The Leader and the Evening Post Echo. Dad had gone everywhere with me in my playing career and very proudly and carefully had kept many scrapbooks. I would be welcomed into the house by my mum whilst my dad would head off to find his scissors and the latest scrapbook that he had on the go. I still have these scrapbooks now and I post some of the items from time to time on Twitter and Facebook and I'm always touched by the reactions of fans that remember those times at Kenilworth Road and me as a player.

David Pleat was a great coach and very much hands on in training, but his individual man management was not so good and, considering he was still a fairly young coach, he didn't really get the dressing room jokes and would react quite strangely to some things said to him, particularly from David Moss and Jake Findlay. When he did try to join in his remarks did not go down too well and would just get silence from the changing room as we would sit there looking around at each other, not really knowing what to say. So, on that front, he was quite an odd character.

There was one time a friend of mine came down from Mansfield to watch me play at Kenilworth Road. I gave him the full tour around the ground and took him in the changing room to meet all my team mates and the management staff and coaches, etc. David Pleat knew full well that I had a mate down to watch. The game was ticking along at 1-1 at around the sixty-minute mark and I could see that our bench were fishing out Lil Fuccillo's number as he'd not been back long from a leg break and was proper blowing out of his back-side. But then, Lil hit one out of nowhere, it screamed into the net, and all of a sudden the numbers were changed and our bench put up number 5, my number, for the player to be substituted. I had always taken being the player to be substituted well before that time and shook the player's hand coming on to replace me and all that, but this time I saw red. Perhaps I felt Pleat was doing it as he knew I had a friend down to watch me and thought I needed bringing down a peg or two after bringing him in for a guided tour. I didn't stay on the bench but stormed down the touchline instead and straight into the changing rooms. I came into the club on the Monday after the match to find that I was down to play the following night, a Tuesday night, away at Hereford United… with the reserves. Pleat had done me for my public show of anger.

We had such great team spirit at Luton Town during my time, there were no clashes of personalities or egos. We were all very relaxed with each other and it reflected how we played together on the pitch. Unlike today in the modern game, our match day warm up consisted of a game of 'one-touch' in the dressing room which involved a circle of players only being able to take one touch, and if you took more than that you were out. I have to say that it got quite competitive! Then we'd head out onto the pitch at ten to three, knock the ball about a bit, perhaps a little stretch, and then we were back into the dressing room and kick off was upon us.

October 31st, 1981, home to Crystal Palace was when the injury happened. I had just been up for a cross from a corner and powered in a header which Paul Barron saved well. Then, when I was back on the edge of my own penalty area I turned my body, but my studs stuck in the turf and I felt my knee rip. I tried to carry on but there was no stability in the right knee at all. I signalled to be substituted, and was replaced by Raddy Antic. John Sheridan took a look at it and told me it was ligament strain and I'd be back playing in two weeks.

Unfortunately, this wasn't the case and it was a long slog back after the operation. The club doctor was a typically daft eccentric GP type; Dr Berry. He would come in each week to look at me and on one occasion he examined me, moved, stretched and manipulated my knee. He stopped, looked up at John Sheridan and announced, "John, I believe the knee is much better, it won't be long now." Only problem was the daft sod was examining the wrong leg! I worked hard to get back to fitness as I had come so close to my dream of playing in the First Division of English football. I eventually got back to some reserve football and played at home to a Leicester City team, however, I had lost a bit of pace, not that I was ever the quickest of defenders anyway, and I now had a limp on my right leg. I was with Rob Johnson for almost a whole year as he was out at the same time as me, but thankfully, for Rob, he fully recovered and went on to have the career in the top flight that he deserved.

I went out on loan to Grimsby and Lincoln City but came back for the last season of my five-year contract in 1983/84 determined to get fit and

Saxby soaring through the air in the Burnley penalty box during the 1979/80 season

to play some First Division football. But it never happened and at the end of the season as my contract had expired, I left the club. My regret is that I didn't get to say goodbye to anyone and that I didn't keep in touch with anyone. Colin Addison took me to Newport County so I was off to Wales.

Willie Maddren, the then-Middlesbrough manager, contacted me to see if I would be interested in a move up to the North East for the 1985-86 season, which I did and got to play with a great bunch of players coming through there, including a very young Gary Pallister, Stuart Ripley, Bernie Slaven and Colin Cooper. All these players would soon take the club back into the First Division in 1988 but I was not to be a part of it. Bruce Rioch came in as manager and took me to one side telling me they'd pay my contract off and that was that. I was finished in professional football at twenty-eight years of age. It took me a long time to get over the absolute disappointment of my injuries at Luton Town and when I was finishing playing at Middlesbrough, Luton were going through their most successful period with the FA Cup semi-final the year before at Villa Park against Everton. They were about to achieve the club's highest ever league finish in the top Division in 1986/87 under John Moore after Pleat had moved to Spurs.

My twelve appearances in 1981/82, thankfully, meant that I qualified for a Division Two Championship Winners' Medal, which I kept and still have today. I did have some match worn shirts from my time at Luton Town and they are now in the safekeeping of my son.

As I said, my biggest regret was losing touch with everyone after leaving in the summer of 1984, especially with Ricky and Kirk Stephens. The fact is that it took me a long time to get over my injury which caused me to leave Luton Town and I didn't have any contact again, not until the recent players' reunion in 2018 at the David Pleat Elite 80's function and thank god that we did, as we got to meet up again with dear old Raddy that night not knowing, of course, what would happen to him so recently. We've all stayed in touch after that night and vowed to keep it that way. There is some talk of a golfing holiday in Spain, where Jake and Kirk spend a lot of time.

These days, I work in Nottingham, about nine miles from home, for Kingfisher Professional Services working in the business credit industry. It's a nice Monday to Friday office job. I used to do some work for Mansfield radio on match days but I haven't been to Field Mill to see a game for a couple of years now, as the grandkids keep me busy on the weekends, but I have promised myself to visit Kenilworth Road more often in the near future.

(BORN 1ST OCTOBER 1959, NEWPORT, WALES)

# MARK AIZLEWOOD

## LUTON TOWN FC 1978-82

*Mark signed for Luton Town in 1978, which was David Pleat's first season as a full-time manager in the football league. Wanted by Arsenal, Mark made his debut with Newport County at the age of sixteen.*

I officially signed for Luton Town on April 1st, 1978. The manager at the time was David Pleat. This was his first ever job as a full-time manager in the football league and people may forget that I was the first player he ever signed. I've always kept in touch with David over the years. He is very proud and to a certain degree protective of that group of players he put together which ultimately achieved the goal of getting the club promoted out of the Second Division and up into the First. That group really bonded and you get that in football if you have success, even if you don't speak to each other for years but then, when you meet up, that connection is instantly there.

I was so lucky because David Pleat was a great planner, always thinking ahead. He had me on his radar for a while even before he became the manager. He watched me a number of times, including a game away in February 1978, I think it was. We lost the game and I was told on the quiet that Luton Town were here watching me. I thought to myself well I was crap today so that'll be that, but within two months I was joining Luton Town and moving up two divisions in the football league, and I wasn't even turning nineteen until October later in the year.

He was an excellent tactician and a great coach and throughout his time as a manager in the game people have always respected his football ability and thorough knowledge.

We had some excellent initial results in that first full season in 1978/79, and by the end we had to win our last but one game to stay up if I remember it correctly. In the modern game David may not have lasted in the job past that first season but thankfully. the chairman and directors kept faith in him, a man who was still a very young manager learning on the job, so to speak.

Going back to before I even joined my local team, Newport County, I had the chance to join Arsenal when I was fourteen. My dad was a steel worker and my mum worked in a factory. We got the chance to go up to London and in those days a trip up to London from South Wales was a big deal. You think nothing of it nowadays but then it all felt quite surreal, it was really special. I'd already had the Arsenal 'Welsh' scout watching me, and I'd already been up to train with them at London Colney a few times and stayed in digs with a very young David O'Leary.

Arsenal were keen for me to sign so that's why they invited my mum and dad to go up there. Now, with the greatest respect to my parents, they were as rough as arseholes; they put us in a five-star hotel on Park Lane, then we went to meet with Bertie Mee. Dad said to me, "Just leave all the talking to me." Bertie Mee was a lovely bloke and a legend at Arsenal but my Dad took advantage of the situation and said to him, "Mr. Mee, myself and my wife have never been to the London's West End to see a show as we can't afford it!" Mr. Mee said, "Is that so, perhaps we could help with that?" I can't even remember who was in the show! Arsenal sorted out a first-class box for us at the Aldwych Theatre and my dad took the tickets and told Mr. Mee, "Thank you very much, we'll make a decision tomorrow."

The next morning, we were having breakfast at the hotel and my dad turned to me and said, "Right, you can tell Arsenal to fuck off now as I've already done a deal for you to go to Newport County!" I was a bit taken aback, but I was fourteen so I just told him 'right you are then, dad'. We went in to see Arsenal and again my dad did all the talking along the lines of thanks very much, it's not for us with Mark moving up to London, he's going to stay in Newport. Basically, my dad just used it as an opportunity to have a night out in the West End of London with my mother.

Like I say, he had already come to an agreement with Newport County for me to sign for them regardless of the interest from Bertie Mee and Arsenal. I would report at Somerton Park, which is no longer there, on a Friday after I had got the bus from school.

A September away day 2-0 defeat at Bristol Rovers early in 1978/79 season

Back in those days the bottom four clubs in the Fourth Division at the end of each season had to apply to the Football League for re-election and it seemed that Newport County were always one of those clubs in this situation. The club was broke, they didn't have a penny! Sometimes, I would have to wait in the office on a Friday while the secretary went into the bar to empty out the one-armed bandit and I would get paid my fiver in coins from the machine, which felt like it weighed a tonne at the time.

County were already, unofficially, paying me £5 a week for 'expenses', although I was still only with them as a school boy. They got their money back though, as they eventually sold me for £50,000 to Luton, but they were paying me this based on the proviso agreement they had with my dad that I would sign for them when I left school and turned sixteen.

I made my full debut at sixteen, the manager at County then was Jimmy Scoular. I was due to make my debut away at Darlington so I was asked to report to the club on the Friday. Now, younger people reading this probably won't remember but back then if you bought Persil washing powder you got free rail tickets. It was all planned well in advance with all the players being instructed to have their wives to buy Persil in their weekly shop so that the club could collect the rail vouchers. My first problem that day was that I had to get the Friday afternoon off of school. My Headmaster said no to my request saying, "No, you're not going to be a footballer, stop the silly pipedream, you have to attend school, I'm not giving you a Friday off for you to travel to Darlington." I was still at school and about to make my debut in the football league, so I wasn't going to give up. I went home and told my dad that I couldn't play after all on Saturday for County. He asked why not and I replied, "The headmaster won't let me have the Friday afternoon off to catch the train with the rest of the team," to which Dad said flatly, "Leave it with me!"

The next day, my dad went to my school to see my headmaster. I sat quietly listening in outside the school office within ten minutes Dad emerged with the headmaster. "Mark, of course you can have the afternoon off school, you'll do the school proud playing for County in the football league," he said. I'm guessing that with my dad, being an old steelworker, went in and threatened him somewhat. Whatever it was, it worked!

During the 1979/80 season

Back to the train, on the said Friday afternoon we were on the platform at Newport Station. There was sixteen of us and the club only had enough Persil coupons for fifteen tickets. Jimmy Scoular, who was a canny Scotsman, said, "Son, you walk up and down the carriages in the train until we get to Crewe!" I had to do this in order to avoid the ticket inspector. That was me, up and down the train for something like four hours. But I did make my football league debut that weekend and I was determined to stay in the team, which is what I did. I played the next thirty-six games for Newport before Pleaty came in for me in March 1978, I was still only eighteen but being transferred to Luton Town for £50,000

I had been playing a mix of left back and further up in midfield for Newport. There had been rumours in the local papers that clubs were interested in me. I think we played away up at Scunthorpe United when I was told that Luton Town were up watching me play. To be blunt, I thought I'd played shit in that game but to be fair to David Pleat he'd watched me, or had me watched on a number of occasions, and I think it was only within a matter a weeks after that I was signing for him at Kenilworth Road.

The best thing that ever happened to me in football was immediately after I signed with David, before the ink was dry on my contract, I forget exactly how much it was that I would be earning in that first contract but it was good money. David Pleat told me to pop into the next room, ushering me in. There he said, "You're on very good money now, son, you'll need to learn how to manage it. Also in that room was a financial advisor, which was a sign of just how forward thinking that David Pleat was in taking the club's duty of care to the next level. That man I met is still my financial advisor to this day! It was one of the pastoral care things that Pleaty did with his players. He knew I needed help on this front, he knew my background, he knew that I was a council house boy from Newport and now I had more money than I knew what to do with.

David was a magnificent training ground manager. He took every training session himself. With that Luton Town side he was one of the first football managers to put a left-footed winger on the right wing and a left-footed winger on the right. They all do it now but Pleaty was innovative.

Sometime before all this happened, I lost my father. He died aged forty-seven, just before I signed apprenticeship forms for the Newport club. He had a stroke thanks to the alcohol and his lifestyle. I believe that if Luton hadn't come in for me, after thirty plus games, it's quite possible I would have stayed in Newport. You see, after my father died, I earned the money in the family and I lived at home with my mother and my sisters. So much depended on me. My brother had never lived with us. He had always lived with my grandmother and grandfather.

But Luton came looking for me and, looking back, that made a man of me. Imagine the scene: You live away from home, far from your family and everything unfamiliar. Under such circumstances that's when football becomes crucial and becomes your life. The reason you've left home in the first place is football. If you are in the first team everything is fine, but if you are not in the first team and you live away from home, it is hell on earth. Still, I have always advised young players to leave home early in order to focus completely on football.

Anyway, there I was in Luton, a professional footballer and living in club accommodation. "I've put you in lodgings with a lovely boy. You will get on very well together," said David Pleat to me. I was placed with Mrs. Gough on Poynters Road in Luton. She was lovely, she came to my wedding to Margaret, bless her. At Mrs. Gough's I was to share with two young lads, one was Tim Smith. He was a nice lad from Gloucester who the club had big hopes for, but he only made two first team appearance before returning back home soon after I joined in 1978. The second was a young lad who'd already broken into the first team and he would become a really good friend for life too, who also came to my wedding; Ricky Hill. Ricky was a very special person and supremely talented player and went on to play for England. I would also soon become good friends with Brian Stein too, but coming from my background in Newport, it was initially a bit of a shock to me and I didn't know what to do. I didn't know how to react to this black person who was about to share accommodation with me. In Newport at that time there were no more than about two or three black pupils in the whole school where I was, Hartridge High. Anyway, Ricky became a very good friend and he, along with Brian Stein, enjoyed going everywhere together.

I was already engaged at the time to a girl from Newport so I was going back home after most of the games. Ricky would go back to North London for a quick visit then we'd head back on a Sunday night or early on the Monday morning. I eventually felt that I had to get married and move Margaret up to Luton with me because I was gambling, drinking and basically going out every night. So, I thought to myself, if I don't get married and settle down I'll never make it as a professional footballer. I went home one weekend and I said to Margaret, "Look, love, I think that we ought to get married!" I bought a house near Leagrave Train Station in Luton with the best intentions in the world of doing it up before we got married and moved in, but after we were actually married she moved in with me and the grass was up over the windows as I hadn't been anywhere near the place. On a side note, we moved in and had great neighbours and I'm still friends with the people that lived next door to us, and, I'll be attending his eightieth birthday party in September up at Bedford Golf Club, up past Warden Hills in Luton. All I remember about those hills was running up and down them in pre-season training with Pleaty. David used to have a bungalow up that way so it was certainly handy for him having those rolling hills nearby for us to get all of that leg work in during the summers.

We moved to Brooklands Close, on the outskirts to the north of Luton, just off Toddington Road. It was a nice place to live. Alan West, he was a lovely guy, would sometimes pick me up and we'd head into training and games together. He was a bit of a rebel by all accounts but then settled down, and he was a really good quality player. Luton were lucky to have got his best playing years as he was at the club under Harry Haslam a long time before I joined.

David Pleat had signed eight new players and we got off to a great start. We won the first game but the season was generally disappointing. We had no choice but to win the last home game, against Fulham I believe, in order to stay up. But during that first year something else happened to me. I began to follow the habits of Ricky Hill and Brian Stein, which were different to what I was familiar with in Casnewydd.

We would spend quite a bit of time betting in the bookie shop. Les Harriott, who was a young professional at the club, would come with us and be a bit of a bookie's runner for us, getting the sandwiches for us. He was a nice kid who never quite made it in professional football.

For twelve months this was the pattern: train, shower, walk to the bottom of Kenilworth Road and then up to the bookies. We would bet on every race, every single one. Then, after leaving there, go back to the accommodation to have tea. From there, we went on to Bletchley to bet on the dogs and from there, if we had any money left, on to the Grosvenor Casino in Luton to keep on betting. Then it was home, sleep, get up, train. At the time I was earning between £300 and £400 a week. That was our life. That's what we did. You would fail to do that now because most players today are better. With us, though, once the training was over at lunchtime, the club's responsibility for the players was also over.

That was the beginning of what was possibly developing into a kind of addictive, dependent personality on my part - gambling, and later on, drinking. I don't know. Who knows when it started? But until I was transferred to Luton Town at the age of eighteen, I had never had a single drop of alcohol. My father and brother were both heavy drinkers, but I had never drunk a drop. But quite a bit, as well as gambling, alcohol was part of life. You would go and hang out with the guys and you would have a drink. After all, I was a young lad living away from home, I had money in my pocket and I had good friends.

The training structure at Luton was excellent. Initially, when I signed, David Pleat had Ken Gutteridge with him as his assistant manager and soon after, David Coates and John Moore were brought in to bolster the coaching staff. Ken moved on from the club within a year or so and then Trevor Hartley came on board. David Coates said something to me that's always stuck as I'm a fully licensed coach and I still say this to my young players coming through: "I will know you're a player when the team is playing rubbish and you're still the best player on the pitch!" That really stayed with me and that's how I look at young players now, as there's a lot of young players who only play well when the team plays well. If the team doesn't play well, their standards drop. Bringing David Coates in to join his coaching staff was a masterstroke on David Pleat's part, as David Coates was ten years older than the rest of the staff and Pleaty himself as well, so he acted as the perfect foil with his extra experience in and around the club which allowed Pleaty to really focus on what he loved: coaching. Not that David Pleat didn't get involved elsewhere, because he was 24-7, seven days a week. He was involved in every aspect of the club threw himself into it even as a still relatively young manager.

I remember a couple of times he would tell me off for coming in to train on my days off. I felt like saying to him, "Well, you're always here!" He would say to me that your body needs time to rest after playing and training, understanding that recovery time was so important whereas other managers would be happy for you to run all day, every day. It's a cliché but he really was ahead of his time with his players' care as well as his training methods, and he was a fantastic training ground and drills coach/manager. Things happened in games during those years under David that looked like they were off the cuff but all the very best moves that look that way are all well drilled and rehearsed passages of play. Plenty of clever set plays and moves to catch out our opponents and we had loads of them. David Moss would cut in from the left wing on his right foot and play into Brian Stein's feet with Lil Fuccillo joining up to support. We worked on that for hours in training, which made it look natural in a match situation.

You can train and work hard all you like but you have to have good players, the right players, and we had a damn good team. We had Brian Stein and Ricky Hill, who both went on to play for England; we had Pricey (Paul Price) at centre half, Welsh international who went on to play for Tottenham; Milija Aleksic who also went to Tottenham; both lads played in FA Cup Finals for Spurs. We had Kirk (Basher) Stephens who was an excellent player at right back, hard as nails but a really good footballer, too. Mal Donaghy was superb throughout his ten years at Kenilworth Road, Luton did well to hold on to him for as long as they did before he eventually moved Manchester United and then onto Chelsea as well. Mal had come over around the same time that I joined in 1978, from Northern Ireland with another young Irish lad called Terry Hayes, a good little midfielder, who I trained and played with in some of the reserve games. Terry was a small but strong lad with a moustache, but never made a first team appearance before heading back to Belfast a year later in 1979. Phil Boersma, the former Liverpool and Middlesbrough player, was still at the club for a short while when I joined but I got to play with him. Phil was as fit as a butcher's dog, he really looked after himself, really into his diet and nutrition watching everything that he put into his body. Young Godfrey Ingram was very much in and around the group then. I even remember David Pleat pulling off an incredible loan move for him when he linked up the New York Cosmos in the American NASL (North American Soccer League) with all its glitz and glamour in the late 1970s and into the early 1980s. It was an amazing move for him as he was still just a kid, a local lad from Luton over in New York, playing and partying with some real high flyers from the world of football, music and showbusiness over there. When I think of Lil Fuccillo, I close my eyes and I can still hear the noise of his leg snapping when he got that horrific leg break away at Brighton in December 1978, as it just echoed all around the Goldstone Ground. That cost him two years of his career and sadly he was never the same player after that – don't get me wrong, he was still a classy, skilful player with great passing vision, but never quite the same and he struggled to hold a regular place in the team, whereas before, he must have been one of the first names on David Pleat's team sheet.

Of course, there was Big Sax (Mike Saxby) as well. Pleaty got him from Mansfield Town in 1979 and for two years he was brilliant at the back for us as well as being a handful at set pieces up the other end of the pitch. Big Sax…he was my mate, he was! He loved a drink and we were drinking partners away from the club. He was a good lad, what you would call a man's man. I remember going to Sax's wedding to Glenis, along with Paddy Grealish and Ricky Hill. He was from a little mining village in Mansfield. It must have been 1980 or 1981 time, a memorable day. I showed a photo that had been taken outside of Sax's mum and dad's house on the morning of the wedding just last week to my wife and she was pissing herself at our clothes; not Ricky, though, of course, he always was and is a timeless style icon. Not forgetting Brian Horton either, he was fantastic for us when he joined in 1981. But the five of us (me, Steiny, Ricky, Les Harriott and Sax) became really good mates and they all came down to my wedding. Basher would come and play snooker with us as well. Most of the lads in and around the team did to be fair to them, they were a great sociable group of lads which you don't always get at football clubs, but we certainly did during that time at Luton.

Pre-season training was always tough, as it should be. It's different these days but back then, you would spend the first two weeks of training without ever seeing a football. I didn't mind the first couple of weeks of

Mark surges through, during a 2-2 draw away at Shrewsbury Town in December 1981

hard graft but I was always happy to see those footballs finally come out on the training ground.

I was quite fortunate in that I was naturally fit. In fact, the club doctor (Doctor Burrows) who examined me for my medical before my move from Newport to Luton, commented that I had the best muscle formation in legs that he'd ever seen; I believe that this guy was not only advising Luton Town but he was also the medical advisor to the English Football Association as well, so that was quite something coming from him.
My fitness was something that I would always have to keep on top of throughout my career. As I was six-foot-one/six-foot-two and by my own admission quite slow. I had to keep myself around a stone under what my natural weight should have been in order to be able to run forever, so to speak. I wasn't very fast but I had stamina and I always said that I'm as slow in the 90th minute as I am in the 1st. So, my strength was being able to wear my opponent down.

The fact that I had been training with semi-professional players, who were proper men by the way, two nights a week on a Tuesday and a Thursday at Newport County since I was a kid at school, really helped prepare me for the physical requirement of the game. Whereas these days, I see some lads at eighteen years of age and I look at them and say that they haven't got their 'football legs' yet.

I played most of the games in my first season. The second season I was in and out but for a nineteen-year-old, I'd played a lot of games in the football league.

I got a few injuries in my time at Luton Town but the most bizarre one was when I walked straight through the plate glass window down at QPR after a match there. In fact, I think it was the very first competitive game played in the football league in England on their newly laid astroturf pitch at the start of the 1981/82 season. I scored Luton's first ever goal on astroturf that night when I equalised after Andy King (former Luton Town favourite, RIP) had put QPR ahead and then my mate Ricky Hill scored the winner. It was dark on the outside stairs but it was lit behind the glass, rendering it invisible, well it was to me, anyway. I was too busy talking to someone and when I turned around all I saw was the stairs which were reflected in the glass. I just thought it was a doorway and so I just continued on and straight through the glass. I was later told that if, when I made impact with the glass, I had stopped, I would have gotten seriously injured as all the glass would have come down on my head, neck and shoulders, but as I'd just carried on walking straight through it was like a scene from a Tom & Jerry cartoon. I then made my way to the bar for a post-match pint with our lads and some of the opposition boys too, just to be sociable. I thought I was fine but then someone pointed out that I'd got some blood coming out of my eye, that I'd cut it. It turned out to be nothing too serious, just a couple of stitches in my eye and that was it. It couldn't have affected me that much as I scored again four days later and this time it was the winner away at Bolton. That shot went in low past their keeper late in the game to give us a third straight win at the start of the season.

One person on the backroom staff that I've not mentioned was our excellent physio, John Sheridan. He was fantastic. He certainly wasn't one of those old school 'trainers' as they were called back in the day, when it was a guy running on with the insides of an old football filled with water and a sponge to treat every injury under the sun. John was a new breed of physio, always looking and striving for knowledge so that he could bestow his best treatment on us players. And you have to remember what John had to overcome, he was a really strong character as he used to take an awful lot of stick, absolute dog's abuse came his way from the opposition fans when he'd come onto the pitch because he had a limp from a bus accident that he'd had earlier on in his life. David Pleat knew he had a good one in

John on the staff and he showed that when he took him to Tottenham with him after David took the job at White Hart Lane in 1986.

I was still only eighteen when that summer Pleaty announced we were going to Florida on a team building break together. I'd never been away and was now suddenly flying to Miami, Florida, with Luton Town. This trip was something like ten days which was something else back then. Looking back on it, with hindsight, it was probably a master stroke by David Pleat. I don't know how he got the club to pay for it but they did and with a lot of new players coming in at the end of season, this trip really helped to define the group. It was pure genius on David's part. It really gave us momentum as a group and I really think that we started the season (1978-79) on such a high because that trip away together really bonded the group.

But that was David Pleat, he knew what would work for us, both as individuals and as a team. Mind you, Pleaty knew everything, he was a walking encyclopaedia and not just about football either. He would casually walk past me and Ricky Hill on the bus on our way to a game, when we'd be looking at the racing page. Suddenly, and un-invited, he would interject and say, "Yeah, he's good over six furlongs, blah blah blah, don't like that jockey, blah blah blah…" then he would walk off without waiting or looking for a reply from us. He'd leave us thinking what the fuck? Going back to his knowledge on players, he knew every player, everywhere, as he still does to this day. My upbringing in Newport had been quite a happy one. I don't think I could say I was ever close to my mother or father, but the same is true of my brother and sisters, too. They didn't come close to them either. I never saw loving, obvious, open signs from anyone in the family as such. To a large extent people left you alone and you were expected to go it alone, but that was the norm back then. It was often me who had to take care of myself.

I'm not saying that's a bad thing because I benefited from that later and became independent. But when I was a child, if I wanted clean clothes, I had to wash them and iron them. I rarely saw my father and even when I did see him he was often drunk. And my mother was always working. I can't remember ever getting a hug or a kiss from either of them, but I don't believe that was something that belonged to them in particular. He belonged to that generation in general. I didn't feel any different to anyone else and it didn't do me any great harm. I had football and on the council housing estate where we lived there were wide, green spaces where I could play with my friends.

What was interesting and entertaining from my point of view, of course, was that I was a right-footed player until I was six or seven years old. Even as a small child I would always kick a ball all over the place. One day I was playing football in the council house where we lived, and as I went for the ball I accidentally kicked the back of the chair. Well, I didn't manage to get to the ball and instead I broke my leg - the 'tib and the fib'. As a result of that I spent the next eight months with my right leg in a full plaster cast. But the minute they removed that and put a smaller plaster on my leg so I could walk again I started kicking a ball once more, but this time using my left foot! Throughout my career, being a left-footed player was a big advantage for me but it was all by chance. Pure luck. Perhaps fate.

Because if you consider that I'm also slow, it's quite possible that I wouldn't have had the opportunities I had if I'd been a right-footed player on top of that. When the plaster was removed, when I was seven years old, I had come to use my left foot naturally. And left-footed players can be selected for games to ensure balance in a team. That was then an advantage throughout my career on the field. I certainly feel that I got a place in the people's team over the years, not necessarily that I was that much better than the others players but because I was left footed; I got the nod to give balance to the team.

All of the hard work came together in that fabulous 1981/82 season. In the summer, David Pleat had moved on Paddy Grealish, Paul Price and Alan West but brought in Brian Horton and installed him as club captain. We were going great guns that season, even overcoming the massive loss of Big Sax at the end of October, and we went from strength to strength. It was a great season for me personally too, until I picked up an injury and was substituted in the first half of a game at home to Wrexham in the middle of March. I managed to play in the following game away at Barnsley but then I had to come out of the side for treatment. David Pleat took no chances with letting it derail the run in for promotion and quickly moved to bring in Richard Money on loan from Liverpool. Richard did really well in the side and I never really got back fit enough to force a claim back into the starting line up. But, I had amassed easily enough appearances to be awarded a Championship winning medal come the end of the season. However, not playing in those final fourteen games towards the end of the season culminated in me deciding to move as I was just getting in to the Welsh national squad and so I needed to be playing

Mark in the kit that he never got to play a first team game in as Luton moved up to the first division in 1982, Mark left for Charlton in the October without kicking a competitive ball in the league

first team football. Rather naively, when I look back on it, especially as Richard was only on loan initially before Luton signed him on a permanent deal from Liverpool, I said to David Pleat, "Look, I want to go as I need to play. I'm used to first team football, I'll not be happy to be a squad player." And so, a deal was arranged for me to go to Charlton Athletic. I didn't really want to leave Luton as I had set up a home there, but to be fair, the move to Charlton turned out to be an excellent one for me personally and I had five very enjoyable years there helping them to regain their top flight status. I finally got to play in the English First Division as I never got the chance to do so with Luton Town, which was a shame really. But at Charlton I discovered a real love of the theatre and dining out in the Westend of London. I just adore Covent Garden in London. Later on, when I lived in Chepstow, I could be in Cardiff in an hour or could turn the car the other way and be in Covent Garden in under two hours. I don't drink anymore, I haven't had a drink since 2005, but I do love the theatre and a nice meal.

I was prepared to leave to get a first team place and so I signed for Charlton Athletic on November 4th, 1982. My first child, Nikki, was born a day later in the Luton & Dunstable Hospital on November 5th, 1982. I had to leave my wife Margaret while she was in labour to catch the coach at junction 11 of the M1 with Charlton to make my debut away at Leeds United on November 6th, 1982, which we won 2-1. It was certainly quite an eventful few days. In those days you didn't get time off as the father if your wife was having a baby. How times change and indeed how time flies as my daughter, Nikki, will be 40 this year!

I joined Charlton when I was twenty-two, but I didn't move to live in Charlton straight away, I stayed in Luton. This was in the days before the arrival of the M25 and it was a bit of an old journey every day down to

Woolwich, I have to admit, but I was confident I could finish it. I would leave about half-past six every morning and I would pull into the Charlton car park with five minutes to spare; training started at 10 o'clock. As we had a newborn daughter, Nikki, and I went back and forth every day. Staying down during the week wasn't an option as it would have meant leaving Margaret and young Nikki on their own. But I was turning up to training at Charlton already feeling knackered from the journey from Luton. I did have Steve 'Chalky' White to share the driving with as he was doing the same journey, as he'd signed for Charlton from Luton as part of the deal that took Paul Walsh to Luton a few months earlier than I did. I have to say that during my first year with Charlton it became quite a struggle in terms of my fitness and physical condition.

Lennie Lawrence soon took over from Ken Craggs at Charlton and it was Lennie that first pointed out to me that I couldn't keep making this journey every day, that I wasn't doing myself any favours, so we moved to Eltham, just down by Chislehurst, which was just five minutes away from the training ground. I went from one extreme to the other.

I probably had some of the happiest times of my career and life when I was playing for Charlton and lived in London. Part of that was because I love the theatre. When you are living in Luton there are not a lot of theatres but when I moved to Charlton and lived in Bromley, it was twenty-five minutes from the West End.

I love the musicals, especially Miss Saigon. I've seen almost every show in the West End having spent a lot of time there. I love the atmosphere of Covent Garden, too. That's my ideal night out. My wife will ask me what I'd like to do and I tend to say, "Let's go to Covent Garden and have a meal."

It was a pleasure for me to play with and against all those players and if you ask if I would do it all again, I'd say yes in a heartbeat. Nobody can ever take that away from you. I've given all my caps and shirts to my kids and they have them set up in their houses, which gives me enormous pride.

The experience of playing professional football has stayed with me for the rest of my life and I always say to young players now, that it's great to play for your hometown club which I did at Newport County. If I played badly or if I played well my life didn't change, because I would still go home to my mum. However, when you move away from all those home comforts to play football, if you don't play well and you're not in the first team then you're whole life is crap! So, it's the making of you if you stand up to that challenge. My advice to young players is to move away from your hometown club if you get the chance so that way football becomes your life. Luton was the start of my journey to football becoming my life and even now, at sixty-two, driving to training on a Tuesday night with Carmarthen Town. I still renew my Coaching Pro-Licence every three years and so away from everything else in my life, football always was, and still is, my outlet whether it was as a player or a coach. Luton Town was fantastic for me and the club will always be very close to my heart. I still feel very connected to the town and always have done.

(BORN 18 MARCH 1952 IN WITNEY, OXFORDSHIRE)

# DAVID JOHN MOSS

LUTON TOWN FC 1978 - 1985

*In his last season at Swindon Town, 1977/78, David Moss felt he'd become a little stale and needed a new challenge. Feeling a little taken for granted to a certain degree at Swindon, he was hearing whispers from different newspaper reporters around the grounds that a scout was watching him and was glowing about his performance. The three clubs that kept getting mentioned were Stoke City, QPR, and Luton Town.*

I actually ran into Alan Durban later on in my career, who by then was manager at Sunderland, though he was at Stoke City when they were rumoured to be lining up a move for me while I was still at Swindon. I ran into him whilst on holiday, well, it was an end of season tour with Luton. He recognised me and introduced himself. We had a chat about football in general and had a nice but brief talk, just a chance meeting so nothing like an illegal approach or anything like that, but from that meeting I knew he would have been a good manager to play for had my career path taken me to Stoke City in 1978 instead of Kenilworth Road.

It was Luton Town who followed up on their interest. I met with Ken Gutteridge who was David Pleat's assistant manager in the early days after taking over from Harry Haslam. It was all above board and I actually met with Ken in the offices at Swindon Town. I didn't actually meet David Pleat until I went to Luton to sign for them. When I did meet David Pleat for the first time I remember thinking that this guy's not much older than me. The contract was signed, no agents back then, wasn't a negotiation; this was the contract offer before me. A four-year contract, the basic pay at Luton Town was never high, but with appearance and win bonuses for

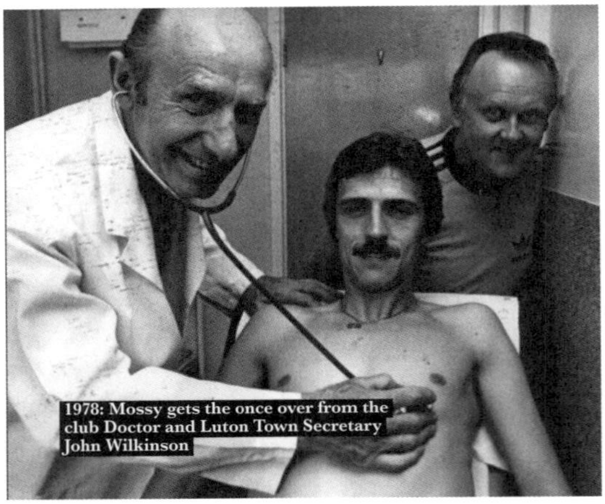
1978: Mossy gets the once over from the club Doctor and Luton Town Secretary John Wilkinson

a club the size of Luton and at the time still in the Second Division, you could earn really good money. I was never on a goal bonus, nor am I a fan of such a bonus as, in my opinion, it can make players selfish on the pitch and shoot from an angle to try to score rather than pass to a team mate who would have a much better opportunity to score, just to try and get the goal bonus for themselves.

I struck up an immediate friendship with Kirk Stephens when we both arrived at the club at the same time – we were put into digs near to the ground and then I eventually went up to digs in Stopsley with a lovely family, a lady called Sissy. John Aston and Don Givens had previously been under her care when they joined the club. Later on, I became very good pals with Richard Money when he joined us on loan from Liverpool in 1982.

I was twenty-six at the time I signed for Luton. I was one of a number of new faces coming into the club along with Basher, Mal and Bob Hatton amongst others. On our first league game versus Oldham, we were paraded out onto the pitch and we stopped and waved to the crowd, introducing ourselves to the Kenilworth Road fans. However, by half time we were back in the changing room 0-1 down. Pleaty was never really a shouter or one to rant and rave, he just calmly went around the changing room reminding individuals of why he'd bought them to the club during the summer and what their specific roles and expectations were. It worked and we won the match 6-1. I was thrilled personally to score two of those six goals as I felt that it helped to justify my large fee at the time of £110,000. I had still been in contract at Swindon Town when Luton came in for me. It was a lot of money for Luton to pay and it was a lot of money for Swindon to receive, so my scoring those two goals in the second half of my debut felt like a weight being lifted somewhat. We did it again a couple of weeks later, putting seven past Cardiff City at Kenilworth Road. It was a bit of a rollercoaster and one that was ultimately frustrating for me as I missed a lot of it through a pelvic strain that I picked up. However, I still ended up with thirteen goals in twenty-nine league games. Pleaty had bought me as a goal scoring winger and I was thrilled to be keeping my end of the deal.

Pleaty had moved on a lot of senior players since becoming manager halfway through the season before I arrived. He knew the club from top to bottom as he'd come into it initially to look after the youth team, then the reserves and then as a coach to the first team, so he had a clear mind who he wanted to keep and which players would not suit the way he wanted to mould his team going forward. He was very single-minded on that front and even players he brought in himself were moved on very quickly if they didn't work out, players like young Steve Sherlock from Man City, the goalkeeper David Lawson from Everton, who Pleaty actually advised to pull out of a local house purchase that he'd lined up after just five first team games. David Lawson quickly found himself out of favour with the subsequent purchase of Jake Findlay. Other players that spring to mind through David Pleat's revolving door were Steve Taylor, Andy Harrow and in my final season at the club, Steve Elliott and Vince Hilaire. All these lads, for one reason or another, just didn't make the grade at that level at Kenilworth Road and Pleaty was very quick to cut his losses in these cases.

After the last game of the 1980/81 season where we'd won 3-0 away at Bolton but still failed to win promotion as results elsewhere went against us, I was off to spend the summer of 1981 playing in the NASL (North American Soccer League) for Tampa Bay Rowdies. It was a great experience and one that I had hoped to repeat but unfortunately, I never did. I spent three months there and took the chance to take the whole family over with me. It was a great life experience for us all. The pitches were a mix, with some weeks on grass and the others on artificial surfaces. The money was really good, I earnt as much in the twelve weeks there that I would in a whole year normally. I got to play with some real characters in that Tampa side including Kevin Keelan, the goalkeeper from Norwich City, John Gorman, Frank Worthington, and two lads from Millwall, Tony Kinsella and Dave Mehmet. The rest of the side was a mix of North and South Americans and South African players.

A number of British-based players had been coming over to the NASL since the mid-1970s, including a fair few from Luton: Paul Price, Alan West, Steve Litt, and the Futcher Brothers. Normally it was arranged on a loan basis, but this had just come to an end and I understand that

Tampa had to buy me for a pound and then Luton had to buy me back for a pound to get around new legislation. Pleaty would ring me up every couple of weeks while I was in America to see how I was doing and to ask what progress I was making. He was always asking questions about what the standard was like, were there any players that could do it in England and he'd ask about training methods too, as he was always thinking of new ways to improve his team with any little advantage going into a new season. The difference was, because I was based in Florida our training sessions were one hour long due to the heat; it was murder. After an hour that was it, you were dripping in sweat and you were drained. The big thing there was taking liquids on board, which we really hadn't got that much into. John Sheridan had gotten into it a little bit when he came to Luton but we'd never been taught about re-fuelling and getting your liquids back into your body. But there, over in the States, and because of the heat in Florida, it was a massive part of the training programme. There were always big tubs packed with ice and sports drinks, and I thought well, this is different, because I was told when I was young that you couldn't drink water during pre-season as it would give you a stitch. I was also not to drink anything other than a cup of tea, which we now know only helps to dehydrate you. It was certainly different times back in the 1970s and into the early 1980s.

Always looking to improve and get players, Pleaty rang me one day and he said, "I've signed a new captain, David: Brian Horton from Brighton." Now, this was a bit of a shock as I'd had a few run-ins with Brian, who was Brighton's captain when I played for Swindon. Brighton, even though in the Third Division, paid big wages and whenever we played against them, Brian (Nobby) used to try and kick me all over the field, winding me up with verbal comments and asking how much I earned. It was all an attempt to get under my skin and I would respond with, "Well, you got me there, mate." I told Pleaty this but he reassured me I'd be okay.

I was late coming back for the start of the 1981/82 season because of playing in the NASL, which saw me miss the first four league games of the season. It felt like I had literally stepped off the plane and onto the pitch at Filbert Street for the away game at Leicester City. I think Steve White got both of our goals in a 2-1 win. I'd met Nobby for the first time on the Thursday before the game and he was absolutely fine with me! We shook hands and had a little chat, and obviously the rest is history, and we became really good mates. He calls me most weeks for a catch up and all that so we're still mates forty years on. Nobby's attitude on the pitch for

Brighton was the same as it was for Luton, he was still on my case but as a team mate not as an opponent. He was demanding, not just of me but of everybody, Ricky, Steiny, Walshy, you name them, he was on their case, but that's the type of bloke he was. We didn't start as friends, there was a lot a previous rivalry when Brighton and Crystal Palace were the big fish paying the big wages and bonuses back in my Third Division days with Swindon Town.

If you're an attacking player or a creative player, you're going to make mistakes and that's where Pleaty was good. He said to me, "The reason I've signed you is I want you to take people on, I want you to cross balls, to try and create, and score goals." That suited me down to the ground because when I was growing up as a young player, I was always criticised for what I couldn't do, i.e., you can't defend, you can't tackle, etc., and then I went to Luton Town and Pleaty told me he was interested in what I could do and wasn't worried about what I couldn't. He was like that, wanting us to play to our strengths, always wanting to get the best out of people. He was good at fitting players in positions and signing them for those reasons. He signed Nobby to be centre midfield player, defensive minded, but Nobby was a better passer of the ball than people gave him credit for. He got people in positions to do the roles that he knew we needed. He was a better passer than Paddy Grealish, Paddy would break things up and he was an honest player and great to have in your team; a brilliant lad.

I never got to keep any kit or shirts from my time at Luton as our kitman, George Rogers would gather it all in at the end of every season and he'd say don't swap your shirts with anyone at the end of the season as it all needs to go to the reserves and youth teams. We were even using the old Admiral gear from the late 1970s as our first team training kit. I do have a couple of boxes sealed up in the loft in which I'm sure there must be some old photos, contracts, etc., from my time at the club.

I never got any international recognition be it youth, Under 23s, B Squad or invitational sides. I think if I'd left Swindon when I was younger than twenty-six and been at other clubs, I might have had a better chance but back then in the early to mid-1970s there were a lot of really good players around. I wasn't from Swindon, I was from Oxfordshire, but I was looked upon as the local lad brought up by Swindon Town from the age of seventeen through the ranks. I struggled to get into the first team but I eventually got my break in the team when Dave Mackay was the manager there. What a great manager and what a great man he was but I got

Mossy gets up close and personal at Kenilworth Road during his first season at the club in 1978/79

nowhere with the previous manager. I was playing in the reserves and just making up the numbers but as soon as Dave Mackay took over he put me into pre-season training with the Swindon first team. He put me on the bench and I'd not even been anywhere near it. Getting to that stage was fantastic and I felt so lucky. It kicked on from there as I went on as a sub and scored a goal and then another. He gave me my debut, which in fact was against Watford, and I made a goal for Peter Noble that all kick started my career. It was all because of Dave Mackay. I call it luck but he took a liking to what he saw in training and thought I had something to offer, so he gave me the opportunity. He didn't change my position as I'd always played out wide but I had a bit of an advantage because I could use both feet, so I was able to play on either wing.

But at the age of twenty-six when I'd been at Swindon for nine years, I felt like I was taken for granted a little, seen as part of the furniture. Over the years players would come and be on twice as much money as I was earning and I have to admit that it did get really frustrating. I would read the football gossip page in the Sunday papers with rumours of certain clubs watching you and all that so I do reckon if I'd moved at twenty-one or twenty-two then maybe I would have gotten some England recognition. But, then again, you have to remember there were some bloody good players around at the time in the late 1970s and early 1980s, some really good wingers, and you had to be a really good player to get into the England squad.

A good friend of mine, Terry Curran, never played for England but he was a bloody good player, absolutely fantastic on his day, almost unplayable. But England always seemed to go for the safe bet preferring the consistent type of wide midfield players rather than unpredictable wingers. Another good winger was young Dave Thomas at QPR who I think started at Burnley. He had a good spell at Goodison Park with

David in action on the wing at home during the 1978/79 season

Everton but he never wore studs, even on those heavy pitches of the day; he always wore moulded studs and in rubber boots you had to be some player with great balance back then, which he was. Tony Morley at Villa was another really good player, Steve Coppell also, who was a work horse up and down that wing. There were a lot of bloody good wide players back in that time ahead of me for England honours.

After a game at Preston in 1979 the legendary Tom Finney said to David Pleat, "I really like your winger." Coming from him that was worth an England cap to me after I'd been out for six weeks earlier that season and not kicked a ball during that time. I think I came on as a sub when we were 0-2 down and I made one with a cross to Ricky Hill, who jumped with the defender and the Preston player ended up looping a header into his own net. I scored one to give us an important away point. But because of this pelvic issue I wasn't training and I came on and chipped the keeper from outside the box. Back then of course, it was still only two points for a win. We needed points at the end of Pleaty's first season to stay up and we beat Fulham at home after we salvaged this point at Preston. It was enough to stay up by two points despite losing away at Wrexham 0-2 in the final league match of the season, a game which I didn't play in, I hasten to add.

A few years later, I think it was away at Charlton and Bobby Robson, who was the England manager by then was watching. He said to Pleaty,

Ready for the first division in the summer of 1982

"David Moss always does well for Luton." That was a nice compliment to receive, however, I think he was really there to watch Ricky and Steiny. I know that Bobby Robson always asked David when he would get to sign Ricky Hill from him, when he was Ipswich Town manager to which Pleaty would say, "I'm not, Bobby, he's not for sale." But do you know, I wish somebody had been allowed to sign Ricky from Luton back then, no disrespect to Luton but he would have really blossomed at Ipswich under Bobby. In that Ipswich side at that time they were up there at the top and he would have been fantastic but to be fair to Ricky, he was happy where he was at Luton. He got his England caps but he should have got a lot more I reckon. He could have gone to Spurs or Arsenal without a shadow of a doubt; he would have shined in those teams. Clubs did come in for him but back then David Pleat had the final say on blocking any move for his players. Football was very different back then, it simply wouldn't happen these days as the players' agents dictate now, and if Ricky had had an agent in those days the agent would have spoken to David Pleat direct telling him Arsenal had been in touch, were willing to offer four times the salary Luton were paying, asking David if they'd be prepared to match that, to which David would have said of course not, Luton can't pay that kind of money. So we, as players, were in the wrong era for having agents dictating and engineering moves for players like they do today. It's fair to say that agents in the modern game are not my favourite subject of conversation. Had the agents been around at that time, would that fabulous team be kept in one piece for so long, to be nurtured and able to grow together? Would it have broken up before it even began? Mal Donaghy would have been gone, Steiny, Basher probably, and Jake Findlay possibly. As I say, it would have been broken up had that group of players emerged today in the modern era with offers of three or four times the money to go here or there and of course, as a player, and I would have been the same. It opens your eyes to your earning potential; it's same as any job that you're in. If you're earning £50,000 a year and someone comes in and offers you £150,000 a year, you'd be interested wouldn't you. It's not about being disloyal or anything, you'd just be thinking that as a family man I can't afford to turn this down. We're led to believe that players like Rooney etc., are on £250,000 a week, and I worked it out that even in my very best year at Luton Town, with all my appearances and win bonuses, which was the 1981/82 promotion year, including a promotion bonus as well, I'd have had to work for ten years to earn £250,000.

When we were in the first division in 1982/83, I would have thought that our basic wages would probably have been the lowest in the division that year. I don't know that for a fact but I'm just trying to think back to the teams that were in the First Division at that time. Even teams like Swansea City and Brighton were paying good money enticing all those old Liverpool players to the Vetch Field under John Toshack. When I look at the likes of Birmingham City, who were down struggling with us, they were a bigger club than us by miles and their wage bill would have been a lot higher than ours. I would say that we were the lowest payers in basic wages, but these clubs probably didn't have as good a time as we did. However, as I've said before, Pleaty was keen on players having contracts with built-in win, appearance and loyalty bonuses paid at the end of each year while you were contracted with the club, which could really push your overall salary up over the course of a season.

At Maine Road on that famous day in 1983, it became very clear that people had realised who we were sat in the stands. I was out as I had been injured two games previously in the disastrous 1-5 home defeat the Saturday beforehand. Everyone else around us won and we dropped from 16th to 21st in the league table and smack into the relegation zone. So I missed the Monday night game at Old Trafford and this one at Man City. I can't for the life of me remember which other players were sat with me but as soon as Raddy scored we all jumped up and went mad. It was clear that it was going to turn ugly so we headed down to the tunnel and into the changing rooms as soon as possible. The Maine Road crowd didn't do themselves any favours that day, both turning on our players physically on the pitch at the final whistle, plus on the coach leaving the ground. The police on board told us all to get down as we drove away as we were treated to a barrage of rocks, cans and god knows what else being propelled at the coach. But we'd done it, we'd stayed up. I often think about what would have happened to that team in the summer had we gone down. It would almost certainly have been decimated. Brian Stein, Ricky Hill, and Mal Donaghy would have been prize targets for many of the big clubs and Paul

Walsh would have certainly gone a year earlier than he did when he joined Liverpool in the summer of 1984.

We never really got any great FA Cup draws from when I first went to the club in 1978. We had York City away in my first season with Luton, but I didn't play as in January 1979 I was still having trouble with my pelvic injury. I remember Steve Sherlock played on the left of midfield and Gary Heale came into the side as well. We got turned over 2-0 there and then the year after we played my old lot, Swindon Town, and lost 2-0 at home to them, which was a real blow to lose to my old club. I scored two goals the year after that in the third round away at Orient, and Godfrey Ingram got the other one. I have a photo on the pitch with Godfrey that I think Gareth Owen must have taken, but then we lost away at Newcastle 2-1 and that's what you don't want: a team from your own division like that at the time. Then, in 1981/82 , we played Swindon Town again and we beat them 2-1. I scored a penalty and Nobby got the winner right near the end. We were very lucky that day as they were better than we'd given them credit for. They had a goal disallowed, and I think it was a very young Paul Rideout who had the goal chalked off. We were lucky, they could have beaten us as they played very well.

That set up the clash with Bobby Robson's Ipswich Town in the fourth round at Kenilworth Road. At the time they were top of the First Division and we were top of the Second. They were a great team, right up there at the time with Liverpool, Villa and Forest. We held them to 0-0 at half time but then Paul Mariner got a couple in the second half and we ended up out losing 3-0. That was a really good insight for us as to what we could come up against the next season if we were to get promoted and play against these types of sides most weeks. However, unfortunately for Ipswich Town, following Bobby Robson's departure that summer for the England job, that great side was eventually broken up with player after player being allowed to leave Portman Road. We never really got any good draws in the FA Cup in my first few seasons at the club. Obviously, the pinnacle in the FA Cup for us was the 1984/85 season, getting to the semi-final and coming up against a brilliant Everton side under Howard Kendall's guidance. They were really emerging as a power house in both England and in European competition, too. I was in my last season at the club and I knew I was finished at that level. Pleaty had been honest with me in the previous summer, when he bought Vince Hilaire to replace me from Crystal Palace with Trevor Aylott leaving Luton as part of the deal and heading to Selhurst Park. It didn't work out for Vince at Luton and he was quickly moved onto Portsmouth. I was a bit part player for that last couple of seasons and I was doing what I could to pass on my experience to the great young lads coming through at the club. I was the sub at Villa Park and I came on to replace Mick Harford. We'd played so well, especially in the first half, but we only had the one goal lead to show for it and we all know what happened in the final minutes to eventually lose 1-2. It was cruel, as that team really deserved a place in a showpiece final in the FA Cup where they would have played Manchester United at Wembley.

I never had any pre-match rituals, habits or superstitions. I did like to go out down the tunnel last though, and be the eleventh man out onto the pitch, but it didn't make or break my day if I hadn't. If a new team mate came in and said they preferred to go out last it didn't bother me; I wasn't superstitious about it to think, oh god I didn't go out last so now I'm bound to have a bad game or we'll lose. This sounds a bit weird, but I used to get the shirt and socks on and always put my shorts on last just before we went out the door. I've known players get themselves psyched up in the dressing room, shouting and bawling to get themselves going to over compensate for nerves. I remember in my early days at Swindon, I would see some of the older players being physically sick before a game, and I'd be sitting there all naïve thinking what the hell's going on. But it was because they'd been building themselves up and they were nervous. Les Sealey would always be really hyped up in the Luton dressing room, he was a great guy, but bordering on insane! I chipped him once in training when he'd not been long It the club, so that would've been mid-1983. He got the ball out of the net and he booted it about three fields away. Then he shouted at me, "Would you fucking well do that in a game?" I said, "Of course, Les," or at least I would try. He just didn't like being beaten full stop, even in training. He actually refused to go in goal for penalties if I wanted to practice taking them, so I had to do it with Alan Judge or one of the young goalkeeper kids.

Pleaty and the club in general were always keen to get the players out into the community whether that was putting on training sessions at local schools, handing out awards or even cutting ribbons at the Barratt Homes openings of showrooms. Car dealer days at Tricentrol and Trimoco were also events the players got invited to, which were quite often myself and Basher. To be fair, I think most of the lads did a lot of stuff like that, and as far as I can remember it wasn't in your contract that we had to attend

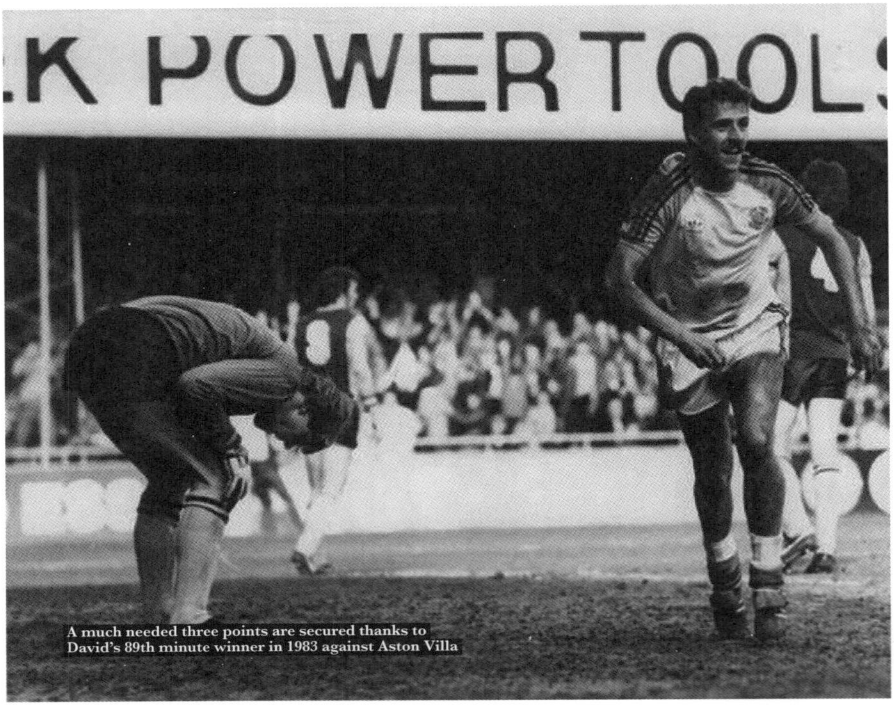

A much needed three points are secured thanks to David's 89th minute winner in 1983 against Aston Villa

a certain amount of these events per season. But it was 'encouraged' and expected of you and we didn't mind doing it most of the time. Pleaty or one of the other staff would just pull you to one side and show you a piece of paper detailing whatever event it was asking if we could attend on behalf of the club tonight or tomorrow. I remember doing a signing in the Arndale Centre in the middle of the town, I can't remember what the occasion was but we got swamped by kids wanting autographs which none of us minded. Mind you, there is a photo somewhere of that day and I don't look happy at all but that was probably about the one-hundredth autograph that I'd signed in a row. It's a cliché but we always felt it important to be happy that there were people willing to queue to meet you and get an autograph, you can only complain when nobody is interested in you anymore.

My final appearance was at Kenilworth Road, ironically, as it wasn't long after the FA Cup semi-final defeat at Villa Park; it was against Everton. In a 2-0 win for the Hatters, the biggest cheer and round of applause of the game was when I came on as a sub replacing Brian Stein. I knew I was nearing my end though, my body was telling me that. I went back to Swindon Town that summer of 1985 which was a mistake, as I was finished and my injuries cut short any emotional return. I tried a little bit of non-league at Trowbridge but packed in all together soon after that.

I linked up again with my mate Nobby when he joined me on the staff at Oxford United, along with Mark Lawrenson who was the club's manager. Mark left soon after over the Dean Saunders transfer debacle to Derby so Brian Horton was installed as manager and he promoted me from working with the youth players to his assistant. The partnership was then repeated at Manchester City between 1993 and 1995 although I felt that the 1983 relegation and my association with Luton Town never endeared the Manchester people to me. The pairing of Brian Horton and me then moved on to Huddersfield Town for two seasons. A short stint in management with Macclesfield Town and as assistant to Mark Wright at Chester followed. I only recently retired from a long association with Liverpool FC in my capacity as Chief Scout for the Merseyside clubs Academy.

I probably appreciate it more now than I did at the time because at the time it's your job and it can change from week to week. Your emotions can change from game to game and if I'm honest I probably didn't enjoy it as much as I should have done. Not just at Luton but overall in my whole career. I enjoy it more now when I think back than when I actually experienced it at the time. It was a bit of a rollercoaster at times, you're up, you're down, and you're feeling good about yourself, and then quickly your mood changes for the worse. You think the world is against you but then suddenly something happens and it all clicks back into place, so maybe now, looking back, I should have enjoyed it more at the time. But, overall, I think we were really lucky for a few years at Kenilworth Road to have what we had with those players. There were some lovable idiots in that dressing room, some really great lads and a fantastic team spirit.

(BORN 13 JULY 1954 IN BLAIRGOWRIE, SCOTLAND)

# JOHN "JAKE" WILLIAMSON FINDLAY

LUTON TOWN FC 1978 - 1985

*On a Tuesday morning in late 1978, twenty-four-year-old Jake Findlay was out training with his Aston Villa team mates when he got a shout across the training pitch. "Jake, the gaffer wants to see you in his office now." Jake went to see his manager, Ron Saunders, who told him that two clubs had come in for him and he could talk to them if he was interested. Upon asking which clubs, Saunders replied, "Charlton Athletic and Luton Town. Have a think about it but the guys from Luton Town are already here and would like to talk to you now if you're interested."*

I went into the next office where I was greeted by the Luton Town manager, David Pleat and his assistant manager at the time, Ken Gutteridge. I had asked for a move two years earlier away from Villa and still being quite a shy and naïve young man, I'd let myself be bullied by Ron Saunders into just keeping quiet and getting on with things. He was like that with a lot of the lads like me, and he had a big ego. I was still looking for a move and the meeting with David Pleat was exactly what I needed as at that time, first John Burridge and then Jimmy Rimmer had been performing amazingly in goal for Villa. Young Nigel Spink was coming through the youth team too, and it was clear he was going to push me further down the pecking order.

Looking back, I feel that perhaps I stayed at Villa four years too long. I should have gone the first season that Ron Saunders came in as we never got along. But that's with the benefit of hindsight, I suppose.

After one hour with David and Ken from Luton I felt very much at ease. David joked and winked at me and said theywere from a little fishing

Shortly before leaving Villa; Jake on the left of this shot with upcoming youth keeper Nigel Spink and John Burridge.

village down south, called Luton. I phoned my wife, Sandra, and told her what had happened, saying I felt I was going nowhere at Villa asked how she'd feel about a move to Luton. Sandra went quiet, then said, "Where's Luton?" "Near London," I said.

I signed with Luton that day and we went down on the Wednesday. We couldn't find the ground so we had to stop and ask where it was, along with the car park and offices. The guy pointed to the last house up on the right telling us they were the offices. We arrived and looked around the ground and Sandra looked at me then said, "Oh, what have we done?" To be fair, coming from Villa Park to Kenilworth Road was quite a change. But it was the beginning of a marvellous four or five years and when people ask me where I enjoyed my football most, I always say Luton Town. Part of my heart was with Villa as it was my first club but there was something really special at Luton. I feel a huge affinity with the club as do so many other players from not only my era but from different generations as well. There's just something about the club that stays with you. When I first went there we were getting crowds of 8,000 to 9,000 but by the early/mid-1980s, we were getting great crowds with sell outs of 20,000 to 21,000 packing into that tremendous little old ground.

The manager created the way it was there, all the lads got on and there were no egos at all whether you were in the firsts, reserves or youth. We all trained together and we all socialised together and this bond was taken out onto the pitch. There were so many different characters in the side, I was the clown off the pitch along with Mossy in the dressing room, but on it I was one of the most respected players as I was very vocal and demanded a lot of myself and my team mates. There was no ego fuelled arsehole players brought into the club. Pleat, when he bought players, didn't just look at their playing ability but he also looked at their characters, too. He was brilliant at getting the right type of players who would fit in. We were a very social group and games permitting, we would all meet up at The Wheatsheaf in Dunstable on a Tuesday/Wednesday night and it wouldn't be just some of the lads, it would be everyone out together. If someone did miss a player night out, boy, did they catch it in the neck the next day from the rest of the lads! Tony Grealish was a good pal of mine at the club but he wasn't there long. Later, he moved near me and Sandra in Birmingham when he moved to West Brom, which wasn't only great for me but also for Sandra as she was also great friends with Tony's wife. You see, that was another thing that bonded us all to the club in those days, the wives all got on well with each other and they'd be included in nights out. We'd all be together in the club, players and wives, then we'd end up in Mr Man's in town for a meal.

There was a health spa in town and the club let the wives use it as well. The day after we won promotion at Kenilworth Road on that wonderful Friday night in April 1982 with the victory against Shrewsbury, all the players and wives met up the following afternoon at this health spa to celebrate with a jacuzzi and Champagne. Midway through all of this me and Sandra had to toddle of from the spa to film the Wallspan Bedrooms advert that ended up in the middle of the commemorative video boxset package that the club put out to celebrate promotion and ultimately the league title, too. The filming took four and half hours, which was made to feel even longer having dragged ourselves away from the Champagne that was flowing back at the spa. However, the Scotsman in me always saw an opportunity for something for free, or so I thought in this case. I didn't get a free bed but what we did get was a set of bedroom furniture for both bedrooms. Happy days at the time, however, six years later on when I was at Coventry City, I received a tax bill for £300 as during an audit after the bedroom company had gone bust, the receivers auditing the company's account found that I'd been given all this furniture and I was due to pay the tax owing on it; some freebie that turned out to be! On the other hand, Tricentrol and Trimoco always looked after us with sponsored cars. Bill Tomlins was a manager at Tricentrol and was in charge of looking after us players with our cars before he joined Luton Town.

When I first joined the club, I found the step up to the pace of the game from Central League reserve football to the English Second Division to be quite a steep learning curve. My reactions and decision making just weren't sharp enough initially and in my first game in December 1978 at home to Preston, I dropped a howler with letting a cross get away from me. We lost 1-2 and then both of the following games were lost; 1-4 away at Leeds United in the quarter final of the league cup and 1-3 away at Brighton in the league. Then things just seemed to click and we won the next match away at Millwall 2-0 giving me my first clean sheet of my Luton Town career.

I had a strange relationship with my first centre half playing in front of me at Luton. Off the field Chris Turner and I were good pals, we got on really well, but on the pitch, we just didn't click. I would come to collect the ball, he wouldn't read that I was coming, and we'd often get in each other's way and collide. It made us both hesitant waiting to see what the other was going to do. I liked to make the 18-yard box mine and run it my way. When Sax came the following summer in 1979 he accepted this and we developed a great understanding. I was a strong, vocal character and I had to be in charge of the penalty box. I had a great back line in front of me with Sax, Paul Price and Mal Donaghy. I never saw my full backs as they were always bombing up the pitch to join in with the attacks. We certainly liked to play out from the back with short sharp passing and attack minded tactics. This was great to play in and attractive to watch but we did leave ourselves open a bit. That all changed in 1981 when Brian Horton came in. He read the game so well and broke up many counter attacks.

I had a great run in the team, hardly missing any games for four seasons. I think Alan Judge came in for the occasional game but I didn't miss many. However, then the injuries started to come more frequently and getting to thirty and beyond they started to take longer to heal, some of which never really did while I was still playing.

In the first season up in the top Division away at Arsenal in March 1983, I fractured my thumb during the game. John Sheridan came on to treat me and he thought it was dislocated so he pulled it and then strapped it up and I played on, but I couldn't catch the ball as I was trying to palm it away and we found ourselves 0-3 down by half time at Highbury. There were no sub goalkeepers on the bench back then so I played on, and we eventually lost the game 4-1 with Mossy getting us a late 88th minute consolation goal. The fracture set in the wrong position from the strapping applied as was shown up a month later from an X-ray. I had to wait for two more weeks until it could be re-broken and then re-set. That was my season finished! Tony Godden was brought in on loan from West Brom and he went to play a pivotal role in those final twelve games of the season culminating in the one that everyone remembers away at Manchester City where dear old Raddy scored the late winner, bless him, to keep us in the First Division.

Affectionately nicknamed 'Ox' by his team mates – Jake seen here in typical athletic flight away at Cardiff City during the 1979/80 season. Paul Price, Tony Grealish and Alan West look on.

I then had a persistent knee injury for two to three years which left me having a bone graft on my neck. This led to another four or five months out on the side lines again. Those injuries led to me never properly regaining match fitness as I couldn't train as hard as I wanted to. It was like all of a sudden I'd gone from being a fit young man to this thirty-year-old who couldn't shake off these knocks. My right knee went on me again in my last year at Coventry City, and that's what finished me off. As soon as I came out of football I got the knee sorted properly. Also, I had a further three bone grafts on my neck and then had a plate inserted in my back, but funnily enough, unlike my friend who's had his hip done, I don't set off any alarms at the airport security walk through!

On the Wednesday night before that 3-3 draw at Anfield in September 1982, we'd played away at Villa and got turned over 4-1. I took a heavy knock on my chest whilst coming out to claim the ball during the game and this put me in doubt for the upcoming game away at Liverpool. We had the Thursday off then came in on Friday. My chest was still sore and bruising had come out but I was passed fit with a good amount of strapping to my ribs. I'd started the game well and had made some good saves in front of the Anfield Kop end of the ground, but then I went to throw the ball out to Kirk Stephens and I felt a twinge. I carried on, though, and then seven or eight minutes later, when I went to throw the

1982; Pre-season photo call at Kenilworth Road

ball out to the left full-back Richard Money, I suddenly couldn't breathe. I had torn my intercostal muscle. I knew what it was straight away as the same thing had happened to me away at Cambridge United in October 1980. I was having a good tussle in the first half with big George Reilly playing his usual taking-no-prisoners' game upfront for Cambridge. He'd almost got me in the first half as I came to collect the ball and his foot was up by my shoulder. In the second half the ball was played forward into my penalty box so I dived on it, but at the same time Reilly came through and hit me full force in my chest. These days he would have been sent off. In those days though, you tried to give as good as you got and I could hold my own. However, with this heavy challenge I was down and couldn't breathe and our physio turned me over so as not to swallow my tongue whilst the club doctor was called from the stands to the pitch. We'd already made our substitution by bringing Raddy Antic on to replace David Moss. We were down to ten men as in those days there was only one sub allowed to be named on the bench. Mal Donaghy took over in goal, as he did in the second half at Anfield two years later. Mal didn't let any more goals in and we scored again in the last minute through Brian Stein to win 3-1.

David Pleat was very approachable even though he did annoy me at the next match after I was injured at Liverpool; we were at home to Brighton. Alan Judge was to play in goal but I still wanted to be included in the pre-match build up and be with the lads. It was at the pre-match meal. Pleat arrived and very bluntly looked at me and said gruffly, "Why are YOU here?" This really pee'd me off and we had words, to put it mildly. I was no longer the young, shy naïve lad from Scotland, but we did respect each other.

The thing that I missed the most after I finished playing was the dressing room; the laughter, the jokes, the wind ups. The dressing room at Luton was fantastic. The closest that I ever got to that again was with John Sillet at Coventry City. We called Mossy and Richard Money 'Clunk and Click' as they were always together. Mossy was great for a laugh but he was really easy to wind up and he'd always bite. Pre-match lunch was always fun, we'd loosen the salt and pepper shakers near Mossy and it would go all over his dinner and he'd stand up and throw it down the table. You'd always know when David Pleat was annoyed as he'd sit there poking his tongue through the inside of his cheek and roll his eyes with his arms folded. If I ever got caught out with the loose salt and pepper I'd never bite, I would just get up and get another dinner. The fiver on a piece of string and tug it away just as it was about to be picked up was always a favourite of ours, too. Soon after Raddy joined us we were away at Swansea when Kirk and I got into his hotel room and put all the bedroom furniture, including his personal things, out on the balcony. We were downstairs in the lobby when Raddy came down from his room and went straight to David Pleat. "Boss, my room, no bed, no nothing, what is this?" David Pleat looked straight over at us and we were already in fits of laughter.

We never went completely over the top, like totally wrecking anything. Another away game we were at Blackburn Rovers, I think it was, when Saxby and Aizlewood were in the opposite room to me and Kirk. When we left a little early to go down for dinner we tied a rope on the handle to our room and attached it to the handle on Sax and Aizlewood's room. We were downstairs and we could tell the boss was getting a bit anxious that those two hadn't come down. So, he turned to Steiny and asked him to nip upstairs and fetch them. A few minutes later, Brian Stein came back downstairs with Sax and Aize pleading their innocence. "Gaffer," they said, "we couldn't get out of our room, someone had tied our room handle so it wouldn't open, Steiny had to let us out!"

We had a club break where the players and wives went to Torremolinos. We'd had a party at mine and Sandra's house on the Saturday and were flying out on the Monday. Dave Coates was in charge of seeing us all on the bus at Kenilworth Road at 7am to take us all to the airport. Coatesy commented, "Look at the state of you lot!" Tony Grealish was still smashed and he actually got thrown off the plane and had to get a later flight, but bizarrely, he still beat us to the hotel where we were staying. David Pleat was to join us two days later that week. As we got into the first training session, a four-mile run back from the beach, we set off with sixteen

December 1982 at home to Watford

players running behind David Coates, but by the time we'd got back to the hotel there was only two of us still with Coatesy. The rest of the lads had dropped off during the run into whatever bar they could find. Two hours later they started to turn up wearing all sorts of sombreros and the like, and Coatesy went around to each of them and had a quiet word. The players knew that while they respected him, they could push their luck a little with him before the boss joined us the next day. No more was said about the matter once David Pleat arrived, fair play to Coatesy.

You have to remember that when I was playing, everything you did during the week was all about leading up to that moment when, following training on the Friday morning, the team sheet would be pinned up for the game the following day – there would only be twelve names on there! The first eleven and only the one sub. None of this today where you take twenty players with nine subs sitting on the bench, and seemingly all too many of them look content to do so whilst continuing to pick up their £40,000 a week.

I mainly had Dave Lawson, initially, and then Judgey pushing me for my place for the first five years that I was at Luton but then, following my thumb injury at Arsenal that left me side-lined for the remainder of the 1982/83 season, my absence was initially covered by Tony Godden being brought in on loan from West Brom. Then Les Sealey came in on a permanent deal from Coventry City during the summer of 1983 and this was followed by Andy Dibble being signed from Cardiff City the season afterwards by David Pleat. To be fair to Les, he came in and was ever present in his first season as the record books show. I didn't make one single first team appearance in that season. I have to be honest, when I wasn't in the side I would get quite down. I didn't like playing in the reserves. I would always prefer to go out on loan so that I could stay sharp by playing competitive football and in front of a crowd like I did when I went out on loan to Barnsley and Derby County.

I only made four first team appearances the following season in 1984/85. The relationship with David Pleat changed and when he spoke to me it was like I could hear his voice but it was the words of Chief Executive John Smith, coming out. I'll admit that I was a little bitter about how things ended at Luton and I moved away from the club to play for Swindon Town, Peterborough United, Portsmouth, and Coventry City, where I was part of the FA Cup winning squad in 1987. There, we beat, of all people, David Pleat and his Tottenham Hotspur team!

I even got to mime on Children's TV show Blue Peter, as the whole squad were invited on during the run up to the Cup Final to air the then infamous song that sides still traditionally put out then. You can still find the clip up on YouTube no doubt. I have to say it wasn't quite the Anfield Rap put out by the Liverpool team the following season.

When John Sillett convinced me not to retire, I signed for Coventry City in 1986 as experienced cover for Steve Ogrizovic. It was a case of third time lucky as I'd almost signed for Coventry City on two separate occasions earlier in my career; Ron Wylie and Gordon Milne had made a bid to Villa for me in 1972. I'd played under Ron Wylie along with Vic Crowe at Villa and we'd won the prestigious FA Youth Cup the year before in 1971 against Liverpool in front of a crowd of 34,000. I was still only eighteen and I was loving life at Villa Park, and so the bid was turned down by Aston Villa.

Then, in 1983, I was originally intended to be part of a swap deal that would take Les Sealey in the opposite direction from Highfield Road to Kenilworth Road. However, my side of the deal fell through and so Bobby Gould signed Raddy Avramovic instead.

Coventry City were kind enough to award me with a testimonial game on August 12th, 1989 against West Brom. It was a pre-season game played for my benefit which I was thankful for, especially as my mum was the guest of honour that day.

I still live in the Birmingham area and have been running a driving school for a number of years, and I recently started working as part of the matchday experience at Villa Park.

(BORN 27 FEBRUARY 1955, COVENTRY)

# KIRK WILLIAM STEPHENS

## LUTON TOWN FC 1978 - 1984

*Starting out in football at his hometown club signing schoolboy forms with Coventry City was just what young Kirk Stephens had dreamed of, however, it was soon to be over, as at fifteen he was released by City and found himself playing for a local factory team called Massey Ferguson Tractors. For a sixteen-year-old this was a footballing education as well as learning how to stand up to the toughness of senior football. Within a few months, a chap called David Kite was scouting for a number of teams as well as David Pleat at Nuneaton Borough. He approached Kirk and took him to a trials match up at Blackpool and also at Peterborough United. Kirk was accompanied by a good friend of his, another local lad from Coventry. Immediately after the trial game the Peterborough Manager, Jim Iley, offered both Kirk and his friend pro contracts on £12 a week.*

My mate signed straight away but I said that I'd need to talk to my dad about it before signing and I would call Jim tomorrow. Back out in the car park I got back in my dad's car to head home when there was a tap at the window. I wound down it down and this fella said, "Hi son, I watched your game and I really liked you, I'd like to sign you and put you straight in the first team for me at Nuneaton Borough. My name's David Pleat, I'm the manager at Nuneaton." I thanked him for his interest and said I'd need to talk it over with my dad and, the same as I'd promised Jim Iley, I told David Pleat that I'd call him tomorrow. Dad told me I'd be better playing men's first team football than playing in Peterborough United's youth and reserve teams. I had started a construction company with my dad so if I went to play for Nuneaton I'd be able to stay at home and keep working with him to build up the business. So, the next day, true to my word, I

Kirk, on the left, circa 1973 Nuneaton team shot, along with his manager David Pleat who would later bring him to Luton Town

called Jim at Peterborough United and told him, thanks for the interest and the offer but I'm going to sign for Nuneaton Borough. It turns out that David Kite had indeed tipped David Pleat off to watch me in the trial match at Peterborough.

One evening six months later, I was walking into training at Nuneaton when David Pleat came out the other way carrying all sort of papers and other bits and pieces. It looked like he'd cleared his desk and it turned out that he had. I asked him what was going on, to which he told me he was leaving Nuneaton Borough as he'd been offered a job scouting at a football league club. He wished me all the best and made me a promise on the spot right there. He said, "I really like you, Kirk, and I'll promise you this, if I ever get a job as a manager at a football league club, I will come back to sign you." I played at Nuneaton for the next six years and really enjoyed it and even though there were lots of offers for me from league clubs, the chairman would always turn down. But I didn't mind as I was happy playing locally and building up the business with Dad.

Over time, David Pleat had gone from scout, to youth team coach, to reserve team coach, to first team coach and then early in 1978, with Harry Haslam leaving to take up the manager's job at Sheffield United, he was promoted to the big job as Luton Town's first team manager. A number of players were quickly sold in order to build his team, his way. Among them, Steve Buckley had already been sold to Derby County and the Futcher brothers were allowed to go to Manchester City. I was contacted through a third party, no agents in those days, not that I ever had or needed one. David Pleat was true to his promise that he'd made to me six years earlier on that training night at Nuneaton. He wanted to sign me and again put me straight away into his first team, but this time at Luton Town in the Second Division of the Football League. I was still playing for Nuneaton Borough, I was twenty-three years old and this move felt right. I called the Nuneaton chairman and said that I'd heard Luton Town wanted to sign me and I wanted to go this time. He said he'd turned Luton down and that he wanted to keep me at Nuneaton and that he had big plans for the club in the form of getting them into the Football League. I told him in no uncertain terms that I had been loyal to the club for six years and not complained about other offers being turned down but now, at twenty-three, this could be my last chance to play league football. He still refused to let me go, telling me I was under contract with Nuneaton. To this I informed him that if you don't let me sign for Luton Town then from this moment I will never play for you again anyway and I will go and play amateur football. At 11:30pm that night, the deal was done for me to leave Nuneaton Borough and sign for David Pleat at Luton Town. I signed the first contract that was put in front of me, no negotiations. It was a three-year contract on £80 a week so I actually took a pay cut to go full time pro as I was earning around £25/£30 a week from football at Nuneaton, plus around £90 a week from the job with my dad. For me, however, football was never about money. The crazy money that players are on now would've been nice of course, but life has been good to me and I was about to have the best six years of my career playing football at Luton.

I was put in digs when I first joined Luton Town, where I lived round the back of Bury Park with landlady, Mrs Howden. Mossy had joined from Swindon Town at the same time and was also in club digs at first, also in Bury Park near me, so we became good friends and socialised in the evenings, often frequenting the cinema at the nearby Odeon. I remember that I made an early mistake with Mrs Howden when I moved in there by saying I was used to early starts working on the construction sites, so after that, every morning, she'd come in to my room at 6:30am and pull the curtains wide open. Trouble was I was so close to the ground and I didn't need to be at training until 9:30am!

I made my football league debut at home to Oldham in the opening game of the 1978/79 season. Including myself, there were seven of us in the starting eleven that day making our debuts in David Pleat's new look side. Steve Sherlock, Chris Turner, Mark Aizlewood, Mal Donaghy, Bob Hatton, David Moss and me. At half time we found ourselves 0-1 down and the fans must have been fearing the worst of Pleat's new team, but we clicked in the second half, scoring six goals without further reply to win our first match 6-1.

I played in the next two games, both of which we lost away at Palace and at Newcastle United before a training incident with David Carr resulting in a cruciate ligament injury. At the time I didn't think it was intentional but later, I became aware that it was and there was a certain

amount of jealousy on his part of the new players coming in and taking his place. I didn't really know the guy but he wasn't around long after and he was transferred to Lincoln City. I'd only just got going at Luton playing three league games and then I was out injured until mid-January 1979.

Jake Findlay and I became great friends when he joined the club a little after the rest of us in the 1978/79 season. Everyone called us 'Toot and Ploot' after the two blue aliens that were famous at the time for the Butlins Holiday Park adverts. Someone called us it one day and it just stuck. Jake and I were always roommates for away games and tours but soon after, Steve White was signed for a lot of money from Bristol Rovers in 1979/80 season when we were all away on a team break in Torremolinos. We'd arrived in the hotel and David Pleat was reading out who was rooming with who. He said, "Jake and Whitey, you're in together." I went ranting at Dave, but he was having none of it and said he was splitting the pair of us for this trip.

That first morning Steve White was up at about at 7:30am, pulling the curtains wide open before he went out on the balcony to do his morning stretches and exercises. Jake was not impressed as we didn't have to be down to the first training session until much later. "Shut those fucking curtains, Whitey," Jake shouted. This went on for a couple of days so, on the third morning, Jake had got some ice-cold buckets ready. As soon as Whitey was back out on the balcony he gave him a good drenching of the cold stuff. I don't think they roomed together again after that!

In the hotel bar on the first night we convinced Steve White that every new player had to perform an initiation task. None of us ever had but we thought it up on the spot and Whitey was game. Being a flexible lad, we said that he had to bend over backwards and walk like a crab out of the bar and into reception. So, he got on the floor, lifted himself up into the backwards crab and did it; fair play to him. However, just as he made it to the reception door and out of the bar, in came David Pleat, David Coates and I think John Sheridan, as well. We were all watching in the bar in fits of laughter with Pleat and company looking down on Whitey and him looking back up at them from the backwards crab position saying, "It's for

THE 1979 APPRENTICES
Back Row: Jan Piotrowski, Tom Murphy, Frankie Bunn, Rob Walker, Martyn Conquest, John Cole
Front Row: Alan Cosby, Rob Johnson, John Woodward, Neil Madden, Ray Brammer

Rob Johnson: 1985 – with pigeon

Rob Johnson: with the authors friend, Paul Bonham (Aylesbury United tracksuit) receiving an award from Rob Johnson, circa 1984

Paul Walsh: 1982

Mark Stein, Mitchell Thomas and Godfrey Ingram meeting in 2021 to celebrate Godfrey getting an all clear following cancer treatment after it was caught by early screening.

Paul Elliott and Ray Daniel in action away at Southampton February 25th 1984 in a significant match where David Pleat had six black players in his starting eleven that day; Mitchell Thomas, Paul Elliott, Ricky Hill, Brian Stein, Ray Daniel and Emeka Nwajiobi - the same six players were also named in the '12' in the previous match at home to Liverpool with Nwajiobi an unused sub

Alan West in action during the 0-0 draw at Stoke City's Victoria Ground in April 1979

David Pleat at the start of his first full season as Manager 1978/79 with his new backroom team: John Moore, Ken Gutteridge and David Coates

David Moss scores on his league debut for Luton Town in the 6-1 win home over Oldham Athletic in August 1978

Cue celebrations…with Bob Hatton and Mal Donaghy, who were both also making their league debuts for Luton that day

Mal Donaghy playing in midfield on his debut along with one of the few remaining players from the Harry Haslam era, Lil Fuccillo. Mark Aizlewood also making his debut keeping a watchful eye and in front of the then roofless Kenilworth Road end open terrace

Bob Hatton in full flight creating havoc in the Charlton Athletic defence during a 3-0 home win in September 1978

Brian Stein is tackled at Ewood Park versus Blackburn Rovers in September 1980

Ricky Hill during the same game with Brian Stein and Paul Price in support

Kirk Stephens and David Moss at the start of the 1980/81 season model the new home shirts incorporating the club's first ever shirt sponsor 'Tricentrol'

*Ricky Hill, Phil Boersma, Godfrey and Terry Hayes enjoy a night out in 1978*

On the morning of Mick Saxby's wedding outside his parents' house

Later that day…

Brian Stein and Tony Grealish in goalmouth action during the 2-0 win over Chelsea on Boxing Day 1980

Godfrey Ingram puts the pressure on the Chelsea defence at Kenilworth Road in 1980 in these two pictures

Ricky Hill uses his guile and elegance as well as his power and skill to beat his Chelsea opponents

Celebrating promotion back to division 1 in 1982 after the 4-1 home win over Shrewsbury Town

Two local Luton born lads, Mitchell Thomas and Wayne Turner, making their way in the Luton Town first team in 1982

Clive Goodyear #5 is mobbed by his team mates after he has scored what turned out to be the games only goal vs Watford 27th December 1982

Les Sealey and his defence foil a QPR corner in a 0-0 draw at Kenilworth Road March 1984

Trevor Aylott in action during the narrow 2-1 defeat at White Hart Lane in April 1984

David Moss in the same match against Tottenham

David Preece making his debut at home to Aston Villa scores the only goal of the game in December 1984

Mick Harford and Peter Nicholas are challenged at St James Park by Newcastle United's Gary Megson in February 1985

David Preece, Peter Nicholas and Steve Foster in action as Arsenal are beaten 3-1 in May 1985

Ricky Hill, Brian Stein and Emeka Nwajiobi in the thick of the action at Sheffield Wednesday in September 1985

Mick Harford in the same match in which he scored two goals but still ended up on the losing side in a 3-2 defeat

Brian Stein on his 28th Birthday scores at Hat-trick against Peter Shilton in a 7-0 victory over Southampton in October 1985

Steve Foster battles with Leicester City's Alan Smith at Kenilworth Road on New Year's Day 1986

LUTON TOWN AND BEDFORD TRUCKS
TOGETHER MEAN BUSINESS

G.S.TWIGG LT
LUTON TOWN

MACKESON
LEEWELL
LTD.
PLANT
SCRAP MERCHANTS OF REPUTE
BALDOCK 893152 · COTTENHAM 50586

WHITBREAD Pale Ale
MACKESON

BEDFORD
GM
COACHES
TRUCKS
VANS
Now the driving force.

BEDFORD
SEED
BRENGREEN
RICHMOND
BY DESIGN.

LUTON TOWN FOOTBALL CLUB
Tricentrol

LUTON TOWN FOOTBALL CLUB

MACKESON ...taste the goodness!

POWER TOOLS

adidas
LUTON TOWN FOOTBALL CLUB
BEDFORD TRUCKS

adidas
LUTON TOWN FOOTBALL CLUB
BEDFORD TRUCKS

LUTON TOWN FOOTBALL CLUB
Tricentrol

Tricentrol

BEDFORD
TRUCKS.

BEDFORD
TRUCKS

adidas
LUTON TOWN
FOOTBALL CLUB
BEDFORD
TRUCKS

BEDFORD

LUTON TOWN
FOOTBALL CLUB

BEDFORD

Tricentrol

VAUXHALL

BEDFORD
TRUCKS

adidas
LUTON TOWN FOOTBALL CLUB
BEDFORD TRUCKS

adidas
LUTON TOWN FOOTBALL CLUB
BEDFORD TRUCKS

TOOLS

my initiation, boss! PRICELESS!

On that break we had a youth team player who had just signed pro with the club. The boss was good in that he would be happy to let us have a beer as training camp wasn't until the afternoon the following day. One night on the tour, this young lad was at the bar. It was fair to say that he'd had a few. He got a bit emotional saying, "I love it with you lot, you don't know what it means to me to be out here with you guys, it's so great to play for my home town club and be with you guys." This went on for a while until Paddy Grealish, having had enough, picked up a silver ashtray from the bar and smacked him round the back of the head with it then asked him how much he was enjoying it now. The young player in question was Wayne Turner. I saw him recently as he's in the building game like me and he mentioned the ashtray round the back of the head incident. He confided in me: "Basher, that ashtray really bloody hurt, but I held it in as I didn't want to cry in front of you lot."

The coaching set up was John Moore, a very disciplined and respected man at the club, David Coates, who you could push it with to have a bit more of a laugh and joke; he was a tremendous coach. Trevor Hartley was a bit more on the periphery of everything and of course we had an excellent physio in John Sheridan. There was one week when John really needed to work his magic for me whilst at the same time trying to hide the real reason of my injury from John Moore and most importantly from David Pleat.

We'd had the Monday off from the club so I was back in the Midlands working in the office on the site where my construction company was. The lads on the job had knocked off. As I was leaving, I noticed there was some loose brickwork which I just couldn't leave, and so I went off to get a long ladder. I propped it up against the wall and climbed to the top. I'd just started to move the loose brickwork when the ladder slipped down the wall with me still on it. I jumped off just before it hit the floor and landed on some rubble, really whacking both my ankles. I was in agony and when I got home, my ankles were black and blue and swelling up.

I got to training early the next day. It was Tuesday and we were playing away at Coventry City on the Saturday, so naturally I was desperate to play. I went in to see John Sheridan but only showed him my right ankle. John looked at it and asked what on earth I had done. I couldn't tell him the truth as he'd have to tell the boss and he would have fined me, but more importantly he would have dropped me straight away for the following

Having recovered from an early season injury, a very young Kirk defends his lines against Blackburn Rovers in his first season as a football league player in a 2-1 home win in February 1979

Saturday away at Coventry City and there was no way I was going to miss that game. So I told John a whopper that I had a puncture on the motorway down from Coventry that morning and had lost it and kicked the metal bar that you use to get the wheel off, catching my ankle on it. John treated the ankle for three hours on the Tuesday and again on the Wednesday. By Thursday I got him to look at my left ankle telling him it had swollen up again hoping he wouldn't notice that it was the other foot he was treating. As he had so many other players at the same time to look after I thought I might just get away with it. Pleat had come in and asked how I was with the ankle. I was desperate to play and John Sheridan had sussed it, he was not fooled at all, but continued to treat it that day, and again on the Friday. On the day of the match I was in at the club for treatment early doors, the coach was leaving to take the team to Coventry at 10am, and Pleat asked John what he thought. John said to take me on the coach and give me a fitness test on the pitch before naming the side. The club doctor, Dr Berry, gave me a cortisone injection which I kid you not was some experience of pain in itself. I went out at 1pm for the fitness test, the ankles feeling great, and I was pinging the ball about with Pleat and Sheridan out on the pitch with me. "It's all good, boss," I said, and I was in the team. Everything was great until fifteen minutes into the second half when the injection started to wear off. I ended up playing through absolute agony for the last twenty minutes of the game. When I got back into the changing room I took my boots and socks off, then my ankles just exploded. I never told Dave the truth about the injury until years later.

I was never a Ricky Hill or a Paul Walsh but always played with heart and desire and I was half decent too, of course. The fans at Luton appreciated this and I always stopped for for a chat with a fan and gave them my autograph. My on-the-field displays enamoured me in the hearts of Luton Town fans and none more so than Boxing Day 1979, away at

Vicarage Road, Watford. Whenever I come back to Luton this is the goal that everyone wants to talk about. I believe it was put down in the club's folklore with 'that' song being sung about Boxing Day for many years at Kenilworth Road. It's funny, as I always get a group of fans and kid them on that it was thirty-odd years ago and I might need a bit of help remembering all the details. I play along further and say, "Wasn't it an early kick off, lads? Weren't they managed by some guy who went to be the England manager, oh, what was his name?" and the guys always shout out, "Yeah, yeah, it was Graham Taylor Basher." I carry it on as if it's all a bit hazy then give them the full blow-by-blow account of the goal. Findlay out to Donaghy, to West onto Grealish, to Hill, to Stein, back to Hill, out to Moss, Bob Hatton spots the reverse run, Moss to Hatton, and I see a gaping hole at the far post but I've got to make up 45 yards to get there. Hatton crosses and I'm there, header in the 89th minute, BANG, GET IN YOU FUCKER, and we've won away at Watford! All the Luton fans in the Rookery End go mad. There's a picture of me and Mick Saxby at the end, me not knowing what to do with myself looking for my Dad, as he went everywhere with me. There were fantastic scenes whilst coming out of the car park at the end of the match. We were in my dad's Jaguar XJS and as it was Boxing Day we were heading straight back to the Midlands to my mum's house. We were surrounded by a sea of jubilant Luton Town supporters all around us and, like a scene from Only Fools and Horses, when Dad beeped the horn on the Jag, the crowd parted to let us through like they did for Del Boy in the famous riot scene on the Trotters' housing estate. As the fans made way for us to drive through I could see that my dad was filling up with pride. All of this joy, adulation, chanting and cheering from the Luton fans was all for his son and what he had just achieved on the football pitch. Dad had come to love Luton Town FC as well. His shoulders were back and his chest was pumped up full with pride, it was quite a moment that I'll never forget.

I often get asked about my only ever sending off whilst with Luton, that came about at Oldham Athletic away in February 1980. It was quite late in the game and the ball went out off the Oldham player, not me, and right in front of the linesman, but he gave it the other way. We were losing 2-1 and I ended up getting sent off for 'thinking'. These were the days when you could talk to the officials, and I said to the linesman, "I think you're a fucking prick." The referee consulted with the linesman and then called me over. "Stephens, I'm going to have to send you off for what you just called my linesman,' he said. I replied, "But ref, I didn't say that he is a fucking prick, I just told him that I THINK he is!"It didn't work and he sent me off anyway. To make matters worse, as I went off close to the Oldham fans some old dear gave me a right old whack with her handbag and, crossing the bridge to the dressing rooms at Boundary Park, I was getting loads of verbal from the home fans surrounding the area. The final straw was when the door to the dressing room was locked, so I kicked it open. Yes, I did throw a few things around in the dressing room but I never trashed it, despite some reports to the contrary. On the Monday after the game I'd calmed down and called Oldham Athletic. "Could I speak to the first team manager, Jimmy Frizzell, please?" They asked who was calling and I told them that it's Kirk Stephens calling from Luton Town football club. Jimmy came to the phone and I said, "Jimmy, it's Kirk Stephens, I'm really sorry for losing my head at your place on Saturday, send me the bill for the door that I kicked and I'll pay for the damages." Jimmy replied, "Kirk, do you really think that you're the first player to kick in a dressing room door?" I appreciated the phone call and the gesture that it wouldn't be necessary to pay for the damages. With that, the episode was closed, apart from my suspension of course.

In September 1982 away at Anfield, Liverpool came the famous 3-3 draw, and Bob Paisley would later be quoted in the national press after the game that Luton Town had come to Anfield and given Liverpool a footballing lesson. It is best remembered for the injury to Jake Findlay after he pulled stomach muscles throwing the ball out in the first half. We all looked around at each other as we hadn't ever planned for a change of keeper and back in 1982, we could only name one substitute on the bench so obviously it was never a keeper named. We didn't even have a goalkeeper top to use as Jake was in too much pain to take the top off. It actually had to be cut off him. I ended up borrowing a Liverpool goalkeeper jersey from the Anfield kitman. I said to Nobby that I fancied it as I was always doing it in training, going in goal for a bit of fun, but this was in front of the famous Anfield Kop end. I turned to the Liverpool fans and put my hands out as if to pray. They loved it and they started singing, 'Shaky for England' and 'There's only one Shakin' Stephens' after the popular leg trembling Welsh Elvis impersonating singer of the time Shakin Stevens, with a V! Ian Rush did score one past me but I have to say there's no shame in that, he scored plenty of goals past better keepers than me. We went in 1-2 down so the boss decided to re-organise. He put Mal Donaghy in goal, who was a bit taller and had actually started out in youth football as a goalkeeper. Wayne Turner moved to right back and I moved

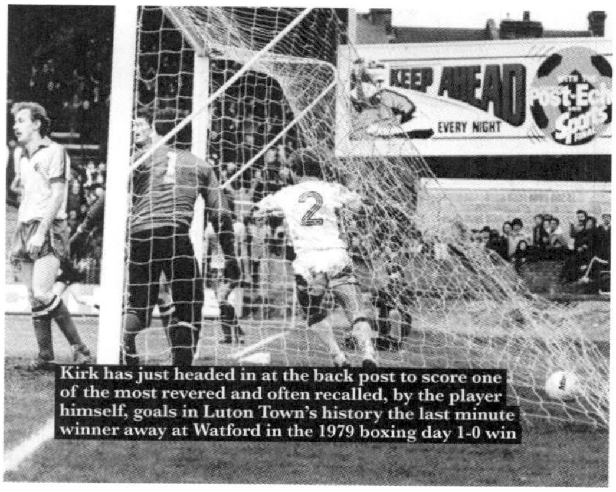


Kirk has just headed in at the back post to score one of the most revered and often recalled, by the player himself, goals in Luton Town's history the last minute winner away at Watford in the 1979 boxing day 1-0 win

into the middle. Mal only let one in and we scored twice in the second half through Mossy and Steiny with his second goal of the match.

I was always very protective of my Number 2 shirt. I was not best pleased when in October 1982 we went down on a Tuesday night to Charlton Athletic away in the second leg of the Milk Cup, having already won the first leg 3-0, so perhaps that's why the boss did what he did... I always liked to get in the changing room early and changed as quickly as possible. I was pretty much changed and ready to go when David Pleat came in to read out the team. 1; Jake Findlay, 2; Mitchell Thomas… I blew up at Dave and asked what was going on why was I dropped. Pleat said he wasn't dropping me, but he was resting me. I said that I didn't want to be rested and why would he leave it until now to tell me that I wasn't playing. I wasn't even on the bench! I couldn't tell you what happened during the match as I spent the game sulking back on the team coach. When we got back to Luton at about midnight, the boss was seeing all the players off the coach back at the club and telling everyone they had the day off the next day. All except when he got to me. "Not you, Stephens, you're in tomorrow." I asked why. He replied, "You didn't play tonight, you were rested and you're in with the reserves tomorrow," And I went off with the steaming hump. I was living back in the Midlands and didn't have a hotel booked so I ended up in Ronelles night club in Luton. At 5am the next morning, I found myself outside the football club waiting for someone like Dick Wassell or George Rogers to arrive to let me in. Dick was the first to arrive and, bless him, he plied me with plenty of coffee. I missed the next two games after that with Wayne Turner taking my precious Number 2 shirt against Nottingham Forest and then Arsenal.

April 1984 at home to Watford is another game that I get asked about a lot with the 'incident' with the Watford and Scotland forward, Mo Johnston. Young Mitchell Thomas had made the left back spot his own and was playing well. We were defending the Oak Road end when the ball broke loose and Mitchell got to it first to clear it and I saw and heard what

Kirk dons the much loved 'Tricentrol' Adidas kit at the dawn of the momentous Division 2 Championship winning season in 1981/82

Mo Johnston did. He knew he was going to be late and he took Mitchell out by slyly kicking his standing foot. Thomas went down and Johnston leant over and shouted at Mitchell, whilst he was still in agony on the floor something racial, questioning his parentage, so I came in and hit Mo Johnston, who ended up laid out on the floor. When Mitchell had cleared the ball the officials and the rest of the players all followed the flight of it, so I wasn't seen taking Johnston out after what he had said and done to Mitchell Thomas. However, the whole of the Oak Road had seen it and starting singing 'Basher, Basher, Basher's gonna get ya.' I thought, shut up you lot, you'll get me strung up. The Watford physio came running on the pitch from their bench to see to Johnston. As he passed me he said, "You fucker, Stephens."

The ref didn't see it so I never even got booked for it. We went in at half time, Pleat closed the dressing room door and headed straight over to me and said, "You'll never play for me again if you ever do that again." The boss HAD seen it. I ripped my shirt off and threw it, telling him to stick the shirt, then the boots came off and the shorts. I was fuming. I was sticking up for my team mate on the pitch who had been physically and verbally assaulted. I went into the toilet and was refusing to go back on for the second half. Nobby Horton calmed me down in the end. "Bash," he said, "don't let us down, the fans down, your family or yourself. Now get your kit

Kirk celebrates promotion to the first division, in 1982, with Brian Horton and later on with his much loved Father

1982/83 up against his boyhood club Coventry City at Kenilworth Road

on and we'll deal with it later." Nobby got through to me and I went back out to play the remainder of the game. There was a double sending off in the second half but it wasn't me. Paul Elliott and Wilf Rostron were both sent off for handbags at ten paces, which meant that Wilf Rostron actually missed the FA Cup Final for Watford against Everton through suspension from this sending off.

At the end of the 1983/84 season, David Pleat called me in and said that Bobby Gould had come in with an offer to take me to Coventry City and did I want to go. "I don't want you to go," he added, "but as it's your home town club it's up to you." I told Dave that I would need some time to mull it over for a few days. It really played on my heart strings as I didn't want to leave my adopted club at Luton but at the same time this was a dream to play for Coventry City. If it had been anyone else I wouldn't have considered it. I was still under contract at Luton, it was never about money. The boss even offered me a 60% pay rise to stay at Luton Town, but in the end the draw of playing for my hometown club as a professional footballer and after I had been released as a fifteen-year-old back in 1970, was too much to turn down. Ashley Grimes had fallen out with Gould and

Kirk, along with Steve White, Lil Fuccillo and Brian Horton keep a close watch on Ipswich Town's Steve McCall in this league clash at Portman Road in 1983

Dave fancied taking Grimes, so a deal was done. Was it the right thing to do? With hindsight, who knows? But, in the end, I couldn't turn down the chance to run out of the tunnel at Highfield Road as a Coventry City player.

It was a sad day when I left Kenilworth Road. I was driving a Ford Escort XR3i with a sunroof at the time and the reporters outside wanted a photo of me sticking my head out of the sunroof waving a last goodbye to Luton Town, but I didn't want to do it.

Similar to the start of my time at Luton, not long after I joined Coventry City I got another bad knee injury after a challenge from Bob Hazel during a game with Leicester City in a 2-0 home win for Coventry in early September 1984. This caused me to miss part of the season and, to be honest, Coventry City never really got to see me at my best as I was never quite the same player again after this injury. I did play for another season in 1985/86 but then retired from professional football after two years of a three-year contract, missing out on an FA Cup Final place at the end of 1987, ironically against David Pleat with his new club, Tottenham.

At Luton with that group of players we had the best camaraderie that

I've ever experienced in football. So many of us still talk to each other all the time and we holiday together for golf and the like. I know that I can phone every one of them today and say let's meet up in Luton in two weeks' time and that all of them, if they physically could, would be there. I spoke to Nobby Horton recently with the sad passing of Raddy Antic and said we'll have to get the lads together and have a memorial drink for him, which we will.

I still live in the Coventry area with my family and continue to run Walsgrave Contractors, the construction company that me and my father began back in the 1970s. For a while in the mid-2000s I was working three evenings a week and on Sundays, with different age groups each year at the Coventry City Academy after its inception under Richard Money.

I still have a few bits of memorabilia from my time at Luton, some programmes and shirts from key games. I also have the away shirt from the famous late win at Manchester City in 1983 that kept us in the first division with only four minutes to go. This shirt is framed and in pride of place on the wall in my snooker room at home.

I speak and text with Dave a couple of times every week, he's been like a father figure to me for almost fifty years. We have villas in Spain quite close to each other. I will always be indebted to him for keeping the promise that he made to me that night in Nuneaton all of those years ago.

(BORN 2 JANUARY 1959, CHIPPING SODBURY)

# STEPHEN JAMES WHITE

## LUTON TOWN FC 1979 – 1982 AND [1-MONTH LOAN IN 1983]

*Stephen joined Luton Town just before Christmas in 1979. Earlier that season he'd scored two goals for Bristol Rovers against Luton. Rovers won the game 3-2 at Eastville. After scoring two goals at Kenilworth Road in a 3-2 loss for Rovers the season before as well, it was probable that David Pleat was keen on signing Stephen at that point.*

I remember driving up the motorway with my dad after the manager at Bristol Rovers said Luton Town had come in for me with a bid which had been accepted, asking if I'd like to speak to them. I was playing for Rovers in what is now the Championship, but was then the old Second Division; I was an aspiring young player wanting to make progress. Luton were top of the league at the time so I told them I was happy to speak with them. We went up there to meet with David Pleat and assistant manager, Ken Gutteridge, and the Hilton Hotel on the side of the motorway near Dunstable. David and Ken were trying to split me and my dad up so I went in Ken's car and Dad went with David in his car. It was just to try to get to know us a bit I suppose. There was a game against Charlton Athletic that night at Kenilworth Road so we watched it in the snow, before we then had talks with David and Ken. I think the chairman showed his face in David's office after the match in which Luton had won 3-0, consolidating their place at the top of the league, and of course I couldn't wait to join! My dad accompanied me, I wouldn't say he was my agent, though perhaps a special agent! I would have only been just twenty then. I'd played for Rovers for two and a half years so I was looking to get away to, I wouldn't say a better club, but a club at a higher level. They offered me a five-year contract and I signed it. Whether I was put on good, average or bad money, I couldn't tell you to this day. I had a loyalty bonus in the contract which would be paid in increments at the end of each year and there was a signing-on fee. I think that was standard practice amongst many clubs at the time. I played football for twenty-one years, scored 275 goals and the only time that I ever had a goal bonus was at my last club, Cardiff City, when I was thirty-seven. I'd have done alright if I'd had a hundred pounds a goal bonus throughout my whole career, wouldn't I! However, back then there were no agents and goal bonuses, it just wasn't a thing then. What do you give a defender for clearing the ball off the line or a goal saving tackle? I don't think forwards should be paid for a goal bonus personally even though I was a forward I just don't agree with them.

'Whitey' scores the only goal in the local derby match with Watford in the 1980/81 clash at Kenilworth Roadl

David Pleat and David Coates, who became the assistant manager soon after Ken Gutteridge left, were both very keen on team bonding and we used to go away at least two or three times a year if we had a spare midweek or an enforced spell with no games due to poor weather in the UK, as well as the end of season team get-aways. We had some great sessions in Torremolinos and Benalmadena, all those types of places on the Southern coast of Spain. There certainly were some stories. One about Saxby springs to mind where he drank what was supposedly a yard of ale but was all a mixture of cocktails. Because he had no money left he drank it straight down and was unconscious before he even hit the floor!

We met the Everton team out in Spain one year, which must have been 1980 or 1981. They were giving it the large one, so to speak, as they were First Division we were just a Second Division team, but Saxby and a few of our lads had some fun drinking games with them. I remember also going out to Eilat one year as well. Bloody hell, they were great times, though.

We also went to Miami and were going down to Disney World in

Steve White fresh and ready to go at the start of the 1981/82 promotion season

Orlando. As I wasn't a massive drinker I was 'hired' to be the chauffeur, driving a 3 litre Buick. The speed limit out there on the freeway was 56 mph. It was about a two or three-hour drive from Miami down to Orlando. From my memory we had Brian Stein, Ricky Hill and Godfrey Ingram sat in the back. Then it was myself, driving, along with Alan West and Saxby, I think, all in the front. On the way home, I was putting my foot down and we had three or four cans of beer being drunk by the lads from a crate we had in the boot. Of course, the boys were supping it back. Of the three lads in the back, to be fair, Godfrey didn't drink so much, Ricky Hill didn't mind a pint now and again and then there was Brian Stein, who liked more than a pint. It was dark by then and out of nowhere we had lights, full beam, right on our tail. Then the blue light came. In America on these freeways, there is a middle section where they're lower than the motorway so of course that's where the police were hiding out of sight. As I said, I was going at over 85 mph in a 56 mph limit, and yes, we were pulled over. I got out of the car and when they saw there were six of us in the car they thought there'd be trouble. There were two officers with their truncheons and their guns drawn from their holsters; it was the whole bloody works. I had to put my hands on the car while I was frisked all over. I was breathalysed, obviously, as they could see all of the other lads were drinking, but that came back all clear. They were really aggressive as they thought there was going to be trouble and of course, I was shitting myself. One of the officers told me to sit in the police car, but I forgot they drive on the opposite side to us and I went to get in the driver's side where another officer was already sat. Suffice to say, I got another 'telling off' for that!

Eventually, they gave me a ticket for speeding. They wanted my address, so I told them that we were over from England on a football tour. After issuing the ticket the police officers then opened the boot on our rented

Buick, removed the remainder of the crate of beer and put it into their police car and that was the last we saw of those beers and the officer. By the time we got back to England, the ticket and the fine had come through the post: $112 USD, which I never paid and I've not been back to America ever since!

That had been an end of season football tour, not just a jolly up – or the Florida Nose, as the boys used to call it. Pleaty or Coatesy would say to us if we could stay in the top four if we're doing well they'd take us on a trip. So of course, Kirk Stephens, Jake Findlay and Mick Saxby, all the naughty boys, were always up for it and they'd been on at Coatesy asking when, where, etc. They couldn't wait to get onto a plane and when we heard 'Florida' we thought Fucking hell, we're spreading our wings a bit here. That became 'Florida Nose'. I don't think we went away the first year that they promised it but the next year they did. That Florida trip must have been 1981, the year before we won the Second Division Championship.

When I first signed for Luton I was put into digs at the bottom of Kenilworth Road in Bury Park with Mrs Howden. I was next door to David Coates so he could keep an eye on me. I wasn't really happy there to be honest. There was another family with a little kid living in the digs as well. She did her best for me, Mrs Howden, but it wasn't that big and I was in a tiny box room with a window looking out onto a brick wall. I was really down for the first six months. In the summer of 1980 I spoke to Pleaty about it and he got me into digs with a local family of well-known Luton Town supporter, Alan Adair and his grandparents Isa and 'Red' Adair, in Stopsley, who were fantastic. The old boy had lost two sons through illness. He was shop steward at Vauxhall's for a long time, 'Red Adair' they used to call him. He was a great character. I think it helped them with that terrible struggle of losing two sons and it helped me also as they were just great to me.

I had a better season in the second year. I think Pleaty initially bought me to put on the bench to start with as Bob Hatton and Steiny were there. The idea was to keep them on their toes. Luton were top of the league and with me coming in for a reasonable transfer fee, the thinking was that it would motivate those players to push on. I didn't play a huge amount of games in that first six months but in the second year, I played a bit more. I think I scored twice against Watford, which helped endear me to the Luton fans. I didn't play regularly in the second year but in the third year we had forty-six games and I played in every minute of every game, four cup ties and forty-two league games. Won twenty-six, drew twelve, lost four, it's the only Championship that I ever won. I had a lot of promotions at Swindon but that was the only time I was in a Championship winning side.

1981/82 season: Steve battles with Leicester City's John O'Neill during a 2-1 home win

We scored some great team goals with that side. I remember the home game with Leicester City, when we beat them 2-1. I scored the opening goal of the game after Lil Fuccillo had picked up possession in the midfield. He then sprayed a diagonal pass out to David Moss for him to run onto. Mossy turned the Leicester City full back inside out, and I think he may have even nutmegged him to go through into the area where he played a delightful cross with just the right amount of power for me to head powerfully back across the goal and into the net in front of the Oak Road end.

David Pleat would swear by David Moss. Sometimes reporters would give him a hard time if we'd had an away game and it hadn't quite come off for us. But he stood by Mossy. David Pleat would say that he was morally so brave, yet some people said he didn't want to tackle back. However, David Moss was the best winger that I ever played with and I'll tell you why: For a centre forward, he was fantastic. He could transfer the ball onto either foot. He would cross from deep, he would cross from the by-line, and he would cross with either foot because he was two-footed and his accuracy was spot-on. You could see how accurate he was by the way he'd smash the penalties in. He was a great wide player and he was one of the main reasons that we scored so many goals. Ricky Hill is also one of the best players that I ever played with. No question, he should have received more England caps. If he'd played for Arsenal or Tottenham from the word go he'd have had seventy-five England caps. A truly great player, he could do the lot. He could run, he could jump, he could head the ball, he could shoot, he could dribble with the ball, and he could turn out, keep possession, tackle… That really was a good team. We had the balance of Fuccillo on the left-hand side, he had really strong legs, however, he wasn't a great athlete but he was very good in close quarters and he tackled well. His distribution, particularly out to Mossy, was exceptionally impressive as well as in the corner to myself or Steiny. Then, Brian Horton was the icing on the cake. He was inspirational. The best captain that I ever played under. If he thought you weren't pulling your weight he wouldn't have it, he'd have you up against the dressing room wall and he'd call you out, whoever it was. Often, in the dressing room at half time, we had words, "You ain't doing this, you ain't doing that," but that was just Brian being a great captain.

I remember before the QPR home game in May 1982, which we needed to win to clinch the Championship with three games to spare, ten minutes before the kick off we had a knock on the changing room door when Pleaty was giving us our last instructions. Dave Coates opened the door and was about to give someone a bollocking because it was so close to kick-off. But who should peak through the crack of the door, Eric Morecambe. He came in and of course did his famous routine with his glasses. Eric asked if it was alright that he just came in to wish the lads good luck. He got this little silver tin out of his top pocket, it was like a snuff box. He started at one end of the changing rooms, I was always round other side with Brian Horton and I think Kirk Stephens was round our side as well, and Eric went around the changing room to all eleven players with the open tin offering everyone a snort on whatever it was inside. It was a great little booster (the humour, not the contents of the snuff tin), it was so funny and it just relaxed everybody. It took the sting out of the situation and David Pleat was quite happy that he came in, in the end. It was a fabulous touch and those are the sorts of things that stay with you as a great memory before such an important game for the club.

That was a great team we had in 1981/82 at Luton. But then, at the end of the season, of course, he part exchanged me for Paul Walsh, which to me was just unbelievable. I was only two and a half years into a five year contract. I was happy at Luton, I was engaged to be married, and we'd just got into the First Division. I had been top scorer right the way through that season and I recall that Steiny overtook me right at the death; I think I had twenty goals and he had twenty-one. Mossy had chipped with sixteen or seventeen goals as well, it really was a great team, Ricky Hill being a magnificent player. Horton, Fuccillo, Mal Donaghy, Saxby and Goodyear had come into the side when Saxby got injured. Kirk Stephens at right back, Money or Aizlewood sometimes at left back, and Jake as the keeper.

The last thing I wanted to do was leave because I was so happy.

It was only about two weeks after the season had finished when David Pleat pulled me in. I said, "It's not happening, David, I'm staying, I've got a five-year contract."David more or less told me if I did stay I wouldn't be playing much and to go home and have a think about it.

I have to say that there were inducements, and in the end, if I was going to have to go, they made it worth my while and Charlton gave me a good contract. Looking back, I probably should have stayed and fought for my place in the team but I've never really been one to keep looking back saying that I should have done this, I should have done that.

The funniest thing about that whole episode was that I'd been to the Ritz Hotel in London on one occasion only and that was when I signed for Charlton. I went off down there with my wife, who'd just won 'Miss Luton 1982', to meet the Charlton manager, Ken Craggs. I'll never forget it because as we got into the lift and arrived at the top, Paul Walsh was there pressing the button to come down. It was so funny. I looked at him and he looked at me and we found ourselves in the lift together. He was going one floor with me and we exchanged pleasantries and I assumed he must have cottoned on wondering if I was part of the deal. Walshy knew the whole story. It was a big move for him and it was sideways/backwards move for me.

So, the deal was done, Ken Craggs was a nice guy who persuaded me to join but as it turned out we had massive problems there. He'd signed about fifteen players. The Charlton chairman was a commodities broker. They'd signed Alan Simonsen, the former European footballer of the year and they must have thrown so much money at him. He turned up in a four-wheel drive Audi Quatro whereas we all had little Volkswagen Sciroccos, or something like that

Steve puts in a shot during the important 2-0 win at home to Norwich City in April 1982

Steve at Highbury against David O'Leary whilst on loan from Charlton Athletic for a month in 1983

to drive around in. He'd been European Player of the Year and played for the past three years at Barcelona, but he was tiny and about eight and half/nine stone. He got kicked all over the shop playing in the English Second Division, but he was a nice man. However, come Christmas time everybody had to go. There were about seven or eight players who were put on the list that they were trying to get money for. I'd scored about thirteen goals up to Christmas but then I got injured and by the time I was coming back from that, Ken Craggs had got the sack and Lennie Lawrence had taken over.

Lennie asked me to go out to Lincoln City on loan to get my fitness back as he knew Colin Murphy the manager up there. They had some good players, John Fashanu, Glenn Cockerill who ended up going for big money to Southampton after he'd turned down an approach to join Luton Town, and the centre half, Trevor Peake, who went to Coventry City where he would win the 1987 FA Cup Final against Spurs and later played and coached at Luton Town. I went up there on a one month loan. I played two games and didn't score in either. At the following match Colin Murphy sat me on the bench as Cockerill or Fashanu were fit again. After that game I went to ask for a meeting with him and said, "Colin, I'm off back down the motorway as I've come up here to play football, you sort it out between you and Lennie Lawrence." With that I got in my car, I remember it was snowing that night, and headed back southwards down the A1. That loan spell was just before Christmas, I think.

At the end of February 1983, I got a call at Charlton to say that David Pleat had asked to take me back to Luton Town on loan. I had a long chat with David a few years ago at Luton Hoo in 2018 for the special 'Elite 80's evening. He came over to our table and said to me, "Do you know, Steve, I have to get this off of my chest. I've always felt so guilty for railroading you down to Charlton after you'd played such a big part in getting us promoted." I replied, "David, it was football, you made a decision to exchange me for a player that you wanted and who you felt could improve the team. It proved to be the right decision and you sold him later on to Liverpool for £700,000 so it was the right thing to do. I bear no grudges whatsoever, it was just football at the time." I appreciated that he let me know the way he was thinking and how he still felt about the decision after all that time. I guess that's the reason he brought me back there on loan when Brian Stein was out for a long time with a broken metatarsal bone, therefore giving me the opportunity to play in the First Division.

We played four games in that loan period that I was back at Luton. We played Ipswich Town away in my first game back on February 26th, 1983, and were beaten 3-0. We got a 0-0 draw at home to West Brom. We went away to Nottingham Forest, and beat them 1-0. Then we got battered at Highbury losing 4-1 to Arsenal. I didn't score but I was involved in securing four points that helped keep Luton Town in the First Division that year (tongue in cheek).

Looking back, some of the lads should have had the chance to go to bigger clubs, the likes of Brian Stein and Ricky Hill. Paul Walsh did get his move to Liverpool and later on young Mitchell Thomas got his move to Tottenham. Speaking of Mitchell, there are three things that you need as a footballer: one is technique, two is athletic capability and the third is intelligence. The more you have of all of those three elements then the better level you'll play at. Mitchell Thomas was one of the best athletes that I'd ever seen. He was a quick learner as well. He wanted to learn, to improve his technique, he wanted to be involved. He always had a smile on his face. A great athlete and standing at six-foot-two, I wasn't surprised that he did well

I played for Bristol Rovers in the FA Cup against Luton at Kenilworth in 1986. We played on the newly laid AstroTurf pitch and lost 4-0. We came off at the end and I kid you not, that pitch was so unforgiving if your touch wasn't spot on. Now, I'd played in the first ever competitive game in this country on an AstroTurf pitch in 1981 when our Luton Town side made history by winning that game 2-1 at QPR. That pitch at Loftus Road was diabolical but it was still better than the other pitches at Preston and Oldham, which were like actual concrete; they were rock hard! You had to cover yourself in Vaseline. I remember Mark Aizlewood and a few others came off the pitch with burns all over their knees, legs, just everywhere, really. I acknowledge that the modern day 4G pitches are almost on a par with a perfect grass pitch, but back then if you didn't pass to feet, the ball would just roll away from you.

David was a very good manager. A very astute manager, no doubt about that. His attention to detail was fantastic and he was a very good judge of a player to bring into the squad as well as a good judge of when a player needed to be moved on. Certainly, one of the best managers that I had in football.

(BORN 7 OCTOBER 1959, KINGS HEATH, BIRMINGHAM)

# GARRY LINDSEY THOMPSON

## PLAYED AGAINST LUTON TOWN 1982-1986 FOR COVENTRY CITY, WEST BROM, SHEFFIELD WEDNESDAY, & ASTON VILLA

*Garry was always exciting to watch playing in this era 'against' David Pleat's Luton sides and he had that habit of scoring the odd goal too, for the opposition. He had a powerful style but he was also a skilful and intelligent footballer, most certainly one of those players that you'd have liked to see join the ranks at Kenilworth Road. Even though he came close to joining Luton Town FC later on in his career when he was at QPR, he never played for David Pleat.*

My impression of David Pleat was formed when I was a young player at Coventry City where I joined at fifteen/sixteenyears of age. I think David was managing close by to Coventry at Nuneaton Borough. His team there had a decent reputation for wanting to play football, and soon after he ended up at Luton Town, I think we saw he and Howard Wilkinson explode onto the scene at the same sort of time. Both of them had a Good reputation. Howard was more of a dour person while David came across as very intelligent, football orientated, both being great football people but having different styles. I played with Howard at Sheffield Wednesday and he was very direct, aggressive on the front foot. David Pleat's sides always gave the impression that they wanted to play, wanted to be a part of the beautiful

Garry with the author's children, Josh and Charlotte in 2012 at a Luton v Aston Villa Legends match

game. Now, for most people at that time, the beautiful game was battling your ass off for the first sixty minutes and when you got on top of the opposition, in the last fifteen-twenty minutes or so you could actually keep the ball and play some nice football, maybe even score another goal. Fans would always remember the last fifteen to twenty minutes of games back then but when I first came through, apart from the Brazil 1970 side, for most games it was like a war zone, where occasionally a game of football broke out. When David Pleat started doing what he was trying to do at Luton there was a lot of interest and a lot of people thought it was a flash in the pan, but you could see his sides develop over the years with some very good footballers. He proved himself to be an excellent manager. He was very knowledgeable, as everyone could hear for themselves, when he added working in TV as a co-commentator on live football to his already impressive CV.

He got the big job that was coming his way at Spurs following his time at Luton. He is what you would call a 'football man'. Having been involved for so many years, he knows players, has good knowledge, always wanted to play with the ball encouraging his teams to express themselves. He's a very genial fella, easy going. My impression of him over the years never changed. When I was a manager for a little while we'd have conversations about players at times, and I think we took a kid on loan from Spurs at one time. He was always very helpful to younger managers, just a generally nice geezer.

Players that I played with who were also at Luton, and three great lads that immediately come to mind are Les Sealey, while I was coming through at Coventry City, then later on at West Brom I played with Tony Grealish. After that I went to the Villa where I played with Paul Elliott following his move from Luton Town.

I'd known Les since I was about fourteen or fifteen. I was a young kid at Coventry,

a schoolboy, and Les was already a first-year apprentice. By the time I joined Coventry he was a professional playing in the reserves. I passed my apprenticeship and ended up going in digs with Les and Valmore Thomas, Danny Thomas's older brother. They basically looked after me for a while. Les, as a geezer, was one of the loudest men that, probably, you'll ever meet. He was always bubbly, always had something to say, he always had an answer. When I look at the dressing room we had then, it included the likes of Tommy Hutchison, big Jim Holton, Bryan King, Mick Coop, Terry Yorath, Johnny Beck, Mick Ferguson, Ian Wallace and Jim Blyth, who was the regular goalkeeper. You had a seasoned, experienced group. Les was not shy to back his own corner, to back himself to be fair to him. That's how people saw him later play for Manchester United and obviously before that at Luton. Very loud, domineering, letting people know what to do. Sometimes the lads would have a go back at him, especially when an opposition player would get a shot away at say 30 yards. He'd save the shot and then he'd come out screaming at the back four and the midfield players and he'd get it back from them saying, "But that's your job, Les, if they have a shot, you're supposed to make a save." But he wasn't having any of it and would always have the last word.

There were arguments, well, not arguments as such, but just funny little moments. I remember when Dave Sexton was the manager, we'd work on shape all week and on a Friday, we'd have a five-a-side competition that always got physical and aggressive. In these games, everyone played different positions. Les would always play centre forward and he was hopeless, but he would always get the winning goal and he'd do a running commentary of the whole game: "Oh, Sealey's done it again, it's all about Sealey," and he'd score the goal and then run off. This had been going on for a few weeks. By now, Danny Thomas was getting the raging hump with him, so the next game when Les had scored a couple of goals, Danny and Les were having words, and as I said previously, Les would always have the last word, we called it 'last-word-syndrome'. However, this time, before we knew it, Les and Danny were throwing punches. Les wasn't a fighter and Danny Thomas ain't the biggest guy in the world, so it was a slightly comical fight, but then you ended up with a situation whereby behind them, the manager Dave Sexton, whose dad was Archie Sexton, the Middle Weight Boxing Champion (though we didn't know that at the time), would be dropping his shoulder and throwing a punch, giving them boxing tips! We'd be pissing ourself laughing knowing the gaffer should be breaking it up was too busy showing Les and Danny some moves! The lads were still going at it with the fisticuffs like babies so we'd take the mickey out of Les for that for a long time, but even then he'd still have to have the last word.

He was a real Arthur Daley type. We called him 'The Spiv' as he had the sheepskin coat and would sell things out the back of his car. He always had options to get you stuff, cars, boots, jeans; anything Les could get hold of from the London markets he would bring it all back up to Coventry to sell it. He used to do a roaring trade! As I said earlier, I was in digs with him so we'd go out a few times but he had a regular girl and I think he ended up marrying her. Les would always be in and out of the digs; we'd be training up at Coventry then he'd shoot off to London for a few days and come back with a load of gear to sell.

Coventry people talk about Les in the semi-final of the 1980/81 League Cup. In the first leg against West Ham at Highfield Road, I think he basically threw one in, let it slip under his body on the goal line from Billy Bond's header and then I did the back pass which went in to the goal. I was blaming him and he was trying to say that I did call 'KEEPERS'. When I went to pick the ball up Les was on his goal line but by the time I went to pass it back to him he was standing next to me, so you can imagine that I took some serious abuse for that. We did an interview afterwards and if you ever see it, Les skilfully managed to basically say it was my fault. But it was okay, it wasn't a horrible situation, and we recovered to win the tie 3-2 when I scored two of the goals at the right end.

When he left Coventry and went to Luton, there were a lot of Coventry fans that didn't like him because he gave them the V-sign one time after a game when he came back with Luton and they'd beaten Coventry. There was a lot of bad feeling towards him but that was him, whichever team he was playing for at the time he was completely committed to, that was his team and he didn't have time for anybody else. I remember playing for the Albion against Luton where me and Steve Foster had kicked lumps out of each other in a good game, a good battle. Fozzie and I were walking off the pitch together chatting at the end of the game and Les said, "Don't talk to him, Fozzie, don't speak to him. He's been trying to kick lumps out of you and trying to take away our bonus, what are you speaking to him for?"

There were also loads of swear words involved in that pitch side rant, at Fozzie as well. Once the game was done, I saw Les in the bar afterwards and he was good as gold, it was just when he was playing he was one hundred per cent on it and that's what you want from your team mates.

When Les went from Luton to Manchester United it looked like he was just going there as a back-up keeper. I was at Crystal Palace at the time where we ended up playing against Manchester United in the FA Cup Final at the end of the 1989/90 season. I was cup tied though so I didn't play and Les wasn't in the United team in the first game. I saw him after the match where Jim Leighton in the United goal had a nightmare in an eventual 3-3 draw. I was saying to Les that there's half a chance the Alex Ferguson might change it for the replay. To be fair to Les that was the quietest that he'd ever been as I think he was taking in the enormity of it all. He did play in the replay in which Manchester United won 1-0 and he was back to his normal self after that.

One of the last times that I saw Les play before he passed was, I think, at West Ham as a goal keeping coach, but he was playing also in a reserve game against us. I was at Northampton Town. Les was in goal for West Ham. We were chatting, just talking as I was walking around the side of the pitch, just casual like how's it going and all that. He was very calm and composed. As soon as the game started, whistle was blown, he was immediately hollering at his back four completely abusing them, then he turned back to me and said, "Ah, you've got to keep them on their toes, ain't ya, kid!" That was him, all the time concentrating on his stuff, hollering and bickering at them just to let them know what he wanted from them to get the job done. He was a very, very, serious individual on the pitch but a load of fun and games off it.

Paddy Grealish came to the Albion after I'd been there for a few months, and I think they signed him and Stevie Hunt at the same time. I already knew Stevie from our time at Coventry. Tony turned up, this little ginger haired cockney geezer who was apparently Irish as well, but one of the broadest cockneys that you've ever met. A really good footballer. He had great ability, ran the game, shut down very well, and was a decent passer of the ball obviously being a Republic of Ireland international and as a midfield pair with Steve McKenzie; they were very good. Paddy did all of the horrible bits, he'd win the ball and keep it moving and organise everybody with all the shouting and hollering but a very good team player, great in the dressing room. He was lovely, always up for a bit of fun.

Cyrille, myself, Paddy and Stevie Hunt became really good mates and along with our wives we'd go out on a Sunday at least once a month. We'd have dinner at one of our houses where someone would cook and go out a lot together as well. Paddy would always organise everyone. I think his old man had a boozer when he was a kid so he was a really social lad. He was the sort of player that you always want in your team and when things weren't going too well he'd raise the spirits. Paddy was always the go-to-guy for a bit of fun but once the game begun, he was on it. Though even during the game he could drop the odd quip and all that. He was a good footballer and a fantastic team mate.

Playing against Paul Elliott in my second game for the Albion, this being after my debut had ended in a 0-0 against Arsenal at home, my second game was Luton away and David Pleat had just signed this kid from Charlton. Paul Elliott was making his debut in the first team just a week shy of his nineteenth birthday and I saw him warming up. He was a tall, lanky, black kid and I thought, he looks like he's pacey and strong, but I'll have him! We proceeded to have ninety minutes of one of the toughest battles you've ever had. I'd just been signed for £225,000 and I'm not sure but I think that Luton had just signed Paul for around £90,000 from Charlton Athletic. After the game, West Brom manager, Ron Wylie, really laid into me: "I've just spent all this money on you and Elliott has battered you all over the place!" He'd really gone into one as the match had ended in a second successive 0-0 draw. I spoke to Paul Elliott a couple of years later when I went to Villa and asked if he remembered that game at Luton. Paul said, "Yeah, you battered me!" It was funny because I had felt exactly the same in that I thought Paul had knocked lumps off me. From then on I always kept an eye out for him, and at first he'd looked very raw but a real player, a defender who looked like he had it all. He was strong, quick, and good in the air. He could attack the ball and anything over the top, he would eat up. He read the game well and he was a good organiser,too. When I played with him at Villa he was a very good team mate, even though he was in the team that went down; there were a lot of other things going on at Villa at the time. Paul got his move to Italy on the back of that so he must have been doing something right.

In both my career as player and assistant manager, whichever club I was involved in would always be treated really friendly by the Luton Town club, including the staff, the officials, everybody. Sometimes, it can be mayhem out on the pitch, but it was never like that at Luton; they always tried to play football and gave you an opportunity to play as well. They were appreciative if you tried to play football, which didn't really happen that often. I imagine when Luton were dropping through the divisions it might have got a bit volatile there but I wasn't playing by then, so I can't really comment. They'd give you a bit of gyp now and again because they'd be supporting their team but it was never the cauldron of hate that you would get when you went to a lot of other places. You always felt that you could have a chance when you went there, you felt like you could get a result as they'd allow you to play. It was never going to be like Wimbledon, where I wouldn't say was nasty but there was that aggressive element, whereas Luton were always a side where you felt you'd get a good game playing against them.

Talking about stand-out players for Luton during the time we played against them then I would have to say that Steiny (Brian) was a different class. He'd score goals for fun, always bright and looking to get beyond you and cause problems, making those little darting runs in behind, and he had a real eye for goal with the likes of Ricky Hill giving him the passes through for Steiny to finish. He was always a danger and looking to stretch the defence with great movement in the box so he was a striker that you'd always keep an eye out for, but the main man was Ricky Hill. Ricky covered ground, he had great balance where he could protect the ball. I watched a video of him just recently and he was a centre forward's dream. He could see the pass to play people in. He represented his country, so it was good for us especially as a black kid growing up. I think Ricky is a couple of years older than me. We played against each other, but you'd appreciate him as he was a very good footballer. He could score as he had the odd goal in him, but some of the passes into the strikers that he made and his protection of the ball was excellent. There were also the likes of Kirk Stephens and Mal Donaghy; they, too, were good footballers, what you would call 'Luton footballers'. They epitomised what the club was about. They were decent on the ball and tenacious, they could compete but really wanted to play football. Then you're talking about the boys who brought the pain, Fozzie and big Mick Harford, they were very… aggressive, shall we say, both were very tough individuals. Even now, when you see Mick out scouting, if he gives you that look you know he ain't playing games. Mick's a serious individual. I used to love to watch him play, he was a very competitive man, aggressive and had goals in his locker. For Luton, with the silky, skilful team that they were, Mick gave them that toughness along with Fozzie. A special mention for Jake Findlay, who left

Villa and went to Luton. Alan West was probably the first Luton player that I remember as he was playing when I was just starting out as a kid and collecting football cards. Brian Horton played there as well, but Paul Walsh, he played with me at QPR for a while and I knew he was a good player when he was at Luton. But when he joined on loan for a month at QPR, I really got to see just what a good footballer he was for myself. Bright, very aggressive, wanting to get behind people and score goals. And he was strong as well, he used to do loads and loads of weights. I used to ask him, "Why are you doing weights?" and he'd say that he wanted to toughen himself up. He was a tough little bugger! Walshy was a very, very good footballer and those are the lads that stood out for me at Luton Town.

I was approached by Luton when I was at QPR. Gerry Francis was the manager at Loftus Road then. I think I was thirty-one. Luton always used to play a certain way but they used to have big Mick Harford to do all the horrible bits as well as scoring a few goals. I was coming towards the end of my career and I wasn't in the QPR team as Les Ferdinand was tearing it up. So, I'm trying to get the odd game, and was told by my financial advisor that David Pleat was interested in taking me to Luton just as cover until the end of that season and to see what happened from there, as there was talk of an eighteen-month contract. I think David just wanted to bring in some experience to his young side and someone decent in the dressing room. I was interested in the move and it looked like it might be happening, but all of a sudden David Pleat dropped his interest. I was told that Gerry Francis had just said no and said that I was an important member of his squad at QPR, so he wanted to keep me there. If I'd have had a choice at the time then I would have gone to Luton as they were always a good footballing side. It's was a team that as a centre forward you'd want to play for as you know they're going to give you what you need, a decent delivery into your feet, your chest, good balls in and around the box that are going to create opportunities for you to score goals, and, given half the chance, I would've joined Luton Town like a shot.

(BORN 17 JANUARY 1953, SOUTH BANK, NEAR MIDDLESBROUGH)

# IAN TURNER

LUTON TOWN FC 1980 ON LOAN FROM WALSALL

Ian proudly shows his 1976 FA Cup winners medal

*On May 1st, 1976, twenty-three-year-old Ian Turner was on top of the football world having just won the FA Cup Final at Wembley, playing in goal for Second Division Southampton against Tommy Docherty's Manchester United. Managed by Lawrie McMenemy and playing alongside the likes of Mick Channon and Peter Osgood they won the cup 1-0 with Ian making a string of saves early in the game and keeping a clean sheet on the big day.*

*Shortly after the FA Cup win in 1976, Ian suffered cartilage problems in his knees and, whilst taking the time for the operation to have the problem removed, he lost his place at Southampton and went to the NASL to play at Fort Lauderdale. He was in good company playing with George Best and Gordon Banks. He'd had loan spells at both Newport County and Lincoln City in 1978 before a chance to sign for Everton came up after a phone call from the then Everton Manager, Gordon Lee. Ian was actually still on loan at Lincoln at the time they wanted to sign him. The fee being talked about with Lincoln was £16,000, which Gordon Lee was happy to pay. But Lawrie McMenemy hearing it was Everton that were interested pushed the asking price up considerably to more than Everton were prepared to pay, so that move never came off and Ian eventually moved to Walsall in 1979 under player manager, Alan Buckley.*

It was 1980 when David Pleat rang me asking me to go to Luton as a back-up goalkeeper. "I need cover for my first-choice goalkeeper Jake

1978; Ian with Gordon Banks and George Best whilst playing for Ft. Lauderdale Strikers in the NASL

Findlay, for the last couple of months of the season and our young reserve keeper, Alan Judge has a bad ankle injury so I don't want to be left with no cover as we're pushing hard for promotion to the First Division, are you interested?" he asked. I didn't need any time to think over the proposition as by now I was playing for Fourth Division Walsall's reserves in the Central League.

We met up at a motorway services on the M6. I agreed to join Luton Town on loan. I was soon training with the full first team squad, the likes of Ricky Hill, Paul Price, Mick Saxby, David Moss and Brian Stein; the training was a different class. Pleat and Ken Gutteridge were proper coaches with great ideas and principals of how the game should be played, it was a far cry from the type of PT trainers, with a run-them-until-you-drop method of training that was standard thinking at the time, if you can outrun the opposition then you will beat them. Luton made me feel part of it all immediately. They were very inclusive straight away and what I liked the most was that David Pleat never strung me along, he was honest and upfront with me from the moment I met him. "I've got a very good number one in Jake Findlay and a promising young reserve keeper in Alan Judge," Pleat said, "but you're twenty-seven and you've got great experience from your time with Lawrie McMenemy at both Grimsby and Southampton, which will prove valuable, plus you've still plenty of time to re-establish yourself in the game."

I played ten reserve games at the back end of the 1979/80 season with Luton Town and can honestly say now, forty years later, I have fondness and great affection for my short time spent at Kenilworth Road. I went from playing in Walsall Reserves in the Central League to being coached magnificently by Pleat and his staff, training and playing with some wonderful players. They were all good people and it gave me a real buzz back for the game of football again after some difficult years with some difficult people. I played against some great teams during my time in Luton's Combination League side and up against some very good players, too. We played away at clubs including Ipswich Town, Fulham, Chelsea, Leicester City, Norwich City and I remember playing at home to Spurs where they won the game 2-1 with a disputed off-side call that never came,

Ian Turner dives at the feet of Detroit Express England forward Trevor Francis

and a young Micky Hazard was left to run through to score after Wayne Turner had equalised for us earlier on in the second half.

I was still a Walsall player and therefore living in the Birmingham area, so I had the pleasure of travelling down to and from Luton every day for training and matches with Bob Hatton. Bob was about to come to the end of his two years at Luton before moving to Sheffield United later that summer. He was great company and he would talk all about the first team games that he was involved with and equally was just as interested in me talking about the reserve team games.

The Luton reserve side that I played in consisted of an enjoyable group of lads to play with, a great crop of home-grown youngsters coming through, and I enjoyed passing on some of my experience to them. Players like Rob Johnson, Wayne Turner, Clive Goodyear and Frank Bunn all went on to play at the top level in the First Division a few years later, the equivalent to the Premier League today.

I found David Pleat to be an excellent young coach and he was very good to me, things weren't black and white with him. He would take your circumstances into account and he was top class, a real gentleman during my time at Luton.

Ian Turner at home in 2016

I do still have the FA Cup winners' medal from that day in 1976 but regrettably, I don't get to go to the football very often at Southampton, mainly because of the cost as I would never, nor would I want to, get away with going on my own without my family. I also tried to call to buy tickets last season but as I wasn't a member I couldn't purchase any. So, being a member of the club's FA Cup winning side didn't go in my favour that day!

After leaving football, I became an engineer in the oil industry and currently live in Southampton having moved back there seven years ago from living and working just outside Stamford in Lincolnshire. I'd previously been working overseas on Oil Refineries in Malaysia and Saudi Arabia but my second wife, Debbie, wanted to be closer to our family on the South Coast. My granddaughter, Sophie, is ten years old and a budding, keen footballer, and I'm particularly proud of her. I built myself a log cabin man-cave in my back garden where Sophie has set up her Xbox and spends time with me. She insists I don't tell her stories about Goldilocks or such like but instead I regale her with tales about my football career, and if it involves me taking a bite out of an opponent's leg whilst playing in the North American Soccer League, then all the better!

(BORN 1ST FEBRUARY 1943, GLASGOW)

# JOHN SHERIDAN

## LUTON TOWN FC PHYSIO 1979 – 1986

*Back in 1979, whilst doing some work with the FA and helping out Tring Town, at the time John Sheridan was blissfully unaware that his life path was about to completely change on the strength of just one phone call. It came from the newly appointed first team manager at Luton Town, David Pleat. He was, at that time, unknown to John and he introduced himself then explained that he'd got John's number from a contact at the FA after hearing good things about him. David then called to ask John if he was interested in joining the staff at Luton Town as their physio, who were then in the Second Division of the football league. John hadn't worked in league football before and was nervous, not least because of his disability.*

I went along to Luton and was interviewed by David Pleat and his assistant manager at the time, Ken Gutteridge. The meeting went well but I didn't think I would get the job and indeed I told my wife this when I got home and she asked how it had gone. However, the phone rang, it was David Pleat again. He said he didn't want to interview anyone else and was really impressed with me and my honesty. I told him I wasn't sure if I had the confidence to be a football league physio, not least a disabled physio. I said that I'd do the reserves and see how we got on from there.

David was and is a superb man, he gave me a chance to work at a football league club that very few others would have done. He insisted upon having the highest possible standards put in place where all the small percentages collectively can make such a big difference.

I joined Luton Town at a marvellous time. A real golden era was emerging where everything just seemed to align with the staff, and along

John, with arms aloft, follows David Pleat onto the Maine Road pitch at the final whistle in May 1983

with David and Ken there was also John Moore and David Coates. Players, such as Mossy, Ricky Hill and a little later on Brian Horton were great people as well as players who really took to me and I am still friends with them now. I happily attend social evenings with them and the occasional round of golf with Mick Harford. And as for the fans, they were great to me straight away and would always cheer and wave to me. I was still worried about my limp and running onto the pitch to treat injured players, though thankfully I didn't have to go on in my first six games and then when I did go on, I grew hardened to the harsh comments made by opposing fans.

I remember later in my career at Luton we were away at Old Trafford on a terrible day weather-wise, pouring down with rain which made the pitch very muddy and slippery, and one of our players was injured at one end of the pitch. I went on and at the same time another of our players had gone down at the Stretford End. I naturally thought the other physio would run on to treat our other player as such was the etiquette, but to my horror they didn't. So, in these terrible conditions, I had to limp from one end of the Old Trafford pitch to the other, slipping about in the mud. I was getting a load of stick from the Manchester United fans but after I treated the second player I stood up, bowed, and pretended to doff my cap to them. They loved this and started to applaud, and I found this was the best

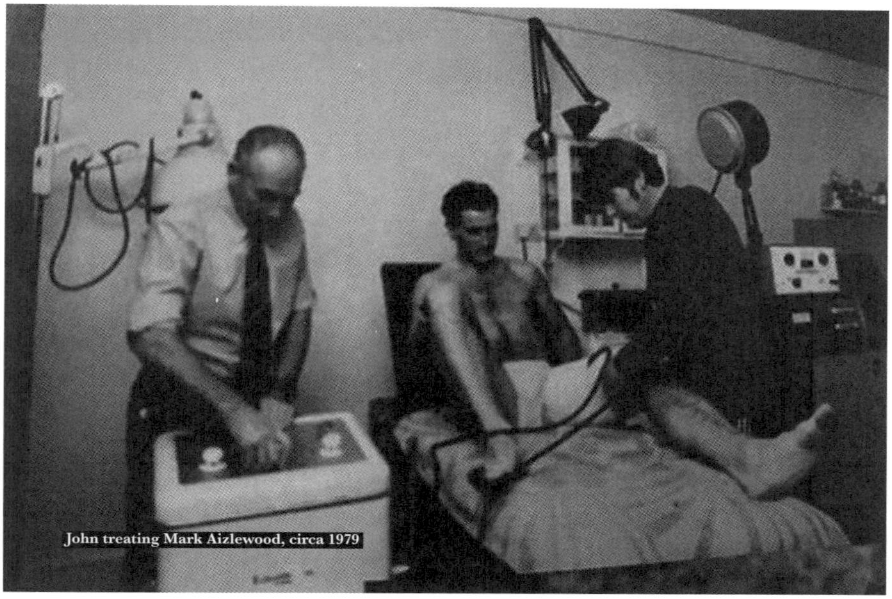

John treating Mark Aizlewood, circa 1979

way to deal with situations like this. In fact, I felt that my limp and pipe gave me a bit of personality for people to remember me by. I remember passing Brian Clough in the early days in the First Division; I think he and others only remembered me at first because of the limp and I was fine with that.

I was also the kitman, so I would arrive early at around 9am on a home-match day. I would set out my medical kit and the playing kit before some players would be in for treatment. Usually, these would be players that weren't in the starting line up for that day as the team would be announced to players and staff the day before so everyone knew what was happening and what was required. We very rarely did late fitness tests on a match day, unless someone had been away with a cold or something, then they would come in to see the Doc, Dr Berry. The players would start to arrive at Kenilworth Road around midday and then we'd go for a pre-match meal up at the Chiltern Hotel or the one on Compton Ave. After that, it was back to the club and players would drift in for strapping and such like, you'd get to know their routine and you would leave them be to run through that. Stan and Ian Sagers would help with the players' pre-match massage rubs. On away matches, I would often go to the opposition ground the afternoon before the match to put out the kit and then to set up my medical room and to make sure that the facilities were adequate before

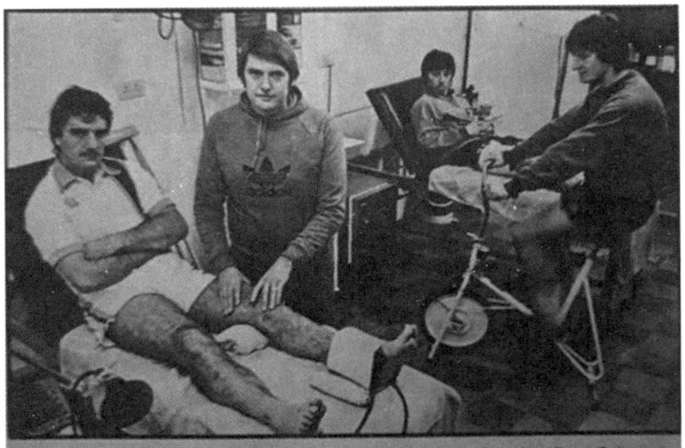

John Sheridan pictured treating Lilly Fuccillo. *Picture: Evening Post Echo*

heading back to the players and staff at the hotel.

So many games stand out from my time at Luton, but I think the best one for pure emotion was the Manchester City match on the last day of the 1982/83 season at Maine Road. Looking around at the players in the hotel that morning everyone knew that we would win the game, which is what we needed to do to stay in the First Division. I remember looking over at Mal Donaghy, usually a quiet character, and he was really up for the game. We just knew that we'd get the win, no matter how late, and when Raddy got that goal after coming on as a substitute with only a few minutes to go, I ran on the pitch after David Pleat, to an outpouring of incredible emotion. Unfortunately, it turned ugly on and off the pitch. Paul Elliott and I were surrounded by Manchester City fans and for a few moments we had to defend ourselves. We were certainly not the aggressors in the situation, which was quickly broken up by horse mounted Police. Then, leaving the ground, a gentleman was run over by the team bus and I went out to help him, but while I did so he spat on me yelling, "You've put us down."

It was so sad to hear of Raddy's sudden passing in 2020. We'd all met up the year before at David Pleat's Elite 80's social evening and it was such a shock when the news came through. When he left Luton in 1984 he said to me, "John, you are a real professional," and this meant a lot to me coming from him. When he'd joined Luton, he couldn't speak any English and I remember taking him home for lunch to help him settle in; he was a lovely man.

The players really loved playing for club in this era, even loan players wanted to stay. I remember Micky Droy coming to the club on loan from Chelsea. After only a few games he got injured, I think away at Manchester United, and he asked me if he could stay at Luton for his treatment. Colin Todd was the same as he came in and was quickly injured around the same time as David was trying to sort out the troublesome centre half position due to Paul Elliott still being out injured from his broken leg. The

2019; John shakes hands with his long time friend David Pleat with Brian Horton enjoying the moment too

situation was finally resolved with the signing of Steve Foster, rescued by David from Aston Villa reserves, and what a player he turned out to be for Luton, a true inspirational character and leader. I went with Paul Elliott to hospital when he was nearing full fitness after the leg break where he had a special pad made to go under the shin pad as it was a mid-tibia break. After he got back to fitness I don't think he played too many games for us, and I don't know if Luton needed the money but Paul soon moved to Aston Villa. He came to see me to ask for my opinion on his knee after the terrible challenge from Dean Saunders in 1992 when playing for Chelsea away at Liverpool. Players kept a trust in you long after they left and played for other clubs. Paul actually gave me a shirt from his days in the Italian League with Pisa from a match against Napoli when he marked none other than Diego Maradona. In fact, I have quite a collection of shirts given to me, mainly from players that I'd looked after a lot during a particular season. Gazza gave me his FA Cup semi-final shirt from the Wembley game against Arsenal in 1991 when he scored that amazing free kick, and Gary Lineker gave me one of his World Cup shirts from Italia 90. I do have a lot from over the years and I have kept them all.

The most disappointing game was another obvious one. The 1985 FA Cup semi-final defeat at Villa Park to Everton. We had played so well for so long in the match and the next day we were all on the floor wondering how we'd lost the match, but we bounced back. I often wonder how far we could have gone had David stayed at Luton, what players he would have signed, and perhaps the club would have continued in its upwards trajectory.

I didn't want to leave Luton, it was my team, the club that I'd supported as a boy. I had to think long and hard about it when David asked me and Trevor Hartley to join him at Tottenham. I certainly couldn't have done the job at Tottenham had it not been for my time at Luton. We had special players for sure at Luton Town but Tottenham was another level where almost all the players were senior internationals, Hoddle, Waddle, Ardiles, Claesen, etc. The money was okay at Luton and I would have happily stayed on but I had to think of my family's security with the offer to join David at Tottenham.

I went on to serve under Terry Venables after David Pleat left Tottenham and ultimately ended up back at Luton via Leicester City. David called me when he went back to Luton to ask me to join him again but there was no way I could go back full time, so I agreed to return on a consultancy basis with Clive Goodyear also back at the club as full time physio. I also went out to Lazio to aid Paul Gascoigne with his return to fitness as he trusted me from our time together at Tottenham and while I was there, Lazio asked me to work with some of their other players. I ended up working not only with Paul but with the likes of Thomas Doll, Karl Heinz Riedle and Giuseppi Signori. Shortly after the World Cup final at Italia 90, I had the pleasure to be the physio for the World XI team that played against Peter Shilton's England XI team in his farewell to international football game played at White Hart Lane. Amongst others on my World XI were Roger Milla, fresh from his moment of fame with Cameroon at Italia 90, and also Franz Beckenbauer.

None of this would have happened to me had it not been for that phone call out of the blue from David Pleat back in 1979.

## (BORN 30TH MARCH 1967, LUTON)

# MARK CADEN BURKE

### LUTON TOWN FC 1982-84

*Mark Burke graced the Kenilworth Road pitch much earlier than when he joined as a promising young Cardinal Newman schoolboy in 1982. There's Ciné film evidence to show Mark taking the field at just short of his eighth birthday. Shot on March 22nd, 1975 against the then-League Champions of England, Leeds United, Mark is seen leading the teams out kicking the ball as a mascot for the day.*

It was a great thrill for me as a local Luton lad as my grandad, who was a steward at Kenilworth Road and used to look after the Maple Road seats, arranged this absolute treat for me for my birthday through my membership in the Junior Hatters. My abiding memories from the game, which was recently shown again on BT Sports and then ITV4 as part of the Big Match Revisited series, was that I managed to miss all three goals in this 2-1 win for Luton. Following me being paraded out onto the pitch, I was then hurried back up the tunnel just before kick-off and into the changing rooms. Within two minutes a big roar went up and someone came up the tunnel yelling, "Yes, one-nil, Johnny Aston." I was still getting my things together when the same voice cried out twelve minutes into the game, "Two-nil to the Town, Peter Anderson." I finally made my way up into the stand to meet up with my grandad to watch the rest of this thrilling encounter against the likes of Joe Jordan, Gordon McQueen, Norman Hunter, Frank and Eddie Gray, Johnny Giles, Terry Yorath... Quite a team, eh! With a few minutes to go, as per normal, my grandad would hurry us out of the ground to miss the crowd and as it happened, miss the last goal too, as Joe Jordan made the most of a mistake by the young Paul Futcher to pull a goal back for Leeds United and to set up a

Mark during a Luton Town youth team match

grandstand finish. Luton held on but I even missed seeing the game the following day when it was shown on TV, as there were no video players back then in 1975 and I'd been taken out for the day for my birthday. I only just got to see the goals from the game recently all these years later with the match finally getting a re-run, but my love for Luton Town certainly started there.

I've got a scrap book somewhere with some dodgy photos of me at Luton, but I can't find it so I don't think anyone believes I played for them! There was a photo taken on the pitch of the whole team together in May 1984 at Kenilworth Road, just before the Southern Junior Floodlit Cup Final second leg against Colchester United, but I can't track that down. I've got the team sheets but I've never seen that picture taken of the team on the pitch.

I went to Cardinal Newman High School in the town and played for St Josephs on a Sunday. John Moore saw me play for St Joe's and from there he invited me for a trial in a match between Luton Town Under 18s and Cambridge United away in a Southern Counties Youth League match. In fact, I think I must hold the record of playing the most matches in that league ever because the good ones coming through used to move quickly up to the reserves and the bad ones were got rid of. I had a couple of years at Luton and then a year at QPR, so I had three years playing in that league. That was my first match away at Cambridge United and I remember it because I came up against Andy Sinton and Mark Cooper who went on to Tottenham. I played centre half, Marc North was playing in goal for us, Garry Parker centre midfield and little Steiny, Mark, up top with Cahal McConville. We had a good little side and came up against a decent team at Cambridge, but I did well so I was invited back again and managed to see the season out while I was in my least year in senior school. That particular season was memorable for me, I call it my claim to fame. I was playing for the youth team and doing really well when the FA Youth

Mark playing for the youth team circa 1982

Cup started which consisted at that time of Stacey North, Mitchell Thomas, Tim Breacker, Ray Daniel, Mark Watts, and Cahal up front with Richard Cadette or Mark Stein. Little Steiny used to be the Number 12.

Luton Town drew Newport County away and because I'd done really well with the Saturday team I got invited along to the training session. It was snowing and icy and the training session took place on the car park in Maple Road by the director, players' and staff entrance. They had some little floodlights up in there. I did really well in this training session so I was excused from school that day and was allowed to travel down to Wales with the youth team to Newport. I was given a tracksuit with all the 'Bedford Trucks' logos on it and I was loving it. There was me still at school and here I am on the first team coach with Stacey and Mitchell and all these great lads. I felt like a was living the dream, feeling like a pro. When we got to Newport, Tim Breacker had a little bit of a knock and that was the reason I was travelling, just in case. Tim had a fitness test, which he passed, but when the staff wrote out the team, sheet they'd put me down as Number 12 as the sub, so poor old Mark Stein got left out because in those days you were only allowed the one sub. Mark had gone all the way down there to sit on the bench but not even as the named sub, so that was my claim to fame that I'd kept Mark Stein out of the team that night. It was a cold night there, I remember running up and down the pitch to keep warm whilst getting a bit of stick off the Newport fans. We won there but I didn't get on unfortunately. I did stay in and around that side though, and I travelled with them that year to Oxford United at their old Manor Ground where we won in a replay after drawing at Kenilworth Road. I was with the team at Norwich City on that run where we got all the way to the semi-finals. In fact, Norwich City was the two legged semi-final that year and I still have the team sheet from the away leg.

I absolutely loved being part of the squad, and you have to remember that at the time I was still a fifth year in senior school playing for my home town team, my team that I supported and that seven years earlier I had been a mascot for against Leeds United. I was on the youth team coach just arriving back at Kenilworth Road on the day of the famous Raddy Antic winner up at Maine Road against Manchester City, the game that kept Luton in the First Division and sent Man City down. I can't remember if we'd been playing at Brighton or Spurs that day with the youth team. Anyway, we'd been following the game on the radio on our way home and we'd literally pulled into the car park in Maple Road just as Raddy scored, so we were all jumping up and down on the coach going mad and celebrating survival. However, it came to decision time at the end of the season and I was thinking it was going to be brilliant as I'm leaving school and going to be taken on as a full time apprentice. I'd been playing the whole season pretty much since I was there and we were all talking amongst ourselves about who was going to be offered the apprenticeships, as in those days you didn't have ten or eleven apprentices getting signed on, you only had the four or five and I missed the boat. I'll never forget it, I laugh about it now, but it broke my heart really. I knocked on Trevor Hartley's office door and went in. "So, Trev, I'm coming to the end of my school year and I was just wanting to know about next year?" I said. I'd gone in there full of confidence but Trevor turned around and said, "Well unfortunately Burkey, we're in the First Division now and we're looking to recruit potential First Division quality players. Had we been back in the Second Division I think we would have taken you on." I just thought, wow, and my whole world fell apart a little bit. However, I look back now and at the time they'd not long since signed Paul Elliott, which meant him and Mal Donaghy in the first team. In the reserves you had Saxby and Clive Goodyear, then backing them up was Stacey North and Mitchell Thomas. That was six quality centre halves so they didn't need another and as they had Marvin Johnson coming up through the schoolboy sides as well, I was just in the wrong place and position, unfortunately.

But, because I was local, they did invite me to the pre-season in the summer going into the 1983/84 season and I did really well when I got the chance to train with the first team occasionally. In the 11v11 full practice matches, there was Paul Walsh and Brian Stein up top against myself and

Stacey North at centre half, and even though it was only a training game, I'll always remember it. We won 1-0, so that was a nice little memory for me as I think it was soon after that Steiny and Walshy were playing together for England against France. I took a lot of what I learnt under Pleaty into my own management and one of those lessons being to have those full 11v11 training games, first team vs mix of reserves and youth. A lot of the time they do end up with the first team losing those training games as the lads out of the team or coming up through the ranks feel they have something to prove. But perhaps that helps drive them to give that bit extra effort, which is great.

We used to train down at the old Brache every day, where Luton Town train, but they've spent some money on the facilities since our day. We'd all meet at Kenilworth Road in the morning and then get on the bus driven by Jim McCabe. We'd drive in the back way down at the bottom off Park Street and Cutenhoe Road. It was that summer where Trevor Hartley 'done us a good one'. They took us for a session in the morning where they'd really run us, and we were quite tired as we broke off for lunch. We went into the changing rooms and Stacey North had found some cricket stumps and a bat and ball in the old groundsman hut. So, we set up a little cricket match, put the stumps in and Trevor Hartley came over and said, "Oh yeah, I play cricket, I'll play a little game with you, I'll bat." Trevor was a good cricketer and there was Stacey and Mitchell and the other boys all bowling at him. Trevor was smashing it everywhere and we were all running around the field trying to get him out. Even though we were having a great time, we just couldn't get him out. Then it came to the end of lunchtime, he called us over and he'd sucked us right in. He said, "How the hell have you got any energy to play cricket? You were obviously not worked hard enough this morning so you're all going to do double this afternoon." A life lesson for me and the other lads by Trevor right there!

I'd now moved on to Luton Sixth Form College and was playing again every Saturday morning week in-week out, going back for the first team games if they were at home at Kenilworth Road. Along with the apprentices we were to help the ground staff fork the pitch at half time. The full apprentices didn't really like it, but I loved it. It was February 1984, half time on the pitch, and I was there with my fork. I remember Luton playing Liverpool and it was lashing down with rain but I didn't have my boots with me so I was wearing a type of crocs that we'd wear back then. I put a pair of tracksuit bottoms over my Farah's (all the cool kids were wearing them) and Sammy Lee was coming towards me. I was a little star struck thinking, Wow, it's Sammy Lee! He then turned to me and said something that I couldn't understand, I just couldn't hear him, but I still just nodded and said, "Yeah, yeah, yeah!" He probably wanted me to go and fork a particular area but I'll never know. The lads I went to school with were ribbing me years later saying, "I remember seeing you on the pitch at half time with Sammy Lee when Luton played Liverpool."

I've still got my autograph book from back when doing the ground duties and one time, when we were playing Manchester United, I wanted to get all of their autographs as they came through. I tell you something, Ray Wilkins that day was different class, what a gentleman he was. He stopped for a little chat while he signed my autograph book writing, Best Wishes, Ray Wilkins. That's another memory that always stayed with me with those United players coming through just up the back by the players tunnel.

We played Millwall in the league cup at Kenilworth Road that year and I was getting absolutely battered, really beaten up by a certain Teddy Sheringham who was a year older than me. He was already the same size then as he was when he broke into the senior team at Millwall: massive. It was something that I learnt from that day as I was really getting battered and I didn't even win one header. John Moore just said to me, "Look, sometimes you know the forwards got the better of you and there's more ways to skin a cat. Go forward as if you're going to challenge for it and at the last second just back off, drop off and he'll end up flicking it on to you." I took that advice into my game, so that night John Moore certainly helped coach me on the spot and show me what to do there. I got on very well with John and when it came to the club making the decision on me, I think he would have kept me on but it was Trevor Hartley and Pleaty who gave it the 'no', so to speak. As I said, perhaps Pleaty was thinking he'd got Paul Elliott, Mal Donaghy and all the ones I mentioned before and was wondering if he really needed me, too. I got the second chance I think, because I was local and I'd done okay, it wasn't costing them anything and Steiny, Mark Stein, who was a year older than me, had been non-contract that year as well.

Pleaty would come to the youth games on a Saturday morning and at half time would come into the dressing room and call me Marshall, Marshall Burke. I think there was a left back called that in the league at Blackburn or Bolton and I did think at the time that Pleaty was keeping an

1984/85 during his non-contract season with QPR

eye on him. Perhaps when he saw me it was in his head: 'Marshall'. I don't really know if there was anything in that but it was something that stuck with me over the years.

All of this was leading up to the two-legged final against Colchester United in April 1984. We went away in the first leg, I wasn't very well actually but I was at Layer Road and didn't play. I think Luton lost 4-1 there in the first game. Then, they came back to Kenilworth Road for the second leg and even to this day it was one of the best midfield performances that I've seen. Garry Parker was unbelievable that night, he absolutely ran the show from centre mid, and little Steiny scored. I think Kingsley Black may have come off the bench that night. After the game John Moore came up to me and said, "Burkey, thanks ever so much for everything that you've done for us, good luck for the future." It didn't come as such a shock to know I wasn't to be offered a full apprenticeship as I'd gone into Trevor Hartley's office that year before to be told as much.

I went to train the pre-season of 1984 with Hitchin Town as Alan West was the player-manager. While I was at Luton I'd still been playing for St Joe's on a Sunday. The season finished and St Joe's and Hitchin Town Youth were the top two teams in the Chiltern Youth League. We played Hitchin and beat them and following that, Hitchin Town invited me down for pre-season. The Hitchin youth team manager at the time was a fella called Jeff Southall, whose son, David, was an apprentice at QPR. The first game of the season, QPR's Youth played Ipswich Town away and they got hammered 5-1, so on the back of that, Chris Gieler, who was in charge of the youth set up at QPR, spoke to Jeff and asked if he'd got any players that could play from the Under 18s team. At first Jeff said no, not really, but then he thought of me, knowing I was training with Hitchin's first team and so he told Chris at QPR that I might be worth looking at. They invited me down for a trial, midweek it was, down at Loftus Road on their plastic pitch where they'd arranged a game against Wimbledon, which was to give Andy Sayer some match practice as he'd been injured and needed some game time as Wimbledon wanted to put him in their first team on the following Saturday. I played directly up against Andy and I marked him out of the game and straight after the match, Chris invited me upstairs and said he wanted to sign me on a non-contract basis and did I want to play for them. So I thought, Well, I'm going to be playing at Loftus Road every other week, yeah definitely. As soon as I had said yes, out came a pair of Adidas astro turf boots! Wow, I thought, I'll definitely do this.

I played for the whole season there, again in the South East Counties League, and I really think I must have held the record for the most appearances in that league. I played that year with Gavin Peacock and Gavin McGuire then at the end of that season, we went to Holland for an Under 21 tournament with the likes of Martin Allen, David Kerslake and Gary Cooper joining up with the Under 18s. It was a great weekend, we did brilliant. I was only used as a squad player coming on, though, as a sub every now and then. The teams we played were unbelievable: East Germany Under 21s, Czechoslovakia Under 21s, Holland Under 21s and then there was Celtic, Ajax, PSV and Feyenoord; it was a great weekend that I'll never forget.

Pat Holland, the former West Ham player, was the manager of the QPR team at the tournament, and we were coming back through Heathrow Airport, walking through the Customs area. I'm a young, naive green kid and I looked at the customs officer and just smiled at him. "Alright, how are you?" I said. Straight away he pulled me over. "Can we have a look in your suitcase?" he said. I'd got nothing to hide but Pat Holland got the hump because we'd got a coach waiting for us. Pat came over trying to hurry me up, telling the customs officer to hurry up and there was nothing to worry about. But the customs guy turned to Pat Holland and said, "Oh, is that so, sir, well I'd like to look in your bag as well now!" The customs guy let me go while Pat had to unpack the whole of his bag. When he caught up with me on the coach he was none too happy. At the end of the year, it was the same as previously at Luton: "Thanks very much for all your efforts this year but we've got nothing for you, unfortunately." And so, that next pre-season in 1985, I was back in training at Hitchin Town and that was it. I've been there ever since, first as a player and now as the first team manager.

(BORN 12TH DECEMBER 1966, LUTON, BEDFORDSHIRE)

# LEE JOHN PAYNE

LUTON TOWN FC 1982-1985 (YOUTH & RESERVE NON-CONTRACT)

*Born and raised in Luton, attending Denbigh Road infants, Wauluds Juniors and Lea Manor High School in the town, as a very young child, Lee could hear the roar from Kenilworth Road from the family home in Norman Road.*

I grew up with that sound in my ear. My family was very much linked with Luton Town Football Club as there was always a little bit of mystery within it because of the famous Joe Payne, who still holds the league scoring record of ten goals in one game back in 1936. There was always a special air of mystery around the fact of us possibly being related as my grandad, along with Dad and his brothers, were all Lutonians. My grandad, bless him, he's passed now, was involved in football. He was renowned amongst the local footballing circles in Bedfordshire for being a very strict referee. He had no qualms of sending players off whatsoever! He was a brilliant referee and he should have made it to the football league referees' list. He worked for Luton Borough Council all of his life; so perhaps the two career paths didn't quite go hand in hand? My father, Ken and my Uncle Brian were both very good local footballers.

My mum does have a footballing claim to fame on her side of the family, though, as my grandmother's uncle, Arthur "Ikey" Bryan, was a South London fishmonger local to Charlton Athletic. He used to walk around the pitch at The Valley with haddock nailed to a large stick and he'd be shouting ,"Addick, get your Addick!" which was how 'Haddock' was pronounced in the South London dialect. This would have been in the late 1930s and famously, this is where Charlton Athletic became known as 'The Addicks' as the club's nickname.

My journey began as a supporter of the club. I used to make the short walk down from our house in Norman Road, along with my brother, Colin, and my dad from around the age of seven. In the Luton side at that time were John Aston, Peter Anderson, and of course, Alan West. We later moved away from Norman Road and to the Marsh Farm Estate.

Lee lining up for his junior school team in Luton

The first medal that I ever won in football was playing for Wauluds Junior School. I was presented with my medal by the Luton Town captain at the time, Alan West. I remember looking up at him and trembling with excitement, I just couldn't believe that Alan was giving me this medal as I'd watched him from the Oak Road terrace and now here he was in front of me. I would only have been around ten or eleven years old so it was a big thrill. On my school team that day was a lad who would play a massive role, not only in football but in my life in general. That lad was Mark Burke. We had two years together being invited by John Moore to play for Luton when we were still in high school. Then we played together again at Hitchin after I'd left Luton and Burkey had spent a year with QPR. I've known Mark since we were kids at school, a lifelong friend!

Going back to my schooldays, to be invited to join the youth team set up at Luton Town, was just something else. Having stood on the terrace countless times, it was really special to now have the opportunity to play for the club. My nemesis (a friendly nemesis at that) in the youth and reserves, was Kingsley Black. Kingsley was a Cardinal Newman lad, but from across town living just off of Farley Hill. 'Kings' was a year younger than me in terms of school years. We were both out and out left wingers and this gave David Pleat, John Moore and Trevor Hartley a dilemma.

David Pleat told me this later on when he tried to sign me for Leicester City, before I moved from Barnet to Newcastle United. He told me that he was always in a dilemma over me and Kingsley. I let him off the hook by telling him that he made the right choice for Luton Town as I think the club received two million pounds for him when Brian Clough signed Kingsley for Nottingham Forest in the early 1990s. Kingsley was a super player, but with him being younger than me, I felt the club always had their eye a little bit more on him.

I was in and around the club from about the age of fourteen or fifteen, so I have great memories of the players that I trained with and was fortunate enough to play with, especially Ricky Hill and Brian Stein. I actually lived with Mark Stein in a little apartment near People's Park in Luton and I played with him a lot in the youth and reserves sides. What a career that he went on to have after he left Luton. There wasn't a great deal to Mark's game, but talk about a natural goalscorer! He would come alive in the opponent's penalty area, in and around the six-yard box. His style of play put me in mind of the great Brazilian forward, Romário. Mark came in one pre-season with us at Barnet when his brother, Edwin was there. He trained with us, but you'd never have known that Mark would progress to be a Premier League player. He just did the solid work well, but nothing to stand out, no ego, no tricks or anything special. You'd know that in a ninety-minute match in the premier league, if you got the ball into 'Little Steiny' he would score. Mark set the Premier League record for number of consecutive games that he scored in, scoring in seven games in a row. This was when he was playing for Chelsea so it would have been 1993/94 season. Mark had hit his prime form by then.

I remember training up at 'The Lux' (Electrolux Sports Ground) with that great Luton team that had just been promoted to the top division of English football in 1982. I was rubbing shoulders with these guys and it was just like a dream for me, as I was this kid from the Marsh Farm Council Estate in Luton.

Speaking of 'The Lux' training ground, I vividly recall an altercation between Jake Findlay and Herbie Smith where they had a full-on fight in the showers after training one day. It was some scuffle let me tell you, as they were two big heavy men! I was watching this as a fifteen-year-old kid. It was like a heavy weight fight, they were sprawling around in the water until eventually the other lads managed to split them up. But there certainly were some big characters looking back at the time. Later on in my career, I played again with Herbie Smith down at Barnet and I reminded him of that incident. Herbie being Herbie was quite proud that I recalled that happening as he felt he'd gotten the better of big Jake that day.

My dad, Ken Payne, was manager at Wealdstone, so I used to go along with him. I'd be in the changing room before the games and I would, occasionally, sit on the bench with him as well. They were in Gola League then, which later became the Vauxhall Conference and is now known as the Vanarama National League. They had a very good side at the time, which included two ex-Luton Town youngsters, Tom Murphy and Nigel Johnson. One particular game, I stood to the side of the dugout. There was a young boy playing for Wealdstone and suddenly I was aware that somebody had come over and stood next to me. This would have been around 1978/1979 so I would have been around eleven or twelve. I looked around and saw it was David Pleat standing right there! So, I nervously put my head down thinking I couldn't believe he was standing right next to me.

The game continued and eventually he looked at me and asked, "Are you a Wealdstone fan?" to which I replied that I was, but at that stage I didn't mention that my dad was the Wealdstone manager. David continued, "I like the left back, what's he like when people run at him?" I couldn't believe he was asking me, this little kid, what I thought of this player he was watching. But David was very much like that, he would source snippets of information; he was like an encyclopaedia of football knowledge. He was amazing at obtaining and valuing information from people, both young and old. I said to him, "He's only just broken into the first team here, but he's been outstanding." He nodded and continued looking out on the pitch saying, "Okay, yeah, I like him." David returned three times to Wealdstone that I know of, however, he never signed the player.

A few years later I was at Luton Town and David was going to put me on a YTS contract, but he was hesitating and I took this opportunity to say, "Gaffer, I'd really like to remind you of a moment that you may recall." He asked me what it was and I continued: "About four or five years ago, when I was a little kid on the terrace at Wealdstone, you stood next to me and asked about the left back they had playing at the time." Immediately, he put his hand up to his head and said, "Stuart Pearce!" I nodded and said, "Yep, it was Stuart Pearce." I've run into David Pleat many times over the years in and around football and the first thing that he always says to me is, "Stuart Pearce, I should've signed him!"

David Pleat never did offer me a contract with Luton Town and I have no issues with that at all. I was a late developer physically, so I left Luton at seventeen years of age and later, I counted all the clubs that I'd played for right up until I finally made my professional debut at twenty-one for Newcastle United in 1988.

I must have played for every single team within Bedfordshire at any level, including Warden Rangers, Offley, Arlesey, Dunstable Town, Baldock, Hitchin Town, Stevenage Borough, Barnet, then of course all the Sunday morning teams that I used to play for too, as you did back then. You'd play on a Saturday afternoon and again on the Sunday morning. I also played for top Luton side St Josephs, as well as the North Home Counties representative side too, alongside the Gallagher brothers (Des and Alan, not Liam and Noel). That team was really strong, but then the local sides were all strong sides back then.

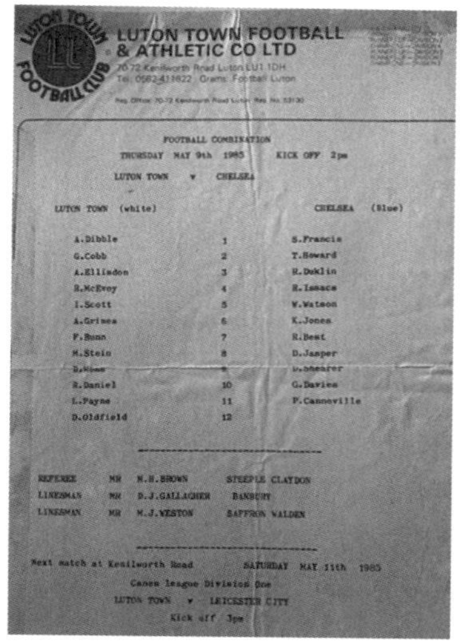
LUTON TOWN FOOTBALL & ATHLETIC CO LTD

FOOTBALL COMBINATION

THURSDAY MAY 9th 1985 KICK OFF 2pm

LUTON TOWN v CHELSEA

| LUTON TOWN (white) | | CHELSEA (Blue) |
|---|---|---|
| A.Dibble | 1 | S.Francis |
| G.Cobb | 2 | T.Howard |
| A.Ellisdon | 3 | R.Duklin |
| R.McEvoy | 4 | R.Isaacs |
| I.Scott | 5 | W.Watson |
| A.Grimes | 6 | K.Jones |
| F.Bunn | 7 | R.Best |
| M.Stein | 8 | D.Jasper |
| [illegible] | [illegible] | D.Shearer |
| R.Daniel | 10 | G.Davies |
| L.Payne | 11 | P.Canoville |
| D.Oldfield | 12 | |

REFEREE MR N.H.BROWN STEEPLE CLAYDON
LINESMAN MR D.J.GALLAGHER BANBURY
LINESMAN MR M.J.WESTON SAFFRON WALDEN

Next match at Kenilworth Road SATURDAY MAY 11th 1985
Canon League Division One
LUTON TOWN v LEICESTER CITY
Kick off 3pm

Lee, number 11 on the team sheet for Luton Town reserves v Chelsea in May 1985

I learnt so much from all of that football education and to top it off, when I went to Hitchin Town in 1985, who was the manager at the time? My hero from Luton Town and the man who presented me with my first medal in football all of those years earlier, Alan West. I used to go to Alan's church in High Town, Luton, and I became a Christian with Alan as my pastor. I've had a very close relationship with Alan and his wife, Cathie, for over forty years. I'm fortunate to have met a lot of special people throughout my life but I have to say that, for me, both Alan and Cathie West were just on another level.

Alan became a Christian, giving his life to Christ, somewhat ironically whilst visiting his in-laws in Christchurch, New Zealand of all places, in the summer of 1976. He was playing in America that summer but spending the small break in the season in New Zealand, before he then came back to England and to his Luton Town team mates to tell them he had devoted his life to Christ. This was the mid to late 1970s so the other players at the club were, initially, sceptical of the whole thing, to put it mildly.

I must have played about fifteen reserve team games at Luton Town, as my dad used to keep the team sheets that they produced and handed out on the entry gate for those games. Looking over them is amazing to see the strength of teams. The games I played in would consist of Mark Stein, Ray Daniel, Ashley Grimes, Andy Dibble, Frankie Bunn, David Oldfield and David Moss. Mossy was coming to the end of his playing days at Luton, but it was an education to play with him as well as those other players. The strength of the opposition was amazing too, and you would play in the stadiums, which made sense as it got the players used to playing at those venues like Stamford Bridge, Highbury, White Hart Lane. It was fantastic and it didn't matter that there was hardly anyone there to watch. The diameters of the stadium pitches are different to modern day Academy venues, it's a different feel, and I think that you even have a different reaction on the ball. It's strange because it's enclosed and there's less wind, it's just a completely different environment to when you're in the stadium and you don't get those experiences nowadays coming through playing in the Under 23s sides. I remember playing at Stamford Bridge and at Highbury for Luton against Chelsea and Arsenal, who also put out really strong sides. The thing for me was that feeling of playing in the stadiums. Despite it being close to empty, you'd look around and think wow, this is Highbury!

Mitchell Thomas lived about four streets away from me on Marsh Farm. I lived on Sherd Close whereas Mitchell lived on Burnt Close. He had a large family including his brothers, Byron and Michael. His dad was big tough fella, but his mum was probably tougher (laughing). We used to play in front of the Purley Shopping Centre on a massive green area and we'd put a goal up in the summer and have twenty lads playing, a proper ten against ten match. There were some really good footballers playing in those games, but interestingly enough Mitchell never really played with us a lot. He wasn't one of those lads where you'd say that Mitchell's definitely going to make it in football. In fact, his younger brother, Michael, was probably better technically, than Mitchell. I remember the word going around that Mitchell had been offered a place at Luton Town as part of the government funded 'YOP' (Youth Opportunities Scheme) and we weren't shocked but we were still a little surprised. What happened to Mitchell was amazing! Over the next six months he developed into this man-monster, seemingly both in height as well as in statue. I recall watching him, probably in one of his very early games in the first team and I had to pinch myself. I couldn't believe that was Mitchell from the Marsh Farm estate, he just looked like he belonged out there, like he'd played there his whole life.

For me, Mitchell was a superstar because knowing him growing up and going to the same school as him, he never gave me the impression that he had that in him. And yet, when he was given the opportunity, if ever there was anyone who made the most of an opportunity then here he was.

When I met up again with him years later, talking to him was like talking to another encyclopaedia of football. He's very quick, articulate, he does still have some of his Marsh Farm traits – his timekeeping – but as a professional still in the industry, he's absolutely top class. His transition from a Marsh Farm boy to being taken on at Luton via the YTS scheme, saw him, within a year, in the first team and looking like the best player on the pitch. He was strong, quick, he bullied opponents, then onto England Under 21s, full squad training camp call ups, before going onto Tottenham Hotspur along with David Pleat when he left, and an FA Cup Finalist in 1987. Later on, Mitchell also played for West Ham and Burnley along with another spell back at Kenilworth Road with Luton; he really was just top class.

Another lad from Marsh Farm was Stacey North. Stacey was taken on as a full-time apprentice and went on to earn a full-time pro contract with Luton. Now Stace, in the beginning, had little bit more class on the football pitch than Mitchell. He looked like he was going to be the one to blossom and really come through to flourish in the first team, but he never really kicked on with his career at Luton like Mitchell did. Stace went out on loan to Wolves just after I left the club. He then played his way into the first team a little before finally leaving for West Brom and then onto Fulham. Sadly, osteoarthritis brought about early retirement not long after Stace went to Fulham. I believe he moved to America to set up a coaching school and as far as I know he's still there. Another Marsh Farm lad finding his way in the world far from his early beginnings, so to speak.

I played and trained with some great lads in the reserves at Luton. Lads like Ray Daniel, who played quite often behind me in the left back spot. You always gained confidence when playing alongside a good pro. Ashley Grimes was the same. When Ash came to the club in 1984 he played a fair few games in the reserves. One thing that did stick with me was that when they played in the reserves, they never came with a bad attitude. You never felt like they weren't giving their all and that was a great example to set with so many of us young lads making up the majority of the reserve side. They went about their business as though they were playing in the first team. It was about getting fit after injury had cost them a first team place or getting noticed to get back knocking on the first team door, it was really quite inspiring.

I was playing with Garry Parker at Kenilworth Road one Saturday afternoon in the reserves. I think we were paying Millwall. John Moore, speaking in his big, strong Scottish accent prior to the game, had instructed me to take all of the free kicks and corners that were on the right-hand side

Lee (extreme left) playing in a pre-season friendly away at St Albans City in 1985

of the pitch, because I was left footed, so that I could swing them by bending the ball in with my left foot rather than a right footed player swinging it in an outwards trajectory.

John had clearly marked all this up on the board in the changing room when he went through his team talk. Within ten minutes of the game starting we were awarded a free kick, almost exactly to the point where John Moore had marked out on the board. I'd gone running over from the left wing to the right-hand side with the intention of following John's instructions to the letter. I was on the ball getting ready to deliver the free kick when Garry Parker came over to me and said, "I'm taking this free kick!" I looked at him hoping that he'd recall John Moore's instructions. Garry had played a lot of games already in the first team so I was also thinking well who am I? I wasn't even officially on the books, I wasn't an apprentice, I wasn't even a junior pro! I was eighteen by now and was still hoping to be awarded a pro contract. I was a non-contract player and I was caught between 'Parks' and John Moore, who was screaming from the dugout, "Lee Payne, you take the free kick!"

Kenilworth Road was empty for this reserve match so John Moore's voice was echoing all around the ground. I tried to reason with Garry saying, "Look, the gaffer…" But Parks just said, "Fuck off, I'm taking it!" I stepped back, looked across to John Moore, held out my arms and shrugged. John Moore was about to go ballistic! At this very moment Garry Parker bent the free kick straight into the top corner of the net, GOAL! Parks just turned to me and then the bench with his hand aloft to salute this goal, and that was Garry Parker. He was supremely confident. What a player he was, he had incredible belief in his own ability and he was right to back himself. He was fantastic, he had an air of genius about him along with a likeable cockiness, too.

We walked up the tunnel together at half time and he looked at me and said, "Don't worry about it, I covered ya there, Lee!" John Moore never said a word in the dressing room about it at half time. But had Garry missed it, we would have got hammered. You just couldn't argue with what he could do with a football.

Lee during his short spell with Barry Fry at Barnet

The funniest player that I ever played with was Wayne Turner. I had difficulty even playing with him because I would get the giggles and once I started I just couldn't stop. Wayne would do the 'Freddie Starr' walk strutting around the changing room, sticking his arse out like Freddie, too. He'd have us in stiches! We were in the changing room one day, it must have been straight after a game; Wayne had quite a talent for calling on his flatulence on demand. He would lean right over to one side, cock his leg up and let rip! We were in there getting showered and changed and there was a knock on the door. It was one of the female staff on the admin team at the club. She said, "We need a couple of pro's to represent the club at the Miss Luton Beauty pageant. It's on this Thursday night at the Pink Elephant." Wayne piped up, "I've already seen the line-up, I think I'll give it a miss!" Wayne was a great lad, really funny. He was a really strong character too, because for a few years he was the butt of the Oak Road Terrace boo boys, they couldn't wait to get on his back, and boy, did they give him some stick! I genuinely think his sense of humour got him through those days, as he not only won them over in the end but was elevated to legendary status as a Luton Town player, not least for scoring the game's only goal in that second FA Cup replay at home to Watford in 1985.

Jumping ahead a little to later on in my career, in the 1987/88 season, I was on my morning drive down the M1, M25 and then A1081 in towards the Underhill ground in Barnet. Wayne Turner and I were both playing for Barry Fry at Barnet by then. I came to a stop and a car pulled up alongside me. I heard BEEP, BEEP, BEEP! I looked across and was Gary Phillips driving (Barnet goalkeeper) and Wayne Turner. Wayne was in the passenger seat and he was calling over to me to wind my window down. Which I did. I asked, "What is it, Wayne?" He shouted, "Payney, it's for you!" At that moment he handed me the telephone receiver from an old-style home telephone that we all had in the 1970s and 80s. Wayne was hanging out of the car shouting, "It's for you, Payney!" Everyone around us must have wondered what those nutters were doing! I don't even want to think what Gary Phillips and Wayne Turner were doing driving around in 1988 with an old-style home telephone in their car…

Honestly, I would have paid money to sit in the back of that car with those two – it would have been like going to work and being entertained by Morecambe & Wise every day.

If I had to say who the most exciting player was that I'd ever seen at Kenilworth Road, then I would probably say it was Wayne's big buddy, Paul Walsh. It was a privilege to see him up close in training. I recall a night game against Birmingham City around 1983. Paul Walsh destroyed their back line, to a degree of almost taking the piss! Noel Blake was playing at the back for Birmingham that night and Walshy must have nutmegged him at least four times during the game. I wouldn't have been surprised if he'd assaulted Paul Walsh that night as Luton were 3-0 by half time! Walshy, on his day, was absolutely unplayable. You just knew he was destined to move on. Luton picked him up from Charlton when he was just nineteen and then within two years Liverpool came knocking for him and he was gone. Walshy, when he turned it on, was mesmerising to watch.

We went and knocked on his door once as we'd find out where the players lived if they were local to us. He lived in a house down in Sundon Park, which is right on the northern edge of Luton. There was about four of us, we'd have only been around fourteen or so at the time. He came to the door with an expression as though to say, 'can I help you lads?' We were just looking at him and he was looking back at us and he was like this spotty teenager with a mop of blond hair. After all, he was still only nineteen. All we could say was, "Alright, Walshy?" He was good as gold, joking with us for a bit, before telling us to sod off!

I joined Barnet in 1987 from Hitchin Town, which is where I'd been playing across two seasons after being let go by Luton Town. Barnet and Hitchin had played each other in a cup game and we got a 0-0 in the first game at Barnet. I had a good game for Hitchin tearing the Barnet full back inside and out. Barry Fry said something cheeky to me as I came off the pitch, as Barry would. In the return game at Top Field we got soundly beaten by Barnet and following that game, the chairman of Hitchin called me into the boardroom. He said, "Lee, we've got some good news for you personally. Barry Fry has offered us five thousand pounds to take you to Barnet. We like you here with us, but we're not going to stand in your way to progress back up the leagues."

A week later I signed for Barnet. Barry had me on the bench, they were at the top of the old GM Vauxhall Conference Division and I came on a few times as a sub. Barnet, at the time, were one of the biggest clubs in the country in non-league football. I played in their reserve side, and I think we played in the London Suburban and the Capital League. Barry had about forty players signed at the club and it was a revolving door even back then.

He loaned me out to Stevenage Borough along with another former Luton Town player, who had also been picked up by Barry, Herbie Smith. That was an experience! When we got there Herbie kicked the training room door open, almost taking it off its hinges. All the Stevenage Borough boys were in there and the door crashed open followed by Herbie Smith and myself. Herbie shouted out, "Herbie's on site!" What a way to introduce yourself to your new team mates. But that was Herbie, he was a big lad and he used his size to intimidate anyone that he met. All I could do was stand behind him trying to hide. My dad later took Herbie to Dunstable Town when he was managing at Creasy Park in the 1988/89 season.

Barry Fry brought me back to Barnet following that loan spell out at Stevenage, and I played in the final game of the season. Barnet needed to win to stand a chance of being promoted to the football league for the first time in their history but on the same day, if Lincoln City won their game as well, then they would be promoted ahead of Barnet. Both teams won their games so Lincoln went up instead of Barnet by two points.

We came back in July 1988 for pre-season, having played a lot of league sides in the pre-season friendlies: Tottenham, Wimbledon, Cambridge United and Luton Town. I think Luton Town was so ingrained in my footballing DNA that they always were involved in my career. I had a great pre-season, I was playing well and feeling good. I was flying. I was now twenty-one years old and had developed physically; I had 'found' my body.

Mitchell Thomas played against us in that game for Tottenham along with a young full back called Brian Statham. I turned Brian inside out in that game. Barry Fry called me into his office and told me that David had been on the phone, which confused me. "David? David who?" I asked. "David Pleat!" Barry replied. "He wants you to go and play for him next week in a trial match at Leicester City for their reserves. David says that he's been watching you and he thinks you're ready now." I said, "I'm not playing, Baz, I don't want to play for David. He had me all that time as a kid at Luton and I was let go!" It was just a typical ego thing at the time; it was all bollocks! Of course, I went and played in that game. But that genuinely was my initial reaction that I didn't want to play in it, because I still felt the hurt of rejection from three years earlier. Barry Fry talked

Luton born; Lee Payne in 1988, finally a professional footballer in the English first division

some sense into me saying, "You never know who else is watching you in these games, you've got to play. The way you're playing, you'll catch someone else's eye."

Barry drove me up to Filbert Street, the then home ground of Leicester City. This particular game was a reserve game in the Central League against Newcastle United on 12th September 1988. I played in the game and did well and that's being modest, as I was later told that I destroyed the Newcastle full back that night! On the drive home, Barry Fry told me that we had four offers on the table already, and to leave it with him as they'd have a deal done by tomorrow lunchtime.

The following day, Barry called me at work, a building site in Welwyn Garden City where I worked as a general labourer. "I've got incredible news for you," he said. "I've sold you to Newcastle United for £125,000." I can't remember which I dropped first, the phone or the broom!

I signed for Willie McFaul at Newcastle United after only playing a handful of games for Barry Fry at Barnet. Willie had sent a couple of people to watch their reserves at Leicester City that night, a club scout and Colin Suggett. Colin was the youth team manager at Newcastle at the time, he'd also played for the club in the 1970s and later became Newcastle United's caretaker manager for a short while. They'd called Willie McFaul to tell him that they had to sign this young winger they'd seen that night playing against Newcastle reserves for Leicester.

I never signed for David Pleat at Leicester City but once again he played a pivotal role in my football career by offering me that trial, which led to another pathway giving me the opportunity to finally play professional football in the First Division at a massive club like Newcastle United.

I had waited so long for my professional debut. My time finally came on 26th October 1988; I was twenty-one years old. It was a massive occasion for me. The game was played at St James Park And I was wearing the famous black and white striped shirts of Newcastle United against

Middlesbrough. We won 3-0. I remember Gary Pallister scoring an own goal to put us a goal up and my great friend Mirandinha, scored the other two.

I played a handful of games for Newcastle United and one of my highlights was playing against Manchester United on a Sunday afternoon live on 'The Big Match'. Mal Donaghy was playing at centre half for Manchester United that day and I said to him as we went off the pitch that I'd been a kid at Luton but never got taken on the books and that I'd played and trained with him during that time and was a big fan of his. Mal was such a kind, quiet man and a gentleman, too. He smiled and said, "Well, you've played against me now son!"

The following week, somewhat ironically, I would be back at my home town club but playing AGAINST them!

Before the game, the media picked up that I was a Luton boy about to go back to play against my home town club that had rejected me three years earlier. They asked me about my Luton Town story and I told them I'd been a fan and then picked up to play as a schoolboy, was never made an official apprentice after leaving school but was kept around as a non-contract player in the youth and reserves before being released/let go finally in 1985. I then told them about the trial match that David Pleat had invited me to play in just three months earlier that year, which resulted in me not signing for David at Leicester but in signing for Newcastle United instead. I said that Pleaty had two chances in my career to sign me but he failed to take either. I also said that it was a special era at Luton and I was a big fan of David Pleat and his teams in the late 1970s and early 1980s.

I thought that was it, just a nice hometown-boy-comes-good story, but I was wrong! The next day I got a phone call from somebody down in Luton, I can't even remember to this day who it was because it upset me so much. It might have been my dad or my grandad? He said to me, "Lee, have you seen the back page of the newspaper?" He wasn't talking about a local paper either, this journalist that I'd spoken to had taken the story to a national newspaper and they'd run it. They'd gone with an image of two fingers being held up in a V-sign with the headline: 'UP YOURS PLEAT!'

I was horrified. I'd been naïve in giving the interview and I was so upset as that was not how I wanted to come across. But that was the angle the newspaper wanted to portray the piece. I learnt an important lesson right there and then. David Pleat, I believe, took it with a pinch of salt and thank god that he did.

It was nice to go back to Kenilworth Road with Newcastle and to have the chance to play against them. It was a 0-0 draw and played on the plastic pitch that Luton still had then. I remember vividly that my boot split during the game and it was flapping like a comedy crocodile toy. I think I caught it in the sand that was on the pitch. I didn't like that surface, it was a pig of a pitch. They laid it the summer that I was told they wouldn't be offering me a contract so I never played on it for any Luton side. It was still great to finally play a competitive game at Kenilworth Road, though. Especially as my all-time hero Ricky Hill was still playing for Luton. Kingsley Black and I came off the pitch together, we had fought so often for the Number 11 shirt in the youth and reserve sides, and here we were, both wearing our respective clubs' Number 11 shirts as First Division professional footballers. We were both Luton born and bred and we'd both been at local Luton side St Joseph's as kids playing for the football team there.

That was a special day for me and all of my family were there to watch. They were all Lutonians going back generations. The fact that I never got to play a professional competitive match for Luton, which had been my dream, meant to go back then was almost like a little bit of compensation with such a big club like Newcastle United, and to play Luton.

I was a Luton boy from Marsh Farm and in that period at Newcastle United I met and befriended a Brazilian international by the name of Mirandinha. He was the first Brazilian to play in the English First Division. He was a superstar and I was just a young pro, but for some reason, God does these wonderful things sometimes in life, we formed a really strong bond. Even after we both left Newcastle United, he went back to Brazil and I ended up moving to Reading when Jim Smith sold me, and then went over to Holland before eventually losing my playing career through injury aged just twenty-five. 'Mira' and I have remained friends and I ended up going to Brazil and spending some time with him in Sao Paulo in the South-East of the country. I married my first wife whilst in Brazil with whom I have two grown-up daughters: Larissa and Gabrielle. My youngest, Gabi, now lives in England. That's when my love affair started with the country and I live in Brazil today after having lived in Spain for the past twenty years.

All of this came from playing with Mirandinha and forming a tight friendship with him at Newcastle United. Which came about from playing in a trial match at Leicester City for… David Pleat.

I played a season under Ian Branfoot at Reading in the Third Division in 1989/90 and enjoyed my time there, scoring three goals in around forty appearances. However, I was abruptly called into the office one day and told that the club needed to sell me and they'd accepted an offer for me from a team over in Holland.

When my playing career ended as a professional footballer I was just twenty-five years old. I played some amateur football in Holland for a while but ended up staying in the game initially as a European Scout based in Holland for Harry Redknapp at West Ham United. In this role I spent a lot of time at the training ground at West Ham for meetings on my player scouting reports. Les Sealey was the goalkeeper coach at West Ham then. I pulled him up one day at the training ground and said, "Les, do you remember booting a young fifteen-year-old trialist up the arse for chipping you off your line during training back at Luton Town?" We were at the Electrolux 'The Lux' training ground and like I said, I'd caught him stranded off his line and so chipped it in and over him. I turned to look at all the lads around me and they were loving it, shouting out their cheers of delight, but some had already started cringing as they knew how Les would react. I didn't celebrate it or anything. But at that point I got a fair old boot up the arse! Les was standing there spitting chips and shouting, "Don't you ever do that to me again, you little wanker!" Years later, when we were together at the West Ham training ground, I asked him if he recalled this incident. He just looked at me with that cheeky look and way that he had about him, paused and then said, "Nah, I can't remember that at all!"

I became acquainted with Glenn Roeder (RIP), who was coaching at West Ham at the time. I spoke to Glenn again when he became the manager at Watford, which was early in my change of career pathway from football scout to football agent. Glenn introduced me to a friend of his; former footballer turned football agent (and former Luton Town player for a brief loan spell), Barry Silkman. I could write a book myself just on the year that I spent working for 'Silky'.

My final list of clubs that I played for includes, Sundon Park Social, St Josephs, Walden Rangers, Offley, Arlesey Town, Baldock Town, Dunstable Town, Luton Town (youth &reserves), Coventry City Reserves, Hitchin Town, Barnet FC, Stevenage Borough, Leicester City Reserves, Newcastle United, Reading FC, BV Veendam, FC Emmen, Gateshead, HHC Hardenberg and WKE.

I looked after a lot of young players and took them to some of the biggest clubs and to the biggest managers in the game. I spent the next twenty-five years of my life as a football agent; how I managed to stay in the game that long I'll never know. Well, I do know the answer to that really: It was just because I loved the game of football so much.

(BORN 22ND FEBRUARY 1962, BEDFORD)

# ROBERT SIMON JOHNSON

LUTON TOWN FC 1978 - 1989

*Born locally to the club, Rob had been on both QPR and Tottenham's books as a schoolboy. Luton Town hadn't even been on his radar until in 1978, he was invited along to a trial match where he did well enough to be offered an apprenticeship. This was at the time where David Pleat had just become the first team manager, with Harry Haslam moving to Sheffield United.*

I was very much a young man with not much experience in how things worked, but it was clear that David had a belief in playing football in a certain way. Control and pass, play with imagination whilst on the ball, this was instilled into me very early on. Pleat wasn't a shouter or a screamer but he was always quick with a put down to keep the players feet on the floor if needed. He certainly appreciated the way that Brian Clough handled things like the press and players and he shared Clough's vision for the way football could and should be played. Ken Gutteridge was the assistant manager when I joined the club but he upset a few of the first team players and was soon to leave. John Moore was my youth team coach, and he is, to this day, a club legend. John taught you about morals and ethics and doing things the right way and the benefits of living your life that way. David Coates was another nice guy, a knowledgeable coach with many fabulous stories going back to his playing days in the 50s and 60s. John Sheridan was the club physio, another really nice guy. It was a strong back room staff but they were not a bunch of yes men; they were very loyal to David and to the club.

I was a schoolboy at both Tottenham and QPR, but I travelled in as I didn't want to leave home. I played for both of their youth teams, training

Rob Johnson in the summer of 1982

at QPR's training ground and they had some amazing players there then, Gerry Francis, Don Masson, Stan Bowles, John Hollins to name a few. They were all heroes to me but I didn't stay because I wanted to be at home. I'd go down there in the summer, travelling on the train to this most incredibly beautiful training centre, but I didn't want to go. It would have done me the world of good to move into digs down there as it would have pushed me harder being away from home. I think it would have made me do more and stand on my own two feet and grow up quicker. For some players that leave home it's the making of them. When I was at Spurs we had Mark Falco in the youth team along with Micky Hazard, and what a player he was, but he was from the Northeast and he was home sick. I remember him coming in and playing in one of the youth team games. He'd been back home as they'd allowed him to go home for ten days and he came back and wasn't as sharp or as fit. The coaches were talking about him saying, "Yeah, he's off the pace a bit because he's been home." Mikey was just one of those that needed to get himself home every now and again to touch base with people, but he stuck it out and he was a great player. Maybe he wouldn't have made it if he was local at a northeast club. Maybe he would have been okay, but I think moving away and to Spurs was the making of him.

I travelled in on the train every day, that was part of the agreement that I had with the club, but Pleat didn't want me to do that. I'd actually signed to stay at Bedford rather than going to Luton as they said they'd allow me to travel but I'd have to pay the fare myself. That was Luton's way of trying to get me into digs near the club but I wanted to stay at home. However, then David actually came to my house and persuaded me to sign and said the club would pay my train fare. It was a big moment in my life for Pleat to come around to my house so that persuaded me it was the right thing to do and I travelled in every day. I think that some lads settle in better if they're in digs. The digs were a home-from-home and the lads were really looked after well. We used to go around a lot to the houses where they were staying and you could see that they were made to feel part of the family. Mrs Gough was a lovely lady, Ricky, Mick Saxby and Tony Grealish among many others all stayed there everyone knew Mrs Gough. These ladies that took the players in were an integral part of the club, very much part of the make-up. There were two landladies that lived next door to each other and Tim Breacker was there along with five or six other players in the two digs, and I think that two of the players even married the landladies' daughters. This was part of the family feeling about Luton Town. I don't think the digs thing still happens anymore, I think it was just of its time, so to speak, but in those days David Pleat was very keen to have these landladies to look after the young players, to cook their meals and look after their laundry as if they were still at home perhaps, having that traditional support unit around them whilst coming into the club.

Milija was the first team goalkeeper when I joined the club. All of the apprentices just loved him. Everything about him exuded style and confidence. He was the nicest man you'd ever meet. He was so nice to everybody. He always had a smile on his face. I remember when David Pleat became manager at the end of January 1978, he wasn't keen on Milija and he wanted a different type of goalkeeper. David wanted somebody who would come and take crosses more. Milija was aware of this but he didn't get the hump, he didn't do anything bad, he didn't show any disrespect to the manager, he kept ploughing on even though he knew that in his heart of hearts that David didn't really want him there.

Trevor Hartley was my reserve team coach when I moved up, he was a really good organiser and a very thorough man. He was the first person that I know of to use video analysis. He was very good for David Pleat on this front as David wasn't quite as good with this sort of organising and detail, so they complimented each other well.

It was brilliant in the reserves under Trevor Hartley. If we won he'd be great, the most affable of chaps, but if we lost we knew what would be coming on Monday… He would run us endlessly up and down Popes Meadow, repeatedly with thirty-second breaks then up again, and then carrying each other, too.

There was a period where we were all doing well in the reserves and the first team were going through a bad spell. Trevor recommended four of five of us reserves to David to be involved in the first team and that same weekend, the first team won their game whilst we went to Watford and got turned over 5-0. We all know what was coming our way on the Monday, however, even with this knowledge one of the reserves, Seamus Heath, still went out and did a marathon, or a half marathon on the Sunday. Seamus was a mad runner and very dedicated, determined to get the most out of every day, always keeping himself busy. Unfortunately for Seamus, when Monday came round and we got off the bus at Popes Meadow, he was in bits after his marathon the day before and apologised to Trevor Hartley that he was in no condition to do the running because of this. Hartley exploded: "Fuck your marathon, I've spent the week pushing some of you for the first team but not now, not for a long time anyway after that performance at Watford." Trevor was like that, he'd need to get it out of his system but by the next day it was done and finished. He was meticulous with the use of video analysis and would show us where we should or shouldn't have been from throw-ins, free kicks, corners – he would show us the video and say you have to be here, an innovation which is taken for granted these days.

I remember the first league game of the season that I was at the club. We were at home against Oldham and we put six goals past them, it was a beautiful sunny day with a full crowd and we absolutely pummelled them. I think it was Kirk Stephens' first game, Lil played and Mal played, too, and I think Milija Aleksic would've been in goal. It was incredible just watching the team score goal after goal after goal. Bob Hatton would've been played too, and it was just a culmination of this pre-season where I've never run so hard in my life amongst all these players. But at first, I didn't know Bob Hatton or David Moss at the time, in fact, I'd never heard of them and yet suddenly here in front of me they were playing football. That was so incredible to watch and the crowd were on their feet; it was almost like every time you sat down you were jumping up again. I thought WOW! as I'd never seen football like it. David Pleat liked to play that type of game where attacking was everything. He didn't concentrate on defending although we were quite strong defensively, but it was more about going forward and with verve and pace, passing the ball. It was great and quite amazing for me as a young lad to be watching in the stands and training with all of these players suddenly. They were something special to me whereas before, I'd been training with them every day and not thinking too much about them. There I was, now at Luton, whereas before I'd not really been at a club where I knew the players so well. I'd gotten to know them over those four or five weeks in pre-season where we travelled away to the Isle of Wight that summer and I'd gone along with them and then suddenly, on this sunny day in August, they're beating and dismantling their opponents on the day, Oldham Athletic, 6-1

David Pleat loved a full-on practice match and it would often be played on the home pitch at Kenilworth Road. First team against the reserves, full training kit on, but we hated it because the first team wouldn't take it seriously, even though the reserves would. We would more often than not win by two or three goals. We'd play practice matches against other clubs too, midweek and during the day. I remember us playing at White Hart Lane a couple of times which was great coming up against the likes of Ardiles, Crooks, Hoddle, Villa, etc., but I couldn't tell you anything about those games. With no crowd to lift you and get the adrenaline pumping they became a non-event, nothing compared to playing a first team match in front of a crowd.

David Pleat knew the type of player that he wanted at the club and he would be quite ruthless with players who he'd bring in if he felt they weren't the right fit for the club, lads like Steve Sherlock from Man City, John Lucas from Manchester United. I remember a big lad, a forward, Andy Harrow, moved his wife and home down from Scotland where he'd been playing part time with Raith Rovers but within two months he was gone, back to Scotland. A little later the same happened with Steve Elliott and Vince Hilaire, both great lads but moved on very quickly by David. Steve Elliott always seemed to score against us when playing for Preston back in the Division Two days, but deemed, very quickly, not to be up to Division One standards.

August 4th, 1982, playing in Finland on a pre-season tour was the date that I had my first ACL injury, a cruciate rupture in my knee. The irony was that it came whilst marking another Luton Town player who was actually playing for our opponents. That man, Seamus Heath, not one to sit still for long, would spend the summer months playing in Scandinavia whilst earning a nice wedge, too. Seamus was playing for the Finnish side and we were running alongside each other when my laces got caught in Seamus's studs. I stopped but he carried on and that's when I felt the knee go. I was lucky that the PCL wasn't damaged. I didn't play again until August 5th, 1983.

When I came back from my first knee operation, John Sheridan came to pick me up from Bedford hospital to drive me back so he could have a look at the knee, this was about three weeks after the surgery. John was such a lovely man, he didn't have to do that but he came to pick me up anyway and take me home, and then he picked me up from home to bring me in and have a look at it. Well, he took the bandage off at which point Kirk Stephens came in followed by all the first team to look. Kirk

Stephens moved in to take a closer look and then he let out the loudest whoop: "What the fuck…lads, lads come and have a look at this, you've never seen anything like it!" You just sit there and you're thinking, I don't want all of this attention but then suddenly you've got all these players around the bed wanting to look at my nine-inch scar! That's football for you and it picks you up in moments like this, making you feel part of the team still, part of the group. In football, if you've got something different, different hair cut or a different shirt it doesn't matter, they'll slaughter you for it; you've got to be strong enough to go through the piss talking. Raddy Antic, who was such a lovely fella, came to look at my scar, too. He looked at me and then he looked at John Sheridan with a concerned expression and then said to John, "In all of my days I've never seen anything like this, will he play again?" This caused me to sit bolt upright and remind them I was in the room, too. John just looked back at Raddy and assured him I would. John was always the most positive man. I don't think he knew for sure if I'd play again but he believed that I would. David Coates came in as well, and he looked at my knee and I saw his face drop and again I was thinking, Oh, for God's sake, but then Coatesy asked John if he could have a word and actually pulled him out of the room to ask the same question Raddy had asked. At this point I was lying there thinking, Do you think that I don't know what you're asking, John? However, looking back it was so funny. None of the lads would do anything to harm you but it was just the environment and the fact they'd play on the emotions of what people would say and just head straight to the core.

I played some pre-season games on loan at Lincoln City under the management of Colin Murphy, who would later team up with David Pleat at both Leicester City and in his second spell back at Luton Town. I went on to play four competitive games under Colin at Lincoln, he was a decent guy but I didn't do myself justice there and he couldn't spin me back to Luton Town quick enough. After a long time out it was probably not what I needed, i.e., to be thrown into Third Division football. I was fit and strong but I needed a spell in the reserves to get myself confident again with the knee in a match situation.

I made my belated first team debut on November 12th, 1983 at home in 1-1 draw with Birmingham City. My next full appearance was on New Year's Eve at Roker Park, Sunderland, at right back. We were playing well and at half time we were 0-0. I personally was doing well again but Nick Pickering, who had his nose broken during the match before, if I

Rob and Ricky Hill close down Tottenham's Tony Galvin in the 0-0 draw against David Pleat new club in October 1986

remember correctly, must have been told by his manager to get in on me during the half time break. I was shepherding the ball out to the touch line when he took his chance to put one on me from behind. Nick was a nice lad but he was perhaps trying too hard to please his manager. Unfortunately, where he caught me resulted in my ACL going in the other knee. To rub salt into the wounds, Gordon Chisholm scored past Les Sealey to put Sunderland a goal up whilst I was on the side line receiving treatment. Ultimately, we lost the game 0-2.

In the first team I would room with Mal Donaghy. Mal was like a big brother, he was the calmest person. Mal never changed and our relationship was always really good. When I got injured for the second time, I'd only played a couple of first team games so I'd not been in Mal's company that much apart from being part of training with the first team. I did play a few games in the reserves to see how the knee felt though, and I knew it was dodgy. Mal was watching this reserve team game from the stands at Kenilworth Road and I was playing in the centre of midfield for the reserves. With this kind of injury it's very hard to explain but in a nutshell, if you turn your head you can fall over because there's no sense in your knee as to what's happening. The best way to explain it is the top half of your leg, your thigh bone (femur) goes one way and your tibia goes the other and you just fall over. It's a really horrible feeling and disconcerting to say the least. I was playing the game, everything was going well, I was playing well within myself and then suddenly, I turned my head quickly and ended up falling over on to my back. I was in pain because my knee dislocated and I was trying to pop it back to the right place. You can get up and walk off with this injury so I did that, but I was feeling pretty down as I'd been out with the first injury to the other knee for a long time. I'd just come back, got injured, knew what had happened and after playing three or four games to test myself, I then knew I'd be facing surgery and several months out of action.I was feeling pretty crap to put it bluntly. As I was walking back in,  shaking my head in my hands, who popped his head in but Mal. He looked at me and could see I was feeling pretty pissed off, but with typical football humour, he said, "So, what happened to you? I didn't see any sniper, where was the sniper?" That broke the moment for me and we just laughed. Then Mal asked what had happened in a more serious tone to which I explained that I knew I'd now need surgery again. It was just the way he came in, he could see it and knew that I was down, but with that football humour he picked me back up straight away. I always remembered that because it's the best way you can deal with that situation when someone's pretty low; it's part and parcel of the game sometimes. Many years later when we were rooming together, he would look at me and say, "Rob, why did you get injured all the time?" I'd ask him what he meant as there were times I'd had a spell of three years without an injury.He'd point out that I was always injured and what was I doing to cause it, but I replied with, "I was just unlucky, I guess." To Mal, it seemed very strange because he never got injured, he never had a lengthy lay off, it never happened to him.

When I came back from the second knee injury in the 1985/86 season, I became the first to play in the First Division after having both my knees reconstructed.

We didn't have agents back in those days, you just went into David Pleat's office and he had a great ploy: He had his desk and his chair at a certain height and he'd had the legs on your chair cut down so that when you sat down you were looking up at him; the affect was amazing. He would get into a serious conversation about how lucky you were to be getting this contract, telling us we'd done alright and he wanted to offer this and that, building you up and making you feel like you'd done really well. However, at the same time you'd feel you were still lucky to be getting this offer and then he'd basically make you a crap offer! That was just what he was like and we all knew it. It was the way he ran the club and he had a certain amount of power to do it.

We all knew David was going to Tottenham in my last year at Luton. I came back from my second injury and played about twenty-odd games in the first team and I'd done pretty well, too. I was feeling pleased with myself and even though my contract was up, David had previously given me a year to prove that I could still play. He gave me a contract telling me he'd give me just enough money to live on as they didn't know if my knees would stand up and if I'd play again. I was very appreciative of that and he went on to tell me that if it didn't work out, they'd look at the end of the year and give me some insurance money so I could start a new life. I accepted his offer and the season of 1985/86 went pretty well for me. I played in around twenty-five matches, one against Chelsea where I was the Man of the Match. I played right back, left back and in midfield as well.

So, there was Pleat, knowing he was off to Tottenham, telling me to sit down in this low chair and said, "Okay, Rob, you've done really well, you've shown now that you can play in several positions and you can make one of the full back positions yours." Mitchell Thomas was about to go to Tottenham along with David Pleat. I was sat there feeling really pleased as this was all very positive, and then David said, "I'm going to give you a three-year contract." I thought it sounded great as bearing in mind eight months previously he'd offered me a contract which was, as he put it, just enough money to live on, he offered me twenty pounds a week more than that. I just looked at him in a daze and said, "What?" He couldn't help smiling, he even put his head down to stop himself laughing. I was trying to speak, saying, "Boss, boss…" thinking that he must have forgotten what he said to me. "Eight months ago you said it was a contract with just enough money to live on, which it was, and now you're telling me that I'm going to be really important to the club and that everyone appreciates me coming back and fighting through the injuries, that I'll be a big boost for the team and you're offering me a three year contract on just twenty quid a week more?" He couldn't help himself from smirking. The other thing about it was he knew that he was going to Tottenham, it was all signed and he was going the following week. It was his last thing to do and I don't know what satisfaction he got from doing it. Anyway, I didn't sign the contract, I told him that I'm not going to sign for that and he replied, "If you don't sign it today you might not get offered it again." I told him that I would have to take my chances and then I walked out. A week later, he went to Spurs and John Moore took over. And John doubled my money! It was just bizarre, I don't know why David did that, it was just his nature.

We had a fines system in place, a tenner for being late, and I was one of the worst culprits because something in my nature made me rebel against it. I used to try and turn up ten seconds before the deadline. We had to be in by 10am so I would try to turn up a minute before just because it annoyed Fozzie and some of the others a bit. Every home game I'd get fined the ten quid and they used to love it, but it used to annoy them when I was just a fraction ahead of time. That was my personality I'm afraid.

There were things that you'd never get away with these days like the

Rob attacks the Charlton Athletic full back in this 1986 Kenilworth Road clash

Christmas carols, something else that Fozzie introduced. The apprentices would have to stand naked on the desk in the middle of the first team dressing room, every single player would sit around, everything was silent as we all had to be quiet, and they were given Christmas carols to learn off by heart three weeks before. The young apprentice players had to stand there in just a pair of wellington boots, holding a brush as a microphone and sing their carol. The worse singer then had to run around the pitch naked. All the staff, coaches and administration staff would come out down to pitch side to watch and cheer the young player as they ran around! There was one lad, Sean Farrell, big lad who played up front, enjoyed it so much that he carried on doing it every year even when he turned pro, even though it was only something the apprentices had to do! Looking back, it seems and sounds very strange but the world was very different then and given that it was Christmas time, it was pretty chilly, too...

Fozzie wanted to organise the defence so he didn't get caught out, but he didn't just organise it to suit him, although it did, it also made the team strong and made us compact and hard to beat. You had the skill and the flair on top of that, whereas Luton before Fozzie was very flowing but we could still concede a lot of goals. When Fozzie came there was a strong discipline as he'd prefer to have a strong player, someone sat in front of him like Peter Nicholas who wasn't that ambitious going forward. That suited Fozzie and it suited the team.

I wasn't a prolific goalscorer (tongue in cheek), but I scored a deflected goal from a long-range drive of mine at home to Burnley in the League Cup. I also 'scored' a goal in front of the Kop at Anfield in an eventual 2-3 defeat in October 1985, but it was disallowed because Emeka was offside. In those days, somebody else could be offside; I'd played a one-two with someone, ran through and put the ball in the net only for Emeka to be given as offside. It would have stood in the modern game but to my huge disappointment it was not allowed to stand. That moment certainly would have been my claim to fame written right there to tell my son all about, to have scored in front of the Kop at Liverpool and to get another 3-3 draw like in 1982, but it wasn't to be. I scored an own goal at home to Norwich though, which my six-year-old son found and showed to me on YouTube! He looked at the footage then turned to me and said, "Daddy, that's awful!" I tried to justify it to him by saying the Norwich player coming in behind would have scored anyway, but he wasn't buying it.

Nobody had any real match day superstitions; some lads would always put the same boot on before the other or not put their shirt on until they were in the tunnel at the last minute, though. Les Sealey, however, used to throw up most games just before a match as he was always so nervous. He used to get over his nerves by shouting at people, kind of putting an act on, on the pitch. He'd get himself enraged to overcome the nerves. I recognise now what he was doing, though I didn't recognise it so much at the time, but these days a good psychologist would recognise what he was doing. We all knew how nervous he got and that he was a bag of nerves a lot of the time.

Les had a bar or a nightclub or something like that after he finished playing, and lost a lot of money on it. He was trying to sell cars at one point, and he'd go to auctions then arrive with a car and try to sell it to some of the younger lads. Like the rest of us, football to Les was great but he always felt there was financial pressure. I don't think that Les ever signed a contract that made him feel financially secure; he was always looking for other ways to make money. I think he felt that his football career was only ever one bad game away from being over. But then, towards the end of his career, he had this fantastic spell where he went to Manchester United as cover for Jim Leighton and ended up winning the FA Cup Final in a replay with Crystal Palace in 1990, and then a year later won the Cup

Rob goes toe to toe with Newcastle United's Billy Whitehurst in August 1986

Winner Cup in a final versus Barcelona. It was such a fantastic way for his footballing career to end and probably very unlikely in some ways because he most likely thought his best days were behind him. But the last part of his career earned him these fantastic highlights. I know he was always worried that his football career would finish, I don't think he was going to stay in the game, although he did stay in football for a while as a goalkeeping coach after he finished playing. I think he always felt that he could make more money doing other things. Les was always bringing stuff into the club to sell and I felt that he was pretending to be someone he wasn't. It felt like an act where he would tell us he could do this great deal, this and that… He was, in all fairness, a genuinely nice person but he just had a side to him that didn't come over very nice. That wasn't the true Les, though, and I feel he put a big act on most of the time to overcome his nerves and a lack of self-belief. The coaches in our day knew certain things about people but they didn't have the training like a sports psychologist would have these days. Compared to the modern-day game it's incredible the amount of staff, especially in the Premier League, the top Division in England, which is where Luton Town were then, but the difference in the staff numbers between then and now is incredible.

John Sheridan was probably one of the most advanced sports physiotherapists of his day. A lot of people speak about him highly but he doesn't get the credit he deserves. John was a gentleman and also very dedicated to his job. Both me and Mick Saxby had dreadful injuries, along with Basher who had the same injury as me (though didn't need an operation), and John had to come up with a diagnosis due to having no scans back then. John's knowledge was incredible and along with support from surgeons – a local one at the Luton and Dunstable Hospital for example – he handled everything professionally and with aplomb. He had a lot to handle with two particularly nasty injuries at the same time.

I personally don't think I thanked John enough as, at the time, I didn't really understand what he'd done. It was almost like I was too ignorant and wrapped up in my own injury and what it required, and even though the surgeon obviously deserves credit, so does John for giving me the programme to follow and helping me recover. I was doing rehab ten hours a day, but as John couldn't spend all that time just with me, he offered me guidance instead. With Mick also, there was so little that John could do in terms of helping him get better because the surgeon that looked at my knee didn't know what was wrong with Sax. It was only when John went to an old professor who decided to open Sax up and have a look that they found the back of his knee cap had come away. I suppose he had a spherical fracture which had taken out the protective surface and it fallen out like a coin, so to speak. When they took the knee cap off and this 'coin' of cartilage fell out, which was to protect the back of the knee, Sax had this small hole in the back of his kneecap which was rubbing when he bent his leg. It must have been excruciating but what can a physio do about that? John was under pressure as in those days people didn't really understand what a physio should and shouldn't do. We all expected him to know everything and to be able to do everything, which is so unreasonable. I had a second injury as well of course, and John really gave me a kick up the backside at one stage because rehab wasn't going right and I'd re-injured the knee, resulting in a torn cartilage, unbeknownst to everyone. However, I was trying to play on with this big swollen knee.

The exercises that John gave me were so innovative. He'd read so much and get me doing a lot of hamstring work, which wasn't something I thought I'd have to concentrate on. But the surgeon was really pleased and he agreed the range of exercises that John had put together for me should be a strong part of the rehab. John's positivity always shone through and sometimes he'd say things like 'you'll be fine' and then two months it'd be obvious we weren't. Sax's injury was bad enough that he needed an X-ray just to see what was wrong, but when the specialists couldn't find anything. John then got involved and took Mick to a surgeon in Scotland. I don't know how John put up with us then as we were miserable gits, constantly questioning why we weren't getting any better. But he did, and he helped us, not just physically but mentally, too. He did the best he possibly could to get us back in training and back on the pitch. Anterior-Cruciate injuries back then usually meant you didn't play again, but his commitment and inner-strength to support us was second to none. He was admired by Pleaty and all the players, that's for sure.

I left Luton Town in 1989 and moved to sign for David Pleat again, as he was at Leicester City by then. There was quite a contingent of former Luton Town players at Leicester at one point, including Marc North, who was there first. Aaron Tighe had a short loan spell there, too. Then Ricky and David Oldfield arrived almost at the same time. It should have been a really good time for us all at Leicester but for one reason or another, it didn't work out that way. I don't know why, but I was in a bad place with my football. It was a funny time and I look back on it with a lot of regret. I think I'd lost my desire to play and to really knuckle down. Leicester weren't doing well, they were badly organised; it was very unlike Pleat. The two coaches he had there were both ex-managers and their coaching wasn't up to much. It was a strange place to be at the time, the Leicester fans were desperate for us to do well but we just couldn't get any team spirit together and then unfortunately, David Pleat was sacked. He then returned to Luton Town completing his 'round trip journey'.

I don't think I appreciated how important Luton Town football club was to me at the time. I kept the Littlewoods Cup final shirt, the tracksuit and the small replica of the trophy that we were all given as medals from 1988 against Arsenal, but I didn't get to keep any other shirts or memorabilia from my time at the club. I think people I met there and the culture of the club helped me grow into a man. Upon reflection, I realise that it was quite a profound time in my life. Forget winning the Littlewoods Cup, I don't think of that as being the pinnacle of it, although winning at Wembley was great, but it was just being at the club at that time and I miss it. Without wanting to sound overly sentimental, it was like a family, good people with good values who taught, coached and trained you well for football, and for life as well. There were ups and downs and I genuinely can't think of a bad thing about the club or my time there. Luton Town was a great grounding for me in my young adulthood and I didn't leave there with any regret. If I had my time over I would go there again.

After a disappointing spell with Leicester City and Barnet, I finished playing at Hitchin Town before moving into physiotherapy, where I linked up for the third time in my career with David Pleat at Sheffield Wednesday. I went on to work with UK Athletics as Senior Physiotherapist and in particular with Jessica Eniss-Hill. I now run my own physiotherapy practice in the Czech Republic where I live with my wife Petra and our son Billy.

(BORN 2 JULY 1965, BICESTER, OXFORDSHIRE)

# TIMOTHY SEAN BREACKER

LUTON TOWN FC 1981-1990

*Tim was born in Bicester but long before the time he came on to Luton Town's radar, his family had moved to St Neots in Cambridgeshire where he spent his school days. Despite being a very promising footballer at school he didn't sign schoolboy forms with any club as his father was set on him completing his schooling first.*

When I joined Luton Town as an apprentice in 1981, the youth team was made up with different layers, in terms of ages, of schoolboys up to the age of 18. I had been offered a trial, after which I was invited to come back to play and train whilst I was still at school. When I was still fifteen, we played in a Midlands Midweek Reserve League. My birthday wasn't until July but I was in the same year as Mitchell and Mark Thomas, who were both in on the Youth Opportunities Scheme. I think they were the first two players in the country to join a professional football league club under that government scheme.

Soon after I had just started as an apprentice when we went to Cambridge in a pre-season game, where there were two sets of elevens put out in the match with the reserves playing first. Me and Frankie Bunn were subs for both games and I got put on with the first team in the second game. I was only sixteen at the time and I couldn't believe it and I still remember that feeling now as I was walking off the pitch. I was known to be from the area coming from St Neots and the manager from Cambridge, John Docherty, came over to me. I thought he was going to congratulate me but he just said, "You still won't make it as a player." I was shocked. I wasn't much more than a schoolboy and I'd never played in front of a

Tim at the 1982 summer media day photo call

crowd before and even though it was only a pre-season game, there was still a couple of thousand there. But then David Pleat came over to me and steered me away saying, "Well done." I'm sure he'd heard what had been said to me. There wasn't even any bad blood as it wasn't like I'd turned down Cambridge to go to Luton, but what he said spurred me on and stayed with me even to this day as a really vivid memory of my playing days. I can only think that what was behind it was he knew I was from the county growing up nearby and he knew about me as a player as he might have seen me playing in the county games. I never got to the bottom of it but as I said, I used it to spur me on to make sure that I did make it.

I'd been to other clubs on trials and even at Luton but I never signed schoolboy forms as my dad was right on my case with doing my exams first. But I just wanted to get through the exams and get to Luton Town. I really enjoyed it under John Moore, Trevor Hartley and Coatesy (David Coates), and obviously David Pleat had a big interest in the youth team. I went straight into digs in Crawley Road when I left school, living very close to Ricky Hill, who used to stay there in one of the digs sometimes on a Friday. To me and the other young lads at the time, Ricky was like a God to us. He was such a supreme player and the idol of all us young ones. I was actually just down the road with another landlady who had just started running digs from her home for the club and I was in with a boy from Sunderland, a goalkeeper, but he didn't last very long. He left soon after and I remember it was winter time and she was quite an old lady, bless her, but I was ill in my bedroom and John Sheridan came to see me. There was a flue by my bed for the central heating and I was in bed ill and breathing out cold air. When I got better and back to training, David Coates pulled me to one side and told me he was moving me into different digs with Mrs Howell up Crawley Green Hill. That was where Brian Horton and a lot of the other lads had been staying for years. It was brilliant that Coatesy got me in there and it helped me massively with my health, it was a proper environment, I think the young keeper Andy Beasley was there, too. I was in digs with Marc North for a little while as well, when he came the year after me. They seemed to always put me in with the goalkeepers, who are always a bit mad; perhaps they thought I could straighten them out a little bit (laughing). Andy Dibble was definitely at the top of the tree for bonkers goalkeepers though, that's for sure – infamous story when he went to Manchester City after leaving Luton and he got stuck in the weeds and the like in a river where he was trying to take a short cut on a pre-season training run. Alec Chamberlain was on the other end of the scale though, as he was the most sensible goalkeeper that I ever met as most of them were mad. None more so than dear ole Les Sealey, RIP. He came to West Ham after I had left Luton Town and by that time he had a pub, which wasn't far from the training ground at West Ham United.

Tim in training down at Vauxhall Motors Brache Sports Ground in 1983

The club's coaching staff were big believers in throwing the young lads in early on. I was a schoolboy and I got thrown into the reserves as a sub and chucked on with around ten minutes to go, this was just to see how you were around the senior players and how you reacted to playing in front of a couple of hundred people in the ground to see if you froze. Well, I presume that's what it was designed for as I never got told that at the time. The thing is, as a youngster, you were always kept on your toes as you knew that after a year, at seventeen, you could be gone, likewise after two and the same after three years. We had two guys down from Sunderland, one was called Alan Lane, who was touted as being the next big thing to come through after he seemingly came from nowhere. We all knew that he'd been promised a one-year pro contract because people talk. But he never made it to that pro contract because he'd been given, even by the standards back then, too much too soon and perhaps he thought he could coast, whereas we were all on it every training session.

There were two other lads around for a short while then, two Welsh lads, Barry Popplewell and Dai (David Owen), but we never knew for sure about contract promises to other lads. I did know about Alan Lane as he'd told me himself that he'd got this guarantee of a year's pro but it turned out to be the worst thing they could have done for him. I presume back then that was the only way they could get him by giving him that verbal agreement, whereas we were just happy working hard and being apprentices. Playing in the reserves on a Saturday had us playing against grown men. We were just sixteen or seventeen, our bodies still developing, and coming up against these experienced guys was hard. Some of them had been in the game a long time so you knew you had to get stronger and also to that level of mental toughness as well. I played against Joe Jordan in a reserve match, I kicked him, just caught him going in for the tackle and he actually chased me. I was absolutely terrified, but it was just one of those things that made you stronger. I also came up against the likes of Trevor Brooking and Glenn Hoddle whilst I was playing for the reserves, which was an excellent setting to be learning and progressing and ultimately pushing on towards becoming a first team player.

We had a great run in the FA Youth Cup in 1983, getting all the way to the semi final, which we unfortunately lost over two legs to the eventual winners Norwich City. I remember David Pleat coming into the changing rooms after the semi-final second leg played away at Norwich City, which we drew 0-0 on the night but we'd already lost the home leg 1-3 at Kenilworth Road. We lost the tie and were devastated as it was like nothing we'd ever played in before, and the Carrow Road game drew around seven or eight thousand supporters that night. But Pleat said to us all, "Look, don't be too downhearted as more of you will have longer careers in the game than the Norwich lads." He was proved correct as I think that only Jeremey Goss, Tony Spearing and Louie Donowa went on to have pro careers where as in our group probably only Michael Shearer, Mark Watts and Cahal McConville didn't.

I remember when I was a young player at the club, maybe even still an apprentice, that there was a bottle of brandy in the first team room. In the old dressing room set up there used to be a sort of fireplace or a shelf and I remember coming across it and thinking, What is a bottle of brandy doing in there? Some of the players would take a swig of it before going out to play, and although I was offered it I never did.

Ricky Hill was a legend with us young apprentices and one day during the week we had a meeting in one of the rooms upstairs. It was just all of us youth team lads along with Trevor Hartley and John Moore, but then in walks Ricky Hill. The whole meeting had been arranged for Ricky to tell us lads all about his match day preparation, how he actually focused and how he didn't just turn up, put his kit on and play, which, when you saw him, you just thought that he did as he made it seem so effortless and easy as he was always so relaxed. He told us just how hard he had worked when he was our age and still did then and that he focused the night before games and still worked hard in training. It was a massive penny-drop moment for me; it made me think, Wow, yeah, I can do that. Something I took forward with me and continued to do throughout my career was spend ages on my own working on whatever I could and it became a good habit almost bordering on a superstition at times. I remember Ricky telling me things that he'd done or that he'd practised when he was my age, and when you're working on your own and somebody like Ricky comes up to you and encourages you to keep going, to keep practicing, that gives you a massive lift. That can be even more so than when a manager or a coach says it to you even though they'd also played the game, but you don't remember them as players. As apprentices we used to sit at the back of the stands and watch Ricky, so this meeting was a really important moment in my career.

We were out on the pitch with the groundman, Dick Wassell at half time during games with our pitch forks replacing all the divots. We'd go down to the dressing room where they had a drying room and all the clothes were hung up, so if it was cold we'd be trying to put on extra sweat shirts over the top of our matchday gear. This usually consisted of a shirt and tie. We'd then go out onto the pitch to the opposite end from the tunnel to work on the divots, because that's where the away fans were back then, on the open Kenilworth Road terrace which was where all the coins had been thrown over by opposition fans. However, we soon got sussed after they questioned why we were all up at that end the pitch.

Tim Breacker fully enjoying this photo day...

I was in the stand at Old Trafford in April 1983, it was the Monday night of the week leading up to famous Maine Road great escape game on the last day of the season. However, I had travelled with the team and I was watching two of my mates from the youth team both making their full first team debuts with Garry Parker and Ray Daniel coming into the starting line-up. I remember just watching them out there and thinking, Wow, my mates are playing at

Manchester United! It again proved there was a pathway for the young players coming through the club.

Tim sets up another attack during the 2-1 home win over Manchester United in the 1984/85 season

I was head apprentice so I looked after the coach's rooms and I remember in 1983 at Christmas time I was told by the coaching staff that I'd have to be on standby over Christmas, which I thought was fantastic as that let me know that I was close to getting into the first team. Fast forward to the March time and I did get my debut. I'm not sure who was pushing for me on the coaching staff but I think it was one of those 'lets just chuck him in' sort of things. Until I got into the first team I'd never played at right back in my life. I made my debut for Luton in midfield alongside Brian Horton away at Ipswich Town. I signed as a wide midfield player and came through the ranks playing in that position. That's what I thought my position was going to be as I'd played on the right and centrally in midfield also, for the reserves at Luton. I think I played one more game in the first team, out on the right side of midfield the week after at home to Everton when Mark Stein made his debut. Ricky was out and I wore the Number 7 shirt and I had Kirk Stephens playing behind me that day at right back. I don't remember much about it apart from that Mal Donaghy was sent off for bringing down Adrian Heath and we ended up losing 3-0. The first team was struggling and under a bit of pressure at the time and it was like a bit of a whirlwind really. So, following those two difficult defeats, both 3-0 losses, I think the staff had second thoughts and felt that perhaps it wasn't a place for the young lads just yet so myself and Mark Stein were back out of the team. Kirk Stephens was the right back at the time but when he got injured and eventually left to go to Coventry City, they chucked me in at right back and the rest is history. Apart from a few games at centre back I never played in any other position again.

A player who I really liked and that I learnt a lot from when I was coming through was Rob Johnson, he was a fantastic lad, a real gentleman. He was very unlucky in his football career as he had an injury that not many players have even once, but he had it twice. He had two horrific cruciate knee injuries, one in each knee, which he came back from both times. He was massively under-rated but I looked up to him when I was a young player and certainly learnt a lot from him. He was technically excellent, defensively sound, could read the game as he had a real football brain, so the opposition found it difficult to get past him. Ultimately, I probably didn't help his career at Luton as I came through, restricting his chances in the right back slot.

When David Moss left the football club in the summer of 1985, I took over his place as the PFA player rep. I was only twenty years old and it wasn't something that I sought out to take on. It came about when, one day we were on the team bus and as a young player you'd always sit down the front, older ones would be down the back, while manager and coaches would also be down the front. David Pleat gave me a folder. I looked up at him and said asked what it was. "You're the new PFA rep," he said. I could see all the players further down the bus sniggered as none of them wanted to do it. However, it actually did me a massive favour as I had to learn about pensions and all things like that. Eventually, I had senior players, some ten years older than me, coming to ask me questions about what was going on so I had to learn everything about the role, but it really did put me in good stead going forward. David Pleat thought it would be good for me and that in the long term I would get the most benefit, and he was right.

On contracts, you'd start off with your two-year apprenticeship. Half way through, after a year, they could get rid of you so if you made it into your second year, you were quite happy with that. If you got a year pro contract offered then that was fantastic. When you were an apprentice you got your digs paid for but when you turned pro then you had to pay for your own accommodation. By the time you'd paid a little bit of tax and paid your digs you were actually no better off than when you were an apprentice. Obviously, however, it was better in terms that you no longer had to carry out all the jobs in and around the ground… That first year as a pro, though, you would be expected to be playing the reserves and working towards knocking on the first team door.

I did alright my first year as a pro and at the end of that twelve months I was told that I was going to get another year's pro contract. At this point a number of senior players were telling me that I should ask for a signing-on fee. I was thinking to myself I couldn't do that, but the older lads kept encouraging me. In the end, I went into Pleaty's office, he told me to sit down then proceeded to tell me what I'd get with the new contract. At this point I said, "Boss, is there any chance of a signing-on fee?" He looked at me with an incredulous expression and hollered, "WHAT?" I could see he was quite taken aback and I started to think that at least I'd asked. But then he turned around and said, "I'll tell you what I'll do, I'll get you some relocation money to help you buy a house as a deposit." I thanked him and left his office, realising I was going to have to buy a house!

Because my parents were in St Neots I found a house to buy there, as I knew the area. Soon after I bought it, I was heading out to training but the boss stopped me. He said, "What are you doing buying a house in St Neots?" I reminded him he'd told me to buy a house and he said, "Not in St Neots! How far is that?' "About thirty miles, boss," I replied. "You're not living there, you'll have to rent it out and stay in digs," he said. I agreed to this but then had to go away and work out how to rent this house out. I sorted it and stayed in digs from that point on. Once I got into the first team I got a better contract and then bought a flat in Luton but kept the house in St Neots so that I always had a rental property. It was something I kept doing as it was easy, but it was almost by default that Pleaty helped me to do it. So, he set me on my way with the PFA role and with the house, which was something that took me through.

At the end of my first full season in the first team I found myself earning a place in an FA Cup semi-final at Villa Park against Everton. That felt surreal to be involved in as it was such a massive game. It was an exciting build up to the day and then along with the massive following from the Luton Town supporters; the atmosphere was fantastic. Despite the end result those are the days you remember. It was in the days before the semi-finals were played at Wembley, as well as the final, but played at a neutral ground, and with the two opposing groups of fans there it was just electric. I was quite close to Ricky when he scored the opening goal in the first half and we were down the end where the Luton supporters were. The noise from the crowd was so loud and we all jumped together, we were screaming at each other in this huddle on the pitch as it was just an amazing moment to take the lead in an FA Cup semi-final. However, sadly it wasn't to be. I can remember little bits of the game but it's amazing how you almost put the whole thing to bed, so to speak, because there was always another game coming just around the corner. We had Norwich City at home, midweek, and then we had Manchester United at home, also in the league, the following game so David and the staff would train our minds, soon

Tim Breacker scores his first ever senior goal for Luton Town away at Newcastle United

enough, onto those games. Everton were The team at the time as well so there was no shame losing having pushed them so close right to the end of extra time. We played them often around that time as well and we had some right old battles whilst they were winning league titles, and cups both domestically and in Europe. Everyone outside of Luton perhaps thought we would get annihilated but we did get so close to getting to the final.

Oddly enough, I did actually attend the FA Cup final that year as back then, and it was a long time ago so things like this used to go on, it was just how it was then, the club used to get tickets for the players. When you were a youngster coming through you didn't even get to see the ticket, you'd just be told you did have a ticket but it had been sold. Somebody would then give you some money and being naïve, you'd accept that was how things were. However, this year I made sure that I actually got the ticket and went to the game. Believe it or not I ended up in the Everton section, but as I was watching I couldn't help thinking that could have been us out there against Manchester United.

At the end of the season that followed the Villa Park semi-final, David Pleat left Luton Town and I remember everyone around the club being quite shocked when he took the manager's job at Tottenham. I met up with Mitchell and he told me that he was going, too. I told him I was pleased for him. But, to be honest, it was a big deal for me as Trevor Hartley and John Sheridan also went with Pleaty. I'd kind of grown up with Mitchell over those previous five years, doing our apprenticeships together and then being in the youth team. It was a big upheaval.

David never came back for me to join him and Mitchell at Tottenham, but later on in my career when he was manager of Sheffield Wednesday and I was still at West Ham, he did ring me in the summer, but nothing happened. It was in the days of when your contract was up you'd go onto a week-to-week deal, which happened to me at West Ham. I was told I would be getting an improved contract but then it wasn't what was promised. That, however, is a long story. The bottom line is that I was on a week-to-week throughout the summer and I was free to speak to people at other clubs, and then it would have to be sorted out at a transfer tribunal for any fee to be passed between the buying and the selling club. I never had an agent right the way through my career although late on, a couple tried to represent me but I pointed out that I'd managed myself and if they could do better then fair enough. But I never signed with an agency. Because I was with the PFA they were good at helping and representing players, anyway.

However, on the back of those changes in the summer of 1986, John Moore, who was a massive figure for me and for my career, ended up being the first team manager of Luton Town with Ray Harford also joining the club at that time as a first team coach under John. I liked John to bits, he was fantastic for me as a young player and as a person.He passed so much good on to me; morals, encouragement, as well as discipline, which everyone needed. He was truly brilliant for me and I could never thank him enough.

I later found out something that perhaps I wished I hadn't. I'd just finished my playing career at QPR and I went onto the staff. I shared an office with our chief scout and it turned out that he was the former chief scout from Arsenal. He told me he'd wanted to sign me from Luton Town for Arsenal back in 1987. He'd strongly recommended me to George Graham as he was just rebuilding the side at Highbury back then. However, George opted for Lee Dixon as he wanted a more 'stay at home' traditional full back, whereas my game was always thinking about going forward and getting crosses in, more like a modern-day full back/wing back, so he signed Lee from Stoke City instead of coming in for me. When I heard this I really didn't know what to make of it and I kind of wished he hadn't told me, but I think he meant it as a compliment. I certainly never got wind of it back then and I was most certainly not aware of any bid if it was ever made. But, as I said earlier, I never had an agent throughout my career so if there ever was any move from Arsenal I was never made aware of it.

I left Luton Town in October 1990 and was the first player signed by

Billy Bonds, the new manager at West Ham United. Although I wasn't looking to leave, the club accepted the offer and that was pretty much it, but I look back with immense pride that such a great professional and a great bloke as Billy Bonds wanted me to be a part of his team.

I continued playing with West Ham for nine seasons before finishing my playing career with two years at QPR. A coaching and scouting career followed with spells at QPR, Plymouth Argyle, Leicester City, Millwall, Charlton Athletic, Bradford City and Bolton Wanderers.

I've ended up living in Market Harborough, Leicestershire, a nice little town with good schools. The people are okay, too, and it's not far from my parents who are still in St Neots in Cambridgeshire. There's a good link to Bicester in Oxfordshire to my wife's family and it's where we were both born. I was with Ian Holloway as his assistant at Leicester City, not for long, but with the kids being in schools we just stayed as it's a good central position in the country for wherever work takes me, whether that's back down to London or North, South, East or West; it's a good base.

*Tim will always be fondly remembered for his time at Kenilworth Road not least for being an integral part of that excellent Luton Town side that progressed through the 1980s and certainly not least for the 1988 League Cup win over Arsenal and of course 'that' goal at the Baseball Ground vs Derby County in May 1990.*

(BORN 9 MARCH 1961, LUTON)

# WAYNE LESLIE TURNER

LUTON TOWN FC 1977 - 1985

*Making his debut for Luton reserves as an apprentice at the age of fifteen, Wayne was originally signed on schoolboy terms the year before. Becoming a hard working and dedicated player, he moved to several different clubs throughout this career, taking up various positions in both defence and as a midfield player, coach, and as manager of Stevenage Borough for a short time in 2002.*

'Boss', 'David', 'Pleaty' are all names I've used for David Pleat over the years, along with a few other names when we've had words throughout our player and manager relationship, usually when he'd dropped me. He was my boss and if I'm talking to him today over a cup of coffee, he's David. We completed a journey from me being a fifteen-year-old school boy to now being a friend and we meet up to share a coffee whenever we can.

Over the years there's not been that many out and out Lutonians playing for the club. As I came through there was myself, Mitchell Thomas, Ray Daniel and a little later, Kingsley Black, the rest of the boys drifted in and drifted out. I grew up near Lewsey Farm and went to Ferrars School and then onto Challney High School. That was a great era as you had Les Harriott, Mick Pacey, myself, and not forgetting Kerry Dixon, all coming out of Challney from our year group. However, David decided not to sign Kerry but signed the three of us (me, Les and Mick) all at the same time. In fact, seven out of the eleven that played for Luton Schools all signed scholarships with clubs. Kerry Dixon was also in the Luton Schools team but didn't sign as scholar anywhere, so we actually had eight of the eleven in that team, something never to be repeated, a real one-off wonder.

David was the reserve team coach at the time that he came to Challney

David Pleat signing Wayne (next to Pleat) in 1976 whilst still at Challney High School; also signing that day were Les Harriott and 1959 FA Cup finalist Dave Pacey's son Mick Pacey.

and he signed me, Les Harriott and Dave Pacey's son Mick, on the same day. Mick Pacey was the most well-known at the time being the son of Luton Town legend, Dave Pacey. Ken Gutteridge was there for the early days with the first team, but I was too young really. I have to mention Danny Bergara, David Coates, and Trevor Hartley, though. David Pleat signed us all, initially on school boy terms as fourteen year olds and then Danny Bergara took us on. Danny was magnificent, absolutely wonderful as a youth coach, he was phenomenal, really ahead of his time in terms of his coaching technique. We all learnt and developed massively under Danny and then he handed us over to David when he went to Sheffield United alongside Harry Haslam. Between those four, including David, they really inspired me to go onto coaching when I finished playing. Danny Bergara used to say that I was a thinking footballer, as I didn't have an abundance of pace, although I could run all day. Therefore, I had to think as a footballer and I was like a coach playing football. I was coaching local teams and winning awards and I won the 'Sos Allen Award' for services to the Lewsey Centre for my work in Luton when I was still young myself at seventeen/eighteen. I was running Lewsey's Under 12s and Under 14s so I knew that I was always going to be a coach. The award was named after a local man Derek 'Sos' Allen who'd played for Limbury Boys' Club as a youth player, and back then, in the 1950s, he'd had spells on both Arsenal and Luton Town's books before moving away. He came back to the Luton area and in later years played in the South Beds League and served on many local league committees. He was still playing on Sundays when he died in 1978 aged just forty-eight. The Luton District and South Beds League went on to name a competition, 'The Sos Allen Cup' in his honour.

When I left that environment at Kenilworth Road I went to Coventry, Brentford and Barnet, and earlier I went out on loan to Lincoln City where Colin Murphy was the manager. He had a different way of playing football and was a totally different type of manager to David. I loved it at Lincoln and it worked for me. But for pure coaching you couldn't get better than the fab four,Danny, David Coates, Trevor Hartley and David Pleat.They were all brilliant in different ways, and they were firm but fair. David Pleat was the first person to coach pattern of play, which really opened my eyes. David would set up a team shape where you would be unopposed then take it into a phase of play towards goal and then into an 11v11. That stayed with me and made a real impression on me far more so than anything else that I've seen. David would continually focus on that; it was where he was at his best. What Trevor Hartley and David Coates were always adamant about was that you should always strike a moving ball, never start any passing drills or start any coaching session with a static ball because in a game, that's considered a re-start. It wasn't about being technically brilliant at passing or receiving a static ball, it had to be on the move and to be able to pass it and control it and then pass it again; it all went hand in hand.

I went to see David Coates to ask him why I wasn't being considered for the first team, as I had been made captain in the reserves at seventeen. He said the main reason I was captain of the reserves meant I wouldn't be getting in the first team anytime soon. He continued, "I think there are better players coming up behind you by the likes of Neil Madden and Rob Johnson." I told him I'd prove him wrong, and I did. I went out on loan to Lincoln City aged twenty, and after I came back I stayed in the first team for three and a half years. So, it was a kick up the arse for me. I don't think he did it for that reason, though, I just think he was being honest. That's how it was then. David Pleat was harsh on the kids in my eyes, definitely giving the benefit of the doubt to the more senior pro's. How he spoke to and treated them in comparison to the lads coming through was chalk and cheese but that's how it was and you had to get on with it and fight your corner, it really was dog eat dog and we had to be incredibly mentally strong.

The Eastern Junior Cup competition was inclusive up to Under 19s so this team was split over three age groups. Godfrey Ingram was a year older than me; Nigel Johnson, he's the lad leaning on me, sadly passed away about fifteen years ago, a really lovely person, bless him, was also a year older than me; and Rob, who was a year younger. That's Gary Sisman

The youth team with Gary Sisman holding aloft the Eastern Junior Cup after a 3-2 win over Ipswich Town, Wayne bottom right

with the cup, he was the captain, the Boy Wonder at that time as he was in the England Youth Team. Godfrey was also in the youth set up with England. However, when Gary came back from one particular England trip, he couldn't get back into our youth team at Luton, it was bonkers, but by now you had Les Harriott and Clive Goodyear at centre half so Gary had to be fitted in at left back, which he hated. Soon after that he got released and signed for Hitchin Town all within the space of a year of playing for England. He actually went into the boss's office as a Luton Town player but came out as a Hitchin one. I was waiting for him that day, and I couldn't believe it because we'd signed pro together on the same day on my seventeenth birthday. Gary is six months older than me so as I signed pro, Luton also signed him as well because of his England situation. As he was involved in the England set up the club had to sign him as a pro at seventeen and a half but by 18 and a half, he was playing for Hitchin. It was as quick as that, which was awful for him.

When I made my debut for Luton's reserves, I was fifteen and still attending Challney Boys' School in the town, so I had to come out of school early on a Tuesday or Wednesday afternoon. In those days we played the games over at Chryslers in Houghton Regis. It was the most magnificent surface that I'd played on, a real top-class pitch. One particular time we were in the dressing rooms getting ready to play against Chelsea. I was playing at left back and was against Charlie Cooke, who by then was thirty-two. My Dad loved him from playing in the 60s and early 70s so this was a really proud moment. I saw Dad pull up in his Eastern Electricity truck, as he was a maintenance man for the electric board, he got out of the truck and started walking across the pitch in his wellies making everyone think that he was there to do some work around the ground. I had my hand over my eyes thinking, Oh, Dad, please go and hide yourself, but he was shouting over to me, "Good luck, Wayne!" You can imagine me lining up against Chelsea while my dad's on the sidelines in his wellies!

I can still name that team today: John Phillips in goal, Graham Wilkins at right back, the centre halves were Steve Wicks and John Dempsey, John Sparrow at left back, then in midfield there was Garry Stanley, who was 'gorgeous' (laughs), and Ian Britton. Wide right was Charlie Cooke, on the left was Clive Walker and then up front they had Tommy Langley and Teddy Maybank. I was fifteen years old coming up against that team.

Playing for us was Dixie Deans, a former Celtic player and Scottish international who was capped twice only a few years earlier in 1974, but on this day he was playing in Luton's reserves with me. Dixie came into the dressing room, and this is the God's honest truth, the boss was taking the team talk as he was still the reserve team coach at the time, and while David was talking I was sat next to Dixie Deans who was smoking a cigarette, swigging a little drop of whiskey, and looking at a nude calendar that he'd 'found' in the dressing room. There was me, a nervous wreck, doing my stretches, and I turned around to see Dixie calm as you like. I think he went out and got both of our goals in a 2-2 draw. That day made a real impression on me coming up against a line up like that Chelsea side, playing on that brilliant surface and Dixie Deans having a pre-match smoke, drop of whiskey and a thumb through a nude calendar with the boss either not noticing, or turning a blind eye!

Also, during this time at the club, we used to play our youth team games at the Co-op ground right up at the top of Stockingstone Road, in Round Green, Stopsley. We'd play the youth team games on a Saturday morning whilst the reserves would play in the afternoon. This particular game, we were playing Swindon Town, I was sub for the youth team because I was playing in the reserves. However, Swindon turned up with only eleven players so Danny Bergara, who was taking the youth team, said to me, "Look, Wayne, they're struggling for numbers so you be sub for Swindon because we've got enough players but they need one more to be their sub." I accepted this from Danny and went into their dressing room, put on a Swindon kit and lined up as sub for them just in case they got an injury. Half way through the second half, they did get an injury. In the meantime, David came up to watch the game before he took the reserves match in the afternoon and Swindon put me on in place of their injured player. I picked up the ball, burst through midfield, got my shot away and it smacked the Luton post and came out. The score at this point was 0-0 so that would have put Swindon in the lead against us. Danny Bergara started screaming

Wayne in the summer of 1981

on the sideline in his broken English with a Spanish accent, "Hey Wayney, Wayney, what are you doing you little shitty? Stop that, stop that, you're injured, you're injured, go down, you little shitty, go down." I looked over and thought, What? I went down and waited for the physio to come on and he said, "Right, you're coming off!" I'd only been on for ten minutes, even though it left them with just ten players and with that, Luton went on to win 3-0. Danny ordered me to go take a shower, so as I was heading for the changing rooms David followed after me and started giving me a bollocking. "What have you come off for, you're not even injured?" he said, then added: "And if you are injured then you can't play for me this afternoon!" I started to protest that I was alright, but he wasn't having any of it. I was well and truly stitched up between the pair of them by helping out Swindon for just ten minutes, and this led to David and Danny having a row over the incident of me coming off.

Those were great days for playing football for the pure joy of it as you'd be playing in the youth team in the morning and then you'd go and play in the reserves in the afternoon. The Combination League on a Saturday afternoon was great because it was so big. You'd being playing against the likes of Arsenal, Chelsea, Tottenham, all the big hitters, and they were fantastic games whilst still really playing for the love of it, but at the same time coming up against some massive names in the reserves, whilst they were coming back having been out injured or having suffered a loss of form and finding themselves out of their respective first teams.

My first team debut was away at Wrexham in the last game of the 1978/79 season. I'd just won Young Player of the Year award a week earlier and I'd been signed as a pro for a little while by then. Now, this was the first time that I'd ever gone away overnight and the first time that I'd ever had a proper pre-match meal. After the team meeting, the boss had told me that I was in the squad, but he hadn't told me that I was playing. I went down to the pre-match meal and it was the best feast that I'd ever seen up until that point in my life. Trouble was, I ate everything; the steak, the chicken, the beans and the potatoes, because coming from one of four boys at home we always had to fight for table rights. For me to see all of that food was like heaven, but I'd forgotten that it was pre-match. About an hour later, David told me I was playing and I spent the next hour running around on Wrexham's pitch with stomach cramps as I had the biggest dinner ever still in my belly! David eventually took me off after about seventy minutes but it was one of those moments when you learn and realise that a pre-match meal is exactly what it says and NOT a feast. I don't remember too much about the game itself, I think we lost 2-0, but I just remember running around in pain. A good friend of mine from later in life told me that he actually sat next to my mum and dad that day at Wrexham. He said that my dad couldn't stop crying as I was making my senior debut in the football league for Luton, but if he'd known how much I'd eaten pre-match then he really would've had a reason to cry.

Mark Aizlewood was suspended after he'd been sent off at Wrexham in my debut in that last game of the 1978/79 season, and his suspension carried over into the new season. I therefore played at left back at home to Cambridge United and away at Bristol Rovers, too. In the Cambridge game I came up against a flying winger for Cambridge, Derrick Christie. Alan Biley, the former Luton Town player was in the Cambridge United team that day as well. Alan was a player who David Pleat had a fair amount of history with, from trying to keep him in check whilst he was on the books at Kenilworth Road. Alan went on to get a move to Derby County soon after and then onto Everton amongst other clubs. I had a game against this flying winger for Cambridge United, and then the next game at Bristol Rovers I came up against another flying winger, Stewart Barrowclough, on the Tuesday night. David told me to get tight to him early on and let him know what I was about. Paul Price, who was our captain, came over to me and said, "Wayne, it's alright what the gaffer said but make sure you smash him in the first minute because you never get booked for the first one. I'm all, "Okay, Paul, that's brilliant, thanks." I went in two footed in the first minute, and as I was crumpled over the top of him the ref was booking me! I looked over the ref's shoulder and saw Paul Price pissing himself. My captain was laughing and now I had to play the next eighty-nine minutes against this flying winger on a yellow card. Paul battered me afterwards and said, "You don't do what I tell you, you do what the gaffer tells you!" Coincidentally, the Bristol Rovers game was Mike Saxby's league debut for Luton Town that night as he'd also been serving a suspension held over from the previous season whilst he was still at Mansfield Town.

Wayne salutes his goal in the 5-0 thrashing of Brighton in September 1983

David was in awe of Brian Clough, he loved him and there was a period where Forest had won the European Cup so they were getting invited to play everywhere. When they didn't go, however, Luton Town would be the substitutes and go in place of Cloughy's Forest. We'd be heading off out to the middle of nowhere during breaks in the regular season due to bad weather in England, Kuwait or Abi Dhabi or somewhere like that without much notice. Around January time in 1981, we got told we were going to play one of these games abroad. We'd gone out there and had a right good laugh, had a few beers as well as playing the football match of course. I don't think David joined us on this particular trip. When we came back, I think it was on the Thursday, we were met by David Pleat who told us we were playing Third Division Rotherham United away in another mid-season friendly to keep us ticking over. So we travelled up the next day having only just returned from our travels. We got absolutely hammered 5-0 and as we came back into the dressing room after the game, the boss sat us all down said, "Look, you've all come back from abroad with a sickness bug and diarrhoea." He looked around the room pointing at players. "Wayne, you've got the shits, Kirk, you've got the shits, and Mossy, you've got terrible shits." He then went straight past Mick Saxby and said to one or two more of the lads, "Yep, you've got sickness and diarrhoea, too." Then Mick Saxby chirps up, "What about me, gaffer?" to which the reply came from the boss, "No, you were just shit!"

Manchester City away in 1983, that 1-0 win. If you see David do that infamous run and dance across the pitch in his beige suit and beige shoes, there's two things here: Without me, Luton would have gone down that day because if I hadn't come off then Raddy wouldn't have gone on and scored, so I saved the club, not Raddy (tongue in cheek, chuckling). The other thing is when the boss goes on that run, if you look at it closely I beat him out the blocks from the dugout with my sweat shirt on running onto the pitch. As the camera follows him and as he catches up with Brian Horton, who I've already made it to and am hugging, David makes it over

Wayne leads the charge ahead of David Pleat at the final whistle of the momentous 1-0 away win at Manchester City in May 1983

to Nobby and elbows me in the chops and gives Brian Horton the biggest hug ever. He doesn't cuddle the pair of us, he gives me the elbow as he just wants his skipper, which is fair enough so I ran off to embrace someone else.

I remember that game so vividly, in a crowd of 45,000 we had 5,000 Luton fans and 40,000 fans were singing 'You're going down, you're going down' for eighty-five minutes of the game. But our five thousand fans were magnificent and turned it on the Man City fans after Raddy scored by singing 'You're going down!' and that's what happened; we won the game 1-0, we stayed up and Man City were relegated. Obviously, the home crowd erupted and it got ugly on the pitch with us players being set upon by some of their supporters. I have some pictures that someone sent to me around a year or two ago on my phone, one where I'm trying to fight my way out and another of Raddy just running off the pitch as me and Paul Elliott are in amongst it with their fans, and I think Trevor Aylott is in the background, too. We managed to get off the pitch but by then it had kicked off in the tunnel with a couple of Man City players. I think it was mainly Dennis Tueart and Nobby Horton, but I wasn't actually involved in the scuffle in the tunnel as we'd only just made it off the pitch after we'd had to fight our way off. It was frightening, but we just did what we had to do.

In March 1984, we played against Ipswich away. David loved two managers, Brian Clough and Bobby Robson, amongst other managers that he got on really well with, but those two, as I remember, really stood out as his favourite to come up against or just to talk football with. At Portman Road this day we lost 3-0. When we got back on the coach, there was a crate of beer at the back as we had to be back on the bus from the players' lounge after the match by 6pm. However, before we left the car park we'd drank all the beers because David had stayed behind talking to the former Ipswich and by then England manager, Bobby Robson for as long as he wanted. When David did get on the bus we were all singing 'Why are we waiting?' and he just looked at us for a few moments, 'gestured' to us and promptly turned around and went back to have another drink with Bobby Robson, making us wait another hour.

The year earlier in September 1983 away at Forest, David was up against another favourite in Brian Clough. As soon as we arrived and put all the kit away in our dressing room, David went 'missing'. We assumed he'd gone to see Cloughy. We never saw him again until five minutes before kick-off looking a little bit 'red cheeked' when he just wished us all the best for the game. As we went out for the kick-off I glanced at the two dug outs and noticed David sitting quite sombre, whereas Cloughy was bouncing around laughing and giggling and without saying that they'd had a drink, I think it spoke for itself. David came in at half time but he was totally subdued and looked a little under the weather. We went out in the second half but couldn't get the goal back after having gone behind and ended up losing the game 1-0. I think David went to see Brian after the game as well, maybe for a top up! I got murdered by their right winger Steve Wigley that day, who went on to be a coach, a decent lad. I think I got 5 out of 10 the next day in the News of the World player ratings. All the lads used to look to see what marks they got the next day in the Sunday papers, which was pathetic. As footballers you're listening to a piss head of a reporter to hear the marks out of 10 that you got where I'd be delighted to get a 7 most weeks.

In October 1984, we'd played about five or six games into the season, when myself and Bunny (Frank Bunn) were 'enjoying' a run in the side, but we had a team crisis meeting on the Monday as we'd had a bad start. This reached crisis point with the final straw losing away to Sunderland at Roker Park 3-0. We were called in for this meeting on the Monday before we headed out to training and David opened up the meeting with, "We've got a massive problem here, lads." He let that hang in the air for a while, then said, "At the moment Wayne and Frank are our best players!" That was a back-handed compliment if ever I heard one!

A month later in November 1984, we were away in Manchester at Old Trafford. In those days we played a sort of formation that was four-three and a half-two and a half. Mossy would be in between midfield/up front and wide left. What that meant was the central midfield player, which was me, would sometimes be outnumbered because you'd have Ricky on the right and me in the middle looking after two, so we were often overloaded in central midfield. Before the game David, was giving his team talk back at the hotel scribbling on his blackboard, going through all the tactics. That day Manchester United's midfield was Remi Moses sitting in front of the back four, with Bryan Robson behind the front two. Jesper Olsen was wide left and Gordon Strachan wide right. Basically, they played a diamond formation in their midfield and my job was to look after Moses and Robson. We were playing this four-three and a half-two and a half and with David continuing his team talk showing the players where to go, he then said to me, "Wayne, what I want you to do is get in the middle of them two and be a right nuisance." There must have been sixty yards front to back. So I questioned it and David repeated his instruction. I hardly touched the ball the whole game. Ricky and Tim Breacker were looking after Jesper Olsen so they were 2 v 1, then you had our left-sided players taking care of Strachan and good old me in the middle with Moses and Robson. That was a cracker being asked to sit in between those two and 'be a REAL nuisance'.

It was true in my head that I was still trying to make it as a professional footballer when I packed up through injury at the age of twenty-nine, because even though you've played ten or so years you were always looking behind at who was coming up after you and you were always looking at the one in front who you were trying to get after. You'd be looking for longer contracts, and if you only had a one-year contract you'd be looking for a two-year contract. You'd be trying to get more money because, as I said, after twenty-four years of age you start to realise that time as a footballer is running out. Even at twenty-four you're thinking you've only got seven or eight years left if you're lucky and you've got to make some money here, so it does open your eyes up as you get older. You're past that youthful honeymoon period of being a professional footballer when you come in

1985; on the day of his 24th Birthday, Wayne scores the famous goal that secured Luton's passage into the FA Cup Quarter Finals finally seeing off Watford with a 1-0 win after three titanic matches

at seventeen. Luton actually signed me on pro forms on my seventeenth birthday, for the main reason I believe, that other clubs wanted to sign me. Luton Town gave me a three-year contract on £30 a week because there was interest from someone else. Perhaps if there hadn't been any interest in me elsewhere maybe they wouldn't have bothered signing me as a pro at that point. From then on I played from seventeen to twenty-four and up until then I certainly wasn't doing it for the money. I was doing it because I loved the club and I loved football and then it all changed. I'd got relentless stick from the crowd, absolutely battered, between the ages of twenty up to twenty-three. One of the reasons for this, I felt, was that I was being used as a continuous 'Polyfilla' player without ever being given the one position to make my own. When I did get my position in the centre of midfield, which is where I had always wanted to play, I became a regular in the side and I played better. Then, to top it all off, I got 'that' goal against Watford in the FA Cup, It was the second replay and it was my twenty-fourth birthday that day. Thereafter, everyone idolised me and I'm an unlikely hero still to this day, but it left me thinking if I hadn't scored that goal in the FA Cup replay what would have happened?

In my last eighteen months at the club I finally became a centre midfield regular. That was important to me because I loved playing in a consistent role. I'm sixty in March (2021) and still now, every birthday, I get people WhatsApping me about that Watford goal. I've got two pictures of it on my wall in the office. The first still of the photo the camera captures me hitting the ball with the whole of The Bobbers Stand behind me still sitting there, and then in the next still it shows the ball going past Tony Coton in the Watford goal. By now the crowd in The Bobbers Stand are up and going mental just a split second after the first image. I have these side by side on the wall in my office.

It was the Millwall game in the FA Cup Quarter Final at Kenilworth

Road in 1985 and my mum, dad and my brothers couldn't get in the ground; it was all smashed up before they got there. The game passed me by. I don't really remember anything of the actual match but a couple of things that did stay with me, we had the Bobbers Stand's orange seats being spun at us during the warm up. As we were out on the pitch going through our stretches, the away end was throwing them at us like frisbees. You knew there was going to be trouble even before the kick off. The match started but we got taken off the pitch by the referee and then brought back on again. Towards the end of the game, we were up the Kenilworth Road end and the ref told us that he was going to blow the whistle when the corner was taken, that he'd blow for full time. As he blew, Les Sealey caught the ball and volleyed it towards the half way line, and he ran so fast that he was past the ball before it had the chance to come back down. He was the first one off as he'd been having things thrown at him from behind his goal in the second half. The morning after we came in for a warm down I remember going around up by the Kenilworth Road end where Les was in goal and there were pool balls, darts, coins, rocks, just about anything and everything had been thrown onto the pitch. Every hooligan from London came up to the town for a night out and smashed it to bits.

David's team talk at Villa Park in the semi-final against Everton, who were the top team in the country at that point in time having gone something like thirty matches unbeaten so we were massive underdogs on the day, was to go out there and do what you could, just be yourselves. He also said to go out early and enjoy the atmosphere and to feed off it. We were wondering what he was talking about as it was still early, but we went out at a quarter to two to find the Holte end was already full, absolutely rammed with our supporters. David told me to go and enjoy it, go and have a look. I got up and went out there first because I just couldn't wait. As I got out onto the side of the pitch, I just waved my programme up to the fans and the whole stand just erupted, then I turned around thinking who's come out with me? but there was nobody with me. It really blew me away, it was the best feeling and as I still had some hair on my head

Wayne battling with Everton's Peter Reid along with Brian Stein in the 1985 FA Cup semi final at Villa Park

back then, my hair just rose up, it was unbelievable, the best feeling ever. I turned around again and eventually, David and the rest of the lads came out onto the pitch as well. I was bursting though, to get that wave and that response from the crowd at an FA Cup semi-final was amazing. How disappointing it was to lose, though. It was a massive disappointment having been 1-0 up with four minutes to go only to eventually lose in extra time to a Derek Mountfield header. People were saying to me afterwards, 'Wayne, well done, brilliant what you have done for the club, you'll get a chance again'. However, FA Cup semi-finals are not like London buses, I knew that it was never going to happen and they were just saying these things to cheer me up and that was the heartbreak. In that game, the staff, which was David Pleat, Trevor Hartley and David Coates sitting in the dugout, took Mick Harford off in extra time and put on David Moss.

I watched a video a number of years ago back in 2004 when I was European scout for Leicester City. I was watching games all over the country and abroad. For some reason my nine-year-old son, Bradley, wanted to watch the semi-final so I got the old video recorder out and we watched the game. Brad kept saying, "You're going to win this, wow, look at you, you'll win this, you're 1-0 up!" I said, "Brad, we don't win this game." I'd never known for that whole time since 1985 to that day in 2004, almost twenty years later, that the staff had taken Mick Harford off. However, what I did realise when I watched it as a coach/chief scout was that nobody was marking Mountfield on the free kick as Mossy wouldn't have marked anyone, but the incredible thing is that I watched that through the week and on the following Saturday I went on a scouting mission to Coventry. I went in the tea room before the game and couldn't believe who was in there… David Pleat, David Coates and Trevor Hartley, all working for different clubs. I walked in and told them what I'd just seen earlier that week, the game that I hadn't seen for twenty years. I said, "Which one of you made the decision to take Mick Harford off in extra time but never got anyone to pick up Mountfield on set plays?" They all, collectively, asked me what I was on about. "Semi-final, twenty years ago, I watched it on Thursday and one of you never got someone to take on Mick Harford's defensive jobs on set pieces, one of you cost me a medal." I was laughing throughout this and as I walked back out of the tea room I left all three of them arguing amongst themselves. I really couldn't get over the irony of bumping into all three of them together only days after having watched the game for first time in twenty years.

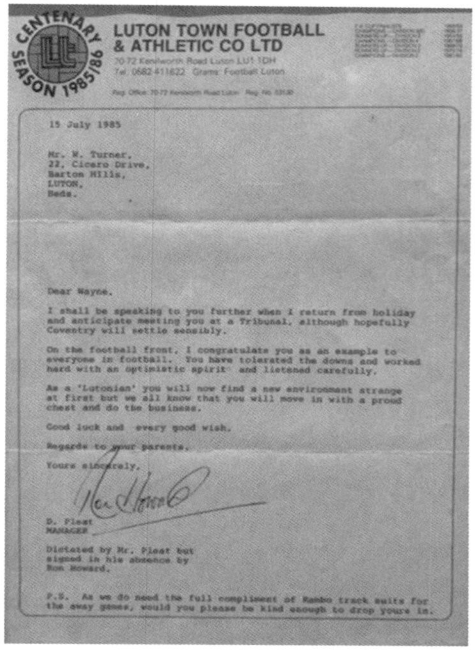
LUTON TOWN FOOTBALL & ATHLETIC CO LTD
70-72 Kenilworth Road Luton LU1 1DH
Tel 0582 411622 Grams: Football Luton

15 July 1985

Mr. W. Turner,
22, Cicero Drive,
Barton Hills,
LUTON,
Beds.

Dear Wayne,

I shall be speaking to you further when I return from holiday and anticipate meeting you at a Tribunal, although hopefully Coventry will settle sensibly.

On the football front, I congratulate you as an example to everyone in football. You have tolerated the downs and worked hard with an optimistic spirit and listened carefully.

As a 'Lutonian' you will now find a new environment strange at first but we all know that you will move in with a proud chest and do the business.

Good luck and every good wish.

Regards to your parents.

Yours sincerely,

D. Pleat
MANAGER

Dictated by Mr. Pleat but signed in his absence by Ron Howard.

P.S. As we do need the full compliment of Rambo track suits for the away games, would you please be kind enough to drop youre in.

After playing in the 1985 semi-final for Luton at Villa Park against Everton, David Pleat and the then chairman of the club David Evans, both sent me letters independently of each other. Both of these letters are now framed and on the wall in my office. The one from David Evans says:

Saturday was the best game that you've ever played, we know that you're leaving, well done, thank you so much.

Then in the letter from the boss, it reads:

Wayne, I congratulate you as an example to everyone in football. You've tolerated the downs and worked hard with an optimistic spirit. All the stuff that you want to hear, but at the bottom of the letter David says, P.S. As we need the full complement of track suits for away games would you please be kind enough to drop yours in.

When I left Luton to go to Coventry City I'd asked David for a two-year deal and £400 a week wage. This wouldn't have put me anywhere near the best paid player at the club but that's what I felt I was worth. I was coming up to eight years at the club in that summer of 1985. However, the boss said to me, "Wayne, there are two problems with that. One, I don't want to pay you £400 a week and two, if you sign a two-year contract in the summer you'll be in line for a testimonial and to be fair, Wayne, you will have been here for ten years, but you've not played in the team for ten years so I don't think that's fair." I was astounded at this. David carried on: "So, I think the best thing to do is to get yourself a move." Thinking right, okay, I went and signed for Coventry City, where I didn't want to be, as I wanted to stay at Luton. It was the only place I wanted to play and I actually cried on the way home driving back to Luton after having signed to move to Coventry City. However, what I did realise at that point when I got to twenty-four years of age was that I needed to earn some money; it wasn't just about playing for the love of it as I had been doing up until then. Also, I'd just bought my first house and I was starting to understand that money made the world go around.

The boss was just such a massive part of the players' lives, especially mine, from the age of fourteen to twenty-four and then I went back with him at Luton Town where I spent several years coaching afterwards, so I got to know him really well. Later in life when I got into the building game with my own company, I did an extension for him over in Radlett, and I got to know him all over again. It's strange, as when you're a young player, you are beholden to this man with him being your manager and having your career in his hands, but when you go back in later life things do change. It was nice now that he needed me and that I could help him. We'd be on an equal level rather than him being my manager and me being his player, so I could carry on with this project with a different mentality in the relationship.

My recollections of the boss, for the most part, are complimentary. Even if they may come across a little twisted at times. However, that's only because that's how it was back then. To be fair, I do remember at the time when David was stone cold honest with me about not being deserving of a testimonial, had I stayed another two years at Luton. That was the big change for me, a big moment in my life. That's when I did go from playing football for the pure love of it, to playing football as a job and for the money. That one situation switched my mindset and I went on to make more money in my career, with it being less successful (through injury) at Coventry City, but I did alright at Brentford, than I did being (semi) successful at Luton Town. In all those years coming through the ranks you just don't get what you deserve and that's just a fact that's not changed too often now, except if you outgrow your respective football club.

In the forty-five years that I have known David, both up close and from a distance, he has become a good friend, still with a real passion for football and a very sharp wit! Nothing I enjoy more than a catch up with David to have a laugh and an in-depth conversation about "The gorgeous game".

(BORN 16TH MARCH 1947, DONCASTER, WEST RIDING OF YORKSHIRE)

# TREVOR HARTLEY

## LUTON TOWN FC COACH 1980 - 1986

*Although born in Doncaster, Trevor moved with his family to London at the tender age of just six weeks old. Trevor attended the Holloway School, representing them at the English Schools tennis championships held at Wimbledon. He played football for Islington Boys, London Grammar Schools, and A.F.A. Public & Grammar Schools XI as well as London Youth. Trevor signed as a professional footballer with West Ham United on 15th July 1964 and made his senior debut away at The Hawthorns against West Bromwich Albion on 28th April 1966.*

*At West Ham he trained and played with Bobby Moore, Martin Peters, Geoff Hurst, Frank Lampard (Senior), Billy Bonds, Harry Redknapp, Trevor Brooking and his future wife's brother, Bobby Howe. Bobby would accompany Trevor to Bournemouth and then forge a name for himself in the booming North American Soccer League as player/coach with Alan Hinton at the Seattle Sounders. Trevor attended all the World Cup matches at Wembley in 1966 cheering on his team mates in the ultimately victorious England side.*

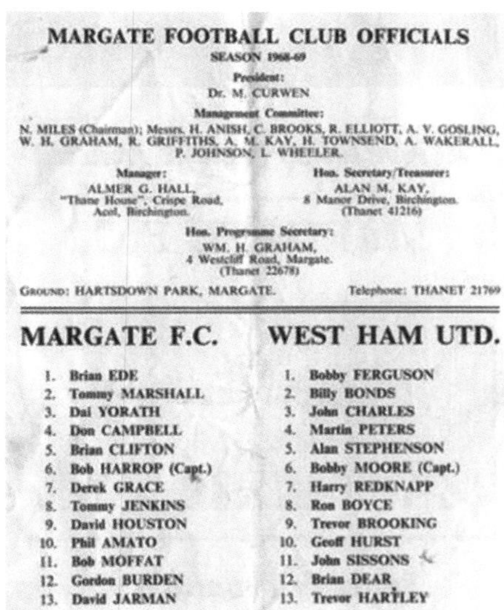

MARGATE FOOTBALL CLUB OFFICIALS

SEASON 1968-69

President:
Dr. M. CURWEN

Management Committee:
N. MILES (Chairman); Messrs. H. ANISH, C. BROOKS, R. ELLIOTT, A. V. GOSLING, W. H. GRAHAM, R. GRIFFITHS, A. M. KAY, H. TOWNSEND, A. WAKERALL, P. JOHNSON, L. WHEELER.

Manager:
ALMER G. HALL,
"Thane House", Crispe Road,
Acol, Birchington.

Hon. Secretary/Treasurer:
ALAN M. KAY,
8 Manor Drive, Birchington.
(Thanet 41216)

Hon. Programme Secretary:
WM. H. GRAHAM,
4 Westcliff Road, Margate.
(Thanet 22678)

GROUND: HARTSDOWN PARK, MARGATE. Telephone: THANET 21769

| MARGATE F.C. | WEST HAM UTD. |
|---|---|
| 1. Brian EDE | 1. Bobby FERGUSON |
| 2. Tommy MARSHALL | 2. Billy BONDS |
| 3. Dai YORATH | 3. John CHARLES |
| 4. Don CAMPBELL | 4. Martin PETERS |
| 5. Brian CLIFTON | 5. Alan STEPHENSON |
| 6. Bob HARROP (Capt.) | 6. Bobby MOORE (Capt.) |
| 7. Derek GRACE | 7. Harry REDKNAPP |
| 8. Tommy JENKINS | 8. Ron BOYCE |
| 9. David HOUSTON | 9. Trevor BROOKING |
| 10. Phil AMATO | 10. Geoff HURST |
| 11. Bob MOFFAT | 11. John SISSONS |
| 12. Gordon BURDEN | 12. Brian DEAR |
| 13. David JARMAN | 13. Trevor HARTLEY |

*Trevor played in a remarkable testimonial match in 1968 for the then Margate FC manager, Almer Hall, who was a former West Ham player. They sent a full-strength team down to the Kent seaside town and the locals were thrilled to see the World Cup winning trio in the West Ham side in Moore, Hurst and Peters. A feast of football was served up with an astonishing 6-6 draw with Martin Peters scoring five goals that night.*

*Trevor went on to play for Bournemouth between 1969 and 1972 scoring three goals in forty-eight appearances for the club before injury curtailed his playing career in June 1972. He joined the Cherries coaching staff.*

*When John Bond left AFC Bournemouth for Norwich in November 1973, the club was briefly run by a committee before Trevor, who was still only twenty-seven years old at the time and reserve team coach, was eventually appointed as his successor. This made him the youngest manager in the football league at the time.*

*One win in their final sixteen games of the 1973/74 season saw the Cherries' promotion bid fall away before Trevor was relieved of his duties shortly after an embarrassing home defeat by Isthmian League champions, Wycombe, in the second round of the FA Cup in January 1975.*

*Following his spell as manager on the Dorset coast, Trevor and his wife, Julie, moved out to Singapore for the next four years, where he had been appointed as director for football to put into place the structure for the game. Trevor would later move out to Malaysia for the position of the National team coach after he left Tottenham having been in joint interim charge along with Doug Livermore for a very short time before Terry Venables came in to take over officially.*

*Upon their return from Singapore with their young family, they moved back into the home they had kept on as a rental property on the outskirts of Bournemouth. But soon after, Trevor was on the move again when he met with David Pleat to discuss a position on the coaching staff at Luton Town, which he accepted.*

I didn't know David Pleat prior to joining Luton Town. We'd already moved back to Bournemouth following our time out in Singapore. Once I'd met him I realised very quickly that I was meeting a really genuinely good football man. He was very good in that I didn't feel pressured to jump straight into a position with the club. He gave me that time and space to consider joining him as we'd not been back in the country for very long. But everything soon fell into place and I was officially joining Luton Town Football Club.

I accepted the role offered to me by David and I was to work with the youth and reserve teams. I joined a great staff that was already in place with David Pleat and David Coates looking after the first team, and I was also to join John Moore. Of course, there was John Sheridan in place as

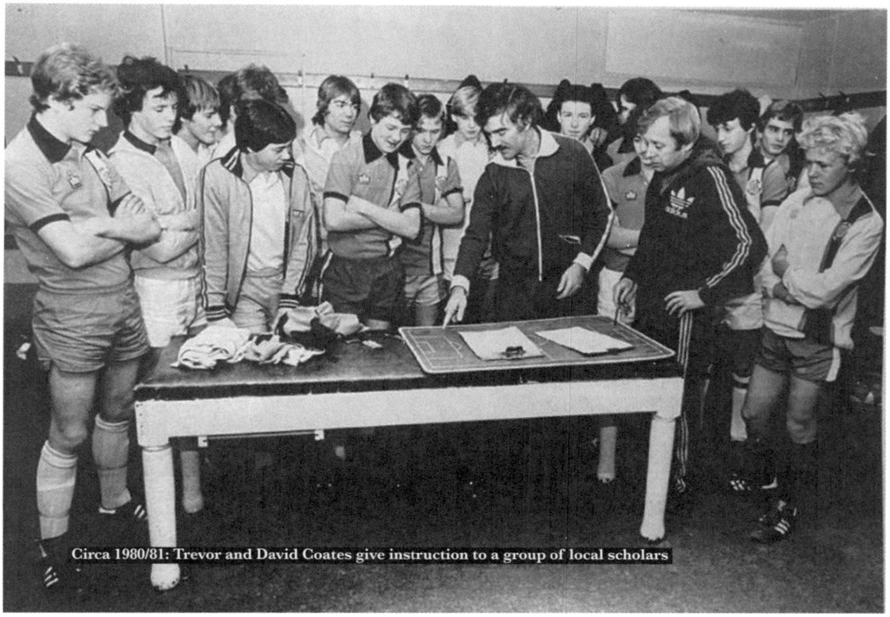

Circa 1980/81: Trevor and David Coates give instruction to a group of local scholars

the club's physiotherapist. I've worked in many countries all over the world but the group of staff at Luton Town were one of the best I've worked with in football.

Initially, at the age of thirty-three, I moved into accommodation ran by one of the club's appointed landladies. She ran 'club digs' that we would normally place lads in who'd joined the club to help them settle with a home-from-home experience. I was keen to have Julie and the children join me once I was settled at the club and we would later find a home in Ampthill just north of Luton, where we have remained ever since.

I used to enjoy taking a mixed age-group team from the youth and reserves along with John Moore, to the annual Blauw-wit competition over in Holland every summer. I don't remember David Pleat ever coming with us, but I know he was very proud of Luton Town's participation. The competition was by invitation only from the organisers.

Some of the boys were a bit of a handful. Ray Brammer was a bit of a lad but there was never any real drama. They were good trips which lasted about four or five days and the players got a lot out of them by playing in a different country and against teams from all over Europe. It really helped to bring on some of the lads like Wayne Turner, Frankie Bunn, Mitchell Thomas, Rob Johnson, Stacey North, and Seamus Heath. I remember

Trevor, 3rd from the right, along with John Moore take control of a mixture of reserves and youth team players circa: 1981

Seamus, he was a good left-sided player with a great left foot, and a bit later David Oldfield and Marvin Johnson would come over as the next crop of players came through at the club.

You saw what the players were made of because it was play, rest, play, rest, full on for the duration of the tournament. Some of the pitches weren't in the greatest of conditions either, as it was always played just after the end of the season and some were like dust bowls. We always did alright there and both the staff and the players enjoyed it.

By the time I arrived at the club, Ken Gutteridge the then assistant manager, had left. The coaching staff set up was quite fluid, it was never rigid, as David Pleat coached so it would be either myself or David Coates who would assist the manager. Mainly, for five years, I took the reserves and the youth teams along with John Moore and I thoroughly enjoyed that role. Then, in the last year in 1985, David invited me to assist him as first team coach.

David (Coates) was the elder statesman on the staff. I think he was ten or twelve years older than the rest of us and had played in the mid-1950s and well in to the mid to late 60s at Hull City, Mansfield and Notts County.

Three important names we used in training were Fred, Sid and Jack – and we would incorporate these into a match. They were used as instructions to the player on the ball who then would either let the ball go through their legs, back heel it, or head it backwards. Mick Harford scored a great goal against Chelsea using that system. Mick shouted out the relevant name and it was back heeled to him catching the Chelsea defence by surprise, leaving Mick to smash the ball into the top corner of the net. It was one of the little things the staff would implement to give us those small advantages that you need in football.

We never said much straight after the match. We would almost always leave it until the Monday or whenever it was if we'd had a midweek match, and we always then had good detailed chats with the players. Sometimes,

I'd wheel in the big old TV and video machine to be able to show the players certain game situations to help them take responsibility on why things happened on the pitch.

They were good days, I certainly enjoyed it at Luton Town. Brian Horton was a great stabiliser for the side that led us to, not only promotion, but the Second Division Championship in 1981/82. It was always going to be a good team, as we'd been building momentum for a couple of seasons by then. They all worked so amazingly hard for one another. Brian Stein really came into his own that season and it's lovely to look back on how that team flourished.

The staff are very proud of the fact that in the period of 1978-86 at Luton Town, the club developed around twenty players who went on to gain international recognition. Mal Donaghy being one of, if not the finest of those players as he played in two World Cup Finals whilst he was still at Luton Town in Spain 1982 and again in Mexico 1986. I ran into Mal quite a few years ago when we were both on a coaching course at Lilleshall; we were on separate courses and that was the last time I saw him and got to speak to him on a one-to-one basis. Always an absolute gentleman on and off the pitch and carried himself well in and around the club; a great ambassador for the game of football.

Initially, with the scouting network in the schools, we would only really look at more local players as in those days transport wasn't so easy to come by. We'd look across all the local schools to invite the best of the young players to train with us. We made sure that we did everything we could so as not to let any talent slip by that might be right under our noses, and we would sign as many as possible.

The club always believed in a strong youth policy. It thrived and would later be a great source of income for the club if and when those players were sold; boys like Kingsley Black, Tim Breacker, Garry Parker, Ray Daniel, and David Oldfield. All those players had come through the midweek invitations to train under the dim floodlights of the Maple Road car park, joining in open sessions with myself and John Moore.

I was always pleased that everyone seemed to enjoy it which gave the coaching staff, including myself, a great sense of job satisfaction. We always worked hard to make sure the sessions were interesting for the boys that came along. Although, I'm not sure that the lads enjoyed running up Popes Meadow as I would put them through their paces up and down that slope.

1982 summer photo call

There was one occasion when I took them to the hills at Ampthill Park. I got some stick from the lads that day, I can tell you. It was hard but the players needed those sessions as it was important fitness wise, especially when you got those horrible extended periods in the season where for one reason or another there would be a spell where you didn't play due to frozen or waterlogged pitches or having been knocked out of the FA Cup, which ended up giving you a blank Saturday or two to deal with.

Jake Findlay was never keen on those long runs, but then saying that he wasn't too keen on short runs either (laughing). But he was a very good goalkeeper and invariably he would come right on matchday. Jake would always get around you with that great big smile of his.

I didn't dwell upon matches when we'd lost, we got it out of our system with constructive talking. Thankfully, in the promotion season, we didn't lose many. We had two early home defeats in September to Cardiff City midweek and then lost heavily at home to Sheffield Wednesday. But that was down to a change in formation where we tried to play Raddy Antic as a sweeper. We could all see that we had a dilemma on where to play Raddy, and sometimes we would play him in midfield whilst other times as a sweeper. He had incredible experience playing all over Europe before David brought him over from Spain. However, Raddy just didn't fit in at times.

Of course, Raddy will always be remembered for coming on as a substitute at Maine Road against Manchester City in May 1983 and scoring what turned out to be the all-important winning goal in keeping Luton in the harsh world of the English First Division had it been saved by a Yugoslav, as John Motson put it during his commentary on Match of the Day.

Personally, I had nothing to do with that team that day, David Pleat asked me to come up to accompany himself along with David Coates and, of course, John Sheridan.

When Raddy scored and the players all piled on top of him all we could

1983 with the age group of players that were preparing to travel to Holland at the end of the season for the annual Blauw-wit tournament.

think of was to calm the players down, get back into position and see the game out – I could see that immediately after the goal Manchester City were getting Steve Kinsey ready to come on as an extra attacker to replace Graham Baker. They didn't need to actually win the game as a point would have been enough to keep them up and to send us down.

You can see all of us caught by the Match of the Day cameras on the pitch imploring the players to get back and to steady themselves. Then, of course, Trevor Aylott headed the ball out of play deep in the Man City half and that ended up taking the last few seconds and the last touch of the ball from a Luton player on that famous day. The whistle went for full time, we'd done enough to stay up, and then David Pleat ran across the pitch to hug Brian Horton. I wasn't aware at the time about the incidents on the pitch where some of our players had been surrounded by Manchester City fans, who had come over from the stands intent on taking out their frustration on some of our lads. I just thought, We've won the match, we've stayed up, how marvellous. It was only later when we were all back together that I found out what had happened following the final whistle.

It was a fantastic day for the club but I had some sympathy for John Benson, who was the Manchester City manager. I had known John a long time going back to our playing days together at Bournemouth in the early 1970s. He had the good grace to congratulate me after the game even though I could see it had destroyed him seeing his side relegated to

Division Two, which ultimately cost him his job. John was a nice man who sadly passed away in 2010.

The lads were so thrilled to be playing again the following season in the top Division. It was all about the players' pride and the prestige of playing at the top level in England. It was never spoken of in terms of financial gain for the club because money just wasn't being thrown at the game back then. It was the thrill of competing again for at least another season against the best teams in the country. Every match was special in the top Division and our boys did well and thoroughly deserved to stay there.

We all had a good night celebrating the win and everyone was very happy. Thankfully, relegation didn't happen so the side stayed together and we kept on with what was a good formula.

Big Steve Foster was a little bit like Jake Findlay in that Steve knew what he wanted to do and more importantly, what he needed to do to be ready for a game. He was another very good player for the club. David bought him in just at the right time, midway through the 1984/85 season when we really needed his type of leadership on the pitch after losing and failing to replace Brian Horton in the summer of 1984. We'd lost Paul Elliott at centre half with a broken leg, we'd tried Micky Droy, Colin Todd and trialled the former Tottenham and Charlton defender, Don McAllister in the reserves for a few games, but nothing was working to fill that gap until Steve Foster came to Kenilworth Road.

Such a shame when you hear of the passing of the players that we coached. Les Sealey was a real shock, I got on really well with Les, he always had something about him and knew to do the right thing at the right time. David Preece was a cracking player, small but he could really tackle hard and his range of passing was fantastic It was such a shame he left us so young like Les Sealey and Marc North. We met up with Raddy Antic and his dear wife at Luton Hoo for the David Pleat Elite 80's evening the year before he passed which was so sad and unexpected, as we'd said on the night how well he looked. Andy King was another great player and I used to play golf with him often over at Millbrook Golf course, along with Mick Harford and Brian Stein.

Golf was and still is very popular with a lot of players, everyone found it was very relaxing and great for the players to spend time away from the football club but still enabling us to keep that bond together by socialising in sport.

When we went away with the club, John Sheridan and I would love to play snooker so it was always a condition that the hotel we'd stay in had a snooker table. Some of the team would play as well but John and I would play on late, as the players would have to go to bed with the match coming up the next day; it was always for fun, we never played for money.

I always enjoyed playing cricket, too. I was never an opening batsman, rather at number 3 or 4 in the batting order. I got a thousand runs in one season, which was my personal best.

I have many good memories looking back on the times back then, and the only bad one that stands out was the Millwall game in 1985. That was a terrible night, so many people were scared stiff. About five minutes before the end of the match the referee had already told us to start making our way down towards the corner of the main stand near to the Oak Road end. We all got back in and were locked in the dressing room but realised our children were still outside. So, we insisted that the steward let us back out of the changing room and into the main stand to get our children to safety. It was a truly terrible night in what should have been a celebration of a great achievement for the club as that win over Millwall meant we'd sealed a place in the FA Cup semi-final, the first time the club had made it that far since 1959.

But the violence and the horrific images made headlines across the daily newspapers and television screens.

The 1985 FA Cup semi-final also ended as a huge disappointment. It was a great occasion for the club, the players gave their all and we were proud of every one of them. For so long it looked as though we were going to beat Everton with Ricky Hill scoring in the first half, but we were pegged back cruelly near the end of normal time and then beaten in extra time. Two years later David, myself and John Sheridan found ourselves back at Villa Park in the 1987 FA Cup semi-final, but this time on the staff at Tottenham and against Watford of all teams. Tottenham won that semi-final comfortably 4-1 but it never made up for the cruel defeat two years earlier with Luton. Those boys really deserved to play at Wembley in an FA Cup Final.

I've often looked back and wondered what became of the lads we had at Luton Town in the early years and what they are doing now. A few years ago, we met up with staff as well as a lot of the senior players at the special 'Elite 80's' evening. That was really nice meeting up with so many of them

2019: Trevor on the right, with Raddy Antic and his wife along with John Sheridan

that night: The Steins, David Moss, Brian Horton, Basher, Wayne Turner, Ray Daniel, Ricky, Walshy, Mitchell Thomas, Steve White, Mike Saxby. It was a real family club and everyone still talks warmly and with genuine fondness

I have a snooker room here in my home with a wall full of memorabilia throughout my career in football both playing at West Ham and Bournemouth and then coaching and managing. I started off playing with Bobby Moore and I ended up coaching so many wonderful players at Luton as well as Tottenham, including Glenn Hoddle. Football has taken me all over the world. I've met and worked with some of the very best and it's given me and my family a very good life!

(BORN 1ST SEPTEMBER 1956, LUTON, BEDFORDSHIRE)

# PETER MEAD

LUTON TOWN FC 1973-77

*Peter Mead was born in Luton, where his mum and dad ran an Off Licence which was owned by his paternal grandmother. The Off Licence was situated on Dunstable Road and to the rear of the property was the old greyhound dog track on Skimpot Lane. The stadium was also used as a speedway track during a short period of time.*

*Peter began his career as an apprentice with Luton Town in 1973 where he spent three years as a professional from 1974 to 1977, without breaking into the first team. During this time, though, he was playing under a young David Pleat as his reserve team manager. After leaving Luton in 1977, he joined Northampton Town and made seventy appearances in the Fourth Division before linking up with the Aylesbury United where he became a popular club captain making well over three-hundred appearances there between 1979 and 1986.*

We lived above the Off Licence on Dunstable Road from 1956 until after the World Cup in 1966. I remember going down to Kenilworth Road to watch the World Cup matches. My dad then bought a post office in nearby Tilsworth, which is in between Dunstable and Leighton Buzzard.

The Off Licence was situated on Dunstable Road and to the rear of the property was where the old Greyhound Dog Track stood on Skimpot Lane.

I remember the first season I joined Luton Town as an apprentice. I was so excited when I started playing matches in that pre-season, and most of the friendly matches took place up at the Stopsley Sports Centre over on the east side of Luton. This was just before David Pleat joined the club as he was learning his trade as a very young manager in non-league football with Nuneaton.

1970's programme signed by Peter

Initially, we had Ray King in charge of the youth team when I joined the club. Ken Whitfield was in charge of the reserves and Roy McCrohan was the first team coach with Harry Haslam as the club's manager.

During my first season, 1973/74, Ray King left the club and that's when Danny Bergara joined Luton to take over the running of the youth team. Danny arriving just pre-dated David Pleat's arrival.

At the end of that season Luton Town were promoted back into the First Division, and following that Ken Whitfield left the club to join Cardiff City.

The following season Danny was still in charge of the youth team. I was awarded a professional contract and that's when David took over as the reserve team manager, which meant I spent my first year as a pro with David Pleat as my manager in the reserves at Luton Town.

The new apprentices would always be allocated specific senior professionals that you would look after. You'd be responsible for cleaning and mending their boots, training shoes and laying out their kit, along with anything else that they asked you to do. I had four pro's to look after: Peter Anderson, John Ryan, Jimmy Ryan, and a young junior pro by the name of Paul Price.

I can go back even further than that, though when I recall watching David Pleat in the 1964/65 season as a player at Luton. I must have been eight or nine years old. He was playing for Luton against Queens Park Rangers at Kenilworth Road, and he scored a goal in that game. It was like a shot-come-cross, it went straight in over Peter Springett in the Ranger's goal. That goal was my first recollection of David and it was when he first introduced the 'David Pleat Shuffle'. He would approach the defender, put his leg over the ball as if he was going to cut inside, but take it with his right foot past the defender and clip the cross over into the penalty box.

As he'd been a winger in his playing days, David certainly loved to have really good orthodox wide players in his teams that he later managed. David Moss is a great example of the type of player that David Pleat was himself.

David left Luton in 1967 to continue his playing career elsewhere. The next time I saw him, he was working in the office at Kenilworth Road. I'd just signed professional so I had gone up to the office to collect my payslip and my pay in one of those beloved square brown wage envelopes that we were given back then.

David was always a forward-thinking coach, he would ask different things of you as a footballer, wanting you to be flexible and open minded to his methods because he liked players to be comfortable on the ball. He wanted you to be able to look after the ball; by that I mean to be able to retain possession of the ball as a team. If you look at the teams that he produced, they were always exceptionally good passing sides.

I was originally a right-back when I was playing as a kid and in the reserve side at Luton for him, and he took me to one side and said, "I want you to play at left back today, don't worry about it, I know that you are right-footed and I want you to use your right foot too, as much as you possibly can, because you're going to have a left-footed winger playing just in front of you. I want him in possession as much possible, so when the ball comes to you just help it on to him so he gets it nice and early in his stride."

If David hadn't have helped me in that way I don't think I would have gone on to play in the football league with Northampton Town. I think I was signed by them from Luton because I could play in both fall back positions on either side of the pitch, so it gave them extra cover. David did this later in his career at both Luton and Tottenham where he played right-footed players at left back.

David Pleat wasn't one of those coaches who, on away trips, would sit down the front without talking to anyone. He would mingle amongst the players and would always be talking and listening to us, explaining his thinking behind tactics and formations. He'd never just change you from one position on the pitch to another without explaining his thought process behind it. He would sometimes say, "I'm about to give you some advice, some of it's good that you want to hear and some of it not so good that you don't, but it'll do you good in the longrun." David was right... I didn't want to hear it! You knew where you stood with him, it was as simple as that.

The only thing I think wasn't in my favour at the time was that I wasn't one of his group of young players that he was bringing in himself; I pre-dated David's return to the club by a year. I joined in 1973 along with Andy King, Lil Fuccillo, Dave Carr, Alan Biley, Martin Chalmers, and Laurence Coyne.

A person who really helped David develop as a coach down at Luton was Danny Bergara. When Danny came over from Spain, nobody had heard of him in the English game. We found out he was Uruguayan and that he was trying to get into coaching here in the UK.

Pasquale Fuccillo Andy King

All the warm ups that you would do, prior to Danny taking us, would be quite regimental. Warming up in pairs, two lines, keeping in straight lines, maintaining the gaps in between. Danny, however, found it quite difficult at first the explain what he wanted from us as his English wasn't great, but he soon improved. The first time he took us for warm up he said, "There's a bag of balls over there, go and get a ball each." There was about twelve of us apprentices and junior professionals in this group with him and we asked him what we should do with the ball. He said to just run with it, carry it at first in a light jog, then put it down and start to dribble. We did that for a few minutes and then he stopped us to do some exercises. Every exercise that we did was with the ball! In fact, everything that Danny asked us to do was with the ball. As we were carrying out this warmup on the outside of the pitch all the first team lads that were with Roy McCrohan stopped and looked over at Danny and us with a 'What the fuck?' expression!

I think Danny really helped David Pleat to bring the technical side of the game into his coaching. Together with Danny looking after the youth team and David as the reserve team manager, they gelled really well. As a group of young players, we couldn't have been in better hands than with these two young coaches.

Most football matches back then in the mid-1970s were all one hundred miles an hour. David had a calmness about him and he wanted us to have the same approach to our gameplay. He would impress upon us that when you're out there on the football pitch you are in charge of the situation, that you have to make those split-second decisions for yourselves and he couldn't make them for us once we were in a game. He said, "I can coach you before and from the sidelines, but I'm not out there with you, so you need to think for yourselves."

I recall reserve games where I would be playing at right back and I'd have Andy King playing in front of me on the right side of midfield. Andy would say, "Meady, as soon as you can, just give me that ball!" It was great to have those players around you who were so willing to have the ball rather than having team mates that just ran away from you, leaving you in the shit, basically! We had players that wanted to get on the ball and make things happen, not wait for it to happen around them.

It was a great experience coming into that environment straight from schoolboy football, to be in the same company at training with these experienced professionals like Jim Ryan, Max Faulkner and Brian Chambers.

David Pleat would say to us young players, "Listen to the experienced pro's, but try to pick out the best bits." He'd say, "If they move away from football and start talking about drinking and the like, don't get involved."

At the time when I was there we had Don Shanks and Graham French; Graham was the loneliest footballer that I ever knew. There was only one person he would talk to and that was Don Shanks, mainly about this, that and the other without going into too much detail… But what a player Graham was! I only played in a match with him once. It was away at

Cambridge United in the old 'Midweek League' that the reserves played in. I'll never forget that night, I was playing at right back with Graham French playing in front of me on the right wing, thinking, Oh fucking hell, what do I do? You had to talk to your team mates on the pitch, but Graham wasn't a talker. Graham came into the dressing room and got changed without saying a word to anyone; he didn't go out before the match for a warmup. We all came back in having been out for a warmup ourselves and Graham was still stone silent, sitting there. The bell went to call us all out to the pitch and I was thinking, For fuck's sake, he's not going to say anything to me! Suddenly, he walked straight over to me and said, "You're the right back, ain't ya?" I said, "Yes, Graham, I am." He continued: "If I call for the ball just give it to me, then you can run past me inside or outside of me and call for the it, but don't be thinking that you're going to get it back. If I were you, rather than burn all that energy just stay tucked in behind me. If I get into any trouble then you're there to help me out." That was it, simple and brilliant and I really have to say what an absolutely talented footballer Graham French was, unbelievably talented in fact, and even in the state he was in that night at Cambridge, where he was only half fit with a chest infection, he couldn't really run.

Graham was an enigma and, like I said, he would rarely talk to anyone; even David Pleat found it difficult to talk to him and they'd played together in the same Luton team in the mid-1960s. But on the pitch, he would go past defenders with such ease that he was almost nonchalant at times. It's well documented that Graham got into trouble with the law and ended up doing a stretch inside following a firearms incident where he received a three-year sentence. The club's first team manager at the time was Harry Haslam and he showed a lot of faith in Graham, especially when he was released from prison; he came back and started training with us again. Harry was a very fair man, he accepted that people made mistakes, made wrong choices in life, but he wouldn't close the door on them. Unfortunately, after a while, it was apparent that Graham wasn't the same man or player that he once was and he eventually left the club. He was rather cruelly dubbed as 'The Poor Man's George Best'.

In my second year as a professional, Wayne Turner was just beginning his apprenticeship having come in straight from school, as most of the lads did of course. It was a good mix, as when you first join at such a young age you're straight in training with senior professionals. Wayne was very serious about his football and worked incredibly hard. He captained the youth and then the reserves when he was just seventeen. We looked out for lads like Wayne as it was only a couple of years since we'd been in the same position coming into full time football from school. I personally remember my early days training alongside the likes of Rodney Fern, Peter Cruse, and Bobby Thomson in particular. He was training with us after he'd been injured. Bobby was another amazing player to be gaining experience from as he'd been fantastic over a number of years at Wolverhampton Wanderers all throughout the 1960s and was capped by England a few times in the mid-1960s. We had the great benefit of Bobby for four years at Luton (1972-1976), he was great for the first team, of course, but also he was priceless for us youngsters coming through. What a fantastic player and an even better person, bless him (RIP).

During pre-season we would be taken out on 'the runs'; we first went to Stopsley and then to Laporte's, as well as Dunstable Downs, and they'd have us running up and down the hills over there. Anyone who knows those Downs will know they're brutal.

The last person you wanted to be paired with on the hill runs was a young local lad called Godfrey Ingram. I have never seen a better hill climber than Godfrey! The runs would be done in 'tiers' with check points, the first check point being Danny Bergara. The next tier you'd hit would be Ken Whitfield or David Pleat, whoever was the reserve team coach by then. Finally, at the top would by the first team coach, Roy McCrohan. You'd do the runs in increments, so you'd hit the first check point, have a breather. Then you'd hit the second one, and another breather. Hit the top, quick breather and then trek all of the way back down again. This would be repeated a couple of times followed by a complete bottom to top run in one go with no breathers! I'll be honest, there wasn't many in the group that could do the hill climb in one go. But for Godfrey, it was a piece of cake. As soon as he came back down, he'd be ready to go again. He was so light and quick across the ground and regardless of it being flat runs or hill runs, he would just glide like it was no effort to him, whilst we'd all be blowing out of our arses and not even making it three quarters of the way up the hill.

It's a shame that Godfrey never held down a place in the first team long enough to establish himself, but boy, what a career he carved out for himself over in America in the 1980s.

Godfrey was certainly a special player and so was Ricky Hill. On my way into the club driving in from Tilsworth I used to pick Ricky up in the mornings; I'd head through Leagrave to David Carr's lodgings, pick him up and then swing up Poynters Road to pick Ricky up as well on the way to 'work'. The senior pro's were really good in that they would look after you. I know that Keith Barber looked out for Ricky whereas John Ryan and Bobby Thomson looked out for me; they'd give me the nod for extra work with them on the pitch after training: Ten minutes, come on Meady, don't worry about your chores, get back out on the pitch with us! Those lads were great at passing on their experience, they really made you feel part of the club as best they could. They'd probably had similar experiences themselves when they were starting out and knew what it meant to a young apprentice. For me personally it was quite surreal; I was this shy sixteen-year-old kid who only three months beforehand had been supporting these guys from the terraces and now, here I was, standing next to them, having a conversation out on the pitch and knocking balls to each other. Fantastic!

The biggest awakening that I had as an apprentice, was the different chores and jobs to do in and around the club, looking after the senior players' boots and general things like that. One of my designated jobs was to look after the away teams' dressing room on match days. It would have to be cleaned straight after the match when they'd all left and gone home. The first thing that had to be done was to pull the plug out of the big communal bath because it took absolutely ages to drain out before I could clean it. While that was draining I could get on with the slipper baths and the rest of the changing room.

I'm pretty sure that this game was against Notts County at home, but I might have remembered the wrong opposition. Anyway, the away team had been kept back in the dressing room for ages after the match. They were getting an absolute bollocking from their manager until they finally all left and I was allowed to go in. I went in and then carried on through the doorway into the baths. I looked down to my left where the big sunken bath was and I'm not kidding you, there had to be five or six 'Richard the III's' floating on top of the water! I'm stood there looking at these turds bobbing about in the water and I'm thinking there's no way I'm going in there! But you had to get fully in there to remove the plug out of the bottom. I went back out and down the hallway to Reg Game's physio room and banged on his door. Reg opened the door and asked what the matter was. I said, "Reg, I'm not doing it, I'm not going in that bath, you come and have a look!" Reg was a grumpy old bastard at the best of times but I managed to persuade him to go to the away team dressing room to have a look for himself. Reg took one look in the bath and said, "Hmm, that's not too good now, is it!" He then clicked his fingers and added, "Come with me." I followed Reg back into his physio room and he disappeared into the store cupboard. Eventually, he re-appeared from the cupboard holding a long bamboo cane with a little fishing net attached to the end. He offered it to me and said, "There you are, boy, fish 'em out and flush 'em down one of the toilets!" I took it and asked Reg, "How come you've got one of these in the physio room cupboard?" Reg slowly shook his head and said, "It happens all the time!" Quite an awakening for me as a sixteen-year-old kid, I can tell you.

Whenever I see David Pleat, if I'm down at Luton Town or around the grounds scouting for Brighton, he always stops to engage in conversation, he'd never just walk straight past you. As a coach he could be hard on you when he had to be. He'd just want to push you to see if you had a bit extra to your game that he might be able to bring out and nurture. He wouldn't say things in a horrible manner but he would say things to wind you up, to test your character. Harry Haslam was completely different, always laughing and joking. Whereas David, whilst he would like a laugh at times, was a more serious character. A very deep-thinking man. He would impress upon you that every moment you are with the club you are representing Luton Town even when you're out and away from the club, and to be mindful that people know you're a professional footballer.

I remember David Pleat turning up at the California Ballroom because he'd heard we were there on a night out and this was a Friday night. He found us and he didn't hold back, he absolutely ripped us all to shreds! He was right do that, too. He spent many a Friday night pulling Alan Biley and one or two others out of nightclubs. He didn't act this way to be mean or cruel. He did it because he cared. If we showed ourselves in a bad light locally around the town then that reflected on him and ultimately on Luton Town Football Club.

Pleaty would look out for you as well, though. I remember when I was a young pro and I was with Alan Biley and Martin Chalmers. This particular time we finished training late and still had our chores to do before we went home. We were absolutely starving after leaving the ground so much later. The first place we came to was a chippy and we got ourselves bag of chips. We were walking along the road, scoffing these chips down out of yesterday's newspaper and then jumped on the bus home. The next morning when we got in for training, Pleaty came over to us, clicked his

Alan Biley

Martin Chalmers

fingers and pointed to the three of us. "Gaffer wants to see you, don't ask what it's about, I've got to come in with you all as well so you'll see," he said.

We all headed into Harry Haslam's office. At the front of his desk, Harry had this gadget thing that would turn over to state his mood: Happy Boss, Grumpy Boss, Horrible Boss, amongst other phrases. We lined up and noticed it said, Upset Boss, and Harry motioned for us to sit down. He then turned to David Pleat and said, "Well, David, what should we do with these lads?" David replied, "I think that I'll leave it up to you, Harry!" Harry Haslam then brought his gaze back upon me, Alan and Martin. "When you three left here last night, what did you do?" We replied in unison, "We went home, gaffer!" Harry sighed and asked, "What did you do BEFORE you got on the bus?" I offered up, "We got some chips!" Harry continued: "Yes, and where did you eat the chips?" Alan piped up, "Out of the newspaper while we were waiting for the bus." Harry leant across his desk and said, "When you leave here, you represent Luton Town FC. As such you most certainly don't let yourselves be seen walking down the street shovelling fish and chips out of a grubby old newspaper! You lads should be model professionals, you shouldn't be eating greasy chips anyway, let alone out in the street for everyone to see. Try some salad with a steak once in a while, boys. If I hear of you boys conducting yourselves like this in public again, you'll be out of the club!" As we all walked out Pleaty turned to us and said, "You boys got away lightly there!". He'd calmed Harry down before we got in that morning so he'd done us a turn.

Although he was a great lad, Alan Biley and David Pleat didn't see eye to eye with each other. Alan was soon to leave the club, which turned out to be the making of him really, as he got his league career going at Cambridge United and went on from there to have a great career with Derby County, Everton, Portsmouth, and Brighton. Luton Town's loss in the end, similar to that of Kerry Dixon, with Kerry never being offered an

apprenticeship having been a local Luton boy, and in fact, he was born right near the ground in Oak Road. Kerry was a supporter with his mates on the terrace and played for Luton Town at schoolboy and youth level. As we know, he went on to have an amazing career, mainly at Chelsea, and played for England, too. But this is all with the power of hindsight and let's be fair, Luton Town under Harry Haslam and then David Pleat didn't do too badly in the proceeding years did they…?

We were young lads on a massive learning curve. It was about teaching us standards. David Pleat would say to us on a Friday, "Right, on the bus tomorrow, collar and tie or you won't be getting on." It didn't matter that we were in the reserves going to somewhere like Plymouth where hardly anyone would be there to see us, it was all about getting us into good habits from an early age. David was always a stickler for smartness, for us to be switched on, be thinking about the game that you're about to play. There would be card games on the coach, as some of those journeys were bloody long as a lot of the motorways had yet to be built. We'd stop for a pre-match meal, something light like poached eggs on toast or something, then get going again. When we were about half an hour away from the ground, David would walk down the coach maintaining eye contact with each of us and say, "Right, lads, get your mind on it, start thinking about the game."

It sounds intense but it was about focusing on all of the small things, which, when they were all added up, would equate to you becoming a bloody good professional footballer. He would let you know when you'd played well and equally so when you hadn't played to your potential. As young players we needed that so we could take that information away with us to self-evaluate our own progression as footballers.

David Pleat would always notice if there was something wrong, if you were behaving differently to normal, if you were reacting in an unusual manner. He got to know his players and their characters. He would never be one to brush over it. He would sit you down and talk to you until he eventually got out of you what was going on and then he would offer a solution to help get the issue out of your system. He didn't have the answer to everything but the fact he would notice and then take the time to talk it through meant a great deal and taught me a lot of things that I took with me right through my adult life.

John Moore was very much like that, too; he and David Pleat were definitely on the same wave length. I made my debut in the Combination League, which was the reserve league played on a Saturday and a step up in standard from the Midweek League. The game was away at Swindon Town and these combination games would get two to three hundred people coming down to watch. They would all be kept together in the main stand and so even with only a few hundred people in, they still made a noticeable noise when you were out on the pitch. It was great playing with a bit of a buzz, an atmosphere that you didn't get playing in the youth team on a Saturday morning or in the one man and his dog Midweek League.

The pace of the game was a different level. I was certainly enjoying it and I felt that I was having a really good game at Swindon. John Moore was also playing that day. He'd been a great player at Luton having come down from Motherwell in Scotland during the 1960s, but he was coming to the end of his playing days. There was a stop in play so John made his way over to me, put his arm around me and in his deep gruff Scottish accent he said to me, "How do you think you're doing, Meady?" I said, "Well, after I got my second wind, I think I'm doing alright, John!" He paused just long enough for me to be hanging off whatever he was going to say next, as though it was going to make or break my career. "Aye, laddie, you are, but can you try even harder?" For him, being a senior pro, he didn't need to do that, it was just in him, it was his way. He sat me down in the dressing room after the match and said, "Whenever you think you're doing well you should always try harder, push yourself to the next level, don't settle for just alright." It was no surprise that in 1978 John Moore joined David Pleat on the first team coaching staff. He became the man responsible for the youth team that produced an amazing stream of wonderful young footballing talent, the list is endless. And, of course, he became the first team manager for one season in 1986 following the inevitable departure of David Pleat from Luton Town when David finally accepted one of the many job offers that no doubt came his way. Luton Town caught the football-watching public's imagination and became the media darling for the first half of the 1980s, playing some electrifying attacking football and scoring goals, and conceding them too, for fun.

I didn't want to leave Luton Town. But I knew I had to if I wanted to have a chance of ever playing first team level in the football league. Going to Northampton Town gave me that opportunity. One of the managers I had at Northampton Town was former Luton Town player, Mike Keen. I loved him, but the fans used to slaughter him at Luton saying he was only in the team because he'd married Alec Stock's daughter. With Alec being the manager at Luton Town at the time, that made Mike Keen the gaffer's son-in-law, which is always bound to bring criticism upon all parties.

If I had stayed one more season at Northampton, I would have had the chance to play with Godfrey Ingram again because that season David Pleat sent him there on loan with a view to a permanent transfer. Godfrey did well and an offer of money was put in to David Pleat and Luton, but Godfrey himself turned the move down preferring to go back and fight for his place in the team back at Luton. The ironic thing was, the season that Northampton released me giving me a free transfer, I thought that I'd had my best season there at the County Ground.

By 1979 and at twenty-three years of age, I found myself out of full-time football and heading over to Aylesbury United. I was still on the roller coaster of football's learning curves going into non-league. I'd gone from being a professional player, where even in the reserves everything is laid out for you in the dressing room, and walked into Aylesbury United for my first game to find there was no kit laid out nor any boots, shin pads, tie-ups, etc. So, I sat down and waited. Suddenly, this big fella bursts in the door with a bag over his shoulder. I later found out that he was Gary Harthill, a winger at the club who played over three hundred games for Aylesbury United. He took one look and me and said, "Who the fuck are you?" I told him, "I'm Peter Mead, I've just joined from Northampton Town." This guy sighs and says, "Oh, fucking hell, another poncey professional!" I asked him where the briefs and shin pads were and another player, a chap called Vince, came in at that moment. Gary Harthill turned to him and said, "Here,

Vinny, young golden bollocks here wants to know where his shin pads and tie-ups are!" What an eye opener that was for me. Going from having everything done for you in the pro game to just being given your boots that you'd have to buy in the first place and that's all you got. I was now training twice a week on a Tuesday and Thursday evening and playing on Saturdays and I had to adjust quickly after being in a professional environment for the six years prior to that. Welcome to the real world, Meady! It took me three months to get used to it. I lasted seven years there playing around three hundred and fifty games for them, so it worked out okay for me.

I've been working in the 'real world' ever since but I also stayed in the game as a scout, because there's nothing better than a life in football and talking football with what you'd call football people. There was one night I was scouting at a game over at Leyton Orient. I saw a bunch of scouts, as there always is, over at the tea hut. I went over and squeezed in amongst everyone. There was Peter Brabrook, the ex-Chelsea and West Ham player, plus Peter Taylor, former Palace and Spurs player, along with a few others. The conversation turned to training sessions when we were all young pro's, it was brilliant, we could have talked for hours. There's a respect amongst ex-footballers from a certain era. Everyone has something to say, but they won't try to talk over you. Each of us has their say because we all respect each other whether we've played for three years in Luton Town's reserves and a couple in the Fourth Division at Northampton, or if we've played for fifteen years in the First Division and represented England. It was a shame that we had to break it up to go and watch the game really. Peter Brabrook told us he was at a game at West Ham and it was doubling up as a celebration of the 1964 FA Cup winning team, winning it against Preston, I think it was. They had been invited by the club to this home game and all had allocated seats reserved for them. Poor planning on the club's behalf meant there were more players than there were reserved seats. Now, Bobby Moore came down the stairs at the old Boleyn Ground and the steward stopped him and informed him that there weren't any more seats available. This is Bobby Moore, the World Cup winning captain of England in 1966 and an absolute legend at West Ham. Peter Brabrook heard this and asked, "Are you having a laugh, steward?" This poor steward was becoming a stammering mess and he could only apologise that they had only allocated this particular number of seats. In the same breath he turned to Bobby Moore and said, "You'll have to go and sit up at the back, Bob!" Peter Brabrook then stood up and said to Bobby, "Skipper, you have my seat, I'll

Peter in 2022 with the author

take the seat up at the back," then he said to the steward, "That's what West Ham should do, Bobby Moore should have his own personal seat whenever he comes here!"

I'm glad that, over the course of the years, I've managed to stay in football as a club scout. I've worked with so many great people who genuinely love football in its purest form. People who love nothing better than to get around a table and talk football. Yes, the game has changed at the very top beyond what anybody could have imagined back in the 1970s. I still love going to games to scout players, though, and I always try to arrive an hour before kick off because that was part of the habit that I got into as a player. I'd always like to give myself plenty of time to prepare before a match.

I've been scouting for Brighton for about five, maybe six seasons now. I went there around the time that Chris Hughton took over as their manager. Before that, I was working for Queens Park Rangers. I also worked for Allan Gemmill and Neil Warnock at Crystal Palace and Dougie Freedman at Bolton. I did a little bit of work with Trevor Hartley as well when he was a chief scout at Luton Town. It's good to stay involved, and being on the scouting network certainly does that.

I got to play for the club that I supported as a boy. It was a great time to be at Luton Town and I wouldn't change it for the world.

(BORN 2 JUNE 1956, BEDFORD)

# PASQUALE 'LIL' FUCCILLO

LUTON TOWN FC 1973 – 1983

*Born to Italian parents, Lil played his debut game for Luton Town in the 1974/75 season as a substitute. His footballing career has seen him play for several clubs, including Peterborough United where he took up the position as manager between 1992-1993. He went on to scout for several teams over the years and is now a scout for Cambridge United.*

I stayed on at school as I wanted to finish my O' Levels. I wanted to do the right thing, education wise, just in case I didn't get a chance as a professional footballer. I went to a 'Rugby' school, by the way. There were two schools adjacent to each other in Bedford. The one that I wanted to go to was full so I had to attend the other, but they were just across the way from each other in the town. This was a rugby school but I always wanted to be a footballer from about the age of eight or nine. I was always with a ball hitting it against a wall every day, which no doubt drove my mum and dad crazy.

The bit of luck I had was in that we had a youth club upstairs at the school which ran every Thursday night and they had lots of teams; basketball, football, just about all types of sports really, so I became attached to that club playing at Under 14s/15s and 16s at Westfield Youth Club.

We were playing a game down in Luton over at the old Vauxhall Motors pitches on a Saturday afternoon and I was approached by George Rogers who was scouting for young players to take them into Luton Town. George was associated with Luton Town for many years. He came over to me after that game and said he'd like to invite me to attend training on Tuesdays

Lil during the 1981 pre-season photo call line-up

and Thursdays, assuring me that Luton Town would cover my train fares to and from Bedford to Luton. We trained just up the road from the central train station in Luton up at the Barracks, known as the Old Drill Hall on Old Bedford Road. That was the start of it all for me; catching the train twice a week to and from Bedford to Luton, training twice a week. It was the beginning of my journey with Luton Town and into professional football.

I was taken on as a full apprentice after I had stayed on at school to complete my exams, so I was actually almost seventeen when I joined in 1973. I started on £6 a week and when I had my seventeenth birthday the money went up to £8 a week. On top of that we got 'digs' money or train/bus fare travel expenses. I didn't move to Luton to be in digs so the club looked after me with expenses and gave my parents some money instead of paying one of the many landladies who ran the accommodation for the young players all across town. I'd catch the train Monday to Saturday when we had games, or Monday to Friday when it was just training.

It was my very first job, on my first day at the club, and I had these old boots with holes in them which I'd brought along with me from home. I arrived at the ground, sat in reception smiling away to myself excited at the thought of going training in a minute. This is how naive I was… Enter Roy McCrohan! Roy was the first team assistant manager and he straight away said, "You don't want those boots Lil, put them away!" All I could muster in reply was, "Oh, okay." Roy continued, "No, you're not training today, don't worry, just come with me." Roy and I began walking alongside the pitch from the players tunnel end and up towards the corner flag at the opposite end of the ground. The groundsman, Dick Wassell, was walking from behind the goal to meet us. Dick had his shed up in that corner of the ground with all his tools and everything stored away. We met up at the corner of the Maple Road enclosure and the Kenilworth Road open terrace, as it was back then and Dick already had some equipment in his hands. "Just grab all of these, Lil," he said. I didn't even think to question it, it was my first ever day at the club so I just went along with it. Roy said,

"I'm just popping up into the offices." These offices were at the top of Kenilworth Road behind the terrace stand and I followed him and then we stopped outside them before he turned to me and said, "Right then, Lil, you've got your brush, you've got your shoes and bags. You see the offices here? You see that hedge? I want it cut!" Roy then proceeded to give me the exact dimensions that he wanted it cut to. "I want everything cleaned and put away, I don't want to see any twigs or leaves on the floor and then you can come back in the ground." He must have seen my face drop as, at that moment, I was thinking that I'd come here to be an apprentice professional footballer and the first thing I get asked to do is cut the hedge outside the club offices which was housed in two semi-detached houses at the top of Kenilworth Road. My chin was on the floor and he smiled. "You haven't made it yet," he reminded me. With that, he just walked away and left me to it. And that was the story of my first day back in 1973 as a footballer with Luton Town.

It was definitely a test of character, a case of, let's see what young Lil is all about, see how he'll react to being given this task as the very first thing that he's asked to do on his very first day with the club.

You can't harp on about the old days when you look back, and even at the people before us when you think of what they had to do. There were players that played part time who had another job to supplement their income from football and I'm talking about senior players here that even played for England and this wasn't all that long before I started in the game. I know a few who were still playing as amateurs even in the 1950s and into the early 1960s. I couldn't really moan, there I was, a full timer, in a football environment, being paid, my parents being paid a little money for my keep, whilst I was having my travel expenses covered by the club.

My fellow apprentices when I joined were Peter Mead, Alan Biley, Martin Chalmers, Andy King, Laurence Coyne, Steve Russell, and Alex Malcolm, along with a couple of other lads. The Futcher boys (Ron and Paul) signed as young lads from Chester City about six months after I joined.

The first year that I was there we had about ten apprentices, which was unusual at football clubs as normally you'd have an intake of six new full-time apprentices, with the rest of the youth team made up of promising local school kids signed on associated schoolboy forms or local trialists who would come and go.

We had different jobs to do around the club, on top of looking after our allocated senior players. I had to look after five players with their matchday kit, training kit along with their training footwear and match boots. You come in first thing in the morning at 9am, you'd get changed yourself and then make sure your players' kit was all ready for training, ensuring they had fresh dry kit and towels, etc. They would let you know what footwear they'd want depending, of course, on the weather, but over time you would get to know what they'd want without them having to ask. Once that was all done the senior pro's would go out, then we would follow. Sometimes, we'd train at the same place as the older players, other times we'd be driven somewhere else.

We'd train for around an hour and half to two hours. When we came back in, there wasn't any food laid on then, there was no talk of nutrition or what types of food that you should take following physical activity. You'd then sort out your five players' kits that had just been used ensuring it had all been put away or sent to the wash room or the drying room. Next job was to clean and polish their footwear, training shoes and boots. If they were soaking from bad weather they'd need to be placed to dry so they'd be ready for the next morning. This included checking their studs and changing any that were worn down or missing. Then we'd have all types of different jobs all across the club. The only place we weren't allowed to go into was the physio room. I would look after the toilets and the bathroom, one of the other lads would look after the dressing rooms and then the other baths in the away dressing rooms and toilets. One lad would have the job of sweeping and cleaning the players' tunnel, which is longer than it looks when you're cleaning it, by the way! The hallways up to the dressing rooms would be cleaned every day. Then, following all of that, when all the jobs were done we had to sit together in the dressing room and wait for the physio, Reg Game, to come make sure he was satisfied that the jobs were done. Only then could we could go home, never before we got his say so. He was a horrible little bastard was Reg, God rest his soul. Reg passed away while he was still working at the club in May 1978. He was like a rottweiler, he would always be grumpy and was sniping away telling us to fuck off! We'd be polite to him, asking if we could go and he'd he'd show his teeth and snarl back, "Are all the jobs done? Hang on, I'll check." But he wouldn't, he'd just go back into his physio room and stay there so we'd have to go to him and ask again. "Reg, can we go now? We've been here thirty minutes; all the jobs are done." But he'd keep you waiting, just out of spite. Then finally he'd say, "Go on then, you can all go."

In the summer, we had the job of painting all of the barriers behind both goals in a bright orange colour. These were the days of the terraces with no seats at all behind both goals so there were a lot of these barriers to re-paint. Everything got the orange paint treatment all the way around the ground, even the handles on everything! If we had some soil delivered we'd have to help with that, too. The shovels would be handed out to each of us, but we'd have to scour the pitch with buckets in hand and clear any stones that had come up before the new soil could be put down.

There was one time that one of my fellow apprentices, Peter Mead, hurt his head quite badly on that Kenilworth Road terrace. It was a sweltering hot summer, beautiful weather and the ten of us were together just mucking about, the hose doing its job watering the pitch. All we'd got on was our shorts and trainers as we were a bunch of vain bastards trying to get a tan. We were all a bit hot and bothered but getting on with the painting of those beloved crash barriers. Peter and I were painting along with six or seven of the other lads when one of the boys said, "I'm gonna get the hose!" Alex Malcolm it was, he had a hold of the hose before when knew it. Alex was a young Scottish lad from Hamilton and played at left full back. He was sniggering now and saying, "I'm gonna water everybody." I must have been right next to him as I told him to keep it away from me because the water was freezing. These hoses were really powerful and we were up on the terrace, about a dozen steps up from the goal. Alex let fly with it at about six of the lads, but Peter Mead, who must have been right by the barrier, went over and hit his head on the bar. He needed twenty stitches in his head from one side to the other following that. To make matters worse, one of the boys picked up an old dirty towel. We

Alex Malcolm

screamed not to put that on Peter's head as it was covered in paint and dirt. Peter was laying there with his head smashed open and we all yelled to go and get the physio, Reg Game. Reg took Peter to the hospital where he was cleaned up properly and stitched up, literally!

We laughed about it afterwards, but the worse thing about it was the dirty old towel that had been on the floor, trodden on, covered in paint and dirt was put on his head. We'd put it right on an area with an open wound, ripe for infection, but we did get it off him sharpish, we just didn't know what we were doing. I'm not suggesting this incident had any bearing on Alex Malcolm's career at Luton Town but he was soon on his way after that and left the club, signing for Northampton Town in the August of 1976.

I regularly meet up with Peter Mead on the scouting circuit as he's still working as a scout for Premier League Brighton. As apprentices we certainly had a good bunch at that time and, importantly, we stuck together.

That was our day-to-day when there was no football in the close season, we just became ground staff, hardly trained at all, whilst waiting for all the Senior pro's to come back to start pre-season training. Behind the goal in the Oak Road stand there were some steps down which took you into a little gym under the stand. We found out later on it was full of asbestos and all sorts down there. We'd go down there and play head tennis for an hour against the staff, and let me tell you that the staff were excellent at head tennis! We were always doing something, even though we could have gone home earlier. We loved staying on. It was nice to get off home but you felt that if you'd left the club without doing anything, you were cheating yourself. After the ground work was done we'd almost always stay on and do some bits in the afternoon, whether it was with the staff or amongst ourselves. We mixed it up and we had a great time just ticking over during the summer months.

Our proper training would start four or five days before the senior professionals came back, starting on the leg and stamina work with cross country runs. When you look back now, some of those runs that we did you just wouldn't be allowed to do now. Like everything in life, things change and you find new ways of doing things if the old ways aren't right for whatever reason. We would do these hills, and how we ever got up them I just really don't know. This would be followed by the six-mile runs every day for five days. Then, on Monday, we'd come in with the senior players so it was like a gradual build up. And that was our life as apprentices. We'd be footballers in the mornings with the pro's, both senior and reserves, and then after training we became the ground staff. We enjoyed it all, and I think it's a shame that young players don't do any of that these days. It wasn't a punishment, it was simply about learning that you had to look after your things and it taught you responsibility.

In our apprentice day sometimes, we'd have to get the hoover out and take it to the Eric Morecambe suite if there'd been a private function up there during the week or on a Friday night. We'd have to get in their sharpish on a Saturday morning to clean it all up in time for the match that day. You couldn't say no to it, it was just part and parcel of your role as a young apprentice learning your trade. It certainly didn't do us any harm, there was nothing horrible in what we were being asked to do.

The older players may have a go at you from time to time and in different ways, especially if you ever got cheeky with them. It'd be a horrible 'muggy day' and one of them would say, "Lil, I want all five pairs of boots taken up to the training ground." He would put a pair on and then he'd say to himself, "Hmm, I don't think these are right, no, I'll take these ones off, these are no good, Lil, I'll try another pair on." In other words, you've been cheeky so you've got five pairs to get ready and if you carry on being cheeky it would soon be ten pairs. Then they'd talk to the other players that you had to look after and he'd say to them, "Make sure all your boots are muddy and horrible as this cheeky little bastard here needs sorting out."

By and large it was all good fun, though. The extra boot cleaning wasn't the best thing to be doing but they were really great times to be in football. The money side, nobody used to talk about it. It was wrong that we didn't as it was your job but we looked at it as if we were playing a sport and getting paid for it. Would young lads run through the proverbial brick wall these days? I don't think so. That's no disrespect to them, but you just feel like you've tapered the desire out of it and they've become softer and softer. On that note, I know that one year at Blackburn Rovers, not long after they won the Premier League back in the mid-1990s, the apprentices that had signed on pro forms weren't allowed to go out and buy a brand new car until the year after becoming a first year professional. If you were eighteen and just signed you couldn't go out and buy a BMW, a Porsche or whatever, until the following year. Guess what, a year to the day they would go straight out and buy one, be it a 4x4, a BMW, or what have you. Young lads are being put on fortunes and at seventeen or eighteen they've still got their nappy on!

Going back a little before we came to the club, Harry Haslam bought four lads down from Manchester United in one deal: Don Givens, Jimmy Ryan, Peter Woods, and Ken Goodeve. From getting to talk to these guys and then training and playing with them, I was told that when they first came here they had this big table in the boardroom where they were sat down with the manager, the secretary, and anyone else at the club of consequence and they were given this presentation of a scroll of a new ground. This was 1969 going into 1970, so Jimmy Ryan thought Oh, fantastic, there'll be a new ground coming soon. We're now in 2022 and still at Kenilworth Road, God bless her, but there's still no new ground!

I remember before all the houses were built over behind the Luton & Dunstable Hospital apparently one of the Directors at Luton Town owned that land all around there. He said the club would build a new ground there. But we all know what happened; he actually ended up selling the land for housing when push came to shove. I was told this later on when I joined the club as a player, by the older players.

What Harry Haslam did, and looking back you know it was designed to harden us up, was have us playing in two leagues. The intention was for us to play more matches in order to toughen us up instead of training. On the Saturday we'd play in the Combination which was a great league where you play all of the London clubs, Crystal Palace, Chelsea, Tottenham and Arsenal. But then we also played in what was known as the Midweek league. That was against Northampton Town, Colchester United, Millwall etc., and in those days they had two teams. We'd do well on the Saturday in the Combination League, win, lose or draw, it was almost always a good game of football. Then, on a Tuesday, we'd go somewhere like Northampton where we'd get battered four or five-nil by a team of big old bruisers. It would be back in the Combination League on the Saturday and we'd win away at Chelsea, but come the following Tuesday night we'd get battered again at somewhere like Millwall. That would carry on and you'd be thinking how can this be good for us playing in such diverse levels of football? We were told, though, that results don't really matter, it's all about what we can get out of you and what can we make of you to help you become a better footballer. And looking back it worked for us, we got grounded very quickly, both on and off the field. We all went on to have good careers and longevity in the game with myself, Alan Biley, Kingy

(Andy King, RIP), and the Futcher twins; Steve Buckley did well, too, and Peter Mead, who had a little bit of a career after Luton at Northampton Town and then with Aylesbury United. You were seeing about a dozen young players become good professionals with good careers in the game, whereas home grown players nowadays are very few and far between.

Luton Town were in the First Division and Harry Haslam was very happy with my development as a first-year professional at the club. I also had Roy McCrohan in my corner trying to get me into the team. I was sub about four or five times that season but only got on the pitch on one occasion. I was sub three times in a row against Derby County at home, Ipswich Town away and then back at home against Wolves. I got on for my debut in the Derby game and we won 1-0, in fact, we won all of those three games. We also won 1-0 at Ipswich Town. Ron Futcher got the only goal in the last minute and we were promptly booed off the pitch as we'd defended for our lives throughout the whole match. We really did get battered but without Ipswich actually laying a glove on us. It was a classic away game; snatch and grab as we came away winning 1-0. All throughout the match Roy was digging Harry Haslam out to get me on the pitch. "Come on, get Lil on, get him in midfield," was all I could hear from Roy. Harry kept saying, "No, he's alright where he is, we'll be ok." As I said, I didn't get on but we got the two points (yes, only two points for a win back then). Afterwards, I thanked Roy for backing me to get on and he said, "Ah, don't worry about it." But it meant a lot to me to have his backing and faith. I was on the bench again the following game, just two days after the win at Portman Road. Again, I failed to get on the pitch but we were scraping for our First Division lives and gained another massive win with a Ron Futcher hat-trick and a 3-2 win.

I'm now going back to my debut in the first team game in December 1974 against Derby County, who were crowned champions of England that season, so this was a huge game: When I got onto the pitch it was like I was trying to run a marathon by myself ten times over. I'd been on for ten to fifteen minutes and when I got back in the dressing room I was panting and my heart felt like it was coming out of my chest! I went in the toilet to get myself out of the way and just to gather myself. In that ten-fifteen minutes that I was on, the ball came out of the box. Their centre half, Colin Todd or Peter Daniel, headed it out and it fell lovely to me. I hit it on the full volley towards their goal but their keeper, Colin Boulton, just picked it out of the air with such ease, which I was naturally disappointed about, as I'd hit it straight at him.

Those few minutes of my debut in the first team went by so quickly. I wanted it to last longer to give me the chance to make more of an impression. The final whistle went and all I could think was Wow, we've beaten Derby 1-0! You have to remember that Derby were an amazing team back then and were crowned as First Division champions in both 1972 under Brian Clough and then again that season in 1975, under Dave Mackay.

This was a big deal to beat them and it was real turning point in the season. After a terrible run of results in the first half of the season, this was actually only Luton's second win of that season. We eventually did go down but we gave it a real fight and that started with this win just before Christmas against Derby.

The joy I felt that night when I went home to my parents' house was pure elation at having played in the first team against the top team in the country at the time, and that we'd beaten them. I was so happy, the pure joy and love of football that I'd had as a child had led me to this moment. I went to bed that night at 11 o'clock and just couldn't keep my eyes shut. I couldn't switch off, I was just thinking about what had happened that afternoon, about all of those great players I'd played against in those fifteen minutes including Bruce Rioch, Archie Gemmill, Colin Todd, Alan Hinton, Francis Lee, Roger Davies, and Henry Newton.

My mum and dad still lived in the terraced house that they managed to buy after we'd all been living in the one room for about three years. My parents had come over to live in Bedford from Italy. This was the 1950s, but families were still living like this with a cooker, wash basin, and toilet all in the one room. And yes, the tin bath was kept outside in the yard being brought in only on bath nights! They got married here in England in 1955 and then had me the following year. First off, we lived in that one room, and I remember us living in three different houses. We were basically really poorly off my dad worked from six to six every day and my mum did what work she could at the same time as having to look after me as well.

We did end up getting relegated back into the Second Division at the end of the 1974/75 season, which was a shame, but being realistic, although we put up a good fight from Christmas time through to the end of April it didn't come as a surprise really in the end. The three straight defeats in a row away from home at the end of March and into April killed us off. Ironically, we lost heavily in the return game against Derby and then again away at Wolves, conceding five goals in both games, and then came the somewhat controversial late defeat at fellow relegation candidates Tottenham, with us going down 2-1 to a late Alfie Conn goal. That one looked offside and subsequently led to Paul Futcher being sent off for his protestations to the linesman, whose flag never came to Luton's aid. That extra point would have saved Luton and put Tottenham down!

I had to bide my time back in the reserves after my several appearances warming the bench in that season in the First Division, and that continued into the following season with Luton back down in the Second Division.

I made my full debut in the league starting away at York City in February 1976. We travelled without knowing the starting eleven, so when we arrived and Harry called my name out in the dressing room, it was a fantastic feeling.

We started the game well, and we looked quite comfortable. Wilf McGuinness was the York City manager. He'd previously been a player at Manchester United in the 1950s under Matt Busby and he also had a short spell as the manager at Old Trafford, too. I picked up the ball midway through the first half, going on a run down the line, beat my marker then put over a side footed cross to Ron Futcher to score. Ten minutes into the second half, with the score at 2-1, the ball got laid back off to me. I looked up and made some space by moving the ball quickly and so I was able to get my shot off. It went straight into the corner of the net. York pulled another back with a quarter of an hour remaining, but we did enough to win the match 3-2. On my full debut, I'd set one goal up and scored a solo goal, which was the eventual matchwinner.

From then on, I trained a lot more with the first team and I kept my place in the starting eleven for all but one of the remaining league games that season. Back then, as a rule, you wouldn't really make your first team debut until you were twenty-one. That seemed to be the age in that era, when perhaps you'd get a few appearances and some games from the bench, but I'm talking about when you'd really be considered as cementing down a place in the team. Myself and Andy King went against the grain with that at Luton and a few other lads around the First Division at other clubs too, but by and large that was the kind of age you'd be looking to be a first team regular. Like I say, I stayed in the team and managed to score another couple of goals towards the run in at the end of the season. I got one away at Oxford United in a 3-1 win and then on the last game of the

Lil scores against Blackpool in an end of season 3-0 home victory in 1976

season, at home to Blackpool. I managed to curl one in around the keeper to cap a 3-0 win to send the home crowd into the summer break happy.

We were full of youthful optimism, it was running throughout that emerging team, and me, Andy King, Ron Futcher and Ricky Hill all felt we had a goal in us every game that we played. What an attacking team we had then, with John Aston, who was a European Cup winner with Manchester United in 1968, down the left and Jimmy Ryan on the right. Once we got into good areas we always felt there was a goal in us, and it's a great feeling to have that confidence, not only in yourself, but in the team around you. That feeling was always there in all the years I was at Luton. It was almost like we wanted to be put under pressure as we always knew we could break out quickly. In modern football terms, we were very good at 'setting the traps' a long time before that became a popular phrase and tactic in modern football. We could always play that way and we got even better at it as time went on. Later on, under David Pleat, we had Mossy, Walshy, Kirk Stephens in tandem with Ricky Hill, who could break devastatingly quick down the right-hand side. I would sit in and hold whereas if myself and Mossy broke out then Ricky would shuffle over and sit in. Everyone knew their jobs and their role within the team.

Going back to Andy King, we'd come through our apprenticeship together. He was another local lad, like myself and, like me, he was also Luton Town through and through. It was a real disappointment when Andy was sold for peanuts to Everton, and Peter Anderson, who likewise went to Belgium to play. The club were in dire straits financially, literally the banks were about to foreclose the accounts and shut the football club. The other clubs looking to pick off our players knew this so they got Andy and Peter at a knock down price, way below their market value. The club had no choice but to accept the offers and the banks were watching and insisting on the sales. Jimmy Husband, a former Everton player, had said to me that the original offer from Everton was for both Andy King and me to go to Goodison Park. In the end Andy went and I stayed. As I stated earlier, neither of us wanted to or were looking to leave as we loved it at Luton.

1976/77 was the beginning of two consecutive seasons where I was ever present in the league side. We had a new signing at the start of that season playing upfront. He was a prolific goalscorer, initially with Motherwell and then with Celtic: John 'Dixie' Deans. He'd turned thirty in the summer that he joined us at Luton, but it still caused a few headlines when he came to us having won plenty of league titles and scored almost one hundred goals for Celtic. Dixie made an immediate impression scoring both goals in the opening day victory over Sheffield United at Kenilworth Road. He was short and stocky but still good in the air despite his lack of height. He went on to score six goals in thirteen starts, which was an excellent return, but he certainly had off-the-field issues with drink. Dixie sure loved a tipple, which naturally caused problems between him and Harry Haslam. The final straw came when he was sent off away at Bolton just before Christmas that year in 1976, and he never played in the first team again.

There was certainly a drinking culture within the game amongst the players all over the country, not just at Luton Town. It was all pub, pub, pub! But that wasn't for me, I was never a pub person. I wasn't a beer drinker. I like a drop of wine these days, though. If pubs had relied on me for their trade then they'd have been shut down and out of business, that's for sure.

I remember Ricky Hill playing in the starting line-up away at Burnley very early in the 1976/77 season. Ricky was only just seventeen and had made an amazing debut from the bench against Bristol Rovers just a few months earlier in April 1976 where he set up a goal for Brian Chambers and then scored one himself in the final five minutes of the match. I think it may have been one of his first games playing away from Kenilworth Road at Turf Moor of all places, and he got dog's abuse from the crowd, which must have been awful for him as a young man finding his way in the game. Ricky being Ricky scored the game's deciding goal with a great header with ten minutes remaining, and we went home with a 2-1 win under our belt.

That's what was good about Luton as an apprentice, you knew you'd always get a chance. And over the years that has always been the case. Young players would always get a chance, and if you were good enough at seventeen like Ricky Hill was, then you would get your chance in the first team. If we'd been at bigger clubs with bigger facilities and with much bigger resources to call upon with many more players to choose from then you would probably find chances in the first team almost nigh on impossible. That's genuinely why I think that many young players have chosen to start their football education at Luton Town. They know they'll get a chance and if that then leads to a move to a big club later on then so be it, all the better.

I had two great seasons when I was ever present in the Luton Town first team in 1976/77 and 1977/78 whilst scoring eleven goals from midfield. In the days long before agents, there were always whispers and rumours floating around football, with hush-hush approaches being made via third parties, usually journalists and others working in the media. One I heard about was that Tommy Docherty was interested, and wanted to take me to Manchester United. I never heard of any follow up or of any approach through the club so I don't know how true that was. At one point, if you believed everything you heard, I was going everywhere! Later on, Harry Haslam wanted me and Ricky Hill to join him and Danny Bergara up at Sheffield United.

I have to say, though, that at the time perhaps I was a little naïve being only eighteen or nineteen. All I wanted to do was to stay at Luton Town and nowhere else. Despite any hearsay offers, or real ones, I just loved Luton Town. It may not have been the best of stadiums but I just whole heartedly loved playing for the club there. I had a great rapport with the club, along with the manager Harry Haslam, who was very good to me at the start of my playing career. We had Pleaty coming in and coaching the reserves and also Danny Bergara who was an excellent coach and went on to manage at Stockport County. He was such a smashing coach especially for us young lads at the club coming up on the first steps of our professional careers.

Paul Price was around too, but he was a year or two older than me. Pricey's brother was already out in Australia involved with the equivalent of the Post Office or the GPO, as we used to call it before it became British Telecom. I think Paul was always contemplating going out to Australia. Paul and I got on really well, we were quite good buddies, and he would often talk about his brother and Australia. What we had in common, of course, was that Paul broke his leg early in his career and he was a great comfort in keeping my spirits up when I later broke mine. Paul went on to gain full international honours with Wales. He would talk to me a lot about the pace of the game on the international scene because it was a bit slower. He thought it was a bit easier than the cut and thrust, full bloodedness of the English football league that was non-stop over a season of forty-six to fifty-odd games, whatever you'd end up playing with your club. At international level you'd get a few days to prepare, then you'd play and some games were at an almost walking pace. I wasn't quite buying into Paul's assessment of international football. If you had Diego Maradona giving you the run around I don't think it would be considered easy.

There was a degree of truth in some of the stories floating around in newspapers back then about me choosing between Italy and England. The Sun newspaper wanted to run a story on Ricky Hill, Brian Stein and myself. We were photographed and the story went along the lines of us being possibilities for the next England Squad and if we were going to be picked or not; none of were sure. I broke my leg a little while afterwards so that scuppered that. I spoke to the Italian federation through a go-between who was based in London and said that whichever country came in for me I'd have to consider my parents' wishes who were both Italian-born and bred. In the end, it was all just talk and no more than that, all of which ended after I broke my leg. I missed two years of my playing career between December 1978 and December 1980 because of that.

I spoke to Wolverhampton Wanderers about going there in a deal. According to them, they were prepared to pay £400,000. I don't think David Pleat knew about that. I'd always played well against Wolves and scored against them on a couple

Lil in action against Watford in the 1-1 draw at Vicarage Road in February 1982

of occasions so the club must have had me on their radar from then. There were no agents in 1978 and John Barnwell, who was a midfielder himself in his playing days at Arsenal and Nottingham Forest and was by then managing Wolves, contacted me just before I broke my leg at Brighton. He went on to sell Steve Daley to Manchester City for about £1.5 million, which was a record fee at the time surpassing the £1 million fee that Nottingham Forest had paid Birmingham City for Trevor Francis early in 1979.

That was the worst part of my career when I broke my leg away at Brighton in December 1978. Followed by breaking it again ten months later when I was trying to come back to fitness. When I look back, we had a club doctor, Dr Berry, who had just come into the club soon afterwards. From memory, it must have been around the following February or March time. Now, Doc Berry wasn't like a doctor who just gives you tablets for a prescription and anything like that, he was there to support the club with injuries, long term or otherwise. He became part of our team, a really smashing fella, with a lovely family. I feel that if he'd been at the club at the time I broke my leg, Doc Berry would have made sure the leg would have been plated. Whereby, I would have been walking within weeks then onto rehab with the physio Roy Johnson (who was soon after replaced by John Sheridan in July 1979), and then on to make a full recovery within a year, probably. I also had a calcium deficiency, which certainly didn't help matters. Eventually, I went to Hitchin to play in a specially arranged friendly match, which I felt went okay until one moment when I had nobody near me, I went to turn and I somehow broke my leg again. It just felt like bubble-gum popping, like it had been glued together and come unstuck. That's the way that I can describe the feeling.

When I broke my leg the first time at Brighton, which was a dreadful tackle by the way, I'd had a shot from the edge of the box about twenty yards out. My foot came back, planted, and then I got hit by the tackle, that's how late he was. The referee was absolutely awful that day. The Brighton player should have been sent off, but he wasn't. Ten minutes later the same player put Mal Donaghy into the stand with another bad challenge, which I was obviously told afterwards as I'd been carted off by then. The break itself didn't hurt, it was like a popping sensation. It went very quiet all around the ground, I was on the floor and was suddenly aware of how deathly silent it had become. It's a strange feeling, you get the shock but there was no real pain. The time it did start to hurt was when I got in the ambulance as all around the old Goldstone Ground stadium at Brighton were pot holes, and they were everywhere!

### *JOHN SHERIDAN: LUTON TOWN PHYSIO 1979-1986*

*Lil's X-RAY before I arrived at club had shown that the fracture had completely healed so he was given the green light to train. Unfortunately, after the second fracture, the X-RAY revealed there had been excess callus around the original break and in fact a partial non-union had been present, so the original X-RAY had given a false diagnosis and this could have not been known when the consultant gave permission for the player to resume training. The game that Lil broke his leg the second time was a friendly against the youth team that had been arranged. The second comeback saw the fracture site protected by a lightweight splint kindly made by Luton & Dunstable Hospital with whom the club had an excellent relationship. The splint added extra protection and was also a psychological boost. During the rest of my career as a physio the splint became the norm after a fracture of the tibia as a fracture of this bone is vulnerable for a fair while afterwards.*

Players these days miss games with a nose bleed, but in our day, we were playing Saturday, Tuesday, Saturday Tuesday, which was great, don't get me wrong. However, when you're travelling backwards and forwards all over England and Wales with knocks, we just carried on playing through with so many niggles and injuries. I was talking to a fellow former player just the other day and he was telling me that in the four hundred games he played he was only really fit for about a quarter of those matches. I said to him, "Yeah, I know, we all had our sore ankles where we'd just strap them up, do whatever we could to get through any fitness test beforehand just to get through the game." I remember games with players failing fitness tests but then agreeing to injections in their thighs to get them out on the pitch, but it was dangerous because you could just keep tearing it and tearing it and end up making it much worse. Players would do almost anything to keep their place in the starting eleven.

When Harry Haslam left Luton mid-way through the 1977/78 season it was horrible. There had been a lot of talk about him being in discussions with the board. His assistant, Roy McCrohan, had gone to coach in America in December 1977 which caused more unrest and seemed to signal a changing of the guard, so to speak. But by mid-January 1978, Harry went on record in the local press and the matchday programme saying that everything was sorted, he hadn't meant to cause unrest but was now looking forward to a future at Luton Town. Then, after the following game away at Charlton, he was gone! Not only Harry but he also took the wonderful Danny Bergara with him to Sheffield United. Like I say, it felt horrible; from my own point of view I had been in the side for two seasons and we were doing great. The previous two seasons we'd gone close to regaining our First Division status under Harry. Finishing five points off promotion in 1975/76 and then four points off it in 1976/77, eventually missing out to Wolves, Chelsea and Nottingham Forest as the promoted sides, we were up there and keeping good company; we weren't struggling.

We were definitely coming up to a transitional period with the playing team that Harry would have to deal with; the likes of John 'Maxi' Faulkner, John Aston and a few others heading towards, not the end of their careers, but certainly the latter stages and there would always need to be that mix of experience and youth coming through. There certainly was plenty of that at Kenilworth Road. There was an air of change needed about the place. I initially brushed off the talk of Harry going to Sheffield United as I didn't take it seriously. We were again competing at the top end of the Second Division whereas Sheffield United seemed to be struggling at the wrong end of the table. I didn't give it any real serious consideration. However, it did happen, and just like that, David Pleat was in charge of the first team.

In just a matter of weeks, Roy McCrohan, Harry Haslam and Danny Bergara were gone! David had been at the club for a few years as the reserve team coach. There was an air of uncertainty amongst the senior players in the dressing room who were unsure about this change with Harry and Roy going, then with David being installed as the manager. No disrespect to David but at the time, the players were asking themselves, "Who's David Pleat?" Harry had certainly been a larger-than-life type of person, whereas Pleaty was completely different. Harry and Roy had put that team together and the players knew that it was going to change. It came very quickly, it was as immediate as just a few weeks into David taking over that players were being moved on and likewise players coming in the other way with a view to replace them. The remainder of that season, 1977/78, certainly continued in that transitional vein and we fell away to a midtable position finishing, ironically, one place below Harry's Sheffield United.

The transition of players went up a gear during the summer break in 1978 with the turnover of players both going out and coming in. Kirk Stephens, Mal Donaghy, Bob Hatton, David Moss, Mark Aizlewood, Chris Turner, and Steve Sherlock came in. Some didn't work out and David was quick to move them back out and bring more in, like goalkeepers Dave Lawson and Jake Findlay, along with striker Steve Taylor. Back then you didn't have the restriction of the transfer window that you have today so David was able to bring in players and move them on whenever he needed to anytime throughout the season. He brought in Barry Silkman on loan, which ended soon after Barry clashed with David's assistant manager, Ken Gutteridge, in an away game at Notts County. David hadn't attended as he was away looking over new players so Ken was in charge on the day, but it didn't go well as we lost 3-1. David also brought in Alan Birchenall late in the season in an attempt to lift the spirit in the dressing room, which, to be fair, worked, as Birch was a great character to have in the camp. The 1978/79 was our worst season and we ended up staying in the Division by the skin of our teeth, staying up by two points. For me personally, as I'd broken my leg in the December that was me finished for the season. To be fair, it was a transitional season and that was the only season that we struggled.

The following season, the team really came together and kicked on under David Pleat. The players he'd brought in the year before that were still at the club really clicked along with the existing youngsters who had started to come into their own; Ricky Hill and Brian Stein were fantastic players and were starting to put their mark on the team. I was out of the team with my leg break and as for my relationship with David, I felt that I was never his player. I was always Harry Haslam's player. So, in a strange way, I did feel like the outcast. I had come through the club before he arrived. Whereas, players like Ricky and Steiny, despite not being the first team manager when they joined Luton, David had been instrumental in their scouting and in them coming to the club then with their subsequent development, along with the coaching skills of Danny Bergara.

I played with Bob Hatton in those early days of David Pleat's managerial career. Bob was brilliant for Luton, it was a master stroke from

David bringing him in with his experience, which would only benefit the young players around him. However, I have to say that we could have scored even more goals with Bob in the side if he just passed the ball once in a while. We had situations where Bob was in a position to square the ball to me or to Mossy or Steiny to score, but he'd shoot from the corner flag before laying the ball off to one of us. You'd think, Bob, I know you have to be greedy as a striker and you'll shoot from anywhere but when you have somebody in a better position where we could just tap it into the net… But he'd say, "Ah, no, no, no, I'll always shoot." He was the most selfish bastard ever, but I mean that in an affectionate way.

Before I got injured at Brighton in December 1978, I was flying under David Pleat having scored seven goals from midfield in just sixteen games. It was one of those streaks that any player, especially a striker, would tell you to try everything to get it in the net, even if it bounced off your backside. That's the confidence that I felt at that time. We started the 1978/79 season with a flyer beating Oldham Athletic 6-1 at home after being a goal down in the first half, which was great as the Oldham players had come off the pitch leading at half time and were really cocky towards us as we walked up the tunnel together. This only helped to fuel our resolve, and just look at the result! We also had goals flying in against Charlton, Cardiff City and Notts County early season at home, but we couldn't get a run of results together and we struggled to win away from Kenilworth Road. Even though confidence was still high, we felt like we could go out and win with attacking flair and score plenty of goals with getting the ball out to Mossy, where he would deliver into the box for Steiny or Bob Hatton to get on the end of. Although, results tailed off and by the end of the season we were uncomfortably close to slipping out of the Second Division and into the Third. That season certainly was when the seeds were sown and the start of the club's journey gaining in reputation as being an attractive and attacking football team. No doubt the club really kicked on under the next evolution of the playing staff under David Pleat. It's consigned to history now, but the brand of football that we played was superb. It wasn't just the number of goals we got but the way we built up play that enabled us to score so many spectacular and well worked goals. It was something special and that was down to the hard work on the training ground put in by David Pleat, his staff and the players. If we were defending we made sure we were ready to spring into attack and our ability to counter attack teams was devastating at times.

We used to call coach, Ken Gutteridge, 'the cone man'. I'm talking about those old-style motorway roadwork type of cones. He'd have them everywhere. He came into the club trying to be a rottweiler. David Pleat didn't like confrontation, so by bringing Ken into the club it gave David what he thought he needed in the form of a rottweiler. Now, I'm not saying that it wasn't the players' fault at times as Ken would stir it up as well. I went to see him when I was out with my broken leg and found him to be immediately dismissive. Whatever it was I was asking about he would instantly shut it down saying, "No, no we can't do that." Not once would there be any give and take with him. He definitely got the players' backs up at times. I remember the constant arguments that he'd have with Steiny. They just clashed and it was certainly a case of I don't like you and you don't like me but they mutually agreed to get on with it. Ken was probably the one more often than not starting the friction. Instead of sorting things out on the quiet he seemed to prefer a loud argument as a way of working things out. He was very much I'm the assistant manager here, you listen to what I've got to say. I think David Pleat was always of the view of freshening things up on the coaching staff, but perhaps Ken's way with us helped David's decision to move him on from the club sooner than perhaps his natural shelf life. However, that was Ken and that was his way and David knew what he was getting when in he brought him in early doors, when he needed an assistant in January 1978.

David Coates was already on the coaching staff before Ken left. He then became the number 2 to David Pleat following Ken's departure. David Coates was totally different and was very good with the players. He'd tell you what was wrong and what was right. I remember one day in training we were working on a throw-in routine. With the first three throw-in's, the team in possession gave the ball away. Coatesy stopped us and said, "The idea of the throw-in is that we keep possession of the ball, don't just throw it and expect to keep it, caress the ball, work the ball, keep the ball." He set us up again and said, "Now, let's get this sorted out, let's have a bit of movement off the ball and we'll see how we get on." From that day on, all of our throw-ins were done in a specific way in order to maintain possession of the ball, not just to toss it in and create a fight-ball situation. That was just from good old-fashioned coaching of good standards.

David Coates loved the gym and we'd head in there as often as possible. We'd play the first couple of five-a-side games and David Coates wouldn't say anything, but by the third game he'd stop us. Bearing in mind we were already a good one-touch team, quick passers of the ball, he'd say, "I've seen what some of you boys are trying to do and it's not right! You're playing off the wall, when you play on a Saturday you haven't got a wall. So, let's use the wall as the touch line and if it touches the wall then it's a throw-in." It was just getting us into good habits, and any changes he made were not just for the sake of it, there was a purpose and invariably it made us better players and then a better team enabling us to keep the ball better.

Later, when I was out scouting and I ran into David Coates, he would light up talking about those days at Luton Town.

Trevor Hartley was brought onto the staff in 1980 as the reserve team manager. Trevor was a quiet man, a clever man. He would articulate himself perfectly in order to get his point over; he was direct and would tell you straight. On a couple of occasions that I wasn't in the first team, I would be with him and he'd say to me, "Lil, what are you doing playing in my team?" I'd reply, "Well, David Pleat has picked his team, I don't pick the team." Trevor would look back at me and say, "Lil, I don't want you in my team, you shouldn't be in the reserves, you have enough talent and you should be playing in the first team." It was Trevor's way of trying to keep my spirits up and also to encourage me to question David Pleat and to strive to get back into the first team as quickly as possible. Trevor would then say to me, "Go and see David, talk to him." I did, not that my chats with David were that frequent, but when I did he would tell me that he'd put me in the reserves because he felt it was a way of ensuring I didn't drop below the expected levels and if I did drop, then someone else would take my place in the first team. Of course, I understood that and I always accepted that the team picked the shirt, and if we're playing well then the shirts yours in that moment in time.

The football that we played with David as manager was enjoyable and as a footballer, even if we weren't winning matches, we always felt like we wanted to play on and keep playing as it was so enjoyable.

Following the two years that I had out I just couldn't get fit! I played and scored at home to Preston in a 4-2 win in December 1980 and I should have kicked on from there, but I just couldn't get my fitness back and only made a further three appearances in the starting eleven during the remainder of the 1980/81 season. John Moore helped me immensely, as we used to go out to the golf course and we'd go for a light jog around there. He'd let me go ten minutes before the rest of the players. I'd still come in last but it wouldn't demoralise you, whereas if you came lagging miles behind the rest of the lads it could get you down. Once I started to play again, I felt like I wanted to go forward but that something was dragging me back.

At the start of the 1981/82 season David Pleat asked me, "How do you feel?" I replied, "I just don't feel good at the minute. After all the training I've done in pre-season I should be further on than I am, it's like I'm switching a light on but there's no light." So, I was out of the team to begin with. We started well with three wins on the bounce but then we had a couple of 'woolly performances' with back-to-back home defeats in September against Sheffield Wednesday and Cardiff City. I came on as a sub on the Tuesday night in the Cardiff defeat, which was my first game that season. I kept my place and was back in the starting line up for the next match four days later, which was the fantastic 4-1 demolition of local rivals Watford. From then I stayed in the team for the majority of the season as we swept to not only promotion, but we won the league, too!

The style of play under David certainly deserved the First Division status that we achieved together. We played some great football and entertained a lot of people, not just Luton fans but a host of admirers across the football family, too. We weren't a kick and rush side, we had players who were all comfortable on the ball we built from midfield with a controlled style of football, and our one touch football was fantastic to play in so it must have been entertaining to watch as well. That's what David Pleat's team were all about, entertaining the crowd. Nothing pleased him more if we played well and something had come off from training during the week, even if we hadn't won or even lost he'd be happy, as long as he felt we'd stuck to his footballing cornerstones, his philosophy.

In the lead up to clinching promotion we failed to win in a run of five games; four draws and one loss. We'd put pressure on ourselves to get over the line as quickly as possible. We all knew how near we were to achieving our goal of promotion to the First Division and I think the nerves crept in. Finally, we clinched promotion by beating Shrewsbury Town at home but it wasn't as easy, as the eventual 4-1 scoreline suggests.

We wanted to win so badly that we didn't play our natural game. When we got the ball, we pumped it up to our forwards instead of remaining calm and playing through the midfield. There was a sigh of relief throughout the team when Brian Stein put us 1-0 up in the first half. However, we got warned at half time by David Pleat that if we didn't settle down into our own rhythm, then Shrewsbury would score. He was right;

they made it 1-1 a quarter of an hour into the second half. However, we finally hit upon our natural game and scored three goals in the final twelve minutes, with Ricky Hill, Steve White and David Moss scoring.

We'd done it and we celebrated up in the directors' box as the fans swarmed onto the pitch to mark our achievement. It was a fantastic night. We were promoted with four games of the season still remaining, a quite remarkable feat. We'd narrowly missed out on promotion in the two seasons before hand, which looking back was probably a blessing as we weren't ready to go up. But with Brian Horton signing from Brighton in the summer of 1981 that really helped us. He'd done it all before and his drive, enthusiasm and experience were to prove invaluable. He was always going to be a manager, you knew that from the moment he walked in the door. He was more than a captain. He became our manager within the team and from the off he had David Pleat's ear, he had great influence and David listened and respected his opinion. They were a great pairing of manager and club captain.

The following season, having been promoted as champions, we were back in the First Division. But I was out of the side again. We were playing Charlton at home in the League Cup in October 1982; we'd all got collar and ties on arriving at the ground, as we did at that time. Wayne Turner had got changed and put the Number 10 shirt on. In fact, he was already getting the strapping from the physio, John Sheridan. David Coates arrived in the home dressing room and called out to three of us, "Lil, Wayne, Billy Kellock, the manager wants to see you all in the office down the corridor!" The three of us were standing in front of the manager's desk and David Pleat says, "Right, here's the team for tonight, Wayne take your Number 10 shirt off, you'll be sub at Number 12. Billy you're dropping down off the bench. Lil you're in starting at Number 10 as you're not going to be playing on Saturday!" That's an example of how Pleaty could be with players at times. So, what happened that evening? Kirk Stephens bombed down the line, crossed to me, I controlled it on my chest, hit it on the volley, roof of the net and we were 2-0 up right before half time as Brian Stein had scored an early penalty to put us a goal up beforehand. Into the second half, Kirk Stephens made an identical run forward, crossed the ball in, I was on the end of it again and caught it lovely straight into the net. We'd won 3-0, and I'd scored twice on my first appearance of the season. At the end of the match, I was running down the line giving the fist up saluting the fans. In the dressing room, instead of saying well done Lil, two great goals on your first game of the season, David said, "Don't ever run down the touchline like that with the fans ever again!" I was sat there thinking, why would you say that? He had to play me the following Saturday as I'd scored two that night. I had a run in the team then for a few games, but I was out again following the Arsenal home game a month after this game at home with Charlton.

The banter was great, like at any football club and if you've got that, then it's a good thing. Following that night against Charlton, the mickey taking carried on from there and every time Wayne Turner walked in he'd get, "Wayne, are you in the 10 or the Number 12 shirt today? You'd better check before you put it on!" Without the banter you just haven't got any team spirit. The dressing room can be a vicious place, but it has to be that way; lively, with everyone on their toes, ready for a piss take or a bit of a prank.

As time went on that season, with Luton Town back in the first division, and as things do at football clubs, nothing really stands still and teams evolve. I wasn't playing as much as I would like now that we were back in the top Division. I felt that I didn't want to leave but I only started eight games in the league that season. I played my last game for Luton Town away at Ipswich on 26th February 1983, we lost 3-0. I was twenty-six, coming up to twenty-seven, so at the time I felt I had to look elsewhere. When the other senior players heard that I might be going to America, they advised me against it saying that I still had my best years ahead of me and I still had a lot to offer here in the English league. I don't have any regrets with eventually leaving Luton, but I do feel I could have been treated a little bit better.

When I left Luton Town late in the 1982/83 season, the manager of the club I joined, Tulsa Roughnecks, was Terry Hennessey, who was the former Welsh international and had a great career at Birmingham City, Nottingham Forest and Derby County. He asked me, "Why have you come to America, Lil?" I said to Terry that back in England I was told there were no other clubs interested in taking me. Terry, with his contacts at Derby County, replied, "I know for a fact that Derby recently offered £70,000 for you!" I didn't know anything about that at all. I felt that David wanted me away from the club as I did something like three weeks under the ten years, which back then traditionally triggered your right to a testimonial match. This is just my feeling about the situation at the time, I've never had this confirmed by David, not that I've ever come out and asked him directly. I think he wanted to have me away from the club and possibly all the better to have me over in America so that I didn't have the award of a testimonial season or match like Paul Price had received for his ten years from 1971 to 1981 before his went to Spurs. In fact, Pricey's testimonial was played in October 1981, which was the season after he'd left Luton Town.

I went to America for just under a year. It was an unbelievable experience. My old Luton team mate, Ron Futcher, played with me over there in Tulsa. I actually went there with a sore knee. I had previously been in training with Luton down at Vauxhall's when I turned and felt a snapping sensation. Everybody thought that I'd broken my leg again. Immediately I said no, there's nothing wrong, it's just a little bit sore on my knee. I carried on training, it didn't hurt that much. That would have been March 1983. Within a couple of weeks of that I went to America to talk to Terry and ended up signing with him at Tulsa Roughnecks, moving over to the US in time for spring training and the early friendly matches in April 1983. So, I missed Luton's run in that season which led to one of the club's most famous games in their history, with the Raddy Antic late winner at Maine Road. That was the one that saved Luton from immediate relegation once again back to the second Division and this time Manchester City, Luton's opponents, were relegated that day in May 1983. I was settling into life in Oklahoma by then with my wife and young son, who had just turned two years old when we went over.

They were mostly English players at Tulsa, only the keeper, the right back, a couple of the midfielders and one of the forwards weren't English. I have to say that the team spirit there was as good as any I ever experienced anywhere in my playing career. We won the conference league that we played in. Then we played a side called Team America in the play off games. The officials clearly wanted this 'Team America' to win, and the referees were 'a little bit naughty', so to speak. It felt like you were playing in Brazil or Argentina where they'd try to nobble the officials. Regardless, though, and as unpopular as it was around the country, we beat them and so we were through to play Vancouver Whitecaps in the semi-finals and in front of 60,000 people. In extra time in those days, if you scored that was it, game over, you'd won. The cross came over and I headed it in to put us through to the final. Again, we were in front of a 60,000 crowd against Toronto Blizzard in the final and we were fortunate enough to win that too, which was fantastic.

My knee was still sore throughout my time in America, I could carry on but it wasn't right. Harry Redknapp phoned me to ask if I wanted to play that winter in the American indoor league but I knew my knee would suffer playing every game on artificial pitches. The artificial surface at Tulsa's home ground was the worst I'd ever played on and certainly didn't do my troublesome knee any favours.

I then came back to England as despite signing a three-year contract when I went out there in 1983, the writing was on the wall for the NASL. Although we were successful, we were playing in front of average crowds of 12,000 fans but still being very well paid, so something had to give, and, within a year the team and then the league itself, folded.

I was back in England and I signed for Southend United who were managed by Bobby Moore by then. To be blunt, that was terrible, just awful on the playing front. On a personal note my son became ill and I got fined two weeks' wages for taking time away to look after my family, so it was never going to work out for me there. I had a spell with Peterborough United and then at Cambridge United before joining Kettering Town in the GM Vauxhall Conference. We did really well that year at Kettering and Barry Fry came in to sign me for Barnet. However, Kettering insisted on a transfer fee of £10,000, which we had a bit of an argument about as I would be going to a direct rival, so it was agreed that I could leave if I moved outside of the league. I went to Wivenhoe Town, which is just outside Colchester, and we won the league we were in there and I got to play with my old Luton Town team mate, Paul Price, for our two years there together finishing in 1991 at the age of thirty-five. From there on I went into coaching, some briefs spells managing, and then into scouting.

From a playing point of view, I have no regrets. The players I played with were fantastic, the rapport was good, and we got on great. Never any bickering, yes there were arguments, of course, but nothing that ever made you feel you didn't want anything to do with them again, it was always sorted out quickly and on we went.

I look back and think to myself, crikey, we had some great years. When I watch games nowadays in my capacity of as a scout at Cambridge United I think, they're nowhere near as good as we were as a team back in that ten-year period at Luton Town, first under Harry Haslam and then David Pleat.

I later worked again with David Pleat when he was in charge at Sheffield Wednesday and there was an enormous amount of work that I got through there for him, but I felt it wasn't really appreciated. But that was us; we always had a little bit of a strange relationship. As a player, I was certainly never one of his favourites and I can honestly say that my conscience is clear in that I've never said anything or acted in any way that was disrespectful towards him. As a forward-thinking coach and manager, I had the utmost respect for him and what he did in his first eight years at Luton Town.

I get on better nowadays with David Pleat and have done in recent years, more so than I have done in a long time, but there's always been a kind standoffish relationship between us and I honestly have never really been able to put my finger on why that is.

What has surprised me the most was that David Pleat put together a squad of around sixteen of us who were all good footballers and I feel that he never gets the recognition from the club, although they respect him. I'm not saying you've got to put a statue up or anything like that, but that ten-year period, I must admit, although I was in it for eight or nine years because of my leg breaks, was the best football that I think Luton Town had ever seen.

(BORN 6TH DECEMBER 1956, EDMONTON, LONDON)

# MARTIN ROBIN SPERRIN

## LUTON TOWN FC 1977 TO 1979

*Martin was brought up in Edmonton, North London. He represented Enfield District Schoolboys and at the age of just twelve, he was asked to train at West Ham where he trained on Tuesdays and Thursdays in the summer at Chadwell Heath, and then Upton Park in the winter. Trained by Frank Lampard Snr and Pat Holland, they didn't sign him as an apprentice at aged sixteen, but did ask him to stay and play with the apprentices in the South East Counties League.*

My dad played for Spurs and Brentford and football was the most important thing in my life as a kid. We lived a five-minute walk to the Spurs ground and were always up there, even taking a ball and playing at half time under the stands at reserve games, no tickets needed in them days, so easy to get in!

I had started an engineering apprenticeship so it was a very busy time working, training and playing Saturday mornings.

When I reached the age of eighteen they let me go, and Geoff Pike and Alvin Martin went on to make pro out of that group.

Shortly after, I had a phone call from the manager of Edgware and went there and got into the first team within a few weeks. I went from boys' football to men's and I loved it!

What a great little club, behind the White Lion pub, but sadly, like so many grounds, it's no longer there. The team used the club house and on a Saturday night they'd have bands on. I remember seeing Chas and Dave there before anyone had heard of them. In my second season at Edgware, most of the players had retired and a new manager brought in some local youngsters. I played centre forward, Brian Stein was right wing and his brother, Edwin, played central midfield. In goal we had a tall lanky youngster who used to turn up on a moped, then walk in with a bag and crash helmet. His name was Dave Beasant (Wimbledon) and I wonder what happened to him.

Martin during the 1978 summer media day

We started the season well in the old Athenian League, winning game after game. We'd formed into a great little group of players and I loved going training and couldn't wait for Saturday to come around.

We drew with Boreham Wood FC in the FA Cup, which was a local derby with them being a top Isthmian league side and with a big following to support them. When the date of the game came out I had a big problem, though; it was the week that I'd booked, miles in advance, a trip to Benidorm with my mates!

When I got back a little worse for wear, the manager was great, saying I'd been pissing it up for a week and to not let him down. We drew the game at Edgware on the Saturday 1-1 and I got our goal. They had a 'veteran' right back playing, who spent most of the game kicking me up in the air and giving us all sorts of verbal abuse.

The replay was on the Monday night with a big crowd in attendance. I couldn't wait for the game to start, we were a very small, youthful side but we did have a big old-fashioned centre half who won everything in the air. We were 2-0 up at half time, me having scored the first. At the start of the second half our big centre half went off with a broken nose caused by their Number 9 who then proceeded to score a hat-trick of headers…

We lost 3-2, and in the final couple of minutes, most uncharacteristically for me, I thought to myself that given a chance I'd get my own back on the mouthy full back that had spent the first game kicking me around. With the last kick of the game he was clearing the ball down the line. I sprinted over to let him have it with my elbow, and it was so late in the game the ref followed the flight of the ball and blew for time!

After the game while sitting with the door to our dressing open, we saw

a stretcher being carried past with the full back that I'd laid one on. Turns out that I'd broken his collarbone. It was all kicking off in the bar as he was the local supporters' hero and I was escorted out to the car park where my girlfriend was nervously waiting and we hurried back to Edgware. Ah, the joys of non-league football in the 1970s.

Whilst all of this was carrying on, I was completely oblivious that both Luton Town and Watford were watching me. The chairman of Edgware rang me the next day and told me Luton and Watford wanted to sign me! You could have knocked me over with a feather! I had given up becoming a pro and it never entered my mind. A day later me, my dad, Brian Stein and I'm not sure if it was his dad too, all went to Kenilworth Road and spent most of the day listening to Harry Haslam, who was a right joker, selling the club to us and we signed two-year contracts. What a whirlwind of a week that was.

David Pleat came into the office in the afternoon after training and introduced himself as the reserve team coach. He said he was at the Boreham Wood game the other night and how unlucky we were and I asked him if he'd stayed until the end. "No," he said, "I left early to miss the traffic!"

I played my first game for Luton reserves on the Saturday not knowing any team mates apart from Brian Stein. We picked Brian up at Cricklewood, in fact, I continued to pick him up there and to drop him back there for the whole time I was at the club.

We played Arsenal reserves, they were second in the combination league and I noticed we were second from bottom! Well, I hit the ground running, scoring two goals in a 2-0 win, whilst being marked by Willie Young the Arsenal, Spurs, and Scottish international. It was a great start.

Soon after me and Brian joined the club, Luton were drawn to play First Division team Manchester City in the league cup, who were the holders and had a great side full of internationals.

The first game was drawn at Kenilworth Road and a draw was once again the outcome of the replay at Maine Road after extra time. There were no penalty shoot-outs in those days so it was on to a second replay to be played on a neutral ground, and Old Trafford was picked as the venue.

I got home from my girlfriend's house on the Sunday before the replay on the following Tuesday night and my mum told me the club had rung telling me to take an overnight bag tomorrow as I was going up with the first team! My first thought was that it was for the experience and not to play. I rang Brian at about midnight to find out if he'd had the same call, which he had, so I picked him up at the bottom of the M1 the next day and we travelled up to Luton together.

We trained at the ground on that Monday and the local paper had sent a photographer to take pictures of me and Brian running up the terraces at Kenilworth Road. Then, before we knew it, we were on the coach and travelling up to Manchester. That night, in the hotel, Harry Haslam pulled me aside on my own and said to me that he would be playing both of us against City. Brian and I would get a half each and I would be starting.

The next morning, the day of the game, Brian and I went down to breakfast and Captain Alan West (a really nice bloke) said to us, "You've made the papers today, boys!" The pictures of us running up the terraces was in all the papers, not just the locals. We couldn't believe us two young lads, who only a few weeks before were playing for Edgware, were now about to step out at Old Trafford.

We trained at Manchester United's training ground that morning and after resting all afternoon we set off to Old Trafford for the game. To my surprise, when Harry named the team, he named me as reserve with Brian starting. I played in the second half, but I admit I felt a little bit let down by Harry for doing that. The game went into extra time and after being 2-0 up we lost 3-2, but it was a great experience.

I enjoyed that first season. Pleaty ran the reserves and helped me a lot. One day he told me that playing up front would help me get stronger, as I was under ten stone and had no muscles. David said we would come in an hour early every day before the rest of the players to use the small gym and weights room behind the Oak Road stand. It had really old fashion weight lifting apparatus in it.

The first morning we did this, I laid on the bench and grabbed hold of the handlebars. David put the rod in the line of weights about half way up and told me to do twenty press ups quickly. Well, I couldn't move it let alone do twenty. In the end, I had just the one weight going up and down

Local Newspaper sent a photographer to snap Martin and Brian training on the terraces at Kenilworth Road in the week following their arrival from non-league Edgware

and I still didn't get to twenty!

This training backfired on me because after doing the weights, then playing in training, my legs were like lumps of lead and I kept falling over the ball. Pleaty said to me on a number of occasions that I should move into digs in Luton but I was happy at home and really didn't want to. In hindsight though, I wish I had, as that way I could have done the weights and extra training in the afternoons.

My second season at Luton started with Pleaty being the new first team manager. Harry Haslam left and had taken the coaches with him to Sheffield Utd. David brought in John Moore and David Coates, two good blokes, and he had signed two forward players in David Moss and Bob Hatton.

I was really looking forward to the new season. Brian had done well with the opportunities he was given and I hoped to do the same given the chance.

However, when we reported back for pre-season training, I was moved into the other dressing room, not included in any of the first teams pre-season warm up matches. Then, when the customary photo of the first team squad for the coming season was taken, Pleaty didn't put me in it. Professional football can be a lonely place when you get treated like that. I lost all my confidence and hated going in to training,

I was giving one opportunity against Sunderland: I was sub and came on for the last half an hour, playing on the right-hand side of midfield, in a game that we lost 3-1. That was it, two substitute appearances for the first team in two seasons at the club.

Eventually, I was more than glad to be given the chance to leave Kenilworth Road to sign for Barnet. It was local to where I lived and it turned out that I was Barry Fry's first signing. Barry was a real Del Boy character, I think that he even sold cars on the side, too. I've seen him kick cups of tea from out of players hands and kick tables across dressing room floors.

Martin, on the left, during his only league appearance at Kenilworth Road as a substitute against Sunderland in April 1978

Barnet, at the time, were in the old Southern league then and Barry wasn't only the manager but would also cut the grass and run the bar amongst many other things.

Another great reason for signing for Barnet was that a player I used to watch as a kid up at the Spurs also played for them: a certain Mr Jimmy Greaves. What a great man and such a nice bloke, too. I had heard about his problems with drink so didn't really know what to expect.

On my first game Barry introduced me to all the players and Jimmy told me to go and change next to him. As we got changed, Jimmy reached under the bench and pulled out an old Sainsbury's carrier bag and took out a pair of rock hard, mud coated football boots and put them on. Then he went back into the bag and pulled out a bottle of what looked like white horse oils, which is what players rubbed into their legs to warm them up. It stank horribly. I remember thinking that Jimmy had brought his own horse oils, knowing there was normally a big bottle of it for everyone. Then, he took the lid off the bottle and drank the lot! It must have been something for his stomach to kill the acid I reckon…

Jimmy played in midfield for us and it was sad to see players from other teams enjoy kicking him up in the air, but I have never seen anyone run with a ball at speed with it so close to his feet, like watching Messi now.

If Barry Fry couldn't take training because he was trying to sign a player, or sell a player more like, then he would ask Jimmy to take the session. Jimmy's idea of training was a lap around the park behind the old Underhill ground, then split into two groups in single file, a ball at the front, fifty yards apart, and you had to hit the other ball first bounce. Once you did it you could go.

I had a loan spell at Wealdstone where Stuart Pearce, a young full back, was coming through whilst working as an electrician, and then I moved again for a couple of seasons at Hendon. I then worked my way around

Martin playing for Barnet with his Tottenham hero Jimmy Greaves

playing for some good Hertfordshire based non-league sides and turning out for Stevenage, Hertford and Ware,

After getting married to Karen (forty-one years now) I moved to the village of Sawbridgeworth where I still live today, and we have two children, Matthew and Kirsty.

I have a kitchen business with my brother, Kevin and we've been going some thirty years now, and many years ago I was in the shop when a potential customer came in. As I looked up I saw that it was Paul Price. He was buying a house where we were doing the kitchens for the new builds. Paul's another great bloke and we had a few games of golf and a couple of nights out before he emigrated to Perth in Australia where I believe he still lives.

I never kept in touch with any of the players at Luton Town but that was really because I wasn't there that long and I didn't live nearby, plus of course, you never had mobile phones in those days. I have seen Brian a couple of times, and he and his wife, who we knew from the Edgware days, came to my fortieth birthday. We had a good chat there, and I said to him that Pleaty talking on the TV is totally different to how he used to talk, and I had to laugh when he agreed and said everyone reckons that he's swallowed a dictionary. I went and watched the Luton Town against Leeds

United game a couple of years ago and met Brian and Kirk Stephens (another great lad) in the bar afterwards, and we said we would have a game of golf together.

Looking back on my time at Luton Town, I enjoyed that first season at Kenilworth Road and will always be thankful for them signing me as a pro. They are always the first result I look for. "UP THE HATTERS!"

(BORN 19 OCTOBER 1957,
CAPE TOWN, SOUTH AFRICA)

# BRIAN STEIN

LUTON TOWN FC 1977 – 1988 AND (1991/92)

*After his family moved to England when Brian was just ten years old, his love of football would see him being signed by Harry Haslam in 1977. Brian went on to score 154 goals for Luton Town throughout his career and made 496 appearances! Playing as a centre-forward, he was and still is one of the most highly regarded former team members of the football club.*

I first played football when I was a young child in South Africa. We didn't have any pitches to play on so we just played in the roads. When we moved to England and settled in North London I loved going to play at the Paddington Recreation centre, and that's where I first started playing organised games of football. There was a guy at Paddington Rec called Albert Hill, who really helped me a lot in building up my confidence as a footballer.

I came from Edgware Town and the first time I walked into the building having travelled on the train from Cricklewood to Luton, I walked to the football ground with my brother, Eddie, and Martin Sperrin. All three of us joined at the same time.

Having arrived I said, "I've signed for Luton," then gave them my name. I was shown inside and told where the dressing rooms were. I went into the reserve team dressing room and was met in there by John Moore, but he said, "No, you're not in this group, you're in the other room with the first team." I knocked on the first team dressing room door then I walked in, not really knowing what was going on because it was my first time as a professional footballer. I remember one of the players saying, as I walked in, "Fucking knock before you come in!" and I was thinking. Oh my God, what's going on here? as this was making me a little bit jumpy. I looked at him and said, "Look John (Moore) has said to me to head to this dressing room." and he repeated himself! making me think I was going to have real fun here. It wasn't a good start and I just thought he was an arsehole. The player was Steve Buckley. There were quite a few players already there in the dressing room and I just didn't know where I was supposed to be.

Martin Sperrin was my lift to the club in the early days, although he was off to Barnet a year later after only making one first team appearance in the league and that was from the subs' bench in a home defeat to Sunderland. I'm not even sure if Eddie lasted much more than a month at Luton. David Pleat was the reserve team coach then.

David came to watch us play after John Moore had recommended us having seen us play for Edgware at Dunstable Town in a Southern League match. I think John had actually played against us for Dunstable that day as he was still fit and playing having not long left Luton Town as a player himself. I think it was John who contacted Luton and said that Edgware have a few players worth watching. He was talking about my brother, Edwin, and my friend, Martin Sperrin, as well as myself.

Pleaty came to watch us and it all seemed to happen at once, as the following week West Ham rang my mum's house to say they were interested in me and the day before that someone from Watford rang as well. When I got home my mum told me that Watford had called asking about me and they'd like to sign me. However, I'd just returned from meeting with Harry Haslam and David Pleat and had already signed for Luton Town.

I didn't even think that you could earn a living out of football but I was willing to take the chance. Martin Sperrin and Edwin did the same thing in taking a chance on full time football, but straight off Luton said that Edwin would be on a month's trial. However, they signed me and Martin straight away. Pleaty liked us two as a pair of strikers whereas Edwin played at the back or in midfield.

Christmas 1977 at home to Sheffield United; Brian scores his first two goals for Luton and earns his team a penalty for Lil Fuccillo to slot home in a 4-0 home victory

Luton Town called and said they'd like me to come up and if I was happy, they'd be pleased to sign me. Harry Haslam was there along with Danny Bergara. Pleaty was the reserve team coach and the physio was Reg Game at the time; quite a character! Reg just said what he thought, swearing at everyone, he didn't give a monkey's, which I was surprised to hear as I was very quiet back then. I felt I had to be careful with what I said.

I had one game in the reserves on the Saturday and on the Tuesday the first team had a third round second replay in the League Cup against Manchester City. Harry Haslam asked Pleaty who the best player was coming through, to which David put my name forward. I was really surprised because we'd played against West Ham on the Saturday against Billy Bonds and I was thinking how quickly your life changes, it was incredible. Playing against Billy Bonds was special to me as I'd been to watch him play for West Ham against Manchester United when my Dad took us to Upton Park when we were kids.

Then, within six months of me and Martin joining Harry Haslam, he got the chance to go to Sheffield United and being a Northerner at heart, he went along with the wonderful Danny Bergara. So the club gave the manager's job to Pleaty and one of the first things I think he did was bring in John Moore to join the coaching staff along with David Coates. David (Coates) was an incredibly good coach. I think he kind of took over when Ken Gutteridge, who was David Pleat's first assistant manager, left the club.

There was a game where I left tickets on the door for my father but my brother, Edwin, had said to his mates to just turn up and say they were Isaiah Stein so they took his tickets, but that was Edwin. My father did turn up but the guy on the players' and officials' entrance wouldn't let him in. My dad wasn't going to take no for an answer so he insisted to see David Pleat right there and then!

This was quite near to kick off and the poor guy on the officials' entrance came reluctantly to the first team dressing room. Pleaty opened the door red faced and said to the guy when he knocked on the dressing room door, "If you ever knock on this door again, then you'll get the sack!" The guy replied, "Well, what do I do? Brian Stein's dad has just walked in with no ticket." Pleaty screamed at the guy, "LET HIM IN!" Everyone in the dressing room looked at me, which was quite embarrassing. My father would go where he wanted. He went in to the boardroom and Pleaty came back down after having gone up there after a game. I was in the big sunken bath with a lot of the lads and Pleaty came in and asked me, "Do you know that your dad's up in the boardroom?" I jumped out the bath, thinking I was gonna get the sack. However, Pleaty said, "No, leave him there, he'll be alright!" Pleaty seemed to change his mind just like that on the spot. David knew what my dad had done for us having been well read up on the situation in South Africa. I was angry at my dad, but I knew he'd do that anyway as that was the sort of person he was.

Myself, along with two of my brothers, Edwin and Mark, set up the Isaiah Stein Foundation in honour to our father. Our dad was a man and a half because I could never have done what he did. We want to go back to South Africa to help further the work that we've begun with the foundation. That's really important to us to be able to do that. My dad always said, education, education, education. Those were his three words. We sponsored a school in Cape Town and to us it's of great importance. It shows the kids that they can achieve things, gives them confidence, shows them what sport can do for the self-esteem of a young person. And that's what it gave me, an enormous sense of worth and pride as to what I had achieved for my family.

I've had an unbelievable career. I went from living at home and giving my mum all of my wages so I could help to give my family something back for what they had done to get us here. At times my dad would to go to Russia, to America, to Canada, he would go all over the world to help gather support to get Apartheid abolished in South Africa. My mum, at times, would have to take us with her to work, and it was amazing to see just how hard she worked. She was a strong woman, even though she didn't think she was, but she certainly was. Both of my parents were unbelievable. What they did for us, their children, is something I could never repay. As I said, I could never have done what my father did because he had been tortured by the South African government as a younger man. When you saw his legs it was unforgivable how cruelly he had been treated and for him to have to endure all of that, I'd think what cowards they were in South Africa at the time.

The family home was in Willesden in North West London and my father would be gone for long periods of time, sometimes for up to six months. I'd ask, "Where's my dad?" and my mum wouldn't even know where he was. That's just how they lived and how it had to be with his movements, being tracked by government agencies around the world and their determination to hinder his efforts to gain support to abolish apartheid in South Africa.

All smiles for the camera in the summer of 1981

He was always campaigning for the release of Nelson Mandela from prison. I firmly believe that my father was instrumental in his eventual release from prison in 1990. This is what my older brother Edwin told me: Apparently, Winnie Mandela used to come to our house all the time back in South Africa and the police knew this as they had spies covering our house. At the time they would have definitely known whenever she came to visit my parents to have a conversation with my father about what they could do to try to get Nelson Mandela released from Robben Island, which is where he was held from 1964-1982. Winnie came to our house four times, but I can't remember any of this first hand as I was still quite young at the time. Edwin was a little older and to be frank, I didn't know my arse from my elbow!

Like I said earlier, I just didn't know that it was possible to play football for a living. I wasn't put into digs when I signed for Luton. Ricky was in digs with a landlady looking after him in Luton with Tim Smith and then later on Mark Aizlewood was put in there with him too, but that wouldn't have suited me as my mum always wanted her sons with her at home. From where we lived in London we could be at the ground for training within forty-five minutes most of the time, depending on the good old traffic and the reliability of Martin Sperrin's car. Eventually, I got my own car as I wasn't surprised when the club let Martin Sperrin leave, or perhaps I was a little bit to be fair to Martin, as I felt he was a decent player, even though neither Harry Haslam or David Pleat could get the best out of him. Edwin only lasted a matter of months and then he was out, too.

Pleaty was very shrewd and you couldn't question his judgment about his signings and who he retained or who he let go. He was the absolute 'Guv'nor' when it came to putting a team together, as he made sure he got to know everyone's character, everything about them, not just as a footballer but every aspect of their lives and how his players lived. I think he was great when he evaluated your character and just everything about you. I was, of course, sorry to see Edwin leave Kenilworth Road. David got to know my parents very well. He would spend hours talking to them in person and on the telephone.

When I was offered a two-year professional contact in November 1977 there were no drawn out negotiations, no agents of course. I was nineteen years old being offered a chance to play full time football, I wasn't going to turn it down. So, I signed, I was told that I would get a basic wage of £55 a week and I was happy with that at the time.

I went from school and onto the Polytechnic in Kilburn. The family was always struggling for money so I was also working on the Saturday in Boots the Chemist in order to help them. I'd get five quid from working at Boots and give it straight to my mother. Going full time in football and earning £55 a week definitely sounded good to me!

I played in the reserves with a guy called Gary Heale. He was a nice enough lad, an Essex boy, if I remember correctly. I didn't know Gary very well, but it was clear from the off that he thought he was going to be the bollocks at Luton. We got thrown in together against Manchester City in a League Cup replay in November 1977, and played at a supposedly neutral ground, Old Trafford, as it was the second replay in the tie. Gary Heale and I started the match and my mate from Edgware Town, Martin Sperrin, was on the bench. Gary got both goals to put us 2-0 ahead but City came back to beat us 3-2. Gary was only bothered that he'd scored the two goals and he was going to be the next big thing.

My friend, Mr Albert Hill, from my early days playing at Paddington Rec, came to watch me play that night. He came all the way up to Manchester to see me play there. He was very proud and I was thrilled for him to see me.

Harry Haslam was still the manager then but David Pleat took the manager's job just a few months after this game in Manchester; I don't think that David rated Gary and he fell away from the first team squad and was sold to Reading later on that year in 1978. He never did score another first team goal at Luton after those two at Old Trafford. He ended up playing in Holland and then settled playing in the American indoor league. That was David Pleat; if he didn't fancy you, you were soon on your way, and he showed this time and time again with a ruthlessness about his decision making that a player wasn't for him.

Late in 1977, I made a few substitute appearances and then right after Christmas 1977, I got my first start in the team on Boxing Day away at Crystal Palace coming in for Jimmy Husband, who dropped down to the subs bench that day. We drew there 3-3. We should have won being 3-1 up at one point but then in what seemed to be the last kick of the game, a very young but already brilliant Kenny Sansom from full back launched a rocket of a shot that flew in to level the game. We always seemed to draw 3-3 down at Selhurst Park in those days. They were always good football matches against Palace.

After my first year, Harry Haslam had left and David Pleat took over as manager and put me on a five-year contract with a pay rise. Pleaty saw more in me than I ever thought possible. It's important at any time in your life for people to show that they have confidence in you. As a twenty-year-old man it made me feel really special. David Pleat was a great manger and a great man. Pleaty was very fair and honest. He was a straight character and he had a lot of respect for people, which I liked about him. What I didn't need would be for someone screaming and swearing right up in my face, it wouldn't bring the best out of me and Pleaty knew that.

I was in the team again the next day at home to Sheffield United, yes, that's right, we used to play back-to-back games over Christmas then; can you imagine the outcry from top level Premier League managers if they were asked to play games like that these days? Anyway, back to 1977, I scored my first goals for Luton hitting a brace that day in a 4-0 win. I also won a penalty for the team as well, which Lil Fuccillo slotted in the net, and Ron Futcher scored the other Town goal. It was like a dream; I could hardly believe it myself!

The senior professionals were good to me, they made me feel welcome after I broke into the team. Jimmy Husband would make me laugh – he'd watch me in training to try and put me off what I was doing. Jimmy would give me that funny look and shout over, "Do you actually know what you're doing?" I'd just reply, "No idea, Jim, why don't you tell me what I should be doing?" It was banter, and if you could give it back a bit you'd be respected for that. If you reacted badly and got the hump then you wouldn't last long. Alan West, Westy, was the club captain, he was really good to me. He'd make a point of coming over to me if I'd missed a chance and say, "Brian, you're doing alright, your movement off the ball is excellent, just keep going, it'll come together." It sounds simple but getting these few words of encouragement really meant the world to me. Westy was a great captain, he was very good at having those brief one-to-one moments in training and during the games, he didn't overdo it but when he did it was spot on. It wasn't just me he would do this with, it was any player that needed it.

I got my other brother, Carl, a trial with Luton Town. He started with us in pre-season. We went to Dunstable Downs as David Pleat would take us there twice a week. You had to get up those hills; up and down three times. Carl phoned me after three days to say he wasn't feeling well and asked me to let David Pleat know that he wouldn't be at training and I was thinking to myself, Oh my god! I spoke to Carl's wife and she said, "Brian, your brother, he came home yesterday, he says that he can't eat, his stomach is twisted!" He'd complained to his wife that the staff at Luton had him running like a dog. She couldn't believe that we had been up and down the hills so much and I told her that's what we do, we have to be fit enough for a long season of football. We had to be super-fit. I won't tell you what she called Carl but it wasn't very complimentary to his stamina! Carl had been playing locally and he always thought that out of all of us he was the best footballer in the family. He did have ability but he just wasn't able to put in the hard work and so without that, you're not going to go any further in the game.

Back to those hill climb runs and this is where Ken came in. Pleaty used to stand at the top, John Sheridan was in the middle, and Ken Gutteridge was in the lower part of the hill run, the first check point so to speak. We'd already done quite a bit of running and we went back up. I started walking because I thought my back had gone on me. Hill running isn't natural, your body isn't used to it. John Sheridan did tell me that it can affect some people with that type of running, but I had Ken Gutteridge screaming at me and he was right up in my face: "Fucking run!" I thought it was fair enough but when he screamed it at me a second time I'd had enough and told him to fuck off because he just didn't show me any respect. I wasn't being lazy; if I could have continued running then I would have, but Ken didn't even ask if I was okay, he just launched into yelling obscenities at me. John Sheridan and David Pleat knew I would have kept running had I been able to. I was shocked and surprised that Ken didn't know me better by then. I felt totally disrespected. David Pleat wasn't happy about it, either. He told Ken to calm down and said, "If Brian says he's injured then he's injured."

Pleaty backed me as he'd never seen me cheat, because I wouldn't;

Brian taking part in some 11v11 training on the Kenilworth Road pitch during a David Pleat led coaching session

why would you? I had his trust and he had my trust, and it's overwhelming for your manager to have that sort of trust in you. It gives you such a rush of pride when people speak well of you and show they have faith in you. That was the same with the physio John Sheridan and all of the other coaches, but Ken was out of order and I felt like he was treating me like a cheat and an idiot even though I was putting my best effort in. Believe me, if any player cheated then Pleaty would know and you wouldn't last long if you didn't change your ideas.

Pleaty knew what he wanted as normally I was almost too polite, well, I certainly was back then because I was brought up to be respectful of people. When we were kids, if a teacher rang my house and informed my parents that I'd been rude to them I wouldn't have been able to go home, but I would never disrespect teachers. I would always keep on the right path. My father would tell us we had to go to school and do the best we could, and add, "If I hear of you being rude to your teachers or headmaster then we're going to have a massive problem!"

This incident was a big thing for me, which led me to stop talking to Ken Gutteridge. I wasn't going to have someone disbelieve in me and think I would cheat the team so to be frank, I just wasn't having it. Pleaty knew that I'd lost any respect for Ken and I just couldn't talk to him. I'm not saying that this was what caused David Pleat to let Ken go but he wasn't at Kenilworth Road for very long, perhaps only little more than a year at the club. I was only twenty or twenty-one by then and I didn't know what others expected of me even though I think I knew what I was doing, but Ken didn't get what I was about at all. We just clashed and I think David Pleat backed me and my honesty, as he had taken the time to get to know me as well as my parents. He had that respect for my character as well as my footballing ability. I know that Ken had similar issues with a number of other players so it must have been instrumental in David's decision to let him go because if you can't get on with the players then, as an assistant manager, you have a problem and it comes down to who is the bigger asset to the club.

The club signed another player from non-league football in 1979/80. This time from Tooting in South London, known as Big Herbie! He was a big South London lad; Luton fans of a certain age will remember him. He was a handful for David Pleat and his staff to manage but they persevered with him because he had the habit of banging in goals in the reserves. He would make his way to meet me on the Edgware Road or a meeting point in Cricklewood and I'd drive him up to Kenilworth Road for training. He wasn't much of a player at that level. Effective in non-league, certainly no higher than that, but David Pleat was always prepared to give players a chance to prove themselves. To be frank, Herbie was what you would call 'a wrong un.' He made one appearance in the first team, getting ten minutes as a sub at home to Manchester City in a League Cup game in November 1980. However, by the following year he was released by Luton Town and back playing at Tooting.

I got my younger brother, Mark, into Luton. He'd been at Tottenham as a youngster and then he went over to Watford because he didn't like it at Tottenham. However, Mark found that he disliked the setup at Watford even more! So, I asked David Pleat if he could come to Luton for a trial to which David agreed. He liked Mark and put him in the youth team at the club. At one point, I think that John Moore was going to let Mark go but Pleaty intervened and said he felt Mark had the potential, so they kept him. Football is about opinions but you also need the right people in your corner sometimes.

I enjoyed my football immensely at Luton Town. Harry Haslam didn't know me, I felt he didn't have that trust in me yet. To be fair, we weren't together very long at the club before he moved on just a few weeks after those Christmas games at Palace and at home to Sheffield United. When, ironically, Sheffield United was the club that Harry left Luton for.

Pleaty certainly had that trust in me almost straight away. He would be out there coaching us every day, whereas Harry Haslam wasn't that type of manager. The training would be left to Roy McCrohan, Pleaty and Danny Bergara. Pleaty was very hands-on and he would love nothing more than to take part himself in full 11v11 training matches on the Kenilworth Road pitch, where we would have the first team playing the reserves.

Roy went to America to coach and then Harry and Danny went to Sheffield United together all with a matter of weeks of each other.

Pleaty ran the whole club, everything, changing that dressing room as soon as he came in. There were no longer people going behind other players' backs to tittle-tattle about this, that and the other, it was just nonsense and David Pleat stamped it out quickly by moving on some very experienced players, which allowed him the funds in the transfer market to re-shape his side. It didn't happen by chance, though. He'd been watching the players that he bought long before he got the manager's job.

David was very good at giving you information in those 11v11 games. He would whistle to stop play and give you advice on where you should be to give yourself a better starting position and to give you more awareness of when to time your run. Also, where the defenders would be until it would instinctively become part of your game and you would take that with you into matches. Pleaty was right more often than not. His attention to detail was incredible. We would just go over things time and time again and it worked.

I played for Bobby Robson in the England set up and he was very similar in his approach to his coaching methods as David Pleat was. In my opinion, David should have been an England manager.

He was brilliant in the transfer market and wasn't afraid to look overseas, either. We often had trialists coming in from around Europe and beyond. I remember a Peruvian international coming into trial called Raoul Goritti in early 1980. But, like the others, he wasn't what David Pleat was looking for.

He finally found his man in Spain, when he signed Raddy Antic from Real Zaragoza. Raddy was technically one of the best footballers that I'd ever seen. In training he would constantly be nutmegging people, including our new captain, Brian Horton, when he joined the club from Brighton a year after Raddy joined us. 'Nobby' Horton didn't like this at all and he would react by going in two-footed in the next challenge. Raddy could see it coming a mile off and he would jump out of the way whilst retaining possession of the ball; honestly, it was so funny. I can honestly say we had so much fun together training with those boys at Luton. The team's heartbeat was like we were all in time with each other. We had one goal in mind and that was to win the promotion from the old Second Division, which we did when we were champions of the Division in 1982. We had just missed out on promotion the year before and we knew how good we were, but we pushed on that season and upped our game.

We were so brave under David Pleat. In our first season up in the First Division we went to Anfield really early on in the season and it was my first time ever playing against Liverpool. It was unbelievable! We headed there with a plan to attack Liverpool, bearing in mind this was still the great all conquering Liverpool side back then, and attack we did.

Standing next to Graeme Souness before the game he was screaming. "Let's fucking do these Southern softies, give them a good beating!" This was as we were lining up in the tunnel, as you come up from below pitch level there and up some steps out onto the pitch. He was trying to intimidate us from the start. Brian Horton was standing with me and we just looked at other and both thought, What a twat! All it did was make us even more determined to take the game to them.

We took the lead in the first half and I scored after we broke quickly from the edge of our own penalty area. Paul Walsh picked the ball up out wide on the left and nutmegged Liverpool defender Mark Lawrenson as he sprinted into the box. He played the ball out to me and I side-footed it into the opposite corner of the net past Bruce Grobbelaar in the Liverpool goal. I'm in my sixties now, that goal was forty years ago, but I can still remember and picture every moment of that match even now. We were in dreamland, but we deserved it. Souness equalised soon after, though, and then Jake Findlay was injured, so he had to go off in the first half. Raddy Antic came on to replace him but our right back went in goal as we were only allowed the one sub then, so we never had a goalkeeper on the bench. They scored again and Souness tried to whack Raddy Antic as soon as he came on the pitch. Ian Rush scored before half time past our makeshift keeper. For the second half we put Mal Donaghy in goal and reshuffled the team. Wayne Turner dropped from midfield to left back, Richard Money moved across in the centre of the defence alongside Clive Goodyear, Kirk Stephens went back to his normal right back position, which I think he was relived about, and finally, Raddy Antic moved into midfield. We looked even better in the second half despite playing without a recognised goalkeeper, and were playing at the home of the English champions.

David Moss scored early in the second half to level the game at 2-2. I then scored down at The Kop end of the ground to put us 3-2 ahead after I latched on to a brilliant pass from Mossy. I kept my head as Grobbelaar advanced from his goal, I dribbled around him and slotted it into the net.

Brian tries to come back from injury too early in February 1983

Liverpool scored again with fifteen minutes left to make the final score a breathless 3-3 draw. The game went out that night across the country on Match of the Day. Luton Town had arrived! The media loved us and David Pleat and for a while we became a lot of people's 'second team' almost overnight.

It was a pleasure to play against the players that were in the First Division. Coming up against Ian Rush and Kenny Dalglish at Liverpool they were just different gravy. Myself and Walshy weren't half bad either. It was great to be competing with these teams and these players. What was the best thing about it though, was that we deserved our place out there on that football pitch on that stage in the English First Division.

I broke a bone in my foot in December 1982 playing at home to Manchester City, which was gutting. One of the City players deliberately stamped on my foot, but they were always doing that anyway. I hadn't really missed any time out injured for about three or four seasons and now we were finally up in the First Division and I got this injury that meant I'd miss five months of the season. I was heartbroken. I'd already scored in the game which we won 3-1. I went to hospital straight after the match and actually took my own car and drove myself. From there I called John Sheridan it was confirmed that it was broken. They put the plaster on and I drove myself home!

I did try to come back at home to Manchester United in the FA Cup at the end of January 1983 and in the league match the following week at home to Liverpool, but it was too early. I'd managed to get through a reserve game against Tottenham beforehand and I got through the Man United and Liverpool games, but then, when I was going through some light running around the pitch, I turned and felt it go again. I'd pushed myself to get back playing too soon and I ended up not playing again until

Brian is finally back and deemed fit enough to play; what a game to come back for – the decisive final game of the season showdown with Manchester City at Maine Road in May 1983

the very last game of the season, away against Manchester City at Maine Road.

David Pleat tried a number of replacements with me being side-lined; David Geddis came in on loan for a second time, Billy Kellock, Frankie Bunn, Steve White was given a chance with a month's loan from Charlton immediately after I broke down in training after the Liverpool home game. Then he managed to get big Trevor Aylott in. The team suffered another injury blow with our goalkeeper Jake Findlay, breaking a finger at Highbury against Arsenal, so David brought in a lovely man and a bloody good goalkeeper, Tony Godden. He came in on loan for the rest of the season from West Brom. I really liked Tony, he was a great guy. Of course, Tony and Trevor both went on to make Luton Town history as part of the team that won on the final day of the season to keep Luton in the First Division.

Trevor Aylott and Kirk Stephens didn't get the recognition for their work to turn over the possession of the ball in the lead up to Trev pushing the ball out to me on the right wing. I got the better of Paul Power at the second attempt to get the ball over into the box, which big Alex Williams in the Man City goal could only parry out to Raddy Antic. Raddy was instinctively lurking on the edge of the City penalty area for him to smash the ball through a crowd of players and into the far corner of the net! We were safe and City, this massive football club, would be relegated on the back of this goal and that transition of play, which was broken up and started by Basher and Big Trev.

The City defenders spent the whole of that game again trying to stamp on my foot as they had done back in December, which had led to my original injury and me missing almost half of the season. I had to play out wide to try to avoid them doing me more damage. Coming back at them in that game was karma. I was playing in front of Trevor Aylott and Paul Walsh, initially, but moved a little wider than I normally would because of the treatment I was getting from their centre halves. If they had managed to do what they'd set out to and broken it again that would have been it, game over! To be on the pitch that day and to be involved in the goal that put them down to the Second Division was definitely karma, without a doubt! It was also another massive show of the faith that David Pleat had in me to take a chance on me being physically fit enough to last the game, and more importantly to be able to affect the match, too.

Coming through in the late 1970s and into the 1980s as a young striker was murder with the treatment that defenders would get away with. The officials let so much go back then, modern day forwards just wouldn't have been able to handle it. There was a lot of physical roughing up, my ankles, toes, my foot broken, I would get whacked on my knees, headbutted or elbowed in the back of the head. You would be watching the flight of a cross coming in when suddenly you'd get a knee in your thigh or in your back; like I say, it was murder out there at times. The defenders back then had it down to an art form. Most of it was sly, but even when it was absolutely bloody blatant the ref would turn a blind eye or wave play on – without a doubt, some referees were intimidated by certain centre halves in those days. It's gone too far the other way these days though, with forwards and defenders alike diving and feigning injury all the time. Could you imagine our full back Kirk Stephens ever doing that? Of course, he wouldn't, if he had he would have been slaughtered by us, his own team mates, it's an absolute joke! They are cheating themselves and the watching fans, it genuinely puts me off watching top level football now.

Speaking of Kirk Stephens, he didn't stand for any nonsense! To be fair, he would be doing all the butting and elbowing in the back to opposition forwards just as it was being dished out to me up at the other end of the pitch. But Kirk could play, too, great at reading the game. An excellent athlete, super fit, and he was a real asset in attack as well because boy, could he bomb forward with the ball when we broke out of defence. Like me, he came out of non-league to join Luton Town.

Guys like Kirk, Mossy, Ricky (my roommate for ten years), and Rob Johnson, all contributed to that team spirit, we couldn't have had a better dressing room spirit than what we had in the late 70s and into the early

80s. We had some great goalkeepers and each of them helped to liven up the dressing room. Jake Findlay and then Les Sealey; Les was one of a kind and I had a lot of time for him. Dibs (Andy Dibble) is still a good friend of mine to this day. We were all friends, not just footballers who came in, played a game of football and then went off again. We became intertwined with each other's lives as well. That spirit remained whilst Pleaty was still with us at the club.

Brian and his younger brother Mark together at Luton Town

I was at a few other clubs too, but never recaptured that feeling of being in it together. The problem was, I would always be comparing to what we had under Pleaty at Kenilworth Road so it never felt good enough elsewhere, it never even came close! I played in France for two years and then had a season back at Luton Town in the early 1990s which was so disappointing, as I came back because David Pleat had returned to the club. I then played one more year in the football league with my brother, Edwin, at Barnet. I scored a lot of goals there but I didn't enjoy the dressing room or how the staff conducted themselves off the pitch. It was difficult but deep down I knew there would never be another Luton type of spirit that we had in that 1978-1986 period.

To be honest, even the dressing room spirit changed at Luton Town straight after David Pleat went to Tottenham in 1986. John Moore came in but he was stabbed in the back by an element within our own dressing toom. He'd brought in Ray Harford and Jim Ryan to work with him as his coaches. John stepped down after a year and the club put Ray in charge. I just didn't feel that I could speak to Ray Harford in the same way that I could with Pleaty, that connection just wasn't there. I wasn't happy that I was feeling this way and thought to myself this is not for me. I wasn't afraid to voice my opinion and that didn't go down well with the new management structure. They were too quick to blame the young lads and I wasn't having it, that's not what Luton Town was all about. It wasn't personal with Ray, but it was his methods, the way he conducted himself that I didn't like. It got to the point where I'd had enough, it had changed too much and too quickly. I didn't like the underhandedness that was going on, cliques were forming in the dressing room and around Ray too, which just wasn't right, and it was too much for me to bear. I wasn't brought up that way to accept bullying and I wasn't going to start putting up with it then.

There weren't many agents in the game then, they were very few and far between. You never got to hear of approaches from other clubs for you unless David Pleat wanted to sell you. He had full authority from the board who he sold. Ron Atkinson tried to get me to go to Manchester United and he rang me when I finally left Luton Town in 1988. "Brian," he said, "that's the second time I've missed out on signing you!" So I asked him when was the first time and he told me he'd tried to sign me in the mid-1980's when he was still managing Manchester United. I didn't want to think I could have played for Manchester United, but at the same time I don't know if I would have gone. I wanted to stay at Luton Town and with David Pleat. David never mentioned any approach from Manchester United to me at the time but I don't hold it against him, Pleaty did what he had to do to protect his and the club's own interests.

The biggest travesty is that in the 1984/85 season, we didn't get to the FA Cup final after playing Everton off the park, certainly in the first half. Meka Nwajiobi had a couple of golden chances to put us out of sight so early in the game. One of the chances he was past the keeper, leaving Neville Southall on the floor. I thought that he'd got to put that one in but he gave Kevin Ratcliffe enough time to recover and clear Everton's lines. I was screaming at Meka to just put it in the back of the net, hit it, hit it! But Meka thought he had all the time in the world. He's a lovely guy but I have to admit I hammered him in the dressing room at half time for not being more clinical in front of goal. We were 1-0 up from Ricky Hill's fantastic strike but you knew that 1-0 against that Everton side would never be enough – had we been 2-0 up at half time it would have been a different story. Everton was the top team in the country in the mid-1980s and I'm sorry to say that we let them off the hook that day. We should have been two or three goals up by the time of the Kevin Sheedy equaliser. That shouldn't have mattered, it would have just been a consolation goal for them. But no, it levelled the game and broke us as it was just a matter of minutes from the final whistle, and then we conceded again in the extra time period that was played.

Back in the dressing room at the end of the match we were devasted. David Pleat didn't have to say much, but he always knew the right words to say. It was simply a case that it just wasn't our day. How right he was because we played really well that day at Villa Park. We were brilliant for so long in that game, but it really does come down to the old adage in football that if you don't take your chances when you're on top, it will come back to bite you!

It should have been us going to Wembley to play the FA Cup final with Manchester United waiting for us.

I ran into Derek Mountfield about ten years ago out in Spain, we just happened to be holidaying out there at the same time. It was incredible that we ran into each other, but you do tend to see ex-players when you're on holiday as there are a lot of us, thankfully, still about. There are parts of Spain that us ex-pro's seem to enjoy returning to. Marbella right down there on the southern coastline of Spain is a big favourite. Not just ex-Luton lads but players from lots of different teams as well. I had to bring up the 1985 FA Cup semi-final again and how spawny they were beating us. Derek, who was the Everton player who popped up to score the Everton winner in extra time that day, just looked at me and said, "Steiny, it was a long time ago, let it go, time to get over it mate!" I accept that of course. It's done and dusted and you have to accept it for what it was, but it's good to run into old players and talk over those days.

David tried to sign myself and Mal Donaghy for a combined fee of a million pounds when he left Luton to manage Tottenham in 1986, but the chairman, David Evans, wouldn't let me go. Mitchell Thomas did go with David to Tottenham but that was only because he was out of contract and the transfer went to a tribunal, which ruled in Tottenham's favour with Mitchell moving to White Hart Lane for only a modest fee. Because of this David Evans was hell bent that he would not sell anyone else to Tottenham, but more over not to David Pleat. He made it very personal and the parting between the two men was far from amicable.

I don't have any shirts from my days playing with Luton Town. I don't even have the shirt from the Wembley win in the League Cup final against Arsenal in April 1988, where I scored two goals including the winner with almost the last kick of the game.

I do have some shirts along with some bits and pieces from my games in the England side, though.

I played a fair few games in the England Under 21s. I was in the full squad three times but only got the one cap for the full team. I played up

It's on its way; Brian beats Winterburn to the fantastic outside of the foot cross from Ashley Grimes to slot home the winner in the very last minute to bring home the Cup in a breath taking 3-2 win.

front in that game with France, with my then-Luton Town team mate Paul Walsh. I was never picked again. I felt it was a bit of a closed shop though, with the England set up. That was just how it was back then. All I could do was try to play best at club level in the First Division with Luton in the hope of getting picked again, but it never came.

My time at Luton was the best time of my life, I have to say that, because the football we played was with such honesty from everyone in the team. Brian Horton was an unbelievable captain. He held you to account for what you'd done and he was right to do so. He was so honest himself as a player and if he thought any of his team mates were giving any less in terms of effort, he would pull you up. There were no favourites with Nobby Horton. He was a stand out as the best captain that I ever played for. Pleaty let Tony Grealish and Paul Price leave the club because he knew what was needed to just finish that rebuilding job to the team to bring in Nobby in 1981. He'd done the same when he let the Futcher brothers, Paul and Ron, leave in 1978 to go to Manchester City for very decent money, which enabled him to put 'his' team together.

It was the proudest moment in my life winning the League Cup Final at Wembley to have my father there with my brothers as well. For myself and my younger brother Mark to be on the pitch winning a show piece final, I was bursting with pride. My mother wasn't there, she was at home in Willesden, listening to it on the radio. Earlier that week I told my mum that I'd got her a ticket. "No, I'm not going," she said, adding that she'd be too nervous being there in the stadium watching.

Brian and Mark Stein the Wembley heroes in the League Cup Final win over Arsenal in 1988

My brother, Mark, was told he wouldn't be starting the final during the week leading up to the game. He was told that he and Ashley Grimes would be the two named subs, with David Preece and Ricky Hill doing enough to prove their fitness for their places in the starting eleven, as they had been out injured and it was a gamble playing them both. As we know, it was a gamble that worked out but Mark went nuts when he was told he wasn't in the team from the start. The problem was created by Ray Harford as he had earlier assured Mark that he would be starting.

I called him from the hotel and said to him, "Mark, I know that you're caught in between and it's not a situation of your making but accept and fucking well get yourself here to the hotel!" He did, getting a cab to where we were staying in Kensington.

The rest is history. Mark took his place on the bench and he got his chance coming in the second half replacing an injured Mick Harford in the 57th minute. Mark was instrumental in the lead up to the winning goal when, with Mark's pace, he left Tony Adams flat footed leaving him with the only option but to haul Mark to the floor. From the resulting free kick, the ball found its way out to Ashley Grimes on the right, he rounded his marker on the by-line and with the outside of his left foot, played in an unbelievable low cross into the Arsenal box. I was able to get to the ball ahead of Nigel Winterburn to slot it home to give us that famous 3-2 win. Luton Town, with two Stein boys in the team, had won the cup at Wembley with 96,000 spectators and millions watching on the television.

It was just as well I scored when I did which as it meant the game didn't go to extra time. If it had that would have been disastrous for us as I was done, my knee had gone! Leading up to the final, I'd been seeing John Sheridan for some private physiotherapy on my knee. John had been with Tottenham for two years by then but he still saw the Luton players privately at his home as he still lived in the town, and I trusted John to treat me rather than the physio we had then at Luton. John Sheridan was the best and he cared about us lads at Luton. He knew everything about us. He had a big heart and you couldn't meet a better man, an absolute gentleman who respected everyone that he treated.

That was the fairy tale ending, perhaps? I hadn't made my mind up to leave Luton before the final. I could have stayed in England but I wanted to go abroad. I had offers from both Spain and Germany as well as France. I also had a call from Ron Atkinson, Everton called about me, too. I had to say no to any offers to stay in England because I wanted to get away from the drinking culture. I was always on the drink every Wednesday but I wanted to change, I wanted to stop drinking. I just felt the best way to do that was to take myself out of the environment of English football.

I went to Caen in France who had just been promoted to Ligue 1 (League 1). I chose them because they actually came over to watch me play. I appreciated that and was impressed by what they had to say. The manager, Robert Nouzaret at Caen, was a lovely guy.

My brother Mark left Luton Town the same summer that I did in 1988. He went on to have a great career first with QPR, then at Oxford United, Stoke City, Chelsea, and Bournemouth, before coming back to Luton in 2000 for a year when he was thirty-four. He's very much like me in that he's his own man and will tell you things how they are. He's a very straight forward and direct person.

The best team that I ever played in was Pleaty's team. David was a great manager. It's not at every club you get that clear and concise message given to you, it was David's consistency of his instruction that made him stand out from everyone else. He was clearly a fan of football, it wasn't his job but his passion. It was like he was being paid to work full time at his hobby, which he did with such energy and enthusiasm.

Pleaty would coach players and would make them better players along with his staff, David Coates, Trevor Hartley, John Moore and even Ken Gutteridge, they all had their part to play.

Football is an easy game, it's a simple game, if you know what you're doing. David Pleat was the master of making the game look easy. That only comes from the hard work being put in place, the building blocks of the foundation of a football team that the watching public never get to see. The lads appreciated his approach. He would say get the ball, run with it but always be looking forward, be positive with your decisions on the ball to take us forward and up the pitch. It you could play within that framework Pleaty was happy to let us express ourselves. David wouldn't linger on the negatives on what players couldn't do, he would always praise and encourage what we did well to make Luton Town a better team.

He always wanted to entertain and we had a lot of respect for each other within the team. When David left it changed, and it was taken in the wrong direction playing wise.

We had a camaraderie and a respect for each other as footballers. We all knew our jobs, what was expected of us. That was the best time that I ever had at the club. Everything just clicked. David made it clear, though, that if we didn't give 100% we'd be out of the team. It didn't matter who you were. David Pleat was quite simply a dream to play for!

I still live locally to Luton in Flitwick, Bedfordshire, and regularly attend the frequent reunions with the players from that era. There's always a special guest of honour whenever we get together: David Pleat, and he's still 'The Gaffer'.

VOLUME 1

# COMING SOON
## VOLUME 2

*Volume 2 OF ' They Played for David Pleat at Luton Town' is due to be published May 2023 featuring the following players:*

*Ricky Hill, Mal Donaghy, Paul Price, Steve Foster, Vince Hilaire, Emeka Nwajiobi, Aaron Tighe, Terry Hayes, Seamus Heath, Mike Newell, Willie Raynes, Edwin Stein, David Oldfield, Marvin Johnson, Kingsley Black, Les Harriott, Neil Madden, Peter Nicholas, Mitchell Thomas with others to be announced soon.*

*If any former players from this era would like to be included in Volume 2 please contact author, Phil Duffy, or publisher, Curtis Sport.*